EDUCATIONAL MEASUREMENT

by
Robert M. W. Travers

Personnel Research Laboratory
Air Force Personnel and Training Research Center

THE MACMILLAN COMPANY • NEW YORK

Preface

In this book an attempt has been made to present an account of the appropriate uses of measurement procedures within a framework of modern education. Considerable emphasis has been placed on the psychological and educational theory underlying the use of particular types of instruments. This is in some contrast to most textbooks on educational measurement, which are designed primarily to familiarize the student of education with an array of techniques and devices which he is expected to be able to use at his own discretion. It is believed that the latter approach does not always equip the student with the ability to exercise sound professional judgment concerning the use of such devices.

The book is organized around certain central problems of education and broad areas of pupil development rather than in terms of the common subject-matter areas or in terms of techniques of measurement. The material is presented in four major sections, of which the first presents the functions of measurement in education and the concepts on which measurement in education is based. The second section discusses the measurement of the intellectual outcomes of education, and the third the measurement of personality development. The final section presents methods of predicting the extent to which pupils are likely to succeed in various programs of study. The writer has found this method of organization the most successful of the many he has tried in teaching courses in this field. It is one which fits well into the curriculum commonly provided for the training of the teacher.

Research and developments in educational measurement on which this volume is based cover a sixty-year period. This period has produced a substantial body of technical knowledge which is essential professional equipment for the teacher. In planning the book the author believed that in most textbooks on educational measurement too little use has been made of this rich inheritance of knowledge. His purpose then became that of writing a text firmly based on this

v

body of knowledge, but suitable as a textbook in a single-semester course in educational measurement. The author's experience in teaching courses in educational measurement in several different types of institutions led him to believe that students of education are capable of acquiring rather more technical and scientific understanding related to the place of measurement in the educational process than they ordinarily acquire. Many instructors with whom this question has been discussed share this opinion, and for this reason prefer to use textbooks on psychological measurement in their courses, believing that these provide more substantial intellectual fare than books on educational measurement. With this in mind the author has attempted to prepare a book on educational measurement at the same technical level as books on psychological measurement. It was believed that such a book would help strengthen a point of weakness in the preparation of teachers.

The volume assumes that the student has had previously a course in educational psychology in which he has acquired a general notion of what is meant by a correlation coefficient, a distribution, and the other elementary statistical concepts which are usually introduced at an early stage in the study of psychology. He is not expected to be able to compute a correlation coefficient or any other simple statistic. Most of the psychological and educational concepts that are discussed are those to which the student of education is introduced in his earliest professional courses. Those which may be new are discussed in sufficient detail to familiarize him with their general nature.

A modern textbook can be produced only if many publishers and individuals generously permit the reproduction of materials which have already appeared elsewhere. The author has substantial indebtedness in this respect. He is indebted to the University of Michigan Press for permission to reproduce large sections of a chapter which he contributed to a symposium published in 1949, entitled *The Measurement of Student Adjustment and Achievement*. This material is incorporated in the last chapter of this volume. He is especially grateful to Dr. G. Frederic Kuder for permission to reproduce sections of an article published in *Educational and Psychological Measurement*, and which seemed to provide appropriate illustrations for parts of Chapter 3. Chapter 6 is based partly on an article by the present writer which was published in the Journal of

Educational Research (Vol. 17, pp. 325–333). The courtesy of Dembar Publications, the publisher of that journal, in permitting the use of this material is acknowledged with appreciation. The illustrations of tests of thinking skill given in Chapter 5, which originally appeared in Smith and Tyler's *Appraising and Recording Student Progress,* are reproduced by permission of the McGraw-Hill Book Company who have recently acquired the book from Harper and Brothers and whose cooperation in this matter is greatly appreciated. The same generosity in granting permission to reproduce material is also gratefully acknowledged in the case of the Columbia University Press for the quotation in Chapter 9 from Symonds' *Adolescent Fantasy,* Dr. H. H. Remmers for the material from a publication of the Purdue Opinion Panel in Chapter 10, and the Psychological Corporation for illustrative items and other materials in Chapters 13 and 14, the Journal Press for illustrative attitude test items reproduced in Chapter 10, Dr. Edward Furst for the analysis of the functions of various types of achievement tests, presented in Chapter 8, and the Department of the Army for the illustrations of test problems measuring work skills presented in Chapter 7. For permission to quote brief materials scattered throughout the volume the author is indebted to Dr. Oscar Buros, whose *Mental Measurement Yearbooks* have proved to be of the greatest value in preparing this volume, to Houghton Mifflin Company, to the Macmillan Company, and to the publishers of the School Review, School and Society, the Society for the Advancement of Education, and the University of Michigan School of Education Bulletin. The American Psychological Association also has been generous in granting permission to quote from its journals. The Psychometric Test Scoring branch of Engineers Northwest, now known as Tescor, kindly permitted the reproduction of one of their special answer sheets in Chapter 11.

A special word of thanks must be given to the Odyssey Press, who published in 1950 a book by the present author entitled *How to Make Achievement Tests.* In parts of Chapter II and Chapter VIII in this volume the author presents a résumé of the material discussed in greater detail in that book, and the author is deeply indebted to the Odyssey Press for permission.

The volume owes much to the fact that an early draft was read and criticized by Dr. Frederick B. Davis who made many suggestions which were most helpful in producing a later revision. Dr. Wimburn Wallace read a late draft and provided one of the most detailed and useful criticisms that any author could want. The book owes much to the extreme care with which he conducted his review. Dr. Elizabeth French provided helpful criticism of Chapter 13 and Dr. Ruth Bishop provided the same for Chapter 3. Anonymous critics consulted by the Macmillan Company have offered numerous suggestions, the adoption of which should make the book more useful to the student of education and to the teacher. Finally, the author must express his indebtedness to his wife, Norma, who spent long hours in helping to prepare the final manuscript.

Work on this volume was undertaken independently of any of the author's official duties in his work for the Air Force. Therefore, designation of the author's present position on the title page does not constitute endorsement or concurrence by the Air Force of any of the views expressed.

R. M. W. T.

Contents

Contents

Contents xix

PART I

Background for Educational Measurement

CHAPTER I

The Nature of Evaluation

What Makes Education Change

It is commonly believed by American educators that progress in education should proceed by some rational process of fact-finding to determine its effectiveness and that this process should be followed by attempts to improve those educational procedures that are found to be ineffective The improved procedures are then examined, and further fact-finding determines whether they actually are or are not better than the previous ones. This procedure is based on the assumption that human beings are basically rational and that if they are presented with facts showing the inadequacy of their practices, they will inevitably attempt to make changes in these practices. Such reasoning seems to be largely fallacious, and the history of education indicates that facts alone, however damning they may be, rarely result in educational change. New practices in teaching can be demonstrated to be effective, but mere demonstration is insufficient to produce educational change. Teachers must first be in a state of "readiness" for change before such changes can be brought about. This fact is well borne out by the work of Joseph Mayer Rice, one of the earliest men to approach educational problems from a research point of view.

Joseph Mayer Rice was at one time a student of the College of the City of New York and later obtained a degree of Doctor of Medicine at Columbia University. After practicing medicine in New York during the years 1881–88, he spent two years in Europe studying pedagogy and psychology at Jena and Leipzig. On his return to America, he became editor of the *Forum,* and, fired by the zeal for educational reform which he had found in the centers of learning in Europe, he

3

persuaded this magazine to send him on a trip inspecting the schools of the United States. During the period from January 7 to June 25, 1892, he visited more than 1,200 teachers in their classrooms in school systems in most of the major cities between Boston and Philadelphia in the East and St. Louis and Minneapolis in the Middle West. In all, he studied thirty-six school systems and also some twenty institutions for the training of teachers.

The results of Rice's observations are recorded in a volume (3) entitled *The Public School System of the United States*, which condemned the mechanical learning that he observed to be the common practice. He noted that children in most schools learned mechanically to read, write, and cipher without acquiring any new ideas.

Rice's argument was that if the three R's were efficiently taught by methods which enlisted the child's interest and at a time when the child was mature enough to learn efficiently, the time devoted to such learnings could be greatly reduced and would then be available for achieving other objectives. He felt certain of the validity both of his observations and of the interpretations given to them, and it seemed to him that reform would follow once the obvious deficiencies of education were pointed out. But nothing could have been farther from the case. Nobody paid any attention either to the observations he had made or to his plea for change. The anticipated cry of public indignation never reached the level of even a murmur.

But Rice was a resourceful person, one of the most resourceful in the history of education. If the public was not influenced by his observations, perhaps what was needed was an army of facts. Rice set out to collect data to support his observations. He embarked upon a testing program to show that current educational practices were wasteful. He built tests in arithmetic, spelling, and languages, but soon found that the collection of evidence of the achievement of an educational objective was difficult, even when the objective was a relatively simple one such as skill in spelling. For example, after he had administered his first spelling test to sixteen thousand children, he went on a tour to discover why some schools had done so well and some so poorly. He had not been gone long on his journey before he found that the differences had nothing at all to do with the method of teaching but were due to "the peculiar manner in which the examinations had been conducted." What had happened was that in some schools over-anxious teachers had given cues to the spelling of particular words by careful enunciations. As a matter of fact, as Rice pointed out, it would be difficult for even the most conscientious teacher not to give cues by this means.

In view of these difficulties Rice developed a second test of spelling and decided to supervise the administration of the test himself. Special care was taken to omit words in which the pronunciation could give away the spelling. This second test and the conditions under which it was administered probably resulted in data which had greater validity. On the basis of these data, Rice concluded (4) that the actual time spent in learning was the least important factor in determining the final spelling skill of the child. He also concluded that, if less time were generally devoted to spelling, the spelling skill of the children would be unaffected but more time would then be available for enriching the curriculum in other respects.

Rice's evaluation studies had far-reaching implications, but at the time they were published they seemed to have no observable effect on education in America; neither was any effect noticeable for many decades that followed. Rice was fundamentally mistaken in believing that educators could be influenced by facts if these facts were presented to them. In general, the path of education does not seem to be changed fundamentally by the presentation of arguments based on carefully collected data, and the effect of the work of Joseph Mayer Rice on the course of American education was so small that in most books on the history of education his name is given only in passing reference. Yet he was a man of very considerable intellectual stature and a reformer whose misfortune seems to have been that he was born before his time.

Educational studies conducted today, like those conducted by Rice, are not carried out for the purposes of satisfying idle curiosity nor principally for the advancement of pure research. Their function is to improve education; consequently, the results of any such studies must be fully understood and appreciated by teachers and others responsible for the program studied if they are to influence practices. The best way to insure such understanding is for the teachers and administrators to be active organizers and participants in the study. There is usually little merit in an outsider conducting a systematic appraisal and presenting the results of his labors to the faculty in the form of a report. As an outsider to the group he is likely to arouse hostility whenever he presents criticisms or suggests change. On the other hand, if he has worked closely with the faculty while conducting the study, he may become accepted as a member of the group and in that capacity may be in a favorable position to offer constructive criticism and suggest change. But the most favorable situation of all for producing educational change occurs when an entire faculty decides that the time has come for some fact-finding and soul-searching. Under such circumstances, facts which demonstrate the need for educational change are most likely to be accepted.

The author believes that it is the teacher who must eventually bear the main responsibility for appraising the outcomes of teaching. While it is hoped that consultants will be available to teachers who want to conduct studies of their own teaching, much of the work of evaluation must still be done by the teacher himself. However, it is important that evaluations made by teachers of their own work should become less informal and more systematic. It is hoped that this volume will offer teachers some help in conducting evaluation studies and serve in the capacity of a special consultant.

It is also anticipated that one result of the development of the so-called evaluation movement will be an increased emphasis on the training of teachers in evaluation techniques. While it is not expected that every teacher will become an expert in measurement, it is nevertheless expected that teachers of the future will be able to appraise more adequately the effectiveness of their own teaching than others have done in the past. It is hoped that this volume will serve as a text in courses on evaluation and educational measurement.

The Nature of Evaluation

Evaluation is the process whereby the values inherent in an event are determined. The term event is used here in a broad sense. Thus, in education, the events evaluated may be an entire institutional program, a part of the program, the planning which resulted in the program, the consequences of the program such as the achievement of the pupils, or any matter related to the program. Since the worth of an educational program must ultimately be evaluated in terms of the changes it produces in the pupils, this aspect of the evaluation process will be discussed at greater length.

The purposes of an educational program are referred to as the objectives or aims of the program. The consequences of the program—that is, the actual changes produced in the pupils—are referred to as the outcomes. Thus the objectives may be described as expected outcomes, keeping in mind that there is often a substantial difference between expected outcomes and actual outcomes.

The evaulation of education in terms of outcomes is not merely a process of determining what the actual outcomes are, but it also involves a judgment of the desirability of whatever outcomes are demonstrated to occur. Suppose it can be shown that students in a certain educational program become more favorable in their attitudes towards certain racial minorities as a result of that program. The measurement of these changes in attitude does not constitute an evaluation. The process of making an evaluation consists not in measuring the change but in judging whether the change is or is not desirable.

Once objectives have been defined and measures of the extent to which they are achieved have been developed, the growth of individuals with respect to these objectives can be appraised without any value judgment being made. In this total process, value judgments are made only in the initial choice of objectives. The entire process from that point on does not involve value judgments, but involves only the assessment of the individual's status with respect to the objectives. It would have been better if the term *assessment* had been reserved for the latter aspect of the program and *evaluation* for only those aspects that involve value judgment. There would be less confusion if this distinction were commonly made. In general, an attempt will be made in this volume to use the term assessment in those cases in which no value judgment is involved and evaluation for those in which a value judgment is involved. This is probably a good intention which cannot be carried out completely in practice because the process of assessment may be related to a total process which involves a value judgment. For example, an observer may make observations on the characteristic behaviors of a class for the purpose of determining the group structure of the children. The observations should be classed as assessments, and yet they may form part of the evaluative process.

Judgments concerning which pupil changes are to be considered desirable are usually made long before actual pupil changes are measured. These judgments are made when the objectives of the program are first established. The objectives should be stated in terms of desirable changes in pupils that the program is to produce; that is, in terms of expected outcomes that are considered worth while.

The only thoroughly acceptable evidence of the effectiveness of an educational program is evidence of desirable changes in pupils. All other evidence is weak and tentative in comparison with evidence that desirable changes actually occur. All other information used in evaluating an educational program deals merely with the conditions under which learning takes place. Until precise knowledge is available concerning the amount and direction of learning that results from any given set of circumstances, the mere description of the circumstances of a program is insufficient for ascertaining the amount of learning that has occurred. Usually knowledge of what actually occurs in educational programs is so uncertain that it is very hazardous to make predictions concerning the amount and direction of learning that is likely to take place under the given conditions. Even the most experienced teachers may make very poor guesses of the amount that their pupils have learned. Outsiders who observe a class and who are less well acquainted than the teacher with all of the factors in the particular situations that affect learning are likely to make even more inadequate guesses. Here again one may expect a considerable amount of improvement in the situation in the future, for eventually research workers will accumulate a very substantial body of information which will enable educators to make at least fairly accurate predictions of what learnings are taking place from a knowledge of the circumstances of learning and of the nature of the learners.

What Is Meant by Education?

In this volume, the term *education* is used in a rather broad sense to include all deliberate attempts to change behavior. On this basis, much education occurs outside the school and includes attempts on the part of the newspapers and magazines to change attitudes, similar attempts by the producers of movies, the makers of political speeches and other speeches, and the organizers of radio and television programs, and to these must be added the efforts of parents, religious workers, playground counsellors, and all other individuals and organizations that attempt to develop what they consider to be desirable changes in behavior. Propaganda campaigns such as those sponsored by various organizations interested in traffic safety, safety in the home, the prevention of forest fires, the improvement of intergroup relations, and countless other causes come within the scope of the present definition of education.

There is no accepted difference in meaning between the terms *education* and *propaganda*, though some writers would make a distinction. Doob (2), for example, who has written extensively on this matter, defines propaganda as "the attempt to affect the personalities and to control the behavior of individuals towards ends considered unscientific or of doubtful value in a society at a particular time." Doob amplifies this by saying that the imparting of "knowledge" which is not accepted by scientific standards or skills which are not adaptive to the immediate situation is propaganda. The attempt to influence the opinion of others in a way which is "bad," "unjust," or "unnecessary" is also propaganda.

Thus Doob draws a distinction between education and propaganda on the basis of certain criteria. First, in the area of information, whatever is accepted as a scientific fact can be taught as education, but if it does not fall into this domain, it is propaganda. Second, an attitude, value, or appreciation which is accepted by the culture can be taught as education, but if it is not generally accepted, it is propaganda. On this basis much of the teaching of Galileo in his time would have been classified as propaganda, and so too would be much of the training that goes on today in teacher-training institutions. On this basis, whenever education struggles forward ahead of its time, it becomes propaganda. This distinction does not seem particularly useful, so from the point of the present writer, the term education refers to any deliberate attempt to change behavior in the direction desired by the person administering the process. Since this volume is concerned with the appraisal of changes that occur in individuals as a result of somebody's effort to achieve some given change, it is concerned with education in this broad sense. It is concerned with the changes in behavior produced by teachers, parents, companions, newspapers, movies, television and radio programs, and by all the other forces in our society which deliberately attempt to modify behavior. There is no particular point in this volume in referring to some of these influences as propagandistic and some as educational.

Relating the Purposes of Education to the Purposes of Evaluation

The process of making evaluations is closely associated with the process of defining the purposes of the program that is being evaluated. Unless the purposes of a program have been clearly defined, it is quite impossible to determine whether the purposes have or have not been achieved.

A common situation, which reflects the lack of coordination of many phases of education, is that which occurs when one group of individuals define the purposes of a program while another group develops evaluative criteria without having these purposes in mind. To a considerable extent, the use of standardized tests of achievement represents this practice. The author of one of these tests is likely to commence his work by defining what he considers to be the desirable outcomes of teaching in the particular area. He is likely to develop a test designed to measure the extent to which these desired outcomes are achieved. However, users of the test are likely to attempt to interpret scores without fully understanding the outcomes that the test is designed to measure. Too often the user of a standardized achievement tests will assume that the educational objectives measured by the tests are his own. Frequently the test user, impressed with the appearance of a printed test, assumes that it must be measuring something significant even if he cannot identify what it is measuring.

Formal Versus Informal Evaluation

While this book is concerned primarily with the making of systematic, formal evaluation studies, it is as well to point out that most evalutions of education are neither systematic nor formal. Both teachers and pupils make judgments concerning the worth of the products of the pupils' efforts, of the classroom materials, of the way in which the class is conducted, of the social relationships in the classroom, and of all other phases of the educational process. Parents and other citizens outside of the school make evaluations, often on the basis of the flimsiest of data. Editorial writers also add their quota of comment and criticism along with those of the taxpayer. Free criticism of education is undoubtedly a symptom of a healthy democracy.

It is also inevitable that most evaluations of education be made on an informal and unsystematic basis, since the cost of systematic evaluation studies are so great that if educational reform were to await such studies, then little change would ever take place. The cost of a systematic appraisal of only a few outcomes of a limited program is always substantial because it involves not only extensive work on the careful definition of desired outcomes, but also in most cases the development of new measuring instruments and the collection of evidence to show that these instruments measure what they are supposed to measure. These steps, preliminary to the actual evaluation studies, may absorb large sums of money, and if, as often happens, the work is unsuccessful and does not produce instruments which are valid for the purposes at hand, the evaluation study may never get beyond the first stages.

At least part of this situation is due to the fact that educational measurement is a relatively new field, and as yet only a very limited number of useful measuring devices have been developed. As time passes there will be a greater selection of measuring instruments available which will simplify enormously the task of conducting evaluation studies.

Aside from the fact that teachers tend to overestimate the amount by which their students develop, there is another important reason for appraising systematically the outcomes of teaching. Many of the things done in teaching are the results of historical accidents and are not the outcomes of careful observations on the effectiveness of specific methods for achieving specific goals. An interesting example pointed out by Bertrand Russell (5) is the teaching of geometry, which until relatively recently was taught in schools as a subject completely independent of arithmetic or algebra. This isolation of geometry from the other mathematical areas goes back to the sixth century B.C., when Pythagoras, after the development of his famous theorem, was led to the discovery of the mathematical problem known as incommensurables. This led both Pythagoras and the Greek mathematicians who followed to believe that geometry must be developed absolutely independently of arithmetic, so for over 2,000 years geometry has been taught in schools in this independent way along Euclidean lines. It is only in recent times that attempts have been made to teach mathematics as a single subject with a careful integration of arithmetic and geometric concepts. Historical accidents of this kind have been enormously important in most teaching fields as well as in other professional areas.

An interesting example of the perpetuation of an outworn teaching procedure was recently publicized as a result of an investigation of a one-room school in the Kentucky mountains (1). In that school the children were receiving training in reading skills by reading aloud the *Canterbury Tales*. These tales have been read by generations of children both here and in England, but to the mountain children in Kentucky the material was uninteresting and unrelated to almost anything in their lives and resulted in a very inadequate development of reading skills. Nobody, it seems, had ever tried to find out systematically whether the reading of the *Canterbury Tales* provided an efficient learning situation. The perpetuation of an inefficient practice would never have occurred if the teacher had realized that part of her job was to carry out systematic studies of a simple nature concerning the effectiveness of her classroom procedures. Every teacher should have the professional competence necessary to undertake simple studies of this kind.

Criteria in the Evaluation of Education

According to *Webster's New International Dictionary* (1945), the term criterion is defined as "a standard of judging; a rule or test, by which facts, principles, opinions, and conduct are tried in forming a correct judgment respecting them." In all evaluation studies, the first and crucial step is that of setting up some standard in terms of which judgments are to be made. If a reading program in an elementary school is to be evaluated, standards must be set up on the basis of which the program can be appraised. These standards are usually established in terms of descriptions of what the children should be able to do at each level. The criteria for evaluating a reading program might include a detailed description of the reading abilities expected of children of specified ages and specified intellectual capacities. These abilities must be carefully defined. If the investigator is interested in evaluating curricular materials in this situation, he must list characteristics of both acceptable and unacceptable materials, or list facts to be considered in classifying materials as acceptable or unacceptable. In this case, as in all other cases in which an evaluation is to be made of an educational program, standards or criteria must be set up before any evaluation can be made. These criteria cannot be established entirely on the basis of facts, but at some stage involve a judgment.

Because the criteria of the success of an educational enterprise are spread along a time dimension, the appraisal of any educational enterprise is a long-term affair. While a learning experience may be designed with the pious hope that it will affect behavior for the rest of the individual's life, it is impractical and usually impossible to record all the consequences of a learning experience if only for the fact that many are not identifiable and others cannot be measured with available instruments. Since the *ultimate* criteria of the success of education may be inextricably embedded in the entire subsequent life history of the individual, it is necessary to evaluate educational experiences in terms of smaller samples of the total life behavior. These smaller samples are not the complete criteria and are sometimes referred to as *proximate* criteria to indicate that these are immediate criteria in contrast to ultimate criteria. It must be remembered, however, that it is rarely possible to demonstrate that the proximate criteria result in appraisals that are the same as those which the ultimate criteria would yield if they were available.

The ultimate criterion of the success of a program of guidance may be the entire future happiness and welfare of the pupil, but the success of the program may have to be evaluated in terms of the extent to which it results in pupils' making what are judged to be sound educational and vocational choices. The latter represents a proximate criterion which is presumed to be related to the ultimate criterion.

In a few selected instances, it is possible to appraise an educational program in terms of ultimate criteria. For example, in a certain war factory, workers were trained to turn out certain simple metal pieces on a lathe. Since the ultimate objective of the training program was to produce the metal pieces at the rate of a given number of acceptable pieces per day, the ultimate criterion of the success of the training program was the number of pieces produced during the time when war needs called for production of these pieces. Proximate criteria in this situation might be the number of pieces produced on certain given days. It is reasonable to suppose that productivity on certain days selected as being representative of the total period might be used as a basis for appraising productivity over the entire period of production. Less valuable as proximate criteria would be productivity during selected hours of the working day. If the workers realized that they were being observed during the criterion hours, it is probable that they would produce more than at other times. In the latter case the proximate criteria would provide poor estimates of the ultimate criterion.

In education, criteria may often be referred to as proximate only for reasons of courtesy, since no stroke of imagination can perceive them to be near to the ultimate criteria. An illustration may clarify this point. There is considerable agreement that the effectiveness of teaching should be appraised in terms of the extent to which given objectives are achieved. Evidence of the extent to which given objectives are achieved can be determined only by measuring pupil growth, and these measurements should form the basic data for the appraisal of teacher effectiveness. In practice, however, it may not be possible to appraise the proficiency of a teacher in this way because suitable measuring instruments are lacking, or because available instruments are insufficiently sensitive, or because pupil growth is influenced by so many variables that the effect of any single one cannot be isolated. Consequently, school administrators often seek other criteria for evaluating the proficiency of those who work under them. One of these so-called proximate criteria is the general impression which the teacher makes on the supervisor, which is used in spite of the fact that there is substantial evidence to show that ratings derived from such general impressions of personality are quite unrelated to the extent to which the objectives of education are achieved. In this case, and it is probable that the same applies throughout the field of measuring teacher proficiency, the proximate criteria which are commonly selected are largely unrelated to ultimate criteria of teacher proficiency.

The remoteness of some of the proximate criteria used from ultimate criteria is a very disturbing feature in education. Some criteria are used largely because tradition has established them as the criteria to be used. Prospective teachers are still appraised in terms of their superficial knowledge of subject matter and professional information. Pupil growth is still often appraised in terms of examinations which measure only the most trivial aspects of education.

What Is Meant by Achievement

In this volume, the term achievement refers to any *desirable* learning that occurs. Since the term *desirable* implies a value judgment, it is obvious that whether a particular learning is referred to as an achievement or not depends upon whether somebody considers it desirable or not. Hence, any behavior that is learned *may* come within this definition of achievement.

It must be remembered that the term *learning* is not limited to the learnings of facts and information. It seems to have been established beyond reasonable doubt that attitudes, interests, and appreciations are also learned. Modern personality theory indicates that many of the personality characteristics of the individual, in addition to those already mentioned, are also learned characteristics. Consequently, desirable personality characteristics are as much an achievement as is knowledge of the history of the United States, although much more is known about how to achieve the one objective than the other. Also, the one objective can be achieved with much greater certainty than the other because the school can control more of the relevant factors.

While the term *achievement* is used in the broad meaning outlined above, it does not imply that most pupil achievements with which the school is concerned should be in the domain of personality. At the present time it seems inevitable that the schools must be concerned to a substantial degree with the development of knowledge, understanding, and skills, and that education must be largely intellectualistic, but this statement must not be taken to imply that other types of learning do not also occur. The fact is that it is only in intellectual fields that the teacher can be very certain of achieving the objectives he has set.

The Teacher as an Objective Observer

The important role which the teacher must play in conducting evaluation studies has already been stressed, but there is one factor which places the teacher in a poor position for conducting such studies, namely, his own ego-involvement in the situation. This means, in simple terms, that the teacher is personally involved in the situation and probably feels that his own prestige is at stake in any evaluation study. The ego-involvement of the teacher has not usually been given proper emphasis in descriptions made by observers of happenings in classrooms largely because such situations have rarely been studied by clinical psychologists. For example, when the writer interviewed teachers to determine the amount of insight they had into their behavior in the classroom, it was found that most of those interviewed had little insight. They seemed to be completely unaware of most of their shortcomings and had little or no insight into the outbursts of hostility which most of them showed from time to time. These outbursts were either not recognized as such or were excused as being in the interest of good discipline. Rarely, if ever, were they recognized for what they were, namely, disorganized behavior tinged with strong hostility toward the pupils. Nearly all the teachers seemed to be good teachers—in their own estimation. Good or bad, they justified their behavior with equal confidence. Any confession of personal weakness in the classroom would weaken their prestige so much in their own eyes that such a confession could not be tolerated at the level of consciousness. Of course, those observed and interviewed in this study belonged to a large city school system in which the teachers are insecure and in which because of their insecurity they can never afford to admit that their performance is anything short of perfect. It is quite possible that in a different situation where self-criticism was encouraged that teachers might show much more insight into themselves.

One result of this deep ego-involvement and lack of insight on the part of the teacher is that he has difficulty in being objective about the interpretation of data related to the classroom situation. This same difficulty in being objective is likely to distort the information which teachers themselves collect, particularly when the information consists of anecdotal records. As Darwin noted, it is a common failing for a person to forget those items of information which run counter to what he desires to prove. For these reasons, it is common for subjective evaluations made by teachers to be worthless. The advantage of basing evaluative studies on objective infomation cannot be overemphasized.

These difficulties which teachers have in conducting their own studies can be largely overcome by improvements in their training in the conduct of research. Moreover, it is necessary to provide teachers with congenial working conditions in which emphasis is placed on helping them evaluate their own work rather than on the rating of the teacher by the supervisor.

The Plan of the Book

The order of presentation of materials in this book is considerably different from that found in most texts on educational measurement. In terms of what has already been said, it seems reasonable that one of the first problems to be discussed should be that of how to define educational objectives. Unless the purposes of education can be accurately described, it is impossible to determine whether they have been achieved. The discussion of this problem is followed by a review of methods that have been used for assessing the extent to which various objectives have been achieved. This review of methods of appraising pupil change covers not only intellectualistic aspects of growth but also those aspects of personality which are not intellectualistic in nature. The chapters on the appraisal of pupil change constitute the main body of the book. These chapters are followed by two which discuss the measurement of aptitudes which the pupil must possess in order to achieve certain given objectives of education.

References

1. *And So They Live,* Documentary Film, New York, New York. Educational Film, Institute of New York University.
2. Doob, Leonard W., *Public Opinion and Propaganda,* New York, Henry Holt and Company, 1948, pp. 600 + VII.
3. Rice, Joseph M., *The Public School System of the United States,* New York, The Century Company, 1893, pp. 308 + VI.

4. Rice Joseph M., "Futility of the Spelling Grind," *Forum,* 1897, 163–172, 410–419.
5. Russell, Bertrand, *History of Western Philosophy,* London, George Allen and Unwin, 1945, pp. 895 + XXVIII.

CHAPTER 2

First Steps in Planning Evaluation Studies

Defining Objectives

The growing interest of teachers in the systematic evaluation of their programs makes it desirable to review some of the problems connected with the basic steps in all evaluation studies; namely, those of defining objectives and establishing evaluative criteria. It is a rather common occurrence for discussions of educational objectives to prove unsatisfactory to all concerned. Such discussions usually become sidetracked on minor details of wording. The cause of this frustrating situation usually remains undiagnosed and the matter of clarifying the objectives of the program is likely to be shelved. However, no faculty group should ever feel embarrassed by this situation, because the task at hand presents one of the most complex and persistent problems of psychology, which is that of establishing a satisfactory classification of human behaviors.

Implicit and Explicit Objectives

It is common practice in educational programs for the objectives of the program to be implicit rather than explicit. This frequently means that the person or persons who designed the programs had goals in mind, but felt no need either for stating the objectives in written form or for defining them in terms of detailed statements. While explicit and detailed definitions of educational objectives are desirable, they are not essential for an effective educational program, provided that the implicit objectives are clearly recognized by those executing the program. On the other hand, *detailed* statements of objectives *are* essential for the effective execution of an evaluation study, largely because objectives stated in general terms are easily misinterpreted or can be interpreted in a variety of ways.

The task of preparing formal statements of objectives presents a basic problem of communication. For example, an instructor giving a course on teaching methods may have a clear concept of just how the teacher-in-training should be able to operate in the classroom as a result of his course. The fact that the instructor has this clear picture of the expected performance of his students does not imply that he can describe to others this mental picture. A man may know his brother intimately but may be unable to tell another the kind of person his brother happens to be. As a matter of fact, it is commonly recognized that the ability to convey such information is rarely found outside of a rather limited group of great writers. Yet until accurate descriptions can be made of the characteristic modes of behavior expected to result from an educational program, the objectives of that program have not been accurately described.

The difficulties of defining educational objectives are not only those which accompany any attempt to communicate ideas. There are also major difficulties associated with the process of defining objectives. The deceptively simple formula commonly prescribed, which calls for the listing of the specific behaviors to be accepted as evidence of the achievement of a given objective, fails to note that the problem is one of establishing a system of classification of human behavior, a task which psychologists have not yet successfully undertaken.

Values in the Selection of Educational Purposes

The various factors that should be taken into consideration in identifying desirable general educational goals cannot be discussed here in any detail. The difficulties of establishing a desirable objective are most acute when we are concerned with general education, and least when vocational or professional education is concerned. In the latter case, the purposes are relatively clear, for the basic aim is to produce individuals who have certain identified competencies, but in the case of general education so many different purposes may be served, so many different consequences may be envisaged, that some basis must be adopted for choosing goals.

The educator may start out with the initial assumption that the child is innately wicked, as some theologians have believed, or that the child is innately good, as Rousseau believed, or that the child is neither innately good nor bad but may acquire these characteristics through training, as the scientist believes. Each of these assumptions leads to entirely different conceptions of education.

The educator may start out with the assumption that values are basically inherent in objects, or he may believe that objects acquire values for an individual because they serve some purpose for him. He may think that the beauty of music is intrinsic to it, in which case a purpose of education becomes that of helping the individual become aware of those external values, or he may believe that music is beautiful because it has certain biological effects on the individual.

The educator is likely to believe either that the aims of education are determined by some kind of application of scientific method or, if he feels that there are such things as absolute values—that is, that things have intrinsic worth in and of themselves—he may feel that aims should be based on some system of absolute values. In the one case, he will think of educational goals in terms of satisfying basic psychological needs. In the other case, he will think of educational goals in terms of the cultivation of the intellect and probably in terms of such concepts as developing unity and integrity of the individual, or even in terms of becoming Godlike or of acquiring the characteristics of a Jesus of Nazareth. If he feels that some kind of scientific approach offers the final solution to the choice of goals, he will probably seek the solution to his problems in the concepts of biology and think of the worth-whileness of learning in a biological community as something measured by survival value. He will think in terms of such biological concepts as *drive* and *need* and talk in terms of pupil growth as if growth, as such, were the ultimate criterion of the effectiveness of education.

This discussion is not presented as a comprehensive presentation of the problems of selecting educational aims. It attempts only to indicate the complexity of the problem and to point out that no satisfactory solution is in sight. It is also stimulated by a recent observation made at a teacher's workshop where the chairman, observing that the first item on the agenda was "Educational Objectives," said to the audience, "Since I suppose we all agree that the primary objective of education is to satisfy needs, we may as well pass on to the second item on the agenda." We cannot afford to be as simple as that.

Characteristics of Educational Objectives as They Are Commonly Stated

Most liberal arts colleges provide little or nothing in the literature they disseminate which might provide some inkling of the purposes of a liberal education, and teachers colleges do little better in the matter. A recent study (3) of a sample of the catalogs of a hundred teacher-training institutions revealed that not one of these institutions offered a detailed description of the outcomes of teacher training beyond the fact that it was alleged to produce persons who were "good teachers." Few high schools define their purposes beyond the fact that they aim at providing a "good general education." This absence of eloquence in the matter is not the result of modesty but must be frankly admitted to reflect an absence of painstaking thought.

On the other hand, a school or other institution is often not much better off after committees of the faculty have pondered long and drawn up detailed lists of objectives, because the outcomes listed bear little relationship to the realities of the situation. All too frequently, such lists of objectives are hopelessly ambitious. The present writer has on numerous occasions reviewed the objectives of high school teachers of English with respect to a year's work on the part of the pupil. These lists of objectives invariably include categories which could not be achieved through ten years of teaching in the area. One outcome which the present writer always criticizes in this connection is the "development of desirable characteristics of personality." This is a thoroughly worthy goal for a teacher, but all that is known of conditions affecting the development of personality indicates that the number of contact hours between pupil and teacher in a year's work is quite insufficient to produce anything except the most superficial and transitory changes.

This does not mean that objectives should be restricted to traditional types of subject-matter knowledge, but it does mean that it is necessary to emphasize the very careful selection of objectives to ensure that those selected can be achieved in a reasonable fraction of the pupils. In the case of a class in English, a change in a specific attitude would be more realistic an objective than a change in the "total personality," because it is known that although personalities can be changed through the concentrated work of the clinician over a long period of time, the process requires intensive effort and the development of special types of social relationships between the person who changes and the one who helps to bring the change about.

Even in the area of knowledge and understanding, it is common for the objectives to be ambitious beyond the realm of reason. Teachers invariably imply in the statement of their objectives that they expect the development of too much understanding in too short a time. Often the amount of understanding anticipated is beyond the ability of the pupil, and a few teachers are even inclined to blame the pupil when the desired amount of understanding is not developed.

All outcomes cannot be achieved in all pupils. At the lower levels of education, it is common to set objectives at levels which it is hoped most can achieve. Despite this good intention, it is common to find that for any given grade many objectives are not achieved in many pupils. As an example, it may be pointed out that at the end of the second grade a considerable percentage of children for all practical purposes cannot read. There are invariably children in the third grade whose reading level is poorer than that of the average child at the end of the first grade. Since the common policy is to promote children from grade to grade regardless of achievement, it is necessary that the objectives of one grade be also accepted as the objectives of the next grade for some of the pupils. For this reason, it is often more practical to specify only the direction of learning rather than the amount, since the latter will vary from pupil to pupil and can be specified for an individual pupil only after an intensive case study has made it possible to predict what he can achieve.

Should Education Develop Goals or Traits?

Even if the values to be achieved by education were well defined, it is doubtful whether this alone would be sufficient as a basis for defining the objectives to be achieved. If it is accepted that children are to grow up in such a way that in their adult life they will support a democratic way of life, it is still an open question as to just what is to be developed. Teachers commonly believe that in order to achieve this ideal it is necessary to develop "traits" such as "cooperativeness," although it is not known whether a trait of this kind can be developed so that the individual will show cooperative behavior in a wide range of situations. Other teachers feel that what needs to be developed is not a number of traits but a system of values which will guide the individual's actions.

The argument in favor of the latter approach is compelling. Of what avail is cooperativeness as a trait if it results in cooperation with a subversive element? On the other hand, a whole range of motives and values (if such elements can be developed) can be used to further the cause of democracy. As far as the development of our society is concerned, it is not so important that certain individuals possess the trait of aggressiveness, but that this aggressiveness be used for furthering the cause of democracy.

The above discussion is largely speculative. The problems are not to be solved by argument but by experimentation. What is said here serves only to point out the weaknesses in much of the discussion related to the development of social characteristics, and that the selection of educational objectives is more than a matter of making value judgments. A sound theory of human behavior is needed in addition.

For economy in teaching it is important that, so far as possible, objectives should be selected which represent functionally related aspects of behavior. It is uneconomic to teach a person how to behave democratically in each and every situation which he is likely to encounter if it is possible for him to generalize from a few experiences in a few situations. Most education is based on the assumption that there will be some transfer of training, and the greater the transfer the greater economy of the learning process.

Procedures for Defining Objectives

The procedures which are commonly adopted for defining objectives are based almost entirely on the pioneer work of Ralph Tyler, who in the early thirties was assigned the task of helping the faculty of Ohio State University improve their examining procedures. The techniques which he developed for this purpose were described in a series of articles in the *Educational Research Bulletin*, and because of their significance the series was later published in book form (4).

However, those who have worked on the systematic evaluation of educational programs agree not only that the best available methods for defining educational objectives are inadequate but also that the best available methods are much superior to those commonly used. The usual formula for defining objectives reads that the first step is to list the objectives in general terms and the second is to define each objective operationally in terms of the behaviors that are to be accepted as evidence that the objective has been achieved. Both of these apparently simple steps need to be examined in order to identify some of the difficulties which they involve.

Step I. Objectives are defined in terms of general statements. For most practical purposes between eight and twelve statements seem to represent a convenient number. This procedure is simply that of dividing up the expected outcomes into a convenient number of domains of behavior. Some examples of such general statements of outcomes of teacher-in-training programs are given below:

> Skill in controlling a class of children.
> Insight into the causes of reading difficulties.
> Understanding of the application of learning theory to the educational process.
> Understanding of the concepts of maturation and educational readiness.
> A tolerant attitude toward the shortcomings of school children.

These examples of general statements of objectives would not be likely to come from an outline of the objectives of a single course, but are selected from various aspects of a teacher-education program for illustrative purposes.

The list of general statements which summarize the objectives must be comprehensive. When a course of study attempts to achieve such varied outcomes as understanding, skill, appreciation, attitudes, and interests, then the list of statements must cover all of these outcomes. The purpose of preparing this list of general statements is essentially that of providing convenient labels for domains of behavior. The labels provide only the crudest indications of the boundaries and content of each domain. It is analogous to a packet labeled "clothes" which does not specify whether the clothes are for children or adults, for men or women, for daytime or evening, for summer or winter. Similarly, the objective "critical thinking" does not indicate whether the critical thinking is to be about social philosophy or hamburgers, but at this stage such details do not matter provided that the person who is defining the objectives knows just what he has in mind.

This step involves the establishment of a taxonomy—that is, a system of classification of all the behaviors that may be considered to be possible outcomes of the given educational program. In this step it is not sufficient to draw up a list of general objectives under which the various outcomes can be classified. It is also desirable that the classification be such that the behaviors in any given category be related functionally within the individual. Unless there is some relationship between the behaviors within a category, it will mean that each behavior will have to be learned independently, a slow and time-consuming process.

In some cases, it is necessary and unavoidable to include domains of behavior in a list of objectives in which the behaviors included are unrelated to one another. For example, the acquisition of a technical vocabulary is such that the learning of the meaning of one term is unlikely to facilitate the learning of the meaning of another term. Every word included in the domain must be learned. In contrast, in the learning of arithmetic addition, training with all possible number combinations is unnecessary, for if a person understands how to add together two 4-digit numbers in a few examples, it is then possible for him to perform a similar operation with other 4-digit number combinations which he has not previously encountered. It is quite obvious that the latter type of objective in which the behaviors are related functionally has many advantages over the former type in which each behavior in the domain must be learned independently.

Sometimes in this preliminary step the behaviors which are expected outcomes can be classified in a number of different ways. That classification should be adopted which groups together behaviors which are psychologically interrelated as far as the learning process is concerned.

Step II. The second steps involves the more precise definition of the domains of behavior which have been labeled in the previous step. This is by far the hardest step in the entire evaluation procedure and one for which adequate techniques have not yet been developed. It has become accepted practice to say that this step involves the listing of specific behaviors which can be accepted as evidence of the achievement of the objective, but this statement grossly oversimplifies what has to be done. These specific behaviors are referred to as evaluative criteria. While this procedure is generally appropriate, it cannot be, and should not be, followed to the letter, as will be evident from examining the following example of an objective of a teacher-education program which has been defined according to accepted practice in terms of relatively specific behaviors. The form in which some of the specific behaviors are listed is undesirable, but they are presented as a basis for discussion.

General Statement of Objective: Insight into the causes of reading difficulties of grade school children.
Evaluative Criteria:
1. Identifies child in grade 2A as one not yet ready to read.
2. Identifies children whose oral reading habits interfere with rapid reading.
3. Selects, administers, and interprets a reading readiness test.
4. Designs a reading program for a given grade which takes into account
   (a) individual differences
   (b) the interests of the children.
5. Selects appropriate words for making flash cards.
6. Recognizes emotional difficulties causing reading difficulties.
7. Criticizes a published reader for deficiencies such as insufficient repetition of words, excessively large vocabulary, and unsuitable sentence structure.

It should be noted that the evaluative criteria vary considerably in specificity. The first is rather specific, while the fourth represents a rather broad category of behavior which could be broken down into a large number of more specific elements. To what extent should the evaluative criteria listed represent relatively specific elements or broader categories of behavior? The answer given in the past has usually been that the elements of behavior should be as specific as possible, but this answer is not satisfactory. An item of behavior such as "identifies child in grade 2A as one not yet ready to read" is specific and identifiable, but it carries with it the disadvantage of not specifying with accuracy the limits of the domain of behavior under consideration. In fact, this item of behavior implies that the prospective teacher has to be able to do this only in grade 2A. On the other hand, if the evaluative criterion in this instance were stated in the form "identifies children in the elementary school who are not yet *ready* to read," the limits of the domain of behavior under consideration become more accurately specified. The latter statement indicates that the student is expected to be able to identify reading readiness at various levels in the elementary school and not just at the 2A level as implied in the original statement. Both the original and the revised statement of this evaluative criterion describe identifiable forms of behavior. While the revised statement loses specificity, it loses nothing in terms of the identifiability of the behavior included in the domain. Consequently, each domain of behavior should be defined through behaviors selected both because they delimit the domain and because they are identifiable.

Objectives are sometimes defined in terms of a continuum. This is done by listing two groups of behaviors: those which characterize the behavior of the individual in whom the objectives are achieved and those which characterize the behavior of the individual in whom the objectives have not been achieved. This system enables the observer to determine the extent to which an individual should be classified in the one group or the other. There is much to be said in favor of this system, since it rarely happens that an objective is achieved in its entirety in any one individual. However, it is usually possible to place an individual on a continuum stretching from a position indicating that an objective has been achieved in its entirety to a position at the opposite end which indicates that no aspect of the objective has been achieved.

A final point should be noted in connection with the second step in defining objectives. It is much more profitable to define a few objectives adequately than to define all objectives vaguely.

Bases for Selecting Behaviors for Defining Objectives

The elements listed as evaluative criteria under each objective must in general be representative of the domains they define; they must delimit the area and they must represent identifiable behavior. Unless the behaviors listed meet these requirements, the corresponding objective has not been properly defined. Each one of these requirements will now be considered in greater detail.

They Must Be Representative. The evaulative criteria listed must be representative of the behavior included in the objective. An all too common practice is to list only those which are readily observed. The objective should be fully defined even if the degree to which pupils achieve each aspect cannot be measured. Another common failure in the definition of educational objectives is to ignore the more subtle outcomes which often are not easily described.

The concept of representativeness is important only when it is not feasible to define objectives in terms which comprehensively and clearly include all behaviors that may be accepted as evidence of the achievement of a goal. An objective such as the acquisition of the technical vocabulary of a trade might be defined by listing *all* of the terms which are to be learned. In this case there is no particular problem involved in making the list of evaluative criteria representative because it is complete and comprehensive. On the other hand, an objective such as *reading comprehension* cannot possibly be defined in terms of all of the situations in which comprehension is to be manifested. Only a representative sample can be listed, and there are difficulties in ensuring that the sample is representative.

They Must Delimit the Domain of Behavior. Several illustrations have already been given of evaluative criteria which, because of their high specificity, failed to indicate the limits of the desired behavior. An evaluative criterion such as "administers a revised Binet Test to six-year-old," is appropriate only if the domain of behavior is to be limited to six-year-olds. If the corresponding objective is to train the student to administer Binet tests to children of all ages, then the evaluative criterion should not refer to a specific age but should specify an age range. Failure to specify the age range is as unsatisfactory as being too specific.

They Must Be Identifiable. Identifiable behaviors are such that observers can agree whether they do or do not occur in a given instance and the description made by the observer of what occurs must correspond to other evidence of what occurs. If a form of behavior such as "shows imagination in handling a class" was listed, it would probably not meet the criterion of identifiability since observers would be likely to show little agreement in appraising teachers for imaginative behavior in the classroom. The main reason for the discrepancy would probably be that the two observers had different concepts of "imaginative behavior." Another reason might be that observers differ in the interpretation to be given to the behavior of a given teacher. For example, a teacher may have organized in her class an ingenious project designed to develop understanding of what constitutes an adequate diet. From the standpoint of one observer the teacher appears to be demonstrating imaginative behavior, but from the standpoint of another observer no evidence of imaginative behavior is supplied because the observer knows that the teacher had available a book in which the unit was fully described. An item or category of behavior is identifiable when the description of it conveys the same concept to all those who read it and there is agreement on the behaviors to be observed.

Limitations on Techniques for Defining Domains of Behavior in Terms of Specific Elements

The technique of defining domains of behavior in terms of specific behavior has limitations. Consider, for example, the problem of defining the goals of teacher education. The ultimate criteria would, presumably, be embodied in a list of teacher behaviors which had been demonstrated to be effective. Yet it is evident that such a list does not take into account important facts. One of these is that a specific behavior may have different consequences in two different contexts. Two teachers who were observed by the writer showed the behavior of clapping their hands in order to quiet the children. In the one case, the children responded immediately to this signal and without any sign of tension. In the other case, by contrast, the clapping of the hands of the teacher received absolutely no response from the children, even though it was repeated quite frequently. The reason for the difference in the response of the children in the two situations was not a result of differences in the basic characteristics of the two groups of children. On the contrary, the different responses were due to differences in the total behavior pattern of the two teachers. One of these teachers behaved in a quiet, well organized manner, and although she gave the appearance of being somewhat aloof from the children, she still managed to play the role of a friend and helper. This teacher was able to clap her hands with great effectiveness. The other teacher behaved as a noisy person in a noisy class. The clapping of her hands was just one more noise, and one noise more added little to the total stimulus presented to the children.

How far the type of situation described above is one which generally prevails is not known at the present time. It is certainly reasonable to hypothesize that a word of praise from a teacher will vary in its effect upon the pupil according to whether the teacher is sparing or generous in laudatory comments. Numerous other examples could be pointed out of behaviors which vary in stimulus value according to the total context in which they are found. Insofar as this type of situation exists, it is not practical to define a given domain of behavior in terms of specific elements.

Levels of Objectives

In most educational programs, objectives and evaluative criteria need to be specified at various levels. In a teacher-education program the ultimate objectives of the program would be defined in terms of the behavior of the trained teacher, but the objectives of most individual courses could not be described in such terms. While one of the ultimate aims of the teacher-education program may be to produce a teacher who can identify the symptoms of serious maladjustment in the child, the first course in educational psychology may do little more in this respect than to familiarize the student with the terms and concepts used in discussing maladjustments. The student must be familiar with the concepts used in describing maladjusted individuals, but he cannot be expected to make diagnoses at such an early stage in his training.

General Method of Assessing Change

Most evaluation studies involve establishing as a fact that certain desirable changes have or have not occurred in the individual. In order to establish whether a change has occurred, it is necessary to measure the individual at two points in time, located in most cases just before and just after the particular educational experience that it is desired to evaluate. For example, in the studies of the effects of films on attitudes a typical design has been for the attitudes of members of a group to be measured before and after viewing a film designed to change the particular attitude. In the better examples of this kind of study a control group which does not view the film is also measured on the same attitude scale at the same interval of time in order to insure that irrelevant factors are not producing any change that may be found.

Sometimes for various reasons it is possible to eliminate the measurement at the beginning of the educational program. For example, in a first course in high school algebra, the teacher may well assume that the pupils come to the course with little or no knowledge of the subject matter. Under these conditions, if the pupils demonstrate knowledge of algebra at the end of the course, this is taken to be sufficient evidence that learning in the desired direction has taken place during the course.

There are hazards involved in making the assumption that a person starts a course with certain minimum qualifications so that whatever behaviors he shows at the end of the course of study which are related to the objectives must be a result of the learning situation. The dangers of making this assumption are much greater in some fields than in others. In a course in English composition at the college freshman level, it is unreasonable to make this assumption since the performance of the student in his final examination is likely to be mainly a result of years of earlier training rather than the immediate outcome of a semester of study. In the latter case, the effect of a single semester's work is very small and, as a matter of fact, may be so small that measuring instruments are not sensitive enough to measure it. These remarks do not reflect on the competence of teachers of freshman English in colleges but merely recognize the fact that the skills involved in effective English composition are so hard to learn and so difficult to teach that little progress can be expected of the student except over a rather long period of time.

In some cases it may be very difficult to design an experiment for determining whether pupil growth has or has not occurred. Diederich (1), in discussing the evaluation of a course in English composition, shows how elaborate a procedure may have to be in a relatively simple study of this kind: *

The teacher should have his students write a paper on a given assignment during the first week of the course and another on exactly the same assignment at the end of the course. Another teacher should then take both sets of papers, remove all identifying marks, and number them in random order, so that no reader would be able to tell which papers had been written at the beginning of the course and which had been written at the end. If the freshness of the ink portrays the more recent papers, they should be stored until they are indistinguishable from the older papers. The two sets of papers should then be shuffled and read in the usual way.

In additional explanatory material, Diederich indicates the difficulties involved in scoring. It may be pointed out, in passing, that even the elaborate procedure suggested in this passage is far from flawless because it is almost inevitable that successive themes written on the same topic will show improvement because the pupil will undoubtedly learn on the first occasion some of the difficulties of treating the topic. On the other hand, themes written on two different topics cannot be compared.

The best-planned evaluation studies in education involve the use of control groups in one form or another. Basically, almost every evaluation study reduces itself to a comparison of the relative effects of two different environments on changes in behavior. Sometimes the educator is interested primarily in the comparison of the relative effectiveness of two methods of achieving certain given goals. If measurement shows that the one method is more effective than the other, then the study gives a definite answer to the problem at hand. However, should the two groups show equal amounts of change in behavior during the experimental period, it cannot be assumed that any of this change was the result of the procedure involved. It may have been a consequence of irrelevant and unidentified influences which affected the two groups equally. In order to show that the latter hypothesis is consistent or inconsistent with the data it is necessary to apply the same measuring technique to a control group which is not subjected to the particular educational program the results of which are being assessed. If it is demonstrated that the

* This quotation is reproduced by kind permission of the *School Review*.

two experimental groups show changes in behavior which the control groups do not show, it may be reasonably inferred that at least a part of the change was a result of the education provided.

Identifying the Causes of Pupil Changes

It is important to be able to identify the aspects of the educational program most important in producing specific outcomes, since this knowledge would make it possible to control the process. The effectiveness of the specific practices of the teacher is one such variable that needs to be appraised. Another is the value of the specific curricular materials. However urgent may be the problem of appraising teacher effectiveness and the worth of curricular materials, it is rarely possible in evaluation studies to identify the contribution of separate variables to pupil growth. The measurement situation is complex and the difficulties of experimentation in education are such that it is not usually practicable to conduct a controlled experiment in which the effects of specific variables can be isolated. Even were it possible to conduct studies in which isolated sources of variability were appraised, it is doubtful whether it would be wise to undertake them. At the present time, it is often possible to persuade teachers to participate in the systematic evaluation of education when it is explained to them that the studies will not indicate the effectiveness of the teacher but will show only whether the program as a whole, with all that it entails, is achieving the kind of change it is designed to achieve. As soon as a study attempts to evaluate the performance of the individual teacher or of specific practices of that teacher, it is likely to become a threat to his security, and teacher cooperation is likely to disappear. Opposition may then even reach the point where the study has to be abandoned. Many well-intentioned investigations of education have had to be abandoned because of the inability of the investigators to obtain teacher cooperation.

Need for Limiting the Scope of Evaluation Studies

It is evident from what has been said that the task of defining all of the objectives of a given program, even of a limited one, is a tremendous task which should be approached with considerable awe of its magnitude. Faculties commonly assume that during the course of an academic year it is possible to define all of the important objectives of their programs. This assumption leads to the planning of an immense amount of work that cannot possibly be undertaken in the time at the disposal of the faculty. The result is that either the final report of the undertaking contains a series of inadequately defined objectives or the project is abandoned as being unfeasible. The Eight Year Study of the Progressive Education Association (2) represents one of the few evaluation enterprises in which objectives were carefully defined and instruments built to measure the extent to which the objectives were achieved. The success of this enterprise was largely a result of the unusual capabilities of those who operated the evaluation program, and it is a tribute to their wisdom to note that they did not attempt to define *all* of the objectives of the thirty experimental schools involved in the program. On the contrary, they limited the scope of the evaluation study to a few objectives which were widely accepted as significant. These objectives represented rather limited domains of behavior in comparison with the total field of behavior which the thirty schools were attempting to develop. By the limitation of the evaluation studies, it became possible to make a systematic and useful investigation. If the program had been broadened to cover a greater number of objectives, it would, like most other evaluation programs, have been a failure, for in this area it is more profitable to do a little adequately than to attempt to do too much.

Summary

This chapter was introduced by a discussion of the problem of selecting educational objectives. It was pointed out that the selection involves a value judgment, but a sound selection must also be based on a theory of behavior. There is little merit in selecting an objective which cannot be achieved because of the psychological limitation of the pupils. In the final analysis, the selection of an educational objective is a reasoned judgment.

The major purpose of this chapter has been to give the student of education skill in defining objectives. Although the procedures described present many unsolved problems, they are nevertheless adequate for planning meaningful studies. It is suggested that the process of defining the objectives of an educational program be undertaken in two stages. First, the general nature of the objectives are described in sentences or brief paragraphs. Second, each objective is defined in terms of a set of evaluative criteria. These evaluative criteria must be identifiable behaviors which are representative of all those which could be listed and which indicate the boundaries of the objective.

The definition of objectives represents only the first stage in the development of the evaluation study. The remaining stages must be planned with the same care and thoughtfulness. It is of particular importance that control groups be included whenever they are necessary for interpreting the final results.

References

1. Diederich, Paul B., "The Measurement of Skill in Writing," *School Review,* 54, 1946, 584–592.
2. Smith, Eugene R., Tyler, Ralph W., and the evaluation staff, *Appraising and Recording Student Progress,* New York, 1942, pp. 550 + XXIII.
3. Travers, Robert M. W., Craig, Robert, and Fenchel, Gerd, "Objectives of Teacher Education," *Journal of Educational Research,* 44, 1951, 641–656.
4. Tyler, Ralph W., *Constructing Achievement Tests,* Columbus, Ohio, Bureau of Educational Research, Ohio State University, 1934, pp. 110 + VI.

CHAPTER 3

The Nature of Measurement

Measurement as a Method of Categorization

The assessment of individuals, whether it is the assessment of the amount of learning that has occurred or the prediction of the amount that is likely to occur, always results in some form of classification of these individuals into categories. In selecting those who are to participate in a given educational program, the final classification is twofold and includes only the categories of acceptance and rejection. The same is true in selecting individuals for jobs. However, in most educational situations, the classification of the individuals into only two categories represents too crude a classification for practical purposes. On the usual letter grade system, there are at least five categories to which individuals are assigned, and sometimes, by assigning plus and minus categories to each letter grade, the number of categories is considerably increased. If an objective test is administered, the individuals may be classified into as many categories as there are scores; for example, if scores range from 32 up to 113, with at least one individual having each score, then there would be eighty-two separate categories. The term *measurement* as it is commonly used in education refers to the classification of individuals into categories and the assignment of numbers to these categories according to some rule.

The number of categories into which individuals are classified when some aspect of them is measured should not be arbitrary. It depends first on the purpose for which the measure is to be used and second on the accuracy with which measurement is made. If measurement is undertaken for accepting or rejecting individuals from a program, then a twofold classification is adequate. On the other hand, if a test is to be given to determine the reading level of a group of eight-year-old children, it may be desirable to classify them on the basis of the test into four or more categories, but there would be little point in dividing them into fifteen or twenty categories insofar as the assignment of each to a definite reading group is concerned.

While the number of categories into which individuals should be classified on the basis of measurement depends on the purpose for which the measure is used, another factor has to be considered. If the scores on an essay test range from 30 to 75, and if the test is unreliable, there is little point in retaining the forty-six categories which represent all possible scores. If the instrument were extremely crude, it might be justifiable to use only two categories. On the other hand, a more refined instrument might be effective in dividing individuals into as many as ten or more categories. The accuracy of the instrument limits the number of categories that can be effectively derived from its use.

Types of Distributions of Measures

Measures of individuals may show distributions of different forms depending on the nature of the characteristic measured and the type of instrument used for making the measurements. A distribution of the ages of children in a certain school is shown in Figure 3.1. This distribution is roughly rectangular, for there are approximately the same number of children of each age. Rectangular distributions of measures are rather rare.

Another type of distribution which is commonly found with certain types of measures is J-shaped. If persons are measured in terms of the number of accidents they have in a particular job in which all of them are working, a distribution similar to that shown in Figure 3.2 will almost certainly be found. Most individuals in the group will have zero accidents and only a few will have several accidents.

The distribution of many biological and psychological measures commonly approximates the shape of a normal distribution. This is a particular type of bell-shaped distribution which has convenient mathematical properties. Figure 3.3. shows the distribution of the

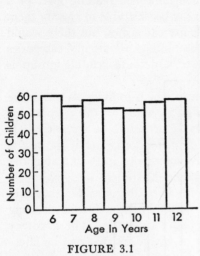

FIGURE 3.1

Distribution showing the number of children of each age in a school. The children in the group indicated as 6 years of age include all the children who have reached their 6th birthday but who have not yet reached their 7th birthday.

FIGURE 3.2

Distribution of accidents among persons working for a given period as operators of spindles and flyers in a textile factory. Data from Newbold (8).

heights of a population of 1,164 adult men. Its shape approximates that of a normal distribution. It can be only an approximation because the normal distribution is a smooth curve, while distributions derived from actual data result in a series of rectangles as shown in the illustrations. It can be seen that if much greater numbers of men had been included in this study of height, and if the steps in measurement had been not one inch but one-tenth inch, the resulting distribution would have been smoother in outline and closer in shape to that of a normal distribution. Even then it would only *approach* a normal distribution because the normal distribution is a *smooth* curve. The term *normal* as it is used in this connection has nothing to do with the psychologist's use of the terms *normality* and *abnormality*.

The normal distribution can be described accurately if only two of its characteristics are known. One of these is the mean or average of the distribution; the other is a measure of the spread of the

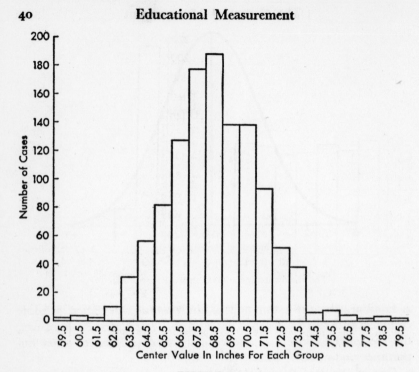

FIGURE 3.3.

Distribution of the heights of 1164 adult males. Data from Fisher (1).

distribution which is known as the standard deviation. The magnitude of the mean and the magnitude of the standard deviation completely describe a distribution that is known to be normal. This can best be understood by examining the representation of a normal distribution shown in Figure 3.4. In this representation the position of the mean is indicated by a line marked M. The standard deviation, sigma (σ), is the distance indicated by the word *sigma*. This distance, which indicates the spread of the distribution, is the horizontal distance from the mean to the point where the shape of the curve changes from convex to concave. The upper part of the curve bulges out (convex), while the lower part is curved inwards (concave), and between these two parts is the point where the curve changes from one type to the other. In this diagram, the base line is marked out in units each equal to one standard deviation.

The technique of calculating the mean of a distribution of scores

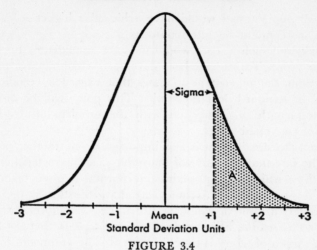

FIGURE 3.4

The diagram represents a normal distribution.

is familiar, but the estimation of the standard deviation is more complex and can be learned by studying Appendix A. However, the uses of the concept of the standard deviation are of great importance and must be considered at this time.

One of the very convenient properties of the normal distribution which is widely applied in the study of test scores is that once the mean and the standard deviation are known, it is possible to determine the percentage of the cases that falls above or below any particular score by consulting a table set up for this purpose.

Consider, for example, the distribution shown in Figure 3.4. A vertical line has been drawn at a distance of one standard deviation above the mean, and it can be said that the shaded area A under the curve to the right of this ordinate includes 15.87 per cent of the total area. Suppose an intelligence test had been given to children on their eleventh birthday and it was known that the scores on this test approximated a normal distribution and had a mean of 50 and a standard deviation of 10. Then a child who had a score of 60 would have a score one standard deviation above the mean. This fact would indicate that his score was exceeded by that of 15.87 per cent of children of his age. On a similar basis, it could be inferred that if a set of scores were normally distributed and if a person's score were 1.5 standard deviations above the mean, then 6.68 per cent of all pupils tested would have achieved a higher score. This person's score might be referred to as a score of $+1.5$ standard deviations, and such a score would indicate immediately his standing in the group. Tables have been developed which make it possible to determine the percentage of cases that exceed a certain score reported in standard deviation units. This point will be discussed at greater length in connection with the problem of developing systems of converted scores.

The normal distribution is also important from another point of view. The fact that measures of many physical characteristics show distributions which are approximately normal is often taken as a basis for assuming that psychological characteristics, if they were appropriately measured, would be distributed in a normal distribution. For this reason, it is common to build tests so that the resulting distribution of scores is roughly normal. The argument does not have too much strength, but it is widely applied.

The Meaning of Scores

Measurement in education provides first what are known as *raw scores*. These scores are usually direct counts of the number of times a specified event has occurred, such as the number of test items answered correctly, the number of books read, the number of errors made in solving a problem, the number of statements endorsed on a questionnaire, and so forth. Sometimes raw scores are time scores, such as the number of seconds or minutes required to complete a given task. These raw scores in the case of tests classify individuals into categories according to the score that they obtain, but the categories used are meaningless without additional data. The statement that a pupil answered 60 items correctly on an achievement test (or, even more specifically, 60 correctly out of 100), has very little meaning. The category 60 must be interpreted before it can be given any meaning. It may be a high score relative to the others tested. It may be low. It may indicate a substantial or a negligible amount of knowledge. A raw score suffers from the defect of being uninterpretable unless additional data are provided.

In order to make scores readily interpretable, it is common to change scores into some type of converted score. The teacher does this when she converts scores on a test into letter grades. The assumption is made by the teacher that each letter grade has some meaning upon which all are agreed, although the fact is that if different teachers were asked to describe the precise meaning of A, B, C, or any other letter, there would be little agreement in the answers. The famous but discredited system of converting raw scores into "percentages" is another attempt on the part of the teacher to convert a relatively meaningless score into one which has some commonly accepted meaning. Here again there would be relatively little agreement among teachers concerning the nature of the achievement represented by a percentage score of 60, 70, or 80. These systems of converted scores are worthy attempts in the right direction, but they lack precision. For this reason, psychologists have invented various types of converted scores which have relatively well-defined meanings. These types of converted scores will now be considered.

Percentile Scores. The simplest form of converted score is the percentile rank, not to be confused with the percentage. The percentile rank or score shows the individual's standing within a specified group by indicating the approximate percentage of those who obtained a lower score. The percentile is easily understood in terms of an example. Suppose that a group of a thousand persons were tested on a long vocabulary test. These persons could be grouped into the ten with the highest scores, the ten with the next highest, and so on down to the ten with the lowest scores. These groups of ten might be numbered from 100 down to 1, or from 99 down to 0. Whichever one of the two systems is used, the numbers assigned to the groups represent the percentile scores of the individuals in that group. A percentile score thus indicates the position of the individual within the group with respect to the characteristic that is being measured. If the system of 1 to 100 is used, then a percentile score of 45 would mean that at least 55 per cent $(100 - 45)$ of the group but not more than 56 per cent of the group obtained better scores. It would also mean that at least 44 per cent of the group obtained a lower score.

We may, of course, arrange individuals within each group of ten in order of score, and then the rank of the individuals within say the 98th percentile would be 98.0, 98.1, 98.2, up to 98.9.

The main advantage of the percentile system of scores, or percentile ranks, as it is commonly called, is that it is easily explained to others and it is conceptually rather simple. The disadvantages of the system are rather numerous. First, percentiles are all too commonly confused with percentage scores of the type commonly used by teachers in assigning grades. Second, percentile scores have very inconvenient mathematical properties which need not be considered here, but the consequence is that they cannot be easily handled in statistical analysis and should never be added or averaged. Third, they inevitably suffer from the disadvantage of indicating only relative standing in a group and do not indicate, without further information, just what the person can do.

Standard Scores. Another type of converted score results from the procedure of multiplying each score by a certain value and then adding a constant. The result of this procedure is to produce a distribution of scores which has a particular value for the mean and in which the scores show a certain specified amount of scatter. The converted scores may be made to have a mean of zero and a standard deviation of one. These are called z-scores, but by multiplying the same raw scores by other values and by adding different constants the converted scores may have other values for the mean and standard deviation.

In this type of converted score, the shape of the distribution of the converted scores is necessarily the same as the shape of the original distribution of raw scores. Thus if the original distribution were rectangular, with an equal number of individuals obtaining each score, the distribution of converted scores would also be rectangular. All the procedure does is to change the numerical values of the mean score and the scatter shown by the scores.

Normalized Scores. Sometimes transformations of scores are used which are such that the converted scores of a specified population are distributed approximately in a normal distribution. T-scores are converted scores which have been developed to approximate a normal distribution which has a mean of 50 and a standard deviation of 10. The system was originally developed by William A. McCall (7) and was such that it normalized the distribution of scores of unselected twelve-year-olds. Today, however, the term T-score is used to refer to any set of normalized scores which have a mean of 50 and a standard deviation of 10. If a system is developed for converting the raw scores of high school freshmen into T-scores, it does not follow that when the test is given to high school seniors the converted scores will be normally distributed. A technique developed by Flanagan to deal with this problem attempts to provide normalized scores derived from several distributions. This special type of scaled score is used in the Cooperative Achievement Tests (2).

There are many conveniences which result from the use of normalized standard scores. If a number of achievement tests have been administered to a group of pupils and if the results have been converted to normalized T-scores, based on all pupils in the same grade in the school system, then it is possible to draw a profile of scores for each pupil and to study his strengths and weaknesses. Such scores can also be added together to give total scores; percentile ranks, however, should never be added, since when this is done very high and very low ranks tend to be given too much weight in the composite.

Normalized scores may be easily converted into percentile ranks by means of a simple table such as Table 3.1. The relationships shown in this table are based on the characteristics of the normal distribution, which have already been discussed. Two systems of normalized standard scores are shown; one has a mean of 50 and a standard deviation of 10, the other, a mean of 100 and a standard deviation of 20.

TABLE 3.1

Conversion of Normalized Standard Scores to Percentile Ranks

Normalized Standard Scores		Corresponding Percentile Rank (Percentiles from 0–99)
Mean = 50 $\sigma = 10$	Mean = 100 $\sigma = 20$	
75	150	99
70	140	97
65	130	93
60	120	84
55	110	69
50	100	50
45	90	30
40	80	15
35	70	6
30	60	2
25	50	0

Age Equivalents and Grade Equivalents. Scores on achievement tests are commonly converted into age or grade equivalents. The grade equivalent for a particular score is usually the grade level for which that score is the median score, that is, the middle score when scores are arranged in order of size. Although a variety of systems is in use, it is common practice to divide the school year into tenths and to make the assumptions that (1) progress is uniform during the ten months of instruction, and (2) no progress occurs during the two months of summer vacation. Thus, if a raw score corresponds to a grade equivalent score of 5.6, it means that this score is the same as the median score of children in the sixth month of the fifth grade. The median score is the middle score when scores are arranged in order of magnitude.

Age equivalents are essentially the same as grade equivalents except that age takes the place of grade. Sometimes age and grade are combined so that age equivalents are based only on children who fall within a limited age range in each grade. This eliminates the retarded and the accelerated children.

Age and grade equivalents are probably the most misused and misinterpreted of all converted scores. One common misinterpretation is the idea that they represent standards which all children should achieve. They tend to obscure the fact that the children in any grade show a great range of grade and age equivalents on any achievement test.

Norms

Once a table has been prepared showing the value of the normalized standard score which corresponds to each raw score for a particular group of pupils who have taken a test, it is possible to use this table for converting the raw scores of other similar pupils who have taken the same test. For example, if a reading test has been given to a large representative sample of pupils at the end of the third grade in a certain city school system, it is possible to convert the scores on the test into percentiles and to draw up a table showing the percentile score corresponding to each raw score. This same table can then be used to convert the raw scores of other pupils completing the third grade into percentile scores and thus to discover how they stand among their peers with respect to their reading ability.

The manuals of published tests commonly supply such tables which make it possible to convert raw scores into percentile scores or other types of scores. These tables should be based on the performance of a particular group whose characteristics should be clearly specified. It has already been pointed out that systems for changing raw scores into converted scores such as standard scores are all based on the performance of a particular group which must be accurately described if the converted scores are to be meaningful. If raw scores are converted into percentiles, then these percentile scores must indicate the standing of individuals with respect to a specified group. Many test manuals provide tables for converting raw scores directly to percentile ranks.

If it is stated that the percentile rank achieved by a pupil on a test is 60, it is a meaningless statement unless information is available concerning the group for which this score corresponds to the 60th percentile rank. It is obvious that a score corresponding to the 60th percentile rank in one group might correspond to the 20th percentile in another. It is, therefore, fundamental to understand that a converted score cannot be interpreted until information is available concerning the group on which the conversion table was based. This group is known as the norm group, against whose performance the scores of individuals are compared. A normalized standard score thus indicates a person's standing with respect to this norm group.

Unless the norm group is properly identified and adequately sampled, the converted scores cannot be interpreted. Hence it is most important in the interpretation of a converted score to know the nature of the data on which the converted scores are based. If an objective test of American history were prepared and if norms were to be provided for "graduating high school seniors," it would be most unsatisfactory if the table for converting scores were based on the graduating high school seniors in one rural high school. A representative sample of graduating high school seniors would have to be tested in order to provide a satisfactory basis for the converted scores. The sample tested must also be adequate in size.

Great care must be exercised in the use of converted scores because often they are based on norm groups irrelevant for the purposes at hand. If a test has been given to a high school senior, there is little value in interpreting his score in terms of a norm group which consists of high school freshmen. The norm group used should always be that with which one wishes to compare the performance of the individual.

The Limitations of Most Systems of Converted Scores

There are, of course, instances in which meaning is lost by the use of converted scores. When a measure consists of the number of books which a child has read during a given semester, the measure is meaningful in and of itself. A fourth grade child who reads fifteen books during a year has spent a very desirable amount of time in this activity even if there are children who have spent much more time reading. A child at a similar level who has read only two books during the year has spent much less time than is deemed desirable at this activity, even though it is better than 50 per cent of the students in a particular school. The statement that a child spends seventeen hours per week watching television is much more meaningful than to state that his standard score for watching television is 65. On the other hand, a raw score on a test needs to be changed into some type of converted score because there is usually no frame of reference within which the raw scores can be given any interpretation.

It needs to be recognized that systems of transmuting scores do not represent the ultimate in providing interpretable scores. They merely provide a system of scores in which an individual's standing in a specified group can be recognized immediately from an examination of his score. From a study of a converted score it is not possible to know in the case of an achievement test whether the score represents a desirable performance in terms of the objectives that have been set for the educational program. For example, if individuals are being trained to understand speech in a foreign language, it is much less important to know the percentile rank on a test of one of these individuals among others in the group than to know the category among the following in which the individual belongs:

a. Can understand accurately the meaning of political speeches, learned addresses, and similar spoken materials.
b. Can get the general gist of political speeches, learned addresses, and similar materials, but may miss the details and fine points.
c. Can understand general conversation about everyday matters only.
d. Can understand only the answers to simple questions and simple directions concerning travel.
e. Can understand only short and simple sentences when they are spoken slowly.

Categories such as these have meaning in terms of the purposes of education. Unless measures of educational achievement can be interpreted in such terms, they must remain vague and relatively meaningless.

Converted scores are mainly reporting and recording devices. In most evaluative studies in education it is sufficient to use raw scores, since the problems studied involve only the direction of change. In addition, evaluation studies are likely to include more and more data other than test scores, and such data are usually directly interpretable in terms of the goals of education.

THE NATURE OF SCALES

Introduction

An understanding of the uses and limitations of educational and psychological measures cannot be divorced from an understanding of the relation of these measures to other widely used types of measuring instruments. A study of this relationship brings out clearly the inadequacies of the former for many purposes.

Types of Measuring Scales

The term *measurement* as it is used in education covers a number of only remotely related processes. Stevens points out that in the process of measurement, social scientists use at least four types of scales. Measurement is defined by Stevens (9) in a broad sense as the assignment of numerals to objects or events according to some rule. His four types of scales are as follows:

Nominal Scales. These scales arrange individuals or events in some arbitrary order, but once the order is established it becomes a means of identifying the individuals or events. An example of this is the assignment of a number to each member of a football squad. Once the numbers are assigned, they serve only to identify the individual. This type of scale is used when observers in the schoolroom record events by writing down the number that corresponds to that event.

Ordinal Scales. These correspond to scales of hardness used at one time by geologists to describe minerals. Various objects of uniform hardness represent points on the scale. The hardness of a given mineral is determined by which of the objects on the scale produces a scratch on it. Very soft objects are scratched easily by the softest object on the scale, while only a diamond will make an appreciable scratch on the hardest. It should be noted that this type of measuring device, because of its crudeness, has now been replaced by more objective and accurate devices for measuring hardness. These devices eliminate to a considerable extent the judgment of the person making the determination. Although this type of scale has been largely replaced by more accurate devices in the physical sciences, it is still commonly used in educational measurement. Most rating scales are of this type and consist of a graded series of descriptions of persons against which individuals to be rated are matched. The degree to which the objectives of a given course are achieved is often rated on a letter scale by A, B, C, D, and E. This scale also would be included by Stevens under the category of ordinal scale. It might be maintained that all psychological and educational measuring scales fall into this category or the previous one and that none of them fall into the two categories that follow.

Interval Scales. These are illustrated by scales such as the Fahrenheit or centigrade temperature scales. The units on these scales are in some sense equal to one another. There is an argument for placing psychological scales based on standard scores in this category except for the fact that the assumptions which have to be made in order to do this would be unacceptable to a very large number of psychologists.

Ratio Scales. The essential characteristic of this type of scale is that measurement is in terms of the ratio of a unit to the magnitude to be measured. Length scales are of this type. The length of a room is measured by the ratio of the length to standard foot scale. It is possible to make a direct comparison between the foot scale and the length of the room because the one can be superimposed upon the other. Examples in psychological measurement are few which permit the use of ratios in measurement in this way. The measurement of loudness is one example. Two sounds superimposed may match a third sound. Usually, however, it is not possible to superimpose one stimulus upon another for the purpose of comparison.

This classification of scales is presented in order to indicate that most scales of measurement used in education are largely of the crudest kind and do not approach the refinement which characterizes the scales commonly used in the physical sciences. As a result there are certain limitations on the use of measurement in education which must now be considered.

Certain Consequences of the Nature of Psychological and Educational Measuring Instruments in Evaluation Studies

Certain characteristics of educational and psychological measures have important consequences for their use in evaluation studies. Consider, for example, the common type of objective test of achievement which is frequently given in schools. These tests provide a score for each child indicating how he compares with certain other groups of children. Now, the very nature of this measuring instrument places limitations on its use. Suppose that one such test measures knowledge of American history and that equivalent forms of the test are given to a group of students before and after taking a course in American history. One student over this period increases his score from 25 to 40, while another shows an increase from 60 to 75. Both show increases of 15 points, but the increases are in different parts of the scale and cannot be compared. A change in score from 25 to 40 might represent a change from almost complete ignorance to one of superficial knowledge of the gross over-all features of our history. The difference between 60 and 75 might represent a difference between the knowledge possessed by the average college graduate and the knowledge of the expert in governmental affairs. The one increase might generally be produced in fourteen-year-old youngsters of average intelligence in six hours of class work, while the other increase might be produced only after years of study and years of experience in the affairs of government. If the two 15-point differences are to be compared in terms of the time taken to produce the corresponding amount of learning, then the difference at the lower end of the scale is not in any way comparable with the corresponding numerical difference at the upper end of the scale. If differences in the amount of change of two individuals is to be compared, then the change must be in comparable parts of the scale and must involve the same test questions. A change of scores from 41 to 54 can be compared with a change of scores from 43 to 51. The one change is necessarily greater than the other. However, if one change in score were 8 and the other 16, it would not be reasonable to conclude that the one change was twice as large as the other. The latter comparison could be made only if it were certain that the units in the scale were all equal.

The importance of this fact is not always appreciated by those who attempt to reform grading systems and who wish to base grades on measured progress rather than on final standing. The growth scores of one child cannot be compared numerically with those of another except where they are derived from the same part of the scale.

A second characteristic of most educational and psychological measuring instruments which limits their value is that they do not usually have a true zero, or, to state the problem more precisely, the point on the scale which represents a true zero is not known. The distinction must be made between a zero on a scale and a true zero which represents a zero quantity of whatever is being measured. An illustration from the field of physics will make the matter clear. A scale commonly used for measuring temperature is the Fahrenheit scale. On this scale the freezing point is 32°, and 0° is of course considerably below the freezing point of water. It is obvious that 0° does not represent the ultimate in coldness, for even terrestrial temperatures drop below this point at certain times and places. It is also obvious that a true zero should represent a complete absence of warmth. The true zero has been determined and is known to be several hundred degrees below the arbitrary zero which has been placed on the Fahrenheit scale. The temperature 0° F. does not represent a meaningful zero at all, but is just an arbitrary point on the scale. Despite this fact, the Fahrenheit scale can be and is widely used for measuring purposes. As a matter of fact, it is only very rarely that it is necessary to convert temperatures into a scale in which the zero on the scale is the true zero of temperature. The arbitrary zero of the Fahrenheit scale is a disadvantage only in exceptional circumstances.

In the case of temperature scales, a true zero of temperature can be determined. This can be done because a great deal is known concerning the nature of heat and it is possible to describe accurately the conditions under which there will be a true absence of heat. It is possible because physics has developed to a relatively advanced state. In the early stages of the development of the physical sciences, it was not possible to give a definite meaning to the term *absolute zero* of temperature because little was known about the nature of heat, but in spite of this limitation many significant researches were carried out. In the same way, it is not possible in the present state of psychological knowledge to give any real meaning to a zero of intelligence. Our concepts related to the meaning of intelligence are still too vague to do this or even to know whether it can be done, but it is still possible to carry out meaningful experiments which involve the use of measures of intelligence.

The consequences of the fact that most psychological scales do not have a true zero need to be considered. Just as it is not defensible to say that a Fahrenheit temperature of 80° is twice as hot as 40°, so too is it equally unreasonable to assert that a student who achieves a T-score of 80 on a test of American history knows twice as much as a student who achieves a T-score of 40 on the same test. Both might know an immense amount about American history, but the test might cover only points of interest to the scholar and specialist. On a college test of American history, both of these students might obtain a perfect score.

In spite of the crudeness of the measuring instruments which are available for use in educational evaluation, guidance, and research, much of great significance has been accomplished through their use.

THE VALIDITY OF PSYCHOLOGICAL AND EDUCATIONAL MEASURES

Validity of Achievement Tests

A distinction is commonly made between tests of aptitude and tests of achievement in that aptitude tests are designed for making predictions concerning future learning behavior, while achievement tests are for measuring what the individual has learned in the past. Thus in validating aptitude tests, the problem is that of determining whether they predict the pupil's ability to learn in particular situations. In validating achievement tests, the problem is that of determining whether they measure the extent to which the pupil can use the learning he has acquired. Aptitude tests must, of course, measure to some extent what a pupil has learned, but they are used mainly for making predictions of future learning behavior.

In the case of most achievement tests, it is not possible to determine whether scores on the tests are closely related to true measures of the achievement they purport to measure. Ultimate criteria of this kind are not generally available, and neither are usable proximate criteria. Hence, it is usually necessary to validate achievement tests by judging whether they satisfy certain conditions necessary for validity. These conditions will now be considered.

Validity by Identification of All Behaviors in the Sample with All Behaviors in the Criterion

Measures of achievement may be valid for assessing what a pupil has learned because all behaviors in the measurement procedure are identical with all behaviors that the pupil has had opportunity to learn. A teacher may be concerned with developing the ability to multiply together two single-digit numbers. The ability is further defined as the ability to undertake these multiplications when the problems are presented in written form and the answer is to be written in a blank space provided. The teacher may prepare a test which asks the students to multiply together pairs of one-digit numbers and to write down the answers. The test is administered under congenial conditions and sufficient time is given each student for him to attempt every problem. The score on such a test is by definition valid because there is complete identity between the behaviors involved in the test situation and the behaviors which are accepted as evidence of the existence of the particular ability.

Another example in which validity of a measurement procedure is established through the identity of the behaviors in the test situation and the behaviors that are accepted as the evidence of the existence of the ability is that of a test for janitors. In the particular situation under discussion, the applicants for positions of janitors were given training in about sixty different tasks which janitors are required to perform. At the end of the course, each man was given every one of the tasks to perform and was scored for specific errors made in each situation. Most of the tasks were sufficiently specific so that the performance in each test situation could be scored as right or wrong. In this example, direct evidence is collected of the achievement of a given ability and the evidence collected is complete. The test is necessarily valid in that it measures whether an individual can do the things he is supposed to be able to do. However, it may not be valid for determining whether he will perform correctly in a job situation. This could be found out only by testing him in an actual job.

Validity by Identification of All Behaviors in the Sample with Some Behaviors in the Criterion

If the test of arithmetic previously described were found to be excessively long and were reduced in length, the resulting instrument would cover only some of the behaviors included in the ability that it was desired to measure. In one sense, this procedure results in a loss of validity but in another sense it does not. The test loses validity because it is possible for a person who knew only those number combinations represented by the test to obtain a high score, and such a person would score as well as a person who knew *all* of the possible number combinations. If, for some reason, a teacher felt that it was very important for her children to make a good showing on the test, it is conceivable that she might give her children drill only on those number combinations included in it. Under these conditions, the test would lose validity as a measure of the ability to multiply together *any* two single-digit numbers. However, in ordinary situations the test *may* not lose validity. Suppose that both the original long form and the short form were both administered to the same group of two hundred children. Suppose that the scores on the one test were closely related to the scores on the other test, and so closely related that if the score on the long test were known, then the score on the short test could be predicted with almost no error at all, and the shorter test would be considered to be as valid an instrument as the longer test. What happens in this case is that the long test becomes the criterion and the short test is validated against this criterion. It must be pointed out that, although the short test was shown to be a valid measure of the criterion in this particular case, it does not follow that it will be valid under all circumstances. If, as was pointed out, the teacher sets high scores on the test as her goal, it will cease to provide a valid measure of the outcome it was originally designed to measure.

The ability to multiply together one-digit numbers is a much simpler one than that encountered in most educational studies. This ability can be defined in terms of 80 separate items of behavior. This assumes that the behavior involved in multiplying 7 by 2 is different from the behavior involved in multiplying 2 by 7. There is evidence to show that this assumption is justifiable. If a test includes only 40 distinct items of this kind, it samples a fraction of the total domain of behavior equal to 40 divided by 80. It is possible in this instance to know exactly what fraction of all behaviors are included in the abilities that are being sampled, but in most other instances it is not possible to do this. If it is desired to measure the ability to apply principles of plain geometry to the solution of common everyday problems, the number of problems which might be solved by such principles is for all practical purposes unlimited. (Assume that the principles of geometry included have been specified and form a short and limited list.) If the student is tested on his ability to make 50 applications, it is not possible to state that he was tested in one-half or one-eighth of all possible applications that might occur. The true value of this fraction is indeterminate, since the number of behaviors involved is not necessarily finite. Neither is it possible by great diligence to include in a criterion measure all the behaviors that are accepted as evidence of the achievement of the ability. All that can be done in this situation is to ensure that the behaviors included in the measure of the ability to apply geometrical principles are in some way representative of all behaviors that might be included in this particular domain. One can never be entirely sure that the behaviors to be elicited by a test situation are actually representative of the total domain.

In a similar way, in the measurement of attitudes it may be desired to appraise how a person may behave in a wide variety of situations. If an educational program attempts to develop in white children a favorable attitude toward Negroes, then the attempt is made to develop desirable behavior in this respect in all situations in which a Negro is either directly involved or involved in concept. By no process imaginable is it possible to list all of the situations included in this category.

In order for a measure to be valid on the basis of possessing identical elements with the elements in the criterion, it is also necessary for there to be general identity of conditions under which the behaviors are to occur. If the criterion in the case of the ability to multiply together two single-digit numbers refers to the ability to do this task under conditions where the individual is not harassed, the measure of this ability will be less valid when it is measured under conditions where the individual is harassed. If a test of the ability of a teacher to control a class is to be measured by a test in which the individual has to solve classroom problems which are described in print in great detail, a teacher may be able to solve all of these problems in the printed test but fail to solve the same problems when they actually occur in the classroom. Under the latter conditions he may become emotionally disturbed and unable to solve any problem in a rational way. In this case, the test situation and the criterion situation are similar in some respects but differ in essential details. These differences in detail may invalidate the entire test.

Face Validity. This is a term which has acquired widespread use during the last decade to refer to the resemblance between the problems in a test and the problems in the criterion situations which the person has been prepared to solve. A few psychologists have gone so far as to suggest that superficial resemblances of this kind are important because it is then easier to explain the purpose of the instrument to the consumer.

An example of *face* validity may clarify the meaning of the term.

In a school for training certain specialists in the U. S. Army, it was found that many men failed to complete the course because of insufficient background in arithmetic. A test was built for screening applicants for admission which covered achievement in arithmetic necessary for passing the course. In order to make the testing situation as acceptable as possible to soldiers, the arithmetic problems all dealt with military situations. It is probable that this did not alter the validity of the instrument, but it did make the men feel that they were being examined on their ability to handle problems which they might have to handle in army life. The flavor of the test had what might be called a public relations value.

Degree of Artificiality of a Test Situation in Relation to Validity of Achievement Tests

Some test situations match almost exactly the criterion situations to which they correspond, except for certain minor conditions such as the presence of an examiner. At the end of a course given to train machinists, it may be possible to test students on exactly those operations they will have to perform in their subsequent jobs. In a test given at the end of a secretarial course, the student may be required to undertake the tasks commonly assigned to secretaries. In both of these situations, the problems assigned in the test situation are identical with those in the criterion situation except for the fact that in an examination a person is likely to be more highly motivated and more tense than in the same situation after employment.

Close similarity between the test situation and the actual situation with which the individual has been trained to cope often has to be sacrificed in order that a test may be produced which can be cheaply and easily administered. It may not be possible to test a person's ability to establish a complete filing system for an office, since to do this it would be necessary for him to work in the office for some time and to be fully aware of its activities and the problems with which it has to cope. So what is usually done is to examine him on his knowledge of filing systems, or to describe a situation in which a filing system has to be established and to ask him how he would deal with the problem. The common substitute for the real situation is one in which a problem is presented in a written form. Such written descriptions, for the most part, provide only a skeleton of detail and, unless they are written by an author of real stature are likely to provide a very poor framework for presenting a problem.

A printed page is always easier to distribute than a mass of equipment, but once test situations have been simplified in this way there is often no limit to the license that the test maker is likely to take in further simplification of the situation. It is all too common practice to simplify problem situations for the purposes of test administration to the point where there is little resemblance left between the situation that the pupil was trained to handle and the situation with which he is confronted. The teacher of high school English may conscientiously state that his primary objective is to teach the children to write in such a way that after they leave school they may be able to communicate their ideas clearly to others. On further discussion, he mentions how later they will have to compose their own business correspondence, write office memoranda, and perhaps prepare office reports, and all these details add to the impression that the teacher has a clear and worth-while purpose in mind. But what does this teacher do to appraise the achievement of pupils in the course? Why, like most other teachers, he asks the children to write a composition on some topic such as "Bees" or "Public Transportation." The resemblance between the total situation that training was alleged to help the pupils to handle and the total situation in which their achievement was appraised seems to be limited to the fact that both involve writing. This last example happens to be drawn from the field of English, but other subject-matter fields yield equally dramatic examples. A teacher of mathematics talks about helping her children to handle common practical mathematical problems, but appraises achievement in terms of their ability to solve abstract numerical problems by mechanical routine.

Written tests often omit essential elements in a given achievement other than those already mentioned. Training programs in leadership have often been terminated with a written test covering the principles of leadership. On a test of this kind, a person may demonstrate a knowledge of how to handle the various leadership problems presented in the test. However, the same individual in the real situation may fail completely because the stresses involved in the handling of people may be too much for him and cause him to become nervous, upset, and disorganized. In this case, the paper-

and-pencil test omits an important central element of the real situation which is crucial in determining the performance of an individual.

Validity of Aptitude Tests

Up to this point in the discussion, reference has been made to the problem of validating tests of achievement—that is, tests which attempt to measure what a person has learned or how he can use that learning. The problem of validating such tests is somewhat different from that of validating aptitude tests. It has already been stated that the difference between an achievement test and an aptitude test lies not in the nature of the test itself but in the purpose for which it is used. Tests built for measuring achievement are commonly used as aptitude tests. For example, tests of achievement in the English language are commonly used for predicting success in college. When they are used for this purpose, they may be referred to as tests of college aptitude.

The validity of aptitude tests is assessed in terms of the extent to which they are successful in predicting the ability to learn in whatever situation they are supposed to predict learning. The problem of validating a test of aptitude resolves itself into that of (1) defining what is to be predicted, (2) measuring the criterion that is thus defined, and (3) determining whether the instrument predicts the criterion. These three steps present the illusion of simplicity, but actually therein lie some of the most difficult problems of applied psychology.

1. *What Is to Be Predicted.* It seems odd that there are often difficulties involved in deciding what is to be predicted. A case which illustrates this problem to an extreme degree is that faced by teachers' colleges which attempt to predict how effective as teachers prospective students will be after training. In this connection, there seems common agreement that the effectiveness of a teacher should be measured in terms of the amount of desirable pupil growth, but we cannot agree on just what constitutes desirable pupil growth or how it should be described. Discussion of this very complex matter rarely progresses beyond the stage of vague generalities.

Another common problem in this area may also be described.

Those concerned with the development of tests of academic aptitude do not agree upon what these tests should predict. Some have been concerned with predicting grades since, it is argued, educational advancement depends upon the student's obtaining good grades. Others have attempted to predict educational achievement as measured by objective tests which, it is claimed, are less contaminated with the irrelevant factors which contaminate grades.

2. *Measuring the Criterion.* Even when a criterion has been defined, there is no guaranty that it is possible to measure it. Even if teacher effectiveness has been well defined, it may still be quite impossible at the present time to measure it. Even if descriptions could be made of the kinds of growth in personality that teachers should help to produce in fourth grade childhen, it is almost certain that little could be done to measure these variables. Personality theory is still in too primitive a stage to permit the development of adequate instruments.

There seems to be a widespread belief among educators that once a criterion has been defined in words, it is an easy matter to develop an instrument for measuring it. Except for the simplest aspects of behavior, nothing could be further from the case. Among other things, this approach completely disregards the important problem of the dimensionality of criteria.

Most criteria that it is desired to predict in education are extremely complex phenomena and cannot be described in terms of a single dimension. For example, it is commonly stated that good social adjustment is a desirable outcome of education, and it is often implied in this statement that it is possible to arrange individuals in order from the best adjusted to the most poorly adjusted. Yet such an implication is completely unwarranted. Social adjustment is a complex phenomenon which can be described only with reference to many variables. A multidimensional system is needed for describing the phenomenon. A child who is socially well adjusted in his home may be socially maladjusted in his school. A child may be well adjusted toward his teacher but aggressive and hostile toward his parents. The term *social adjustment* refers to a number of distinct and independent dimensions of behavior.

3. *Determining Whether the Instrument Predicts the Criterion.* The traditional method of doing this has been to establish a correlation between the predictor variable and the criterion measure. Until

recently, the idea was commonly maintained that the larger the correlation, the happier the educator or the psychologist should be, but this type of thinking is not entirely satisfactory. Large correlations between predictors and criteria are often a result of spurious and irrelevant elements.

Gulliksen (3) has pointed out that the common tendency in the past has been for the psychologist to be satisfied with a relatively high correlation between a test and a criterion, often without understanding why that relationship exists. The correlations thus achieved often have little meaning and are a by-product of conditions which are strictly irrelevant. Gulliksen illustrates this point by referring to a case in which a reading test was found to correlate well with grades in navy gunners' schools. This was because the training program in these schools gave undue emphasis to the study of reading manuals. When more practical work was introduced, the validity of this test fell. Another example of apparent validity resulting from irrelevant variables is the fact that the number of credits taken in foreign language courses in high school correlates positively with grades in college. The reason for this seems to be that the abler students take foreign languages in high school and also obtain superior grades in college.

In order to designate the validity of an aptitude test based on a rational relationship and to distinguish it from the coincidental validity, Gulliksen has introduced the expression *intrinsic correlational validity*. In the field of achievement tests, Gulliksen uses the corresponding expression *intrinsic content validity*, but this term seems to confuse the issue because achievement tests must be valid with respect to the processes they measure as well as with respect to the content, through which the measurement is made. An achievement test may measure an irrelevant psychological process with a relevant type of content.

What is sought in education is instruments which can in some way be used for making predictions about the future behavior of the individual. It is important that there should be some rational relationship between behavior in the test situation from which predictions are made and behavior in the situations in which predictions are to be made. Unless the nature of this relationship is properly understood, any guidance based on the instruments is likely to be dangerous. In addition to the examples already given, the following hypothetical example illustrates the dangers which are inherent in an instrument used blindly for predictive purposes without any insight into the reasons why it appears to have predictive value (10).*

Consider, for example, a hypothetical case of a large industrial concern employing many scientists. Some of these scientists are later placed in high administrative positions while some continue to do research. Suppose that the personnel department in this concern decided to develop an instrument which would discriminate between those newly-appointed scientists who would be likely to be promoted to a high-level administrative work and those who would stay in research. The purpose of this instrument was to select a greater number of those who could be promoted later to high administrative positions. In this situation, the test technicians followed the procedure of drawing up a biographical inventory which was administered to the group of scientists who had been promoted to high-level administrative positions and to a group who had been with the company an equal length of time but who had remained in research. It was found that quite a large number of the biographical items discriminated between the two groups, and by assigning proper weights to these items it was possible to develop a scoring system for the inventory which could be applied to new applicants for research positions. On this basis, it became possible to select a larger number of scientists who had scores nearer to the administrators than to the research worker. Let us suppose that this scale was used over a period of years and studies indicated that it did predict with considerable accuracy those who would acquire administrative positions and that, therefore, it was decided to publish the scale under the title "Scale of Administrative Ability." The scale was also shown to be correlated with the ratings given these administrators by the top officials of the concern. This scale became widely used and was praised extensively by executives and was on its way to becoming a publishing success when a psychologist examined it with some care and observed that the responses which were given high loadings had no apparent relationship to success in an administrative capacity. For example, a person was given credit on the Administrative Scale for having a rural background, for coming from a family of skilled craftsmen, for not coming from a family that earned a living in a retail business in a large city. The scale bore little relationship to the purposes for which it was built, but as the technicians said, "it worked." The item weights were nonsensical but in view of the fact that the scale had been shown to

* The material quoted is reproduced by kind permission of Dr. G. Frederic Kuder, editor, *Educational and Psychological Measurement*.

have selective value, the scale and the procedure for building it seemed to be defensible. Many technicians felt justified in concluding that it was just additional evidence to show that the only way to build a measuring instrument is to try out large numbers of items, for who can tell which items will work?

However, this does not end the fable, for the scientist who noted the peculiar nature of the discriminating items in the scale went on to study the conditions under which the scale had been built and "validated." He soon discovered that the management of the manufacturing concern was strongly anti-semitic and excluded from promotions to high positions those who were Jewish. Occasionally, it happened that a research worker who was Jewish was given an administrative post and when this happened, the chances were that because of prejudice he would be given a low rating for administrative effectiveness.

The scale which the test technicians developed by a blind statistical method merely discriminated between a Jewish and a non-Jewish background and emphasized the sociological factors associated with this variable. When the scale was used in other places, it would tend to exclude from positions those who came from Jewish homes. It would, in effect, be a device which perpetrated a wholly unjustifiable prejudice.

One cannot help wondering how often instruments built by test technicians do just this kind of thing. The technician's approach may have consequences such as these, though in general, it does not. However, it is a basically dangerous technique. Similar examples of the dangers of this technique may be found in other fields. In contrast, the scientific approach to the construction of tests not only produces instruments of more certain value but also advances knowledge in a systematic way.

It is, therefore, not enough that a test have apparently predictive value. If it is to have intrinsic validity, it is necessary for there to be an identifiable relationship between the behavior called for by the instrument and the criterion behavior. It is most important that instruments used for making predictions in educational guidance have intrinsic validity.

Expected Levels of Validity

Since the time of the early workers in the field of psychological measurement, the hope has been implicit in validation studies that tests will eventually be found which will correlate 1.00 with criteria.

This aim is not satisfactory because it ignores certain relevant factors in the prediction problem, as may be shown by considering a specific case.

Consider the problem of building a test which will correlate to a maximum degree with performance in college as measured by college grades over a period of two or more years. It is quite unreasonable to suppose that if the best possible test were built it would correlate perfectly with college grades even if the latter provided a perfectly reliable criterion. This maximum level of predictability cannot be achieved because conditions in the college situation itself may result in the unexpected raising or lowering of average grades. A student who receives early and adequate counseling may replan his program and change his career from one of failure to one of success. Another student may be handicapped throughout his program by unexpected financial problems which blight his entire college career.

These unpredictable and unexpected events may limit to a remarkable degree the extent to which predictions can be made of behavior in a given situation and thus, even with the perfect test battery, relatively low correlations may sometimes be expected between test scores and the variable that it is desired to predict. In the case of the prediction of college grades, few tests have shown validity coefficients higher than 0.7, and one is tempted to hypothesize that this may represent the maximum degree of relationship that can be reasonably expected to occur under optimum conditions.

RELIABILITY AS A CHARACTERISTIC OF MEASURING INSTRUMENTS

The Meaning of Reliability

The reliability of a measure is commonly defined as the degree to which it measures consistently or accurately whatever it does measure. All measurement involves a certain amount of error. In measuring a living room with a linen tape, the measured dimensions will only approximate the true dimensions, for in making the measurements the tape may have been stretched too little or too much. By using a rigid steel tape such as surveyors use, the error of measurement can be reduced, but it cannot be eliminated. In physical measurement, the errors of measurement are relatively small and sometimes do not exceed one part in a million. In the biological sciences on the other hand, substantial errors are involved in most measurement; and hence there is relatively less consistency found when measurement is repeated. Some educational and psychological measurement often involves such substantial errors of measurement as to render it worthless. Owing to the fact that this is a relatively common occurrence, it is necessary in education to have an estimate of the size of this error whenever measurements are made in order to know whether they can or cannot be considered meaningful. Usually an estimate of the over-all reliability of a measure is expressed in terms of a coefficient of reliability which in the case of a perfectly reliable measuring instrument would be equal to 1.00. In a completely unreliable measuring instrument which did not measure anything consistently, the value of this coefficient would be 0.00.

A coefficient of reliability gives a general over-all appraisal of the consistency of measurement, but it may happen that measurement is more accurate in one part of the scale than in another. The coefficient of reliability does not indicate whether or not this is so.

Reliability of a test under ideal circumstances would be determined by administering the test twice under identical conditions to the group in which the test was to reveal individual differences. This cannot be done, since each time a test is administered to a group, it becomes a somewhat different test for that group. Practice and familiarity with the material modify the responses of the individual to the test situation. Thus it is possible only to *estimate* what the reliability under ideal conditions would be, since the conditions necessary for *measuring* it cannot be produced. There are at least four ways in which reliability is commonly estimated.

1. *The Test-Retest Method.* This method involves the administration of the same measuring instrument on repeated occasions. It provides only an estimate of the reliability, since individuals do not respond twice in the same way to the same situation and some learning occurs on the first occasion which is utilized on the second occasion. Some individuals learn more than others by taking a test, and consequently increases in scores vary from one person to another. Therefore, in most cases, the procedure is more like administering somewhat different tests on two occasions rather than in administering the same test twice. Since the reliability of the test is determined by computing

the correlation between the scores on successive administrations, it can be seen that the source of variability mentioned, together with the other sources, will tend to lower the reliability expressed as a correlation coefficient.

This method of estimating reliability of scores is rather meaningless when used to estimate the reliability of data such as the number of books read by children while in the third grade or the number of hours per week spent in group activity in kindergarten. Scores of this kind cannot be compared with scores achieved during the following year because growth will have produced changes which makes it unreasonable to assume that the measures are comparable.

2. *The Equivalent-Form Method.* This method requires the use of two equivalent forms of the instrument which are administered to the same group. The weaknesses present in the previous method are inherent in this method. Individuals tend to show improvement from one form to the next and also show changes in their performance from hour to hour. The assumption must also be made that the two forms are "equivalent," but there is often difficulty in establishing equivalence.

3. *Part-Score Methods.* These methods of estimating reliability are based upon the concept that, with a reliable test, a score based on one sample of the items should be correlated with a score obtained from another sample. This is really an extension of the idea of estimating reliability from two equivalent forms of a test. In the latter case, it is assumed that the two forms of a test represent samples of the same domain of behavior, and for similar reasons it may be assumed that the items in a test can be divided up into two tests of half the original length, each of which also samples the same domain of behavior The reliability of the total instrument is obviously related to the correlation between these two half tests.

The problem immediately arises as to how a test should be split in order to obtain two scores. It is evident that it is not essential to split the test before it is administered, since the scores can be obtained from separate groups of items after the test is administered, although it must be conceded that a test item may change in characteristics such as difficulty if it is taken out of, or left in, context. A somewhat crude way of splitting the test is to divide it into the odd-numbered and even-numbered items. A more refined method consists of matching items in the two halves both for content and difficulty. The latter method results in two half-length tests which are so far as possible similar.

The correlation between scores from the two halves of the test will provide an estimate of the reliability of each of the half-length tests. By the application of a statistical formula, it is then possible to estimate the reliability for the full length of test. This formula is given in Appendix B.

The procedure which has been just outlined assumes that the standard deviations of the two halves are equal, but formulas have been developed which eliminate the necessity for making this assumption.

Part-score methods of estimating reliability must not be applied to speeded tests because under such conditions they will grossly overestimate reliability. The fact that there is some speed element in most tests means that in general they are likely to overestimate the reliability.

4. *Methods Based on Statistical Deductions from Distributions of Scores.* The best known of these methods was developed by G. F. Kuder and M. W. Richardson (5), who provided a number of formulas which are widely applied. In order to use these formulas it is usually necessary to make some assumption which is often not fully justified. In the case of one of these formulas, it is necessary to assume that all items measure the same functions; in the case of another it is necessary to assume that all the items are equal in difficulty and show equal interrelationships.

There has been some discussion in recent time as to just what is measured by the coefficients derived from these methods (see Loevinger, 6), but the fact remains that the Kuder-Richardson coefficients of reliability usually approximate closely those obtained from equivalent-form methods except where the tests are highly speeded.

The Standard Error of a Score

A concept related to reliability is that of the standard error of a score. When most measurements, either physical or psychological, are repeated a number of times, it is usual to find that there is some variation in the values obtained. In physical measurements this

variation is small, although often of consequence. It is for this reason
that the surveyor repeats his readings and arranges his instrument
so that errors from successive readings may be compensating. In
psychological measurement, substantial variation occurs from one
occasion when a measurement is made with a test to the next occasion when the measurement is repeated with an equivalent form of
the same test. Of course, the higher the correlation between the two
forms, the smaller the variation is likely to be. If it were possible to
administer a measurement procedure many times to an individual
under the same conditions, the resulting scores would show a certain
amount of scatter. The standard deviation of these scores would be
their standard error. It can be easily understood that a measuring
instrument might provide more consistent measures in one part of
the scale than in another. For example, an intelligence test might
provide relatively consistent measures for high-scoring individuals
but highly inconsistent measures for persons scoring near the average.
Thus the standard error of a score may vary in different parts of the
scale.

It is rarely possible to obtain the standard error of a score at a
particular point on a scale because of the insuperable difficulties of
repeating measurement under identical conditions. However, it is
possible to estimate the standard error of scores in general derived
from the test. The standard error of measurement for a test provides
an estimate of how much scores are likely to vary if measurement
is repeated under identical conditions, but it does not take into
account the fact that the standard error of a score is often much
larger in one part of a scale than another. The standard error of
measurement for a test is estimated by computing the value of
$\sigma\sqrt{1-r_{12}}$ in which σ is the standard deviation of the scores on the
test and r_{12} is its estimated reliability under the conditions for which
the standard error of measurement is to be estimated. Thus if a test
were administered and the standard deviation of the scores obtained
was 10 and if the estimated reliability was 0.91, the standard
error of measurement for a score on that test would be equal to
$10\sqrt{1-0.91}=3.0$.

This would mean that if it were possible to measure a person
repeatedly *under identical conditions*, his scores would *tend* to form
a distribution which would have a standard deviation of 3.0. If
these scores were normally distributed, we could then say from our

knowledge of the normal distribution that 95 per cent of them would fall within a range of ±6 points of the obtained value.

The advantages of the standard error of measurement over the correlation coefficient as a method of expressing the reliability of a test are obvious. The standard error of measurement is, in general, much more readily interpreted and understood by the teacher than is reliability expressed by a correlation coefficient, and it tends to draw attention to the fact that minor differences and changes in score are inconsequential.

Some Conditions Affecting Estimated Reliability

Numerous factors affect the reliability of a particular measure. Some of these are primarily characteristics of the test and others primarily characteristics of the situations in which the test is used. Each one of the following factors affects the reliability of a measure.

First, if the number of elements in a measure is increased by adding elements which are homogeneous with those already included, the reliability is likely to be increased. For example, if an investigator is concerned with the number of hours which each one of a number of children spends in front of television receivers, he might obtain a record of the time spent during a given week. However, for some children the week might not have been typical, since their receivers might have been out of order, others would have been sick, and still others would have encountered other unusual events. Consequently, if the same measure were repeated, there would be divergencies between the first and the second measures. But if each of these measures covered not a week but a month, then these atypical events would be of much less significance in estimating the average amount of time spent each day in front of a television receiver. The longer the period of observation, the more accurate would be the estimate of the average amount of time spent each day in this activity.

Second, the reliability of a measure will depend also on the group on whom the measurements are made. In this connection, it must be pointed out that for a measure to be reliable, it must show the same differences between the same individuals from one application to another. When differences between individuals are smaller than those which the measuring device is designed to measure, the differences measured will not appear consistently from one attempt at appraisal to the next. For example, a test developed to measure knowledge of the names of tools consisted of 120 multiple-choice test items. When this test was administered to all the high school seniors in a small city, it was found to have a split-half reliability of 0.95 and the scores ranged from 20 up to 115. However, when the same test was administered to a group of machinists, the scores ranged from 106 to 117 and the reliability estimated from this group was 0.2. In the case of the machinists, differences in scores would be considered almost meaningless, and this is reflected in the low reliability coefficient derived from this group.

Third, the estimated reliability of an instrument is affected by variations in the conditions under which it is administered, but the numerous relevant factors included in this category need not be enumerated here.

Reproducibility and Homogeneity of Measuring Instruments

Psychological measuring devices are characterized in varying degrees by a property which has not yet been considered. This property is known as reproducibility. It is easiest to understand this concept by examining the following two short tests, one of which illustrates high reproducibility and the other low:

Test A	*Test B*
1. $15 \times 23 =$	1. What is the meaning of the word *taboo*?
2. If $X = 3$, then $2X^2 + 4X^2 + X^3 =$	2. What is the meaning of the word *ketone*?
3. $\dfrac{d}{dX} \, 4X^3 =$	3. What is the meaning of the word *syllogism*?

If the mathematics test were administered, the right and wrong answers would almost certainly fall into one of the following four patterns produced by four different pupils:

	Pupil 1	*Pupil 2*	*Pupil 3*	*Pupil 4*
Problem 1	Wrong	Right	Right	Right
Problem 2	Wrong	Wrong	Right	Right
Problem 3	Wrong	Wrong	Wrong	Right

In responding to the items in the test, the pupil is able to answer all items correctly up to a particular point and fails all items beyond that point. Of course, the items would not have to be presented in order of difficulty. A test which manifests this property is referred to as a highly reproducible test. It should be noted that in such a test, a score of 1 always means that Problem 1 was answered correctly, a score of 2 that the Problems 1 and 2 were answered correctly, and so on. From the score on such a test it is always possible to determine with some precision which items were answered correctly. Some researchers, impressed with the fact that on such a test the pattern of responses can be reproduced from the score, refer to such scales as reproducible (4).

Now, consider in contrast the three-item vocabulary test. A person may be able to answer any one of these three test items without being able to answer the other two. If it is known that a person achieved a score of one item right, there is no way of knowing which item he answered correctly. His pattern of right and wrong answers cannot be *reproduced* from his score. This vocabulary test has almost zero reproducibility.

Tests which are reproducible are sometimes referred to as homogeneous tests (6) but this term *homogeneous* is also used to refer to other properties of tests. Sometimes it refers to the fact that the items of a test are similar (or homogeneous) in content, but this is an entirely different matter from reproducibility. Sometimes it refers to a property of tests related to reproducibility which may be described as the power of the test to make discriminations among pupils.

In educational measurement one usually seeks to avoid tests like Test B in which there is little or no relationship between the ability to answer one item and the ability to answer another. Rather, one seeks to develop tests which provide scores that reflect a definite pattern of response.

Summary

1. The purpose of this chapter has been to familiarize the reader with some of the characteristics of measuring instruments used in education. It is important that the reader be familiar with these

characteristics, for he will then recognize some of the limitations ⟨ the instruments he uses.

2. The shape of the distribution of scores derived from a particular measurement procedure will vary according to what is measured and according to how it is measured. While many measures of human characteristics are distributed approximately in the form of a normal distribution, others are not. Tests are commonly built so that they will produce a distribution of scores which is approximately normal.

3. In most educational measurement procedures, raw scores are converted into other forms of scores which are more easily interpreted. The type of converted score which is most easily understood is the percentile score, or percentile rank, as it is commonly called. A much more useful system of converted scores are normalized scores of which T-scores are those most frequently used. Age equivalents and grade equivalents are also widely used, but are commonly misinterpreted.

4. Tables for converting raw scores into a more interpretable form of score are referred to as norms. Norms should be based on the performance of a well-identified group described as the norm group.

5. Most scales of measurement used in education are relatively crude, and because of their crudeness certain limitations are imposed on their uses. Rarely can it be said in education that one score represents twice as much of what is being measured as another; neither is it usually possible to compare the amount of improvement shown by one pupil with that shown by another.

6. Instruments used for educational measurement should be more than just collections of test items, but should be such that they discriminate among pupils on a meaningful dimension.

7. Tests are sometimes classified as aptitude tests or as achievement tests according to whether they are used for predicting a pupil's ability to learn or according to whether they measure what a person has learned or how he can apply what has been learned.

8. The validity of a test for measuring achievement and the validity of a test for predicting the pupil's ability to learn are determined by different procedures. Of particular importance is the fact that otherwise irrelevant aspects of the measurement situation may seriously limit the inferences that can be made from test scores.

9. An important characteristic of measuring instruments is reliability, which can only be estimated and never directly measured. Various methods of estimating reliability are available. A concept related to reliability is that of the standard error of a score.

References

1. Fisher, R. A., *Statistical Methods for Research Workers,* London, Oliver and Boyd, 1936, pp. 339 + XII.
2. Flanagan, J. C., *A Bulletin Reporting the Basic Principles and Procedures Used in the Development of Their System of Scaled Scores,* New York, Cooperative Test Service, 1939, pp. 41.
3. Gulliksen, Harold, "Intrinsic Validity," *The American Psychologist,* 10, 1950, 511–517.
4. Guttman, Louis, "A Basis for Scaling Quantitative Data," *American Sociological Review,* 9, 1944, 139–150.
5. Kuder, G. F. and Richardson, M. W., "The Theory of the Estimation of Test Reliability," *Psychometrika,* 2, 1937, 251–260.
6. Loevinger, Jane, "A Systematic Approach to the Construction and Evaluation of Tests of Ability," *Psychological Monographs,* 61, No. 4, 1947, pp. 49 + III.
7. McCall, William A., *Measurement,* New York, The Macmillan Company, 1939, pp. 535 + XV.
8. Newbold, E. M., *A Contribution to the Study of the Human Factor in the Causation of Accidents.* Industrial Fatigue Research Board. Report No. 34, London, His Majesty's Stationery Office, 1926, pp. 74 + V.
9. Stevens, S. S., "On the Theory of Scales of Measurement," *Science,* 103, 1946, 677–680.
10. Travers, Robert M. W., "Rational Hypotheses in Educational and Psychological Measurement," *Educational and Psychological Measurement,* 11, 1951, 371–379.

PART II

Measuring the Intellectual Outcomes of Education

CHAPTER 4

The Measurement of Knowledge and Understanding

The Intellectual Objectives of Education

The previous chapter was concerned with the general nature of measurement procedures in psychology and education. The chapters which follow are devoted to the discussion of achievement variables that are commonly measured in education. Of all of these variables, those related to the intellectual development of the individual are not only the ones which receive the greatest emphasis in instruction but they also are the ones most frequently measured. It is probably inevitable that this is so, for much is known concerning effective procedures for producing intellectual development but relatively little concerning the effectiveness of methods of making changes in other aspects of the individual.

Central among the objectives related to the development of intelligent behavior are those pertaining to the acquisition of factual information, knowledge of principles and generalizations, and the ability to perform a great range of operations such as reasoning operations, problem-solving operations, operations involving the use of numbers, operations related to the manipulation of words, and a great range of other operations which require the manipulation of symbols, ideas, and objects. The ability to perform operations of these types are referred to here as skills, and thus it is customary to speak of thinking skills, reading skills, arithmetic skills, library skills, and so forth. The measurement of these skills will be considered in detail in the two chapters that follow.

This chapter is concerned with the measurement of the pupil's acquisition of information, knowledge, and understanding. By the acquisition of information is meant the learning of what is commonly called a fact, which is usually expressed in the form of a statement such as "Coal is mined in Pennsylvania," or "Cornwallis was defeated at Yorktown," or "Swift wrote *Gulliver's Travels*." Although the schools of Rice's time, according to his account of what he observed, emphasized the learning of such isolated facts by dreary class recitation, the tendency today is for facts to be learned in relation to other facts so that they are, as it is said, *understood*. In this discussion of the measurement of the pupil's information and understanding, it will be convenient to accept as a definition that the extent to which a fact is understood depends upon the extent to which the pupil can identify the relation of this fact to other facts. The child who has learned that *coal burns* and that *iron rusts* has little understanding of these phenomena unless he knows that the two phenomena are related in that both are examples of elements combining with oxygen. It is thus possible to measure the amount of factual information which a pupil has acquired and also his knowledge of the interrelationship of these facts. This chapter is concerned with the measurement of these two aspects of intellectual development which are distinguished here from reasoning skills, thinking skills, and the other intellectual operations that are frequently mentioned as major educational objectives.

The student of education who wishes to obtain more detailed insight into the distinction between information, understanding, and skill as the terms are used here is referred to an extended discussion of the matter presented in a book by Werkmeister (5).

The Measurement of Knowledge

In most educational programs that have ever been developed, the effectiveness of the program has usually been judged in terms of the amount of knowledge acquired. In the past this has been to a considerable extent the result of the fact that knowledge has been stressed as a major outcome of education. In the "mechanical schools" which Joseph Mayer Rice described, the ability of the pupils to report back items of information on which they had been drilled constituted the basic evidence of the effectiveness of the education provided. At the present time, teachers are much less concerned than they were in the last century with the acquisition of information as an end in itself, and other objectives are stressed, but tests and examinations given in most classes are still largely devoted to the measurement of the amount of information which the pupils have acquired. This apparent inconsistency between the stated purposes of education and the devices commonly used for measuring the results of teaching is a consequence of the fact that tests of information are easy to build. It is simple for a teacher to construct a quiz which will require the students to recall names of places and people, dates of events, and similar facts, but it is much more difficult for him to build a test which measures the ability of the pupil to think and solve problems.

The testing movement has also given considerable encouragement to those concerned with the measurement of the information possessed by the pupil, and each year millions of printed and published tests of information are administered to school children. The publishers of such tests commonly argue that teacher-made tests are usually of poor quality and that much is to be gained by the use of a professionally prepared test on which the amount of information possessed by a child can be compared with the amount possessed by other children of the same age. This argument needs to be examined rather carefully, because the flaws in it are not easily perceived. In order to identify these flaws, it seems desirable to study the major events in the history of the development of standardized tests.

The Pennsylvania Study

A landmark of basic importance in the measurement of knowledge is the Pennsylvania Study published by Wood and Learned (4) in 1938 after more than a decade of study. The purpose of the study was to review the current system of schooling in the light of objective evidence concerning its obtained results. Wood and Learned also hoped that the series of tests developed as a part of the study might prove to be useful substitutes for the system of determining level of educational achievement in terms of the number of courses which students have taken. They hoped that a profile of test scores would show what knowledge a student actually possessed, while a transcript shows only what courses he has taken. From the point of view of Wood and Learned, education was considered to be "unavoidably intellectual," and knowledge was necessarily the dominating feature among educational outcomes. Wood and Learned summarize their position in the following words (4, pp. 4–5):

Fortunately, the element of knowledge is the one element which has been recognized as constituting the core of any genuine educational product. It is because different bodies of knowledge are to be acquired that curricula differ among themselves. So complete has knowledge held the field that up to the present day in schools and colleges, its possession readily insures advancement while expressed stipulations as to other qualities that may be desired are negligible in comparison. It is difficult, in fact, to name any other element of educational importance that an institution will normally fix as a differentiating requirement for promotion from class to class. Certainly, the most important supplementary traits, such as "character," "attitude," "social efficiency," or "creative ability," are not conspicuous features of a school or college population as a result of any specific stipulation on the part of the institutions, whatever its ideals or influence may be. It is the actual or assumed possession of knowledge that counts; a failure in character of attitude must be sensational indeed, in order to disqualify any student either for admission or for graduation.

Fortunately, Wood and Learned, while apparently endorsing an intellectualistic approach to education, had a very broad conception of knowledge, and did not, like so many, limit their conception of it to isolated elements of information learned by heart. In the following words, they give their meaning of the term *knowledge* (4, pp. 5–6):

Thus, according to this view, all education is unavoidably intellectual. Its business is to make clear which ideas are true and valuable, which dubious or trivial, which deserve emotional support, and why. But it is considered absurd for education to attempt to proceed without ideas, or to abjure the conviction that true and important ideas are the first requisite in guiding profitably the emotional life of a normal individual.

The inquiry which is now reporting subscribes to this same point of view. Fundamental to its procedure is the premise that education consists in thinking, in the perception of meaning and relationships among ideas which are true and important, and in the marshaling of an individual's natural emotions behind ideas in proportion to their truth and importance.

In these paragraphs, the term *knowledge* is used to cover all process and content which in this chapter come under the categories of "knowledge," "understanding," and "thinking." It does not recognize, as is recognized here, that the pupil's acquisition of information is no guaranty that the pupil will develop in thinking skill.

Two "comprehensive" examinations were constructed for this inquiry into the effectiveness of education in achieving the goals of intellectual development. One was given to college seniors in 1928, and the other to college students when sophomores in 1930 and again when seniors in 1932. In addition, in May, 1928, the study tested the secondary school seniors of Pennsylvania, using a series of tests of intelligence, English, mathematics, history, science, and language.

The general outline of the college senior examination of 1928 throws some additional light on the educational objectives which Wood and Learned intended to measure:

First Session

Part I. The Physical World
  A. *The Natural Scene*—salient traits of the physical and living world as it appears to the naïve observer.
  B. *Tools of Scientific Investigation*
    1. Mathematics
    2. Scientific method—experimental procedure, "inductive logic," philosophies of science, attitudes and interests of the scientist.
  C. *Analytic Sciences*—physics, chemistry
    1. Basic concepts, "laws," procedures
    2. Ability to handle problems
  D. *Earth Sciences*—astronomy, geology, geography
  E. *Sciences of Life*—biology, botany, zoology, physiology
    1. The development of living forms, including man
    2. The functioning of living organisms—metabolism, reproduction, heredity, organized activity

Second Session

Part II. The Social World

A. *Tools of Scientific Investigation*
1. Basic concepts of social sciences—psychology, anthropology, sociology
2. Statistical method, historical method
3. Language equipment (select two)
   a. Greek
   b. Latin
   c. French
   d. German
   e. Spanish
   f. Italian

B. *Ancient Cultures*
1. Primitive cultures—prehistoric and contemporary, including basic cultural techniques
2. Greek civilization
   a. Geographical basis, social and economic institutions, religious life, political history, the plastic arts
   b. Greek literature and philosophy
3. Near Eastern civilizations
   Geographical basis, social and economic institutions, religious life, artistic achievements
4. Hellenistic and Roman civilizations
   Economic and legal institutions, political history, Latin literature, religious organization (origins of Christianity)

Third Session

C. *Western Civilization—Preindustrial Period*
1. Social and economic institutions, to 1850
2. Political history and institutions, to 1870
3. Intellectual development, including religious, scientific, and philosophical thought, to 1859
4. Literature
   a. English
   b. French, German, and other European literatures
5. The plastic arts and music

Fourth Session

D. *Contemporary Western Civilization*
 1. Contemporary economic life
    Industrial techniques, economic organizations, agricultural organizations, world trade, and "economic geography"
 2. Contemporary political life
 3. Social theories
    economic theory, political theory, radical social theories and programs
 4. Social and personal relations
 5. Legal institutions, concepts, and procedures
 6. Domestic institutions and attitudes
 7. Moral attitudes, standards, and theories
 8. Educational institutions, theories, standards
 9. Science as an institution in our culture
 10. Religious and philosophical life and theories
 11. Literary situation in Western civilization
 12. The plastic arts and music
 13. Nationalistic ways of life and ideals
 14. Interrelationships between these social institutions
E. *Non-Western Civilizations*
 Chinese, Japanese, Indian, Moslem

The objective examination, if judged by this outline above, would seem to incorporate an intellectualistic philosophy of education in which broad knowledge plus effective thinking skills form the supreme outcomes. The tests were referred to as "tests of general education," an expression which has become widely used in recent years to denote batteries of tests often of unidentifiable purpose. The reader should note that in the outline some emphasis is given to various aspects of thinking skill, but the emphasis is on information, and no indication is given of the depth of understanding to be achieved.

In terms of the promise offered by the outline, the examination itself was rather disappointing. Most of it measured superficial factual knowledge and did not begin to measure knowledge in the way in which Wood and Learned had defined it. Consider, for example, the following two items which are rather typical of the test materials as a whole:

Atmospheric pressure is ordinarily about (1) 15 lbs. per sq. in. (2) 15 lbs. per sq. ft. (3) 32 lbs. per sq. in. (4) 32 lbs. per sq. ft.

The Book of the Dead was a collection of (1) prayers and magical charms for the dead (2) biographies of famous dead pharaohs (3) recipes for embalming the dead (4) imprecations addressed to Pharaoh's enemies.

The ability to answer these items correctly does not provide any evidence of understanding but indicates only that the individual possesses certain factual knowledge which may have been learned on a rote basis without any insight into its implications. The same criticism is true of much of the other material in the tests. In the literature section, the names of famous writers have to be matched with the titles of famous books. The examinee who has read *about* books could achieve as good a score as the examinee who has read the books. In the fine arts test, the names of artists are matched with the names of famous paintings. This is knowledge in the most restricted sense of the term. In all, in the tests administered in 1928, twelve hours were occupied in testing, and most of this time was devoted to the assessment of the number of isolated facts possessed by the student.

The criticisms which have been mentioned relate to remediable characteristics of the tests. There is no doubt that tests of understanding more similar to those envisaged by Wood and Learned could be developed. However, the tests raised a much more serious issue which must be considered.

The outline of the tests seems to be based on the assumption that general education consists of the acquisition of information and understanding covering the entire range of human knowledge. Essential knowledge seems to be defined as elementary knowledge in every field, but surely this is a tremendously ambitious goal for education. There are certainly few students who can be expected to have more than a fragmentary knowledge of a few areas, and if this is so, the testing battery of the type used by Wood and Learned becomes unrelated to realistically set goals of education.

If there is no essential body of knowledge which all should acquire, then it is no longer possible to use a single battery of tests for measuring the achievement of all students. This is a problem of central importance which must be faced in the development of all large-scale testing programs. Batteries of tests still continue to appear which are based on the assumption that there is a body of essential knowledge which all pupils should acquire and that tests of achievement should measure the extent to which the pupil has acquired this knowledge. Such batteries raise the question of who is to decide what knowledge is essential and what is unessential. Too often, the test writer sets himself up as the ultimate judge in the matter, a position which he would find extremely difficult to defend.

Some of the Consequences of the Pennsylvania Study

Results of the study must be interpreted in light of the fact that the tests measured little else than knowledge of facts, but they are nevertheless of some interest, and there is no doubt that the tests gave great impetus to the advance of educational measurement. It was clearly demonstrated that colleges in Pennsylvania differed substantially from one another in the amount of knowledge which both the seniors and freshmen possessed. It showed that many graduating seniors knew less than the average entering freshmen and that many prospective teachers had less knowledge than the pupils they were expecting to teach.

However, it failed to do one thing it was supposed to do; namely, to demonstrate how a widely used system of objective tests could be used as a substitute for the present system of awarding credit on the basis of the number of hours spent in class. One important reason for this failure seems to have been that the study was based on the assumption that there is a relatively fixed body of knowledge with which everybody should have some familiarity. Unless there is such a body of information and unless agreement can be reached as to its constituent elements, this approach to the appraisal of the effectiveness of education cannot be applied. It would seem that the ever expanding frontiers of knowledge are likely to make this approach more and more a dream of the past.

Whatever may have been the merits of the Pennsylvania Study as an educational enquiry, it had certain important effects on American education. It stimulated substantial interest in the development of objective methods of measuring the students' knowledge, and it gave impetus to the idea that there is an identifiable body of knowledge which all students should possess and which should be measured by some common measuring device. Ben D. Wood, extending the implications of this philosophy and working with the American Council on Education, established the Cooperative Test Service which became primarily an agency for publishing achievement tests at the secondary school and college level, while William S. Learned, acting through the Carnegie Foundation for the Advancement of Teaching, established the Graduate Record Examination, an instrument for appraising the outcomes of a college education and to be used primarily by graduate schools in the assessment of the qualifications of applicants for admission.

The programs of the Cooperative Test Service and the Graduate Record Examination during the first ten years of their existence seemed to be based upon the same philosophy as that of the Pennsylvania Study. Both emphasized the measurement of a fixed body of information which all individuals at a given educational level should possess. Of course, individuals may also be specialists and may have extensive knowledge over and above the common body of essentials, but the basic body of information is something which all should possess, and is the mark and result of a general education. The Graduate Record Examination as it was originally developed presents a clear picture of this kind of outlook, for the tests of which it consisted included the "profile series," which all examinees were required to take, although each examinee could also take a test in his area of specialization. The profile tests consisted of a series of objective examinations in the areas of physics, chemistry, English, social studies, literature, fine arts, biological sciences, and mathematics. These profile tests were taken by all candidates and resembled those administered in the Pennsylvania Study in that they measured primarily the student's fund of available factual information. Whatever may have been claimed to the contrary, the writer feels that these tests, with the exception of the mathematics test, did little to measure understanding but emphasized primarily the assessment of information at a rather superficial level. To some extent, this was a result of the choice of the types of items used in the test. For example, the extensive use of matching items in this series is symptomatic of tests which measure superficial information. The tests stressed extensity of knowledge rather than depth of understanding.

The strict secrecy enforced in the use of the Graduate Record Examination during its first ten years preserved it successfully from the criticism which it should have received and which might have resulted in its early revision. Few of those who administered the examination ever saw the contents of the test booklets, which were sealed when the examinee first received them and resealed at the end of the examination before they were handed back to the proctor. Every copy was numbered, and although an occasional copy may have gone astray, it was difficult for most psychologists to obtain a copy for review. It was possible for a person who held the position of dean to have a copy for inspection, and others whom he chose were allowed to inspect it in his presence, but few educators competent to evaluate it were ever invited to undertake this inspection. In all, experience with this instrument has convinced the present writer that an examination, held secret in this way, fails to receive healthy criticism and revision. It is to the credit of the Educational Testing Service, which now manages the project, that it has recently revised the tests very extensively, and has permitted the review and criticism of the instruments in professional publications. The new area tests which have replaced the profile tests since early in 1955 minimize the measurement of information, but emphasize the appraisal of the student's understanding of what he has learned. In many respects they resemble and should be classed with the tests of intellectual skills to be considered in the next chapter.

The present heir at the college level to the type of testing initiated in the Pennsylvania Study is the Cooperative General Culture Test (3), which has now run into a dozen different forms, all of which seem to follow an almost identical pattern. This test consists of six parts, which bear the following titles:

Part I.   Current Social Problems
Part II.   History and Social Studies
Part III. Literature
Part IV.   Science
Part V.   Fine Arts
Part VI.   Mathematics

The test consists of a series of multiple-choice questions with five alternatives offered for each question. The educational objective measured is strictly informational in character except for Part VI, which deals with mathematical skills. In a review of the test, Bloom (2) has pointed out that the content presumably defines what is meant by "general culture" and, since the test is used in over a hundred different colleges, students are likely to accept the idea that to accumulate information and to become generally cultured means the same thing. Bloom goes on to point out that if the objectives which the test apparently measures are compared with commonly accepted objectives of general education, there is a major discrepancy. For example, in comparing the objectives of the literature section of the General Culture Test with the objectives of teaching literature given in *A Design for General Education* (1) Bloom draws the conclusion that the test measures only one minor aspect of the objectives listed in the report. He points out that the literature section, which is of the literary acquaintance type, does not require the student to have read much literature to obtain a high score. Reading about literature should produce about as much increment in test scores as reading literature. Bloom's summary of his own review (2) provides a condensed account of the limitations of this test: *

Summary. In general, the test has many shortcomings. As a measure of general education, it is decidedly inadequate in both the subject-matter sampled and the types of objectives listed. For the most part, the emphasis is on knowledge rather than on the ability and skill objectives which are emphasized in *A Design for General Education* [1] as well as in the other statements on general education. The knowledge is sampled by items which measure rather superficial acquaintance with the subject matter fields listed. Although such knowledge may be a prerequisite to the more complex abilities and skills, only the most reckless test interpreter would claim that measurement of one provides a good index of the other.

As a test of acquaintance, with a great variety of subject matter, it is a useful test. As an index of the individual's general culture, general education, or liberal education, it is quite inadequate. Perhaps the major criticism of the test is that it attempts to do an almost impossible task—the measurement of the product of two or more years of education in 180 minutes.

* Reproduced by kind permission of Oscar K. Buros, editor, *Third Mental Measurement Yearbook*.

THE MEASUREMENT OF KNOWLEDGE AS AN OUTCOME OF SPECIALIZED EDUCATION

From the previous remarks the reader should not conclude that the measurement of knowledge is a profitless task for the teacher to undertake. The discussion up to this point has been concerned with the measurement of knowledge as an outcome of general education where it is assumed that there is an essential core of information which characterizes the educated man. It has not been assumed that the measurement of knowledge has little value in this context but that the use of standardized tests for this purpose has little merit. The writer believes that knowledge is an important outcome, but that it must be left to the teacher to measure this outcome, since the knowledge acquired by his students may be entirely different from that acquired by some other teacher's students. However, it must be remembered that much knowledge is acquired not for the purpose of enriching the individual's background but for achieving proficiency in some specialized area. In specialized areas of study there may be some agreement concerning what is essential knowledge, and under such conditions the use of published tests may be of some value.

Appropriate Uses of Published Tests of Information

The extent to which a published test of knowledge and understanding can be usefully applied to assess the student's knowledge in a given area depends to a considerable extent on the degree to which the subject matter presents an orderly structure in which certain facts have to be learned before certain other facts can be acquired. Physics approaches closely to this kind of a content area. In the teaching of physics it would be quite impossible to teach the kinetic theory of gases unless the student already understood the concepts of momentum and kinetic energy; neither would it be possible for the student to understand the basis of electrical units if he did not understand the concepts of work and energy. The subject matter of physics is highly structured and can be mastered only by an orderly study of concepts in proper sequence. In contrast, a content area such as sociology can be approached in different ways, and two instructors who developed introductory courses independently might include entirely different content. The subject matter of sociology just does not show the orderly structure characteristic of the subject matter of physics.

The subject matter taught in schools does not for the most part present the ordered and logical structure of physics. Consider, for example, fifth grade social studies as it is taught in a number of different schools with which the writer is familiar. In one school, the major effort in fifth grade social studies is devoted to acquiring knowledge about the local community, its early struggle for survival, the origin of its people, the sources of its later industrial development, the employment opportunities it is likely to provide in the future, the services supplied by local government, and so forth. A second school, in another state, devotes a substantial fraction of the fifth grade to a study of the revolutionary period, with emphasis on the struggle for American liberation and the economic problems faced by the colonists. A third school, in uniformity with the policy of the state in which it is located, devotes the fifth year to the history of the state. Since in the last school system state history is studied every second year up to the time of graduation from high school, only a very small segment of state history is studied in the fifth grade, but it is studied in minute detail.

It is clear that in these three grades entirely different factual material is studied in the time devoted to social studies. If knowledge acquired in the area of social studies is to be measured at the end of the fifth grade year, the same test of social studies knowledge cannot be appropriately used in these three classrooms. A test appropriate for measuring the objectives related to social studies knowledge in one of the classrooms would be quite inappropriate in the other two. If the three teachers involved were brought together, they would probably agree that they could not build a common test for the three classes. It is probable that they would also agree that they should attempt to measure the knowledge that their pupils had acquired, but by means of three different but appropriate tests built by the teachers themselves. These three teachers might perhaps be tempted to examine published tests in the social studies area, but would soon discover that none were designed to measure the acquisition of the type of information covered by their respective curricula. If they were experienced teachers they would probably know well that a test entitled "Fifth Grade Social Studies" would probably have little use in a particular fifth grade.

The fact that the objectives related to social studies information are different for the three classes does not mean that they do not also have common objectives. They may well do, and the extent to which some of these common objectives are achieved may possibly be appropriately measured by published tests. The measurement of such objectives as are collectively described by the term critical thinking—common adjectives of teaching in the social studies— will be considered in the next chapter.

The case of social studies in the fifth grade is typical rather than the exception. In the teaching of almost any subject-matter field, at the elementary or high school level, so much knowledge is available that the teacher has almost unlimited choice. Since time in the classroom is brief, only a very small sample of this subject matter can be introduced, and two teachers teaching at the same grade level in the same school may select substantially different samples of facts and information. There are exceptions to this statement. In physics and to a lesser extent in chemistry, the subject matter must be presented in a definite order. In mathematics, the subject matter represents an ordered system in which, for example, addition and subtraction must be learned before long division. However, the major exception is in the learning of some of the work skills, for in these it seems possible to identify a definite body of information which the successful practitioner should know. An automobile mechanic must know the names of the parts of a car, their location, and interrelationship. He must also know the names and functions of the tools he uses. So too is it in other fields of vocational specialization. The assessment of pupil information in such areas by standardized published tests can be a sound procedure and will be discussed in the chapter on the assessment of work skills. It should also be observed here that in those occupations requiring complex skills, such as medicine and law, it has become customary to measure by state-wide examinations the knowledge of those who wish to qualify. This is a thoroughly defensible procedure, for there is a basic body of knowledge which all practitioners should possess.

Teacher-Made Tests of Knowledge

Insofar as our viewpoint is sound it implies that in most programs of general education it is necessary for the teacher to build his own tests of knowledge. Nothing that is written in this chapter should be taken to imply that the writer does not endorse knowledge as an important outcome of education. He does, but he knows no way of defining an essential body of knowledge which should characterize all individuals and be the mark of the possession of a general education.

The instructor who builds his own test of knowledge must have a detailed outline of the knowledges which he expects his students to acquire and he must have based his selection of content on reasoned judgment. The test which he builds must sample this content adequately and meet the criteria of a satisfactory measuring instrument. The techniques of building such a device will be discussed in a later chapter.

Summary

In the introduction to this chapter, a distinction was made between knowledge and understanding on the one hand and skills such as thinking skills on the other. The traditional emphasis in public education has been on the acquisition of knowledge, and for this reason examination and testing procedures in schools have tended to emphasize the measurement of the amount of factual information which the pupil has acquired.

Early attempts to introduce standardized achievement tests into schools seem to have been dominated by the philosophy that the acquisition of information was a goal of central importance. The Pennsylvania Study was dominated by this influence in its ambitious attempt to provide tests as an objective basis for assigning grades to be recorded on transcripts. The Graduate Record Examination and the early products of the Cooperative Test Service also fell under this same influence, although it should be pointed out that the later products of both of these projects have shown substantial departures from their original policy.

The early major ventures in testing which have been considered were based on the assumption that there is a body of essential knowledge which all pupils should acquire as a result of a sound education. This assumption does not seem to be defensible, and classroom observation clearly shows that there are major differences between communities in the knowledge which pupils acquire at particular grade levels. For this reason, tests which measure factual information must be largely those which teachers themselves build.

Finally, it was pointed out that standardized tests of information can be used appropriately in areas of vocational training, for in most such areas there is a well-defined body of knowledge which the person entering the occupation must have.

References

1. *A Design for General Education,* Washington, D. C., American Council on Education, 1944, pp. 186 + VII.
2. Bloom, Benjamin S. Review No. 4, *The Third Mental Measurement Yearbook* (Editor, Buros, Oscar K.), New Brunswick, New Jersey, Rutgers University Press, 1949, pp. 1246 + XIV.
3. *Cooperative General Culture Test* (Revised Series), Princeton, New Jersey, Cooperative Test Division of the Educational Testing Service, Form X, 1944.
4. Learned, William S. and Wood, Ben D., *The Student and His Knowledge,* New York, The Carnegie Foundation for the Advancement of Teaching, 1938, pp. 406 + XX.
5. Werkmeister, W. H., *The Basis and Structure of Knowledge,* New York, Harper and Brothers, 1950, pp. 451 + XI.

CHAPTER 5

The Trend Toward the Measurement of Skills Considered Basic Outcomes of General Education

Skills as the Core of General Education

The broadening of the curriculum which took place between the First and Second World Wars resulted in the raising of serious questions concerning the validity of the viewpoint that the core of all education must be a common body of knowledge with which all pupils must become familiar. If additional subjects could be added almost without limit, and if traditional methods of organizing knowledge were to be discarded, then a single body of knowledge could no longer be considered as *a* salient, or *the* salient, outcome of general education. What then could be considered the common outcomes of a general education?

Various testing programs came into being which attempted to measure a common core other than knowledge and which the authors of the tests claimed to be the essential focus of all education. Those who felt that information was not the common core have often suggested that various thinking skills might form the essential element of a general education.

One of the first testing batteries that rejected information as an essential outcome was the Iowa Every Pupil Testing Program, which was inaugurated at almost the same time as the Pennsylvania Study and came into being as a service to the high schools of the state of Iowa. In 1935 it was extended down to grades 6, 7, and 8, and in

1940 additional tests were made available for grades 3, 4, and 5. In the 1940 edition of these tests for grades 3 through 8, four tests were included, namely, silent reading comprehension, work study skills, basic language skills, and basic arithmetic skills. It is to be noted that the names of these tests do not include any knowledge category as such, but place emphasis on the ability to perform a number of useful acts. The tendency in the development of this series of tests over the years has been to push into the background the measurement of knowledge as such, and this same trend is reflected in other tests in which the University of Iowa has exercised considerable influence.

While the Every Pupil Tests were developed as a part of a state testing program and have been intimately associated with Iowa, since 1950 it has been possible for schools in other states to obtain the tests and a complete scoring service from Science Research Associates.

The skills measured by the Iowa Every Pupil Tests were somewhat limited in scope and, except for the test of work study skills, did not emphasize those objectives which the so-called progressive education movement had stressed. It remained for the staff of an ambitious project known as the Eight Year Study to explore the possibility of measuring some of the other skills and particularly thinking skills which many modern teachers believe to be among the most important outcomes of general education.

The Eight Year Study was established in 1932 for the purpose of studying the newer type of curriculum that was then emerging in many schools. In its initial stages, thirty cooperating schools agreed to provide a laboratory through which the study could be conducted, and observational studies were initiated in these schools. It was soon realized, however, that little could be accomplished unless systematic attempts were made to collect verifiable evidence concerning the nature of the changes produced in pupils by various types of curricula. In order to achieve this purpose, an evaluation staff was established which set as its first goal the identification of common objectives stressed by the thirty schools. The educational objective most commonly mentioned in conferences and discussions with the faculties was the ability to think, and thus a major part of the efforts of the evaluation staff became devoted to the analysis and measurement of this objective.

Thinking Skills

While much is said and written about thinking as an objective of a liberal education, observation in classrooms leads one to suspect that many teachers have faith that somehow the objective is mystically achieved even if no special effort is made to achieve it. Even more surprising than classroom practices in relation to this objective are the kinds of examinations given by many teachers who claim that thinking is their supreme objective. These tests are commonly measures of nothing but the amount of factual information acquired. The writer can see little reason for believing that most typical school or college curricula help students to learn to think and can find little or no evidence to show that they do. In this respect, many teachers are living in a dreamworld of wishful thinking and will probably continue to do so until evidence collected over long years and in various places forces curricula revision.

The absence of attempts to measure thinking skill as an educational outcome is also a result of the fact that educational psychologists have been interested in the measurement of thinking only insofar as it supplies evidence of "intelligence," "G factor," "academic aptitude," or whatever it is that is measured by most tests of intelligence. Since the aim of these tests has been largely that of measuring potentiality rather than achievement, educability rather than the results of education, little has been done to develop measures of whatever thinking skill are influenced in their development by special learning experiences.

In the Eight Year Study (15), an attempt was made to classify acts of thinking into a few well-defined categories and then to develop objective tests of each one of the categories. While the classification was not claimed to be comprehensive, it included those aspects of thinking which might be described in general terms by the following names:

1. The ability to interpret data.
2. The ability to apply principles of science.
3. The ability to apply principles of logic.
4. An understanding of the nature of proof.

Each of these four categories covers a rather broad domain of behavior, and practical considerations made it necessary to consider only limited aspects of each domain. In the case of the ability to interpret data, the abilities measured were limited to the following elements: *

A. The Ability to Perceive Relationships in Data
 1. The ability to make comparisons.
 2. The ability to identify common elements among data.
 3. The ability to read data.
 4. The ability to make simple computations from data.
 5. The ability to understand symbols used and methods of representation.
B. The Ability to Recognize the Limitations of Data
 1. The ability to identify additional data needed for drawing a given conclusion.
 2. The ability to withhold judgment until all necessary data are available.
 3. The ability to make justifiable generalizations from data.
 4. The ability to identify unwarranted interpretations.
 5. The ability to make qualified inferences regarding trends.

A number of other outcomes within the same general domain, such as the ability to evaluate the dependability of data or the ability to evaluate critically the conclusions drawn by others, were not selected for study, mainly for the reason that it did not seem practical to study every aspect of the ability to interpret data.

In addition, the final instrument designed to measure the ability to interpret data was made in such a way that the data contained in it were presented in various forms—graphical, tabular, verbal, and so forth—and these data were chosen from various subject-matter fields, were concerned with various areas of living, and presented a variety of relationships.

Figure 5.1 † shows an illustration of the type of test developed. Each part of the test presents some data, and in this case the data are in graphical form. The data are followed by a series of state-

* The list of outcomes to be measured as given here is not presented in this form in the text to which reference is made. The present list represents an abstraction from several pages of text. Undoubtedly, the test itself was based on some tabulation of this kind.

† By permission from *Appraising and Recording Student Progress*, by Eugene R. Smith and Ralph W. Tyler. Copyright, 1942, by McGraw-Hill Book Company, Inc.

ments which in terms of the data must be classified as true, probably true, false, probably false, or insufficient to be classified into any of these categories.

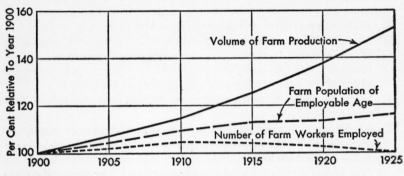

FIGURE 5.1

Illustration of test problems for measuring skill in the interpretation of data.

These Data Alone
(1) are sufficient to make the statement true.
(2) are sufficient to indicate that the statement is probably true.
(3) are not sufficient to indicate whether there is any degree of truth or falsity in the statement.
(4) are sufficient to indicate that the statement is probably false.
(5) are sufficient to make the statement false.

Problem 1. This chart shows production, population, and employment on farms in the United States for each fifth year between 1900 and 1925.

Statements
1. The ratio of agricultural production to the number of farm workers increased every five years between 1900 and 1925.
2. The increase in agricultural production between 1910 and 1925 was due to more widespread use of farm machinery.
3. The average number of farm workers employed during the period 1920 to 1925 was higher than during the period 1915 to 1920.
4. The government should give relief to farm workers who are unemployed.
5. Between 1900 and 1925, the amount of fruit produced on farms in the United States increased about 50 per cent.

6. During the entire period between 1905 and 1925 there was an excess of farm population of employable age over the number of people needed to operate farms.
7. Wages paid farm workers in 1925 were low because there were more laborers than could be employed.
8. More workers were employed on farms in 1925 than in 1900.
9. Since 1900, there has been an increase in production per worker in manufacturing similar to the increase in agriculture.
10. Between 1900 and 1925, the volume of farm production increased over 50 per cent.
11. Farmers increased production after 1910 in order to take advantage of rapidly rising prices.
12. The average amount of farm production was higher in the period 1925 to 1930 than in the period 1920 to 1925.
13. Between 1900 and 1925, there was an increase in the farm population of employable age in the Middle West, the largest farming area in the United States.
14. Farm population of employable age was lower in 1930 than in 1900.
15. The production of wheat, the largest agricultural crop in the United States, was as great in 1915 as in 1925.

The system for scoring the test is somewhat complicated. The record sheet used in the Eight Year Study allows places for several scores. The scores fall into the following four categories:

1. *General Accuracy.* This over-all score measures the extent to which the responses of the student agree with the approved key for the test. Since it is to some extent a matter of judgment whether a statement is true or probably true, the approved key was based on the judgments of a group of so-called experts. The general accuracy score could be broken down according to whether the keyed response was in the true or false category, the false or probably false category, or the insufficient data category.
2. *Caution.* This score measures the tendency of the student to be overcautious in interpreting the data. If the student classifies a statement in the category of "insufficient data," when he should have classified the statement as probably true, he is showing excessive caution. The caution score is the number of overcautious reactions made on the test.
3. *Beyond Data.* This measures the tendency to overgeneralize from the data; that is, it is the opposite of the caution score. How-

ever, it is possible for the student to accumulate points both on this scale and on the caution scale, since a person may vacillate between showing excessive caution and lack of caution. Hence, separate scores are needed for this and the previous category.

4. *Crude Error.* This is simply the number of gross errors, which are those which occur when a person should have marked a statement as true or probably true but marked it as false or probably false, or the reverse.

In addition to these categories, omissions are also scored. It can be seen from this elaborate scoring scheme that the purpose is to provide a representation of the characteristic way in which the thinking of the student usually proceeds. It is not just an assessment in terms of a norm of the over-all achievement of the student in this area. Rather do the data provide something of the nature of a case study in which some of the individual's thinking habits are portrayed. As an illustration of the kinds of interpretations that may be given to profiles on this test, Table 5.1 shows the scores of a single test and the interpretation of this profile made by Smith, Tyler, and their associates.

TABLE 5.1

Illustration of a Profile from the Interpretation of Data Test (15, p. 420)

Category	Jane's Scores	Class Median
General Accuracy	54	57
Accuracy with Probably True and Probably False	35	38
Accuracy with Insufficient Data	51	58
Accuracy with True and False	76	73
Overcaution	48	21
Going Beyond Data	43	36
Crude Errors	11	8

In techniques of getting meaning from quantitative data requiring precise thinking, Jane is near the average for her class. Her scores on accuracy are slightly below the median. This indicates inability to recognize the limitations of data. An examination of types of errors shows a greater than average tendency to go beyond the data, or accept generalities ignoring the limitations of the data. Not only is this score among the highest in the class (significant, since most of her scores are close to the median), but the proportion of errors in this direction in comparison to those in the direction of overcaution is also larger than that of the class (Beyond Data: Overcaution = 43:18, Class = 36:21). Her score on crude errors is one of the highest in the class.

One difficulty in this type of test is that it attempts to measure too much in too short a time. The result is that the part scores, because they are based on few items, tend to have inadequate reliability for the guidance or assessment of the individual pupil.

Various other tests were prepared by the committee on evaluation in the Eight Year Study, and of these one of the most famous is that which attempts to measure the ability to apply scientific principles. The form of the problems follows a more or less standard pattern throughout the test. An incident is described in which some action is taken; for example, a motorist inflates his tires during the day while undertaking a hot desert journey. He lets some of the air out of his tires in the evening to prevent a blowout during the night. The student must first of all indicate whether he agrees, disagrees, or is uncertain about the value of the action taken by the motorist, and then is required to check from a list of suggested reasons the ones which support his decision. Some of these statements represent the correct principles, sometimes stated in various alternate forms, some statements represent principles which do not apply, some are incorrectly stated principles, and some appeal to teleology, analogy, and ridicule.

The scoring system for the test of the ability to apply principles of science is even more complicated than the test of the ability to interpret data. Altogether, twenty scores are computed for each student if the complete scoring system is applied, and from a study of these scores it is possible to determine the type of error that the student is making and undesirable habits of thought possessed within the domain circumscribed by the test.

It is of interest to note that, in anticipation of a demand, many of the instruments developed in the Eight Year Study were published by the Educational Testing Service, Princeton, New Jersey. However, the demand never developed and in 1952 all but the Interest Index were retired from the list of available tests. In order that research workers might still be able to use the instruments, the Educational Testing Service established a system whereby copies of sets of materials for each test might be borrowed for sufficient time to have them reproduced by the prospective user. About the only limitation placed on the reproduction of the tests is that copies may not be sold.

Other Measures of Thinking Skill

The work of the evaluation staff of the Eight Year Study represents the most ambitious attempt yet made to identify certain thinking skills which seem to be amenable to training and to define and measure those skills. The relative lack of information concerning the nature of thinking and the lack of interest which psychologists have shown in recent years in the subjective aspect of the thinking process, together with the absence of studies of the trainability of thinking skills, have made it necessary for educators to start almost from the beginning both in planning teaching in this area and in developing evaluation instruments.

A result of lack of knowledge in this area is that each person who attempts to develop a measure of important outcomes produces a different instrument than that produced by his predecessors. For example, Goodwin Watson and Edward M. Glaser (16) developed a series of tests of critical thinking which call for many of the behaviors elicited by the tests of thinking skill produced by the evaluation staff of the Eight Year Study. They also elicit behaviors which are rather different. These tests require the student to make warranted generalizations from data, to make justifiable inferences, to discriminate between strong and weak arguments supporting a position or viewpoint, and to recognize unstated assumptions in reasoning.

Those who have produced similar test problems and have included them in so-called tests of intelligence have commonly assumed that these skills are relatively untrainable. It seems more reasonable to assume that for each individual there is a ceiling on his trainability, a limit which he cannot pass because of the way in which his body and particularly his nervous system happen to be built. It also seems reasonable to assume that few individuals ever reach their limit of trainability in thinking skills, and that consequently these skills offer reasonable educational objectives.

There is one central difficulty in interpreting scores on such tests. This difficulty arises from the fact that the problems presented usually require the student to read carefully the materials presented. In other words, reading skill of quite a high order is necessary before the individual can demonstrate thinking skill. If he cannot read accurately, he cannot possibly solve the problems that the reading passages present. Watson and Glaser note in this connection that practice and remedial instruction in reading may often raise a person's score on their test, and that poor work habits may cause a student to have a relatively low score. In other words, as a result of the method of presentation of the problems, it is almost unavoidable that they may, on occasion, measure variables wholly irrelevant to the purpose at hand. One is certainly left wondering whether the various studies which attempt to demonstrate the effects of an educational program on intelligence test scores may not do just that kind of thing.

Tests of Thinking Skills in Content Areas

Another trend in the measurement of various skills is to measure them in relation to certain content areas. It is evident that reading skills and thinking skills can be measured independently with social studies materials and natural science materials.

The Iowa Tests of Educational Development (8) can be thought of as an extension of the Iowa Every Pupil Tests of Basic Skills developed for use in grades 3 to 8. However, the series of tests does include two which are tests of information rather than of skills. The tests indicate in their title that they measure general educational development, which would seem on the surface at least to be a nice, respectable kind of outcome to which nobody could possibly object, but the reader may rightly ask just what this means. The descriptive leaflet (7) which accompanied the prospectus of the tests when they were first made available reiterated: "They provide a dependable measure of the general educational background, growth and development of individual students," but such reiterations add little to the meaning of the concept. The leaflet did add that they give the teacher "a reliable picture of the learning ability and present scholastic development of each student" and then, without further discussion of what the tests measure, statements follow concerning the value of the tests for vocational and educational counseling. Little more definite information about the tests could be obtained from the manual, "How to Use the Test Results" (6).

Perhaps this is unduly hard on the tests, but other evidence supports this viewpoint. It is true that the descriptive leaflet provides brief descriptions of the content of each one of the subtests, and one presumes that these brief descriptions are given in order to provide some basis for interpretation. The descriptions are as follows:

Test 1. Understanding of Basic Social Concepts—A test to measure the student's general knowledge and understanding of the situation of modern society. Every person needs this background knowledge if he is to do competent thinking about current problems.

Test 2. Correctness in Writing—A test to determine the student's mastery of the four basic elements in correct writing—punctuation, usage, capitalization, and spelling. This test does not measure the ability to state rules, but the ability to use them.

Test 3. Background in the Natural Sciences—a test to determine the student's general knowledge and understanding of common material phenomena, and of important contributions to modern civilization. Like Test 1, this test is not limited to the content of the present High School curriculum. Instead, items are selected on the basis of what the generally educated person should know.

Test 4. Ability to Do Quantitative Thinking—A test to measure general problem solving ability of the practical sort. The problems sample understanding of life insurance, installment buying, ability to estimate the cost of simple home construction and repair, and similar problems.

Test 5. Ability to Interpret Reading Materials in the Social Studies—A test to measure the student's ability to interpret and evaluate reading selections taken from textbooks, magazines, and newspapers. Ability to evaluate, to understand implications, and to comprehend what is specifically stated in the selection are measured in this test.

Test 6. Ability to Interpret Reading Materials in the Natural Sciences—Like Test 5, this test measures the student's ability to interpret and evaluate reading selections. This test differs from Test 5 only in subject matter.

Test 7. Ability to Interpret Literary Materials—A test which presents a variety of selections from World Literature—all the major types of literature are presented. Recognition of mood and of the writer's purpose are among the points of comprehension tested.

Test 8. General Vocabulary—a test which affords a measure not only of the student's ability to handle words, but also of his general aptitude for learning.

Test 9. Uses of Sources of Information—A test which measures the student's ability to turn to the sources of information which are most likely to contain the solution to a particular problem.

Tests 5, 6, and 7 in this series are particularly relevant for the present discussion. It is to be noted that they are not tests of information, for, as the titles denote, the emphasis is on *interpretation*. The latter is presumably some aspect of thinking ability and is measured by presenting the student with a passage in the relevant subject-matter field and then asking him to interpret the meaning of the paragraph. The questions are all in the multiple-choice or best-answer form. Just what such tests measure is not entirely clear. They may measure knowledge of the subject-matter field, but these tests probably do not, since they require the examinee to call upon his background of general knowledge in interpreting the passages.

It should be noted that, although this battery does give emphasis to the ability to interpret material in various subject-matter fields, it also emphasizes the idea that tests of *essential* or *basic* knowledge have a place in the assessment of educational development. One can be, with reason, a little critical of a test which claims to measure basic knowledge in a certain subject-matter field, and although it is a common practice for some test publishers to make such claims, it must be kept in mind that what is considered essential or basic depends on some person's judgment.

It must be said, in fairness to the distributors of these instruments, that the description given of them in the 1954 catalog of Science Research Associates is more reasonable in its inferences. It does not refer to any of the tests as measuring *essential* knowledge, but it retains the reference to *basic* knowledge.

Another direct outgrowth of the Iowa Tests of Educational Development was a series of tests prepared by the United States Armed Forces Institute to measure the "general educational development" of veterans applying for admission to college who did not have high school diplomas from accredited high schools. These tests were known as the *United States Armed Forces Institute Tests of General Educational Development* and included the following four tests in forms for both high school and college level:

Test 1. Correctness and effectiveness of expression.
Test 2. Interpretation of reading materials in the social studies.
Test 3. Interpretation of reading materials in the natural sciences.
Test 4. Interpretation of literary materials.

The following is the description of the tests given in the catalog of the Cooperative Test Division of the Educational Testing Service (2) during a period of many years when that organization acted as distributor:

The Tests of General Educational Development are designed to measure the extent to which *all* of the past educational experiences of the individual tested—including the experiences gained in military service—have contributed to his general educational development, or to his ability to carry on successfully in a program of general education of the type which the academic high school and the first two years of the liberal arts college aim to provide. The emphasis is placed on intellectual power rather than detailed content, upon the acquisition of broad but definite generalizations, concepts and ideas, and particularly upon the abilities to comprehend exactly, to evaluate critically, and to think clearly in terms of such concepts and ideas, rather than upon the detailed facts from which the ideas and generalizations were originally derived. These tests are *not* to be considered as end-of-course achievement examinations.

Each of these tests is to be administered under work-limit conditions; that is, each student should be given as much time as he needs to complete the test. A period of two hours per test is generally adequate for nearly all persons to whom the tests may be given.

This description * provides some clarification of what the tests are alleged to measure but fails to define the key expression *general educational development*. The statement that "the emphasis is placed on intellectual power rather than detailed content" suggests that the tests measure some aspect of thinking skill rather than knowledge. Examination of the tests reveal that Test 1 measures

---

* These tests are no longer distributed by Educational Testing Service but may be obtained from Veterans Testing Service of the American Council on Education, 5741 Drexel Avenue, Chicago 7, Illinois.

recognition of correct or incorrect spelling and correct or incorrect usage according to the so-called rules of grammar. When the writer worked through the test in order to determine what it seemed to measure, little was found in it which by any stretch of the imagination would be likely to measure "effectiveness of expression." It is hard to see why the authors did not call it a test of usage.

Tests 2, 3, and 4 are reading tests—that is, each test consists of a series of reading passages which are followed by certain questions. Some of these questions can be answered only after reading the passage, while others can be answered independently. A great variety of mental processes are measured by these tests.

In order to illustrate the range of achievements that may be measured by such tests, a problem of the general type under discussion is presented in Table 5.2. The problems presented in this illustration (which does not come from any published test) do not exhaust the variety of functions that such items may measure, for these are very numerous.

It is of general interest to note that tests very similar to those included in the Tests of General Educational Development were used by Edward L. Thorndike some twenty years earlier in the Thorndike Intelligence Tests. Thorndike too was interested in the measurement of mental processes rather than in knowledge of content, but the measures derived from his tests were referred to as measures of intelligence, and not as measures of educational development. The reader should ponder over this difference.

There can be no doubt that, through reading tests, the measurement of thinking skill in a subject-matter field has great potentiality as a technique of measurement. The tests which use this technique at the present time must be considered to be largely experimental and exploratory. The shortcomings in the technique seem to result from the fact that little has as yet been done to make an analysis and classification of the various thought processes that may enter into solving the items. The fact that a test consists of a paragraph does not ensure that any particular thought process is involved. Once the thought processes have been properly defined, it will be possible to build tests which measure more and more precisely some definite and identifiable category of behavior, and something much more meaningful than "general educational development."

TABLE 5.2

Illustration of a Reading Test Used for Measuring Various Aspects of Achievement in a Technical Area. (The correct answer to each item is marked with an asterisk)

An artificial kidney is a blood washing machine for removing toxic substances from the blood. Most artificial kidneys pass the blood through long cellophane tubes immersed in saline solution. Substances are added to prevent the blood from clotting. The poisons and crystalloids in the blood pass through the cellophane while the blood cells and proteins are retained. Some machines now in use may remove as much as one ounce of urea in an hour which is much more efficient than the human kidney.

Test Question	*Comments on the Test Question*
What property of cellophane is made use of in the device described?	
*1. Permeability to certain substances 2. Extreme thinness 3. Impermeability to saline 4. Affinity for poisons in the blood	This item involves little more than a restatement of the gist of the paragraph.
Under which one of the following circumstances would it be most likely for a patient to have his blood washed?	
*1. During a temporary injury to a kidney 2. During an operation for removal of a kidney 3. During chronic kidney disease. 4. During periods of excessive function of the kidney.	This item requires the examinee to use other knowledge related to the paragraph.
Which one of the following substances is most likely to be added to the blood before it enters the cellophane tubes?	
*1. Heparin 2. Saline 3. Haemoglobin 4. Thrombokynase	This item calls for *specific* knowledge in addition to that provided by the passage.
What physical mechanism is used in the device?	
*1. Differential diffusion 2. Pressure transmission 3. Precipitation 4. Differential solubility	This item calls for general knowledge of a principle in order to interpret the passage.

Thinking Skills in Relation to Subject-Matter Fields

One strong argument in favor of an integrated curriculum, in which work is not divided into traditional subject-matter fields, is that it is then possible to organize work in terms of meaningful objectives. On this basis, skill in writing or arithmetic is learned through executing various projects, and the same holds true for other educational objectives. Under the conditions of an integrated program, one might expect that thinking skills could be learned as skills of general value, while if these skills were learned in a specific subject-matter field, one might have doubts as to whether the individual would apply them in other areas. Furst (4, 5) attempted to compare the outcomes of a program constructed in terms of broad areas of learning with those of a program built along traditional subject-matter lines. He found that a student's level of performance in a certain thinking skill in one subject-matter area bears little relationship to his level of performance in the same skill in another subject-matter area. In other words, his study indicated that, for example, the ability to judge the validity of data in physical sciences bears little relationship to the student's ability to judge the validity of data in the social sciences. The thinking skills studied were acquired in relation to subject-matter fields and not as skills that could be generally applied. This was as true for the students in the integrated curriculum as for those in the traditional type of curriculum.

Insofar as this study is valid, it suggests that, at the present time, it is more reasonable to measure these skills with respect to certain subject-matter areas than to attempt to measure them as general skills. Of course, it is quite possible that the teachers in both curricula in the study might have been so oriented that they tended to teach and think in terms of subject-matter areas. What is not clear at all is the extent to which the student must have mastered the content of a field before he can undertake complex thinking in the area. Process and content, as Lorge (9) has pointed out, are only semantic distinctions and are inextricably bound up with one another.

The Present Status of Measurement of Thinking Skills

The trend toward emphasizing thinking skills in education has been paralleled by attempts to measure the extent to which these outcomes are achieved. By far the best planned of these instruments are those developed by the staff of the Eight Year Study. It will be recalled that the tests in the Eight Year Study do not measure thinking skill in traditional, narrow subject-matter fields. They are based on the assumption that if effective thinking is to be learned, then it should be learned so that it has applications to a wide range of situations. However, it is possible that the school curriculum may be such at the present time that thinking skill, if it is to be learned at all, is learned in limited subject-matter fields. Furst's study (5) supports this point of view, and if such is the case, measuring instruments of the kind represented by the Tests of General Educational Development are more appropriate for measuring expected outcomes than are those of the Eight Year Study.

Although it has been pointed out that the type of test represented by the *Tests of General Educational Development* lack the rigorous type of planning which characterized the development of tests in the Eight Year Study, they still represent instruments of considerable interest. The teacher should be familiar with the criticisms presented here, but these criticisms should not blind him to the uses of the instruments.

However, before the teacher uses a device such as that entitled *Interpretation of Reading Materials in the Social Studies,* he should attempt to make an analysis of what the test appears to measure. The teacher should read the test, answer the questions, and then ask himself "How many of the test items measure only knowledge of technical vocabulary?", "How many measure the ability to draw inferences from data?", "How many require the pupil to draw generalizations from data?" and so forth. After the teacher has made this kind of analysis of the test, he will be in a good position to judge the relevance of the instrument to the purposes he has in mind.

STUDY SKILLS

At every level of education, teachers emphasize the importance of the development of study skills which in certain aspects are thinking skills. It is also customary for teachers to complain bitterly about the inadequacy of the study skills of their students and to blame these inadequacies on the teachers at lower levels in the system. This system of putting the blame onto the shoulders of others does little to solve the problem. In fairness, it must be said that much has been done on the positive side to build study skills by systematic efforts on the part of many classroom teachers as well as by teachers of special classes assembled for that purpose. Study skills, in the broad sense of the term, may be classified in the following main categories, which are not distinct but overlapping:

1. Reading skills. To some extent, these are considered in this volume under the heading of language skills, but the study-skill specialist is interested in diagnosing the causes of reading difficulties.
2. Writing skills, including the preparation of reports. These skills vary from the mechanics of writing and include such matters as punctuation and capitalization up to high-level thinking skills involved in organizing the concepts to be presented in writing and some of the more subtle aspects of methods of presentation.
3. Listening skills and note-taking skills.
4. Skills related to the organization of ideas. These receive some attention in the chapter on language skills. Reading is one and only one of the processes requiring the organization of ideas.
5. Skills related to the scheduling and planning of work.
6. Skill in the taking of examinations. This may include a variety of skills from handwriting up to the use of cues in answering objective test questions.
7. Data-gathering skills and library skills.

Publications for improving study habits vary in size from pamphlets such as that prepared by Wrenn (17) to larger manuals such as that produced by Robinson (13). The extensive use of these devices makes it desirable to consider methods for appraising their effectiveness. The ultimate criterion of the success of such materials is the extent to which there is a change in the performance of the student in his work. Most studies in this area have used changes in the average grades of the student as the criterion of effectiveness, though some have used the extent to which the students did or did not achieve their educational objective, such as that of graduating from college. Evaluative criteria of this kind have been used in studies for measuring the outcome of training in study skills. The results vary from the negative findings of Eckert and Jones (3) in one situation to the positive findings of Sherburne (14) in another.

The usefulness of grades or the completion of an educational program as a criterion of the effectiveness of training in study skills may be questioned. In at least one instance of which the author is aware, training in effective study habits was accompanied by the giving of a number of hints concerning which sections of courses were considered easy and which were run by instructors who were lenient in their method of grading or who were easily influenced by appropriate apple polishing. Extraneous variables of that kind are likely to contaminate the results of any study, for "knowing the ropes" is a different ability from effectiveness as a learner. Only when both the experimental and the control groups have programs of study established before the experimental training program begins is it possible to evaluate study-skill training in this way.

Any systematic investigation of study skills cannot rely upon grades and the achievement of educational goals as the sole criterion of the effectiveness of training. Even if improvement in grades is shown and even if this improvement is maintained over a considerable period, it is still desirable to determine which aspects of training were the effective ones. Did the student show an improved record because of improved reading habits, or because he learned to budget his time, or because he learned how to present his knowledge best on examination, or because of something else which he learned? Questions such as these must be answered and can be answered only by measuring each of the specific variables for which special remedial training has been given. In the next chapter various measures will be discussed of the variables such as reading comprehension and writing skill, but some of the most important aspects of study skills cannot be measured in a test situation and can be appraised only in terms of what the student actually does. The ability of the student to budget his time and plan his work must be assessed by observing how he budgets his time and plans his work. A test of his knowledge of how he should plan his day and his work will probably yield very different results from those obtained by observing his customary routine. In this case, in particular, it is not so much the knowledge of how to plan time that matters as it is aspects of personality which permit or inhibit the individual from behaving in the way he knows he should behave.

There is also the problem of permanence of the changes produced in any remedial program in the area of study habits. There is at least basis for arguing that the defects in the study habits of many students are a result of deep-seated defects in their personality, while remedial work, directed toward relatively superficial results, may produce changes which can be measured by tests. These changes may be transitory. Study-habit deficiencies are so closely related to personality problems that the assessment of progress may require the techniques of the clinician. Also, a given type of difficulty may have many causes which vary in the extent to which they are remediable.

The Inventory Method of Determining Deficiencies in Study Habits

A number of inventories on which the student may record the type of difficulties he is encountering in school have been developed. These inventories are mainly of value as a basis for conducting an interview, since it commonly happens that students may have little insight into the real sources of their problems. The best-known problem check list at the present time was developed by Mooney. This inventory has been prepared in a junior high school (11) and a high school form (10). There has also been a special form for student nurses and for rural youth, but these are no longer used. A form for adults and a college form have also been made available. These form a comprehensive check list of the trials and tribulations of the adolescent. They were prepared on the basis of substantial data relating to the actual problems of high school students such as may be obtained from interviews with pupils, from an analysis of case records, from an analysis of paragraphs written by students about their problems, from pupils' written expressions of educational needs, and from other miscellaneous sources in the literature. The check list itself provides a long list of troubles such as "shyness," "too easily led by other people," "too self-centered," and "heavy home responsibility." There are altogether three hundred items in the list. Some of them deal with inadequacies in study skills, faulty study habits, and related sources of scholastic failure. The student is asked to read the list slowly and underline any items which suggest something that troubles him. When he has completed this first step, he is to go back over the items he has underlined and circle the numbers of those "which are of most concern" to him. Finally he is asked to write a summary of his problems. The student's inventory is not scored, but is used as it stands as an account of the student's troubles.

Mooney (12) has suggested a number of approaches to the validation of the Problem Check List. They are as follows:

1. Students who have taken the Problem Check List are asked, "Do you feel that the items you have marked on the list give a well-rounded picture of your problems?" The fact that 92 per cent of college students studied responded in the affirmative is offered as evidence of validity. The meaning of the term *validity* in this instance is crucial in evaluating the worth of this evidence. If validity means that the student checks the items on the list which he *states* to be his problems, it is one thing. It is another if validity is to mean that the student checks the problems which are his in terms of a clinical diagnosis. In order to clarify the latter, it may be pointed out that individuals often have very limited insight in the nature of their own problems, and as insight is achieved they may find that their problems are very different from those they had previously imagined them to be. The fact that students feel that the check list provides a well-rounded picture of their problems is evidence of only the first type of validity just mentioned, which many will argue is a misuse of the word validity.

2. The second type of evidence of validity presented by Mooney is of a different type. It involves the demonstration that changes in the student's personal problems are accompanied by changes in the entries made on the check list. In the experiment reported, two groups which were rather small for the purpose and consisting of seventy men and forty-six women were given the check list. Nine days later they were asked to indicate on a mimeographed schedule any problems that had been solved during that period and any new problems that had arisen. The check list was then readministered, and 83 per cent of the changes indicated by the student on the mimeographed schedule were shown up in a comparison of the two performances on the check list. This is to be expected, regardless of the validity of the inventory. Individuals who fill in check lists such as the one under consideration are likely to be ego-involved enough to show consistency in their two records and to make these records consistent with other evidence which they have given to the experimenter. The reports made by the students on the schedules and the reports made on the check list are not separate items of evidence

and are not comparable with independent observations of two observers. The two series of data are contaminated one with the other and there are powerful psychological forces operating to make them consistent.

3. The third approach to the problem of validation is much more promising than the other two, since it partly overcomes the criticism that students may not have insight into their own problems. This more promising approach is that of selecting groups who on the basis of other evidence have identifiable problems. These groups are then administered the problem check list to see whether the responses reflect these problems. Mooney reports an unpublished study by Stogdill and Benton (12) in which the Problem Check List was administered to two groups with thirty-five undergraduates in each. One group consisted of a class in remedial study skills, while the other consisted of a mental hygiene class. The group undergoing training in remedial study skills showed a significantly greater frequency in the checking of items such as "don't know how to study effectively," "fearing failure in college," "not doing anything well," "daydreaming," "teachers lack interest in students," "needing to know vocational abilities," "unable to concentrate well," "slow reading," and other similar items. The mental hygiene class showed a significantly greater frequency in the checking of items such as "going into debt for college," "feeling unfair," "confused in religious beliefs," "parents expecting too much of me," "not enough time to myself," and "wanting courses I am not allowed to take." Certainly this appears to be some evidence that the problems checked on the list are problems which one might expect the students in these groups to check.

This study does seem to present some evidence that the problems checked on the list are the *stated* problems of the individual. However, the record of any individual must be interpreted with the greatest of caution, for it is common knowledge among clinicians that the individual often has little understanding of his own problems, and his own efforts to verbalize them may result in statements which give a completely distorted picture of the true state of affairs. States of anxiety, for example, may become attached to this or that object even though these objects may provide no real basis for anxiety. The important thing is to determine the *cause* of the anxiety and not the objects to which it may happen to become attached. It is possible that the Problem Check List may be more valuable in identifying individuals who suffer from anxiety states than in identifying sources of anxiety, but this is a matter which will have to be investigated through some well-conducted clinical studies in which individuals who have filled out the list are subjected to clinical interviews.

THE SELECTION OF PUBLISHED TESTS FOR USE IN A SCHOOL PROGRAM

Standards for Selecting Published Tests

It should be clear from what has been said that the main value to the teacher of a published test is in its measurement of the skills which are commonly considered to be important objectives of education. Since this is the case it is most desirable that the teacher be able to exercise good judgment in the selection of tests for purchase and subsequent use in his classroom or in a school-wide organized testing program. The selection of such instruments requires the exercise of sound professional judgment and is far from being the simple matter which it is commonly supposed to be. The American Psychological Association has long recognized that decisions pertaining to the selection of published tests are difficult to make and has drawn up a list of what should be the essential features of a test worthy of consideration (1). Since this list of essential and desirable features of a good published instrument is a rather technical document, only those aspects of it which have particular relevance to teachers can be summarized here.

Prior to the final selection of an achievement test for measuring some important skill, the teacher should obtain a sample kit of materials from the publisher and review these materials, asking at least the following questions:

1. Does the test have a manual which describes clearly just when the test can be appropriately used? In the case of an achievement test, the manual should state the grade level for which the test is appropriate and the type of training for which it is designed to measure the outcomes. However, the teacher must remember that the test items themselves in a very real sense define the educational objectives

to be measured by a test and the teacher should read each item, asking himself the question, "Does the fact that the pupil is able to answer this test item provide evidence that he has achieved in some degree the educational objective it is desired to measure?" Sometimes it is desirable to count the number of items related to each of several outcomes.

2. Does the manual provide necessary information for the interpretation of test scores? In the use of an achievement test the teacher may want to know what scores have been achieved by other pupils of comparable age, ability, and training, in order to be able to assess the effectiveness of his own teaching. Often, information of this type is not given, or only the performance on a nationwide sample of pupils is given. Such data can be misleading. For example, pupils in Texas who take a second grade reading test may achieve much higher scores than pupils in New York City just because in Texas it is customary to begin the teaching of reading in the first grade. If the norms are based on a sample of children from both of these areas, they will have little meaning for the individual teacher. Many test manuals present "national norms," as if these were a special sign of distinction. Needed more often are norms based on samples of children of specified age groups who have been exposed to a well-described program of education. It is also important that norms be based on groups of substantial size in order to reduce the possibility that some special circumstances may have produced unusually high or unusually low scores.

3. Does the manual indicate the kinds of inferences that can be made from test scores and the basis on which such inferences can be justified? This question refers to the validity of the test for the purposes for which it is said to be appropriate. If an achievement test in the area of reading is described as useful for identifying those students who need remedial teaching in this area, then the manual should cite studies which support the claim that the test will do just that. If a test manual states that the test measures certain skills in the social studies which are common objectives of high school teaching, it should also provide evidence to support this statement. It should refer to studies which show that objectives related to the test are common objectives and that the test items have a rational relationship to those objectives. Of course, there will be many occasions when the teacher will be interested in making comparison within

his own school; for instance, when he compares the performances of pupils before and after a particular unit of instruction. In such cases the norms given in the manual will be inconsequential.

The teacher must not accept broad generalizations unsupported by evidence as a basis for using a test. Rather should a teacher select for use those tests which are supported by manuals which present well-qualified statements concerning their uses, which indicate that thoughtfulness and thoroughness went into their construction, and which provide substantial evidence that the inferences which it is desired to make from the scores can be validly made.

4. Is the test known to have adequate reliability in the situation in which it is to be used? The test manual should indicate clearly just how the reliability of the test was estimated, the numerical value of the coefficient of reliability obtained, and the group on which it was obtained. Few commercial tests will have reported reliability coefficients of less than 0.85, but sometimes these are obtained with data from groups which have a much wider range of ability than the one to be tested. For example, a certain test of achievement in arithmetic is reported to have "a test-retest reliability of 0.89 when used with an unselected group of 1,000 high school students." If the teacher expects to use the test on a ninth grade group, he may expect that the test will have a substantially lower reliability with that group, since ninth graders have a more restricted range of arithmetic skills than high school pupils ranging from the ninth to the twelfth grade. For this reason, among ninth grade pupils, the test may not demonstrate differences of the type which the teacher may be interested in demonstrating.

5. Are the procedures for administering the test sufficiently simple and economical that it can be administered within the facilities available and within the budget provided by the school? Most published tests of achievement require little special equipment, but a few, such as certain tests of stenographic abilities, may require special equipment. Certain tests which involve a speed element must be timed with a stop watch, since an ordinary watch permits too wide a margin of error. As far as the cost is concerned, it should be noted that a test which requires the use of a separate answer sheet usually costs less per administration because the booklets are reusable. It should also be noted that a separate answer sheet permits rapid and efficient scoring. Tests in which the answers are recorded directly

in the test booklet are extremely laborious to score, for a separate key must be used for each page, and the pages must be turned and the keys changed. Many tests in which such a scoring procedure is necessary may take as long as fifteen minutes to score, while the corresponding tests which use a separate answer sheet can be scored in less than one minute.

The purpose of the preceding paragraphs has been to outline the type of inquiry that the teacher should make before deciding to use a particular published test of achievement. Mere reliance on the professional reputation of the publisher is insufficient, for many of the most competent test publishers produce tests which are recommended only for certain limited experimental purposes which the teacher is unlikely to have in mind. Finally, it needs to be pointed out that the title on the cover page of a test is often misleading. As was pointed out earlier, a test which is entitled "Effectiveness of Expression" may turn out to be a test of the so-called rules of grammar which relate only in a very indirect way to effectiveness of expression.

The Study of Published Tests of Skills Acquired in General Education

The preceding sections of this chapter have been planned to help the teacher and the prospective teacher to judge the merits of tests and to evaluate the evidence concerning their usefulness. It is important to obtain practice in the critical evaluation of tests, and to do this the student is advised to obtain specimen sets for study. The student should ask the instructor in the course to obtain the specimen materials for him, since most reputable test publishers will not send test materials to persons who have not been individually qualified to receive such materials. An alternative is to ask the instructor to endorse the student as qualified to receive the tests.

In order to help the student locate materials for review, Table 5.3 is provided, which lists a number of tests together with the names and addresses of the publishers. Since it has been emphasized in this book that a published test of a skill stressed in general education has a more defensible use than one which claims to measure essential knowledge within a subject-matter area, the tests listed are mainly in skill areas.

Although numerous tests of arithmetic and reading skills have been obtainable for twenty-five years, it is only within the last decade that tests of some of the other skills acquired in general education have been available. Even today the choice is limited, and, for many skills, published tests are not yet available. Another limiting condition in drawing up Table 5.3 is that many publishers of batteries of achievement tests seem to feel that skill tests are appropriate mainly in the lower grades, while the older children should be tested for information and understanding in traditional subject-matter areas.

It is not the purpose of this book to recommend tests, for it is hoped that the prospective teacher who reads this volume will acquire the skill necessary for judging the merits of the particular tests he may review. The appearance of a test in Table 5.3 does not constitute endorsement. The table is published only to help the reader locate tests for further study. It should also be noted that few reading tests are included, because these are listed separately in the next chapter. Also, the fact that a test battery is listed for a given level does not mean that a similar battery of tests in the same series is not published at a higher level. In conclusion, it must be said that the list is not intended to be a complete one at the time of publication and, since the student will wish to obtain a specimen set of the *latest edition* of any test ordered, no dates of publication are entered in the table.

Summary

1. Transition in general education from an emphasis on the acquisition of information to an emphasis on the acquisition of skills has been paralleled by attempts in the field of educational measurement to develop tests of the latter type of outcome. The Iowa Every Pupil Testing Program represented the major pioneering effort in this new trend in the measurement of pupil growth and has been the precursor of many large-scale testing programs devoted to the measurement of skills.

2. A substantial stimulus was given to the movement to measure skills as outcomes of general education by the Eight Year Study, which was one of the largest and most influential research projects

TABLE 5.3
Some Tests of Skills Acquired in General Education

Title of Test	Publisher or Distributor	Level of Test	General Nature of Skills Which the Test Is Designed to Measure
Stanford Achievement Test	World Book Co. Yonkers-on-Hudson New York	Grades 1.9–3.5	Paragraph meaning Vocabulary Spelling Arithmetic reasoning Arithmetic computation
		Grades 3.0–4.9	As above plus language
		Grades 5–6	As above plus social studies, science, and study skills
		Grades 7–9	As above
Metropolitan Achievement Test	World Book Co. Yonkers-on-Hudson New York	Grade 1	Matching words to pictures Recognizing printed words Identifying words which refer to colors, numbers. Things to eat, etc. Numbers
		Grade 2	Reading Arithmetic Spelling
		Grades 3–4	Reading Arithmetic Language usage Spelling
Iowa Every Pupil Tests of Basic Skills (New edition)	Houghton Mifflin Co. 432 Fourth Ave. New York 16, N. Y.	Grades 3–5	Reading comprehension Work study skills Language skills Arithmetic

TABLE 5.3 (cont.)
Some Tests of Skills Acquired in General Education

Title of Test	Publisher or Distributor	Level of Test	General Nature of Skills Which the Test Is Designed to Measure
Iowa Tests of Educational Development	Science Research Associates, Inc. 57 West Grand Ave. Chicago 10, Ill.	Grades 5–9 Grades 9–13	As above Understanding social concepts Background in natural sciences Correctness in writing Quantitative thinking Interpreting social studies materials Interpreting literary materials Vocabulary Uses of sources of information
Tests of General Educational Development	Veterans Testing Service of the American Council on Education, 5741 Drexel Ave. Chicago 7, Ill.	High School College Level	Correctness and effectiveness of expression Interpretation of reading materials in the social studies Interpretation of reading materials in the natural sciences Interpretation of literary materials General mathematics Correctness and effectiveness of expression Interpretation of reading materials in the social studies Interpretation of reading materials in the natural sciences Interpretation of literary materials
Cooperative Dictionary Test	Educational Testing Service Princeton, N. J.	Grades 7–12	Skills related to the use of a dictionary

TABLE 5.3 (conc.)
Some Tests of Skills Acquired in General Education

Title of Test	Publisher or Distributor	Level of Test	General Nature of Skills Which the Test Is Designed to Measure
Survey of Study Habits	Educational Records Bureau 21 Audubon Ave., N. Y. 32, N. Y.	Grades 12–14 Grades 8–14	As above Efficiency of study habits
Test of Critical Thinking	University of Oregon Press Eugene, Oregon	Grades 7–9	A wide range of thinking skills
Gray-Votaw General Achievement Test (revised edition)	Steck Company Austin, Texas	Grades 1–3	Reading comprehension Vocabulary Spelling Arithmetic reasoning Arithmetic computation
Progressive Achievement Tests	California Test Bureau 5916 Hollywood Blvd. Los Angeles 28, California	Grades 1–3 Grades 4–6	Vocabulary Reading comprehension Arithmetic reasoning Arithmetic fundamentals Language Skills similar to those measured at the Grades 1–3 level
Study Habits Inventory Revised Edition	Stanford University Press Stanford, California	Grades 12–16	Efficiency of study habits
Test of Study Skills	Steck Co. Austin, Texas	Grades 4–9	Test pupil's knowledge of sources of information and ability to use certain thinking skills
Watson-Glaser Tests of Critical Thinking	World Book Co. Yonkers-on-Hudson New York	Grades 9–16	Battery I. Discrimination reasoning Battery II. Logical reasoning

that has ever been undertaken in education. This study demonstrated the feasibility of measuring many of the thinking skills which are mentioned in lists of objectives.

3. The skills of pupils related to study habits can be studied by means of inventories and check lists, as well as by the conventional type of skill test. The Mooney check lists represent major ventures in this direction, although they also include a substantial amount of material pertaining to aspects of the pupil's difficulties other than those related to ineffective study skills.

4. It is believed that the outcomes discussed in this chapter can be measured in school-wide and system-wide testing programs without forcing the curriculum into the pattern of uniformity that has been the case when tests of information have been widely used.

5. It is important that the teacher exercise sound professional judgment in the selection of published tests. The points of special importance that the teacher should consider in the appraisal of published tests were discussed, and since these were presented in a much condensed form, no attempt will be made to summarize them further here.

References

1. American Psychological Association, Committee on Test Standards, Technical Recommendations for Psychological Tests and Diagnostic Techniques. Supplement to *Psychological Bulletin*, 51, 1954, pp. 38.

2. *Cooperative Test Division Catalog*, Princeton, New Jersey, Educational Testing Service, 1949.

3. Eckert, Ruth E. and Jones, Edward S., *Value of "How to Study" Course for College Students*, Buffalo, New York, University of Buffalo Studies, 10, No. 2, 1935, pp. 46.

4. Furst, Edward J., "Effect of the Organization of Learning Experiences Upon the Organization of Learning Outcomes. I. Study of the Problem by Means of Correlation Analysis," *Journal of Experimental Education*, 18, 1950, 215–28.

5. Furst, Edward J., "Effect of the Organization of Learning Outcomes. II. Study of the Problem by Means of Factor Analysis," *Journal of Experimental Education*, 18, 1950, 343–352.

6. Iowa Tests of Educational Development, *How to Use the Test Results*, Chicago, Science Research Associates, 1946, pp. 36.

7. Iowa Tests of Educational Development, *Descriptive Leaflet*, Chicago, Science Research Assocites (no date).

8. Lindquist, E. F., *Iowa Tests of Educational Development*, Chicago, Illinois, Science Research Associates, 1942.

9. Lorge, Irving D., "Trends in the Measurement of Achievement," in *Measurement and Prediction of Adjustment and Achievement*, edited by Donahue, Wilma T., Coombs, Clyde H., and Travers, Robert M. W., Ann Arbor, Michigan, University of Michigan Press, 1949, pp. 256.

10. Mooney, Ross L., *Problem Check List*, High School Form, New York, The Psychological Corporation, 1950, pp. 6.

11. Mooney, Ross L., *Problem Check List*, Junior High School Form, New York, The Psychological Corporation, 1950, pp. 6.

12. Mooney, Ross L. and Gordon, Leonard V., *The Mooney Problem Check Lists*, New York, The Psychological Corporation, 1950, pp. 15.

13. Robinson, Francis P., *Effective Study*. New York, Harper and Brothers, 1946, pp. 262 + IX.

14. Sherburne, J. S., *Problems and Outcomes of a College Remedial Program*, Ph.D. Dissertation, Ohio State University, 1938, pp. 411.

15. Smith, Eugene R., Tyler, Ralph W., and the evaluation staff, *Appraising and Recording Student Progress*, New York, Harper and Brothers, 1942, pp. 55 + XXIII.

16. Watson, Goodwin and Glaser, Edward M., *Tests of Critical Thinking*, Yonkers, New York, World Book Company, 1942.

17. Wrenn, Gilbert S., *Practical Study Aids* (Fifteenth printing), Stanford, California, Stanford University Press, 1946, pp. 16.

CHAPTER 6

Assessment in the Communication Skills*

Introduction

The development of thinking skills is intimately connected with the development of language; at least there seems to be no question that the adequacy of thinking depends partly on the extent to which the individual has developed a system of signs and symbols through which he can manipulate ideas. Since language is the very medium of thought, the appraisal of skill in the use of language becomes a matter of great interest not only to the teacher of English but to any teacher interested in the development of thinking skills. One word of caution is needed at this point. While language skills are needed for effective thought, it does not follow that a person who has well-developed language skills is necessarily an effective thinker. Language is a *necessary but not a sufficient* condition for effective thinking. It is for this reason that an entire chapter is devoted to this topic.

The previous paragraph should not be taken to imply that language serves only the purpose of facilitating thought, for obviously it serves many other functions. It is, of course, primarily a means of communication, but in our culture it is also an important medium for providing certain types of aesthetic experiences. These functions

* This chapter represents a revision and extension of an article written by the same author entitled "The Measurement of the Outcomes of the Teaching of English," published in the *Journal of Educational Research*, 17, 1949, 325–333. The author gratefully acknowledges the permission given by Professor A. S. Barr to do this.

of language must also be measured in the assessment of pupil development.

The Measurement of Outcomes Related to Expression

The measurement of the student's ability to express ideas in various forms has usually provided the basis for evaluating student progress in language skills, and for generations the essay or theme has been the English teacher's chief means of measuring this outcome.

The objectives which teachers attempt to achieve or to measure through theme writing are numerous. They include the development of such varied abilities as the following:

The ability to write grammatically correct English.
The ability to organize ideas.
The ability to express ideas of interest to others.
The ability to transmit concepts from one person to another by means of accurate verbal description.
The ability to express ideas in a form which is both clear and interesting.
The ability to produce an aesthetically worth-while composition.
The ability to spell correctly.
The ability to punctuate and paragraph.

All of these abilities and others, it is claimed, can be measured adequately in a student's theme. The traditional method of appraising a student's composition is for the teacher to make an over-all evaluation of it on the basis of general impression. By this method the teacher is appraising the composition in terms of his own general concept of what a desirable composition should be. Sometimes the teacher's concept of a good composition is fairly clear and can be made explicit, but often it has been formulated only in general terms. The evidence indicates that over-all impressions are usually based on rather superficial qualities of the composition. If such an appraisal of a composition is to have definite meaning, it is necessary for the teacher to determine just what weight is to be attached to each of these factors. This is just a way of stating that all teaching is aimed at a number of objectives, but that certain objectives are stressed more than others, and that an evaluation instrument should give the greatest emphasis to those objectives that receive the greatest stress. For example, one authority in this field (14) defines seven variables that should be measured in a composition. These seven are sense, spelling, punctuation and paragraphing, grammar and syntax, accuracy and vocabulary, power of expression, and the general impression given by the total composition. He recommends measuring each of these items separately before combining them into a total, and he believes that the examiner should determine what weights are to be assigned to each category. The various composition rating scales which have been developed (16, 17, 18, 19, 32, 34, 36) are all based on this kind of a concept. They all attempt to break down a composition into various measurable components and to give a weight to each. While analytic procedures do have some merit in that they force the teacher to make an analysis of what is being measured, composition rating scales have not had very widespread usage mainly for the reason that they have stressed analysis to the point where the scoring of a composition requires more time than the teacher can reasonably devote to it. Consequently, in recent times there has been a tendency for many authorities, including Stalnaker (27, 28), to recommend a compromise between the detailed, analytic rating-scale method and the over-all general impression method. In this compromise method the teacher rates the composition on the basis of over-all impression, but defines the main aspects that are to be kept in mind in forming this impression.

It should be noted that some of the skills involved in written compositions cannot be evaluated at all. There seems no possible way by which one can measure the extent to which an individual is able to express his own ideas clearly, since apparent inadequacy of expression may be either a symptom of lack of ideas or a symptom of the inability to express ideas.

Up to this point, only the teacher's evaluations of a student's product have been considered. There are, however, judgments other than those of the teacher which may be given consideration in evaluating a student's literary efforts. In discussing this question one writer (14) points out that the usual formula for developing writing skills is the formula of writing "anything about something for anybody," in which only the something is specified. When this formula is used as a teaching device it becomes very difficult to appraise the student's accomplishment because neither the student nor the teacher knows precisely what is to be accomplished. People outside of school never have to write "anything about something for anybody," and most adults would find such a task difficult, if not impossible. In life outside of school, people write with a particular audience in view, and most of the things they write are rather short. In adult life, the success of a written composition is judged, not always in terms of the kinds of judgments made by teachers about the composition of students, but in terms of whether the composition achieves a particular objective.

This is an important point, for it stresses the fact that expression can be evaluated adequately only in terms of the purpose which it serves. There has been a marked tendency for certain writers on the subject of the teaching of English to stress this fact. Hartog (14), for example, takes the view of the great Dr. Johnson that the usual form of essay is necessarily "an irregular, ill-digested piece," and is inclined to feel that the student should always write with a clearly defined purpose in view. He should know whether his composition is to be written in order to inform, or to amuse, or to inspire, or to perform some other function; and his composition should be evaluated by the audience consisting usually of classmates who decide whether it did actually inform them, or inspire them, or amuse them. This method of appraising student composition has merit, since all writing outside of school is done with a particular purpose in view and evaluations are performed in terms of the success of the composition in achieving that purpose. From this viewpoint, compositions should be rather short, for, apart from the fact that most of those written to meet daily needs actually are short, it is much easier to make evaluations of short compositions than of long ones.

There is one aspect of written compositions where new methods of appraisal are needed. That is in their aesthetic quality. In this connection Dewey (4) makes a useful distinction between an *expression* and a *statement*. He points out that the former has aesthetic value only, while the latter serves primarily to inform. The scientist makes statements, the artist makes expressions. The scientist makes statements which tell how to do certain things, but the expressions of the artist do not direct the observer what to do; they are made because they produce a certain experience in those who perceive them. Dewey (4, p. 85) states, for example, "The poetic as distinct from the prosaic, aesthetic art as distinct from the scientific, expression as distinct from statement, does something different from leading to an experience. It constitutes one." Up to this point the discussion of the evaluation of written compositions has been limited to the evaluation of the student's ability to make statements. However, techniques for evaluating the student's ability to make aesthetic expressions must also be considered.

The ability to produce an expression which has aesthetic value as distinct from a statement has rarely been assessed and there is little in the technical literature on the measurement of this ability. However, one recent study (26) of the ability of children to make artistic expressions presents results of significance in the present connection.

A major difficulty in the appraisal of the free, poetic compositions of children is that the poem of one child is so wholly different from the poem of another that the two productions are incommensurable. They must be evaluated on different scales because of differences in form, in content, and in other important variables. It becomes much easier to compare the poems of different children if the poems are written within the same frame of reference, and an ingenious attempt to do this is described in the study under discussion. The assessment technique was that of presenting the student with part of a poem and asking him to add a few lines of original composition. For example, in one of the questions the students were presented with the line, "I saw old autumn in the misty morn," and were asked to add three lines to continue the opening. Here are examples of how two students completed this task:

Example 1.   I saw old autumn in the misty morn
             Adorned in fading glories, like a king
             Grown old with age; the flaunted red of dawn,
             The gaudy leaves, concealed a dying thing.

Example 2.   I saw old autumn in the misty morn
             With grey-clouded sky in the dreary dawn
             But the sun soon came up and the clouds went away,
             And eventually it was a lovely day.

There can be little doubt that the second of these productions is greatly inferior to the first, and it seems to be fairly easy for teachers to evaluate the merit of a series of these compositions. Study has shown that when two teachers make independent evaluations of the merit of the student's responses in this test, there is rather good agreement between the evaluations. The reliability of the appraisal process in this situation is high and in marked contrast with the unreliability of the process of grading poems produced in situations where no restrictions are placed on the kind of creation which the student is expected to produce. Before leaving this technique it is worth giving a few more examples of the kinds of problem situations presented by this poetry completion test:

Shining like slugs,
The cars came fast;
Across the night
Their glances glowed;   (Finish this description of cars
With purring hearts   at night by adding two lines)
Approached and passed.

Men cannot swim
As fishes do,   (Add a second verse of four lines)
They only slave
A hard way through.

Another of the remarkable facts about this type of measuring technique is that the children in the study were able to produce so much original material in so short a space of time. In the test described by Smith (26), the children were required to add two, three, or four lines to nineteen different selections. It is surprising to find that many children were able to do this entire task in less than thirty-five minutes, and that the younger children in secondary schools had much less difficulty with the task than older children. The children used in the experimental work on the test would correspond roughly in ability to those in an academic curriculum in an American secondary school.

The possibilities inherent in the free-answer type of measuring instrument have not been fully recognized by those concerned with educational measurement. Unfortunately, the emphasis on the development of objective best-answer types of tests has largely obscured from view the possibility of other forms of measurement. One result of this tendency has been a widespread attempt to use objective tests for measuring indirectly the ability of the student to write or to speak. It is argued on the basis of rather flimsy evidence that if, for example, a student can discriminate between a clearly worded statement and an ambiguous statement, he is more likely to write clear statements than if he cannot make the discrimination. Numerous objective tests of the mechanics of expression have been developed for the purpose of measuring by very indirect means the ability of the student to communicate ideas. Other objective tests have attempted to measure the ability to organize ideas. However, for two reasons, the development of these tests has been largely an unhealthy influence. First, it has encouraged a very indirect method of measuring the outcomes of instruction. Second, many of these tests have not only provided a poor basis for evaluating the student's communication skills, but they have encouraged the perpetuation of many undesirable teaching practices. Fries (10) has pointed out in this connection that most language usage or grammar tests which have been produced are based on so-called common errors, but a large fraction of these so-called common errors are accepted by scholars as satisfactory usage. "On the whole," Fries states, "the methods of the present approach in the schools assume that the problem of language usage is a simple one of mistakes and correct language which can easily be separated according to perfectly definite measures and therefore they attempt to make the pupil 'conscious of the rules' by which to determine the correct language. From the scientific point of view in language, however, such methods are fundamentally unsound for language usage cannot be separated into two simple classes."

Probably the only major exception to this statement is in the use of objective spelling tests, where there is ample evidence to show that the student's ability to spell can be measured much more adequately through the use of an objective test than through the perusal of the student's written composition.

Something must be said about the evaluation of oral compositions. Objectives related to oral composition have been given increased emphasis at all levels in recent years because it has at last been recognized that in life in general there is a greater need for oral composition than for written composition. However, the evaluation of oral compositions presents all the difficulties associated with the evaluation of the written composition and an additional difficulty besides; namely, that oral compositions are fleeting, transitory phenomena which cannot be reviewed repeatedly for evaluation purposes unless they are recorded. However, much can be done to improve the usual rather rough evaluations of oral compositions. Improvements can be made in evaluating oral compositions by standardizing the situation in which the oral composition is made and by attempting to evaluate the compositions by comparing them with a graded series of compositions. At least one attempt to do this has been published in a reputable educational journal (22). In this article, it was pointed out that just as the quality of a sample of handwriting may be measured by the Thorndike Scale (30) by comparing it with a series of samples graded in quality, so too may the quality of a student's oral composition be measured by comparing it with a series of samples. The article goes on to describe scales for classifying grade school pupils' verbal responses to a story, picture, or object. While this technique is still experimental, it does seem to be a profitable one to develop. However, teachers who use this measuring technique will still have to develop their own scales, for the recorded scales used in the study cannot be purchased. In this connection, it is worth noting that various researchers (2, 13, 9) have developed simple paper-and-pencil scales for measuring certain aspects of oral expression. The rating scales thus developed have been published in journals and are available for use.

Appraising the Student's Understanding of Written and Spoken Language

Up to this point, discussion has been centered on the appraisal of oral and written compositions. Consideration must also be given to the appraisal of the development of the student's understanding of the ideas of others conveyed through written language or speech. Reading comprehension and aural (listening) comprehension are important objectives which all teachers, regardless of field, attempt to achieve in pupils. Since emphasis in schools has been on the development of reading skills rather than on listening skills, most of the work on appraisal has been done in the area of reading rather than in listening. As a matter of fact, the writer could find only one major educational research on the measurement of listening skills (11), though there are thousands on the appraisal of reading skills. The development of listening skills remains very largely an unexplored field.

Reading skills have been most adequately measured at the elementary school level, where the main purpose of testing has been diagnosed; that is, to determine the causes of reading difficulties. Special mechanical devices have also been devised for studying the mechanics of the reading process, but Traxler (33), after a careful review of the results achieved with such devices, concludes that there is little evidence to justify their use. In any case, the mechanical devices produced for studying the reading difficulties of children are not practical devices for the classroom teacher, and even in the hands of the expert are of questionable value.

The measurement of reading skills at the secondary school and college level is much less satisfactory than at the elementary school level. This is evident from the fact that different tests of reading skills at these higher levels seem to measure different variables.

In order to illustrate the variety of skills which a single reading comprehension test may attempt to measure, the following partially complete list of objectives is given:

Recognizing the purpose of the author.
Identifying the main ideas conveyed.
Identifying the main techniques used by the writer in transmitting his ideas.
Recognizing the author's philosophy.
Recognizing the meaning of certain figures of speech.
Identifying the meaning of particular words.
Identifying errors in reasoning.
Identifying references made by the author.
Identifying the meaning of particular words as they are used in context.
Identifying implications of the author's arguments.
Understanding the nature of the characters portrayed by the author.
Recognizing humor.
Recognizing the use of alliteration and other devices used by the author.

Tests of reading differ greatly in the skills that they are designed to measure. Many of the earlier tests of reading provided the pupil with a long paragraph of simple material and determined how much of it he could read in a given period of time. It was usual to check on the conscientiousness of the pupil's reading by giving him some objective tests items covering the factual content of the part of the selection he had read. Tests which follow this pattern are designed to measure whether the pupil has mastered the mechanics of speedy reading, but many reading experts question whether this is a variable of central importance.

More recently developed tests have tended to place much less emphasis on the speed factor. These tests are usually intended to measure the level of difficulty of the material which the pupil can understand. This is done by providing a series of short selections which vary in difficulty, complexity, and subtlety. A few objective test items which follow each selection are used for determining whether the pupil has understood the main ideas presented. Examples of well-developed tests of this type at the secondary school and college level are those published by the Cooperative Test Division of the Educational Testing Service. These tests measure two main aspects of the reading process. One is the understanding of the meaning of words, which is measured by a vocabulary test. The other is comprehension, which is measured by the technique described in this paragraph. The comprehension score that is usually derived from these tests depends to some extent on the speed of reading, but a rather complicated scoring procedure can be used if it is desired to measure comprehension independent of speed.

Attempts to break down reading skills into fundamental components will be discussed at greater length in the section of this chapter which deals with diagnostic tests, but one other development in this field of measurement must be discussed here. It seems clear that both comprehension and speed of reading depend upon the pupil's familiarity with the content field. Reading tests commonly derive their content from literature similar to that with which the pupil has some familiarity, but there are a few tests which measure reading skill in specialized areas such as social science and physical science. Such tests, which were discussed briefly in the last chapter, usually measure comprehension and are not speeded.

One of the interesting outcomes of the use of tests of reading comprehension is the finding (11) that measures of reading comprehension provide useful measures of listening comprehension. At the late secondary school and adult level there is a marked tendency for the poor reader to be the poor listener. Until good tests of listening comprehension have been developed, tests of reading comprehension may be used with some validity for predicting skill in that area. The lack of adequate evaluation instruments in measures of listening comprehension reflects the fact that little is known concerning the extent to which listening skills can be trained.

A special problem in the appraisal of reading comprehension is the appraisal of the student's understanding and appreciation of poetry, and it is a field of measurement which has attracted some of the most ingenious workers. Abbott and Trabue (1), who carried out a pioneer investigation in this field, considered that an important indication of the appreciation of poetry would lie in the individual's ability to distinguish good poetry from poor poetry. It seems reasonable to assume that a person who cannot distinguish between poetry judged by experts to be good and poetry judged to be poor could not have any appreciation of poetry, and such critical discernment is an important constituent of the appreciative process.

Abbott and Trabue selected a large number of poems which are recognized as works of considerable merit. These poems were modified in ways that destroyed their original worth in varying degrees. Some were converted into sentimental versions of the original, others into prosaic versions. Altogether, three new versions of each poem were prepared and then together with the original were submitted to a number of experts, including poets, literary editors, critics, and professors of literature. If these experts did not agree that the original was the best of the four versions, then the series was discarded. In some cases, it seems, a change in a poem actually improved it.

After four versions of each of over a hundred poems had been so examined, two short series of thirteen poems each were selected for the two forms of the final test. Each of these series represented material of graded difficulty from Mother Goose up to Milton or Browning. In the test itself each page was devoted to the four versions of each of a single poem, and the subject was instructed to "read the poems, A, B, C, D, trying to think how they would sound if read aloud. Write 'Best' on the dotted line above the one you like best as poetry. Write 'Worst' above the one you like least."

These tests were given to a large number of children in elementary and high schools and to students in college in order to determine how far young people of different ages were able to discriminate between the merits of one version of a poem and those of another. It is obvious that the students whose taste corresponded most closely with that of the experts would be able to choose correctly the best version of each of the thirteen series and would thus score thirteen points. On the other hand, the person who just guessed would score on the average between three and four points. At all levels it was found that an appreciable proportion of the subjects tested did no better than they would be expected to do by chance. For example, among fifty-six children in the fifth grade, twenty-nine scored less than they might have been expected to do by chance, and the fine qualities of the best version of these poems won recognition from only a relatively small fraction of the college group. In the higher grades of the elementary school there was practically no appreciation of the merits of the various versions of the poem. It is difficult to see how children could possibly appreciate such poetry when they were unable to distinguish the good versions from those that are both atrocious and idiotic. The situation in the high school was not much better, where the students still showed little taste, and even in college a large number of students were unable to distinguish good and poor versions of relatively simple poems.

Not only did students of certain ages fail to choose the best versions, but many of them showed a definite preference for the poor version, and particularly those poor versions in which the original poem had been sentimentalized. There was a steady increase in the preference shown for the sentimental versions throughout high school. This evaluation technique strongly suggests that the poetic material which children in high school are expected to appreciate bears no relation at all to the interests of their age. It seems almost self-evident that children cannot develop an appreciation for material which they do not understand, which has for them no real interest, and which they describe as dull and unintelligible. Before leaving this technique, it may be noted that there has recently been increased interest in its use through the publication of studies using it (25, 35).

The failure of children to appreciate and enjoy much of the poetry with which they come into contact does not however seem to be a result of the nature of poetry but a consequence of the type of material that is selected for school children. This was indicated rather clearly in an evaluation study by Manicoff (20), which showed that the intensive study of suitable poetry in the seventh, eighth, and ninth grades resulted in an increased interest in poetry and an increase in the amount of poetry read voluntarily.

The children who had poetry read to them regularly also showed a greater increase in their scores on a test of poetry appreciation than the children who did not have this experience.

In the Manicoff study, the extensive reading of poetry also seemed to have some effect on the amount of creative writing undertaken by students who had never attempted anything like that previously.

Fifty per cent of the pupils in the seventh grade, 49 per cent in the eighth, and 27 per cent in the ninth, who had never previously written original verse, managed to produce some during the experiment. In a control group there was almost no change in the amount of creative writing.

The Diagnostic Test of Reading

Another development in the measurement of language skills has been the diagnostic type of test, thus named because it is designed to identify those aspects of learning in a given area in which the individual has been least successful. For example, diagnostic reading tests measure various aspects of reading skills and provide scores for each aspect. It is claimed that an examination of this profile of scores may help to identify these aspects of the skill with which the child is having the greatest difficulty and which may be preventing progress from taking place in other aspects of the skill. There are difficulties inherent in the process of developing diagnostic achievement tests. One is that if the test is to have diagnostic value, then it is necessary for each part to have high reliability. Since each part has to be fairly short, adequate reliability is often difficult to obtain. Another problem is that before the test can be used for diagnostic purposes it is necessary to show not only that each part measures what it is supposed to measure but that the elements measured are the essential ones in the total skill.

It is also important to be aware of the fact that a test which measures over-all achievement in a particular area must include small samples of the subject matter or skill to be learned from a great many different aspects of the domain of learning. Each small sample is insufficient for making deductions concerning the pupil's proficiency in that aspect of the total achievement to be measured. In contrast, a diagnostic test includes rather large samples from limited aspects of the area of achievement. It is intended for making a check at certain crucial points, or at points which are judged to be crucial.

In the strict sense of the term, diagnostic tests do not diagnose the causes of learning difficulty. They indicate only the aspects of learning in which the individual has had difficulty and not the cause of this difficulty.

At all levels there has been a great proliferation of reading tests which have provided increasingly complex profiles of scores.

TABLE 6.1

Scores Derived from Three Readings Tests

I	II	III
Iowa Silent Reading Test: Advanced Test, Form A. Revised (12)	California Reading Test, Form AA Intermediate (31)	Nelson-Denny Reading Test for Colleges and High Schools, Forms A and B (21)
Word Meaning A. Social science B. Science C. Mathematics D. English	*Vocabulary* Social science Science Mathematics English	*Vocabulary*
Paragraph Meaning A. Science B. Literature	*Interpretation*	*Paragraph Meaning*
Paragraph Organization A. Selection of central idea B. Outlining		
Sentence Meaning		
Location of Information A. Use of the index B. Selection of key words	*Reference Skills*	
	Following Directions	

The early tests developed by Thorndike and his associates as a part of a battery were designed to measure intelligence and provided no analysis of the various aspects of reading. Later tests by other authors tended to provide several measures of reading skills. There seems almost no limit to the number of scores that reading tests may be made to yield, but the number provided by any test should not be taken as an index of the value of the test. Table 6.1 shows the name given to the various scores provided by three different reading tests which offer a marked contrast in the range of skills which they are intended to measure. By coincidence, the oldest and the newest of these tests provide the most complex profiles of scores. In choosing

TABLE 6.2

Some Tests of Reading Skills

Title of Test	Publisher or Distributor	Level of Test	General Nature of Skills Which the Test Is Designed to Measure
California Reading Test	California Test Bureau	Grades 1–4.5	Vocabulary Reading comprehension
		Grades 4–6	Same as above
		Grades 7–9	Same as above
		Grades 9–14	Same as above
Diagnostic Reading Test	Committee on Diagnostic Reading Tests, Inc. 419 West 119th Street New York 27, N. Y.	Grades 7–13	Test I Vocabulary Reading comprehension Test II Silent Comprehension Auditory comprehension Test III Rate of general reading Rate of science reading Rate of social studies reading Test IV Oral word attack Silent word attack
Gates Reading Diagnostic Tests—Revised Edition	Bureau of Publications Teachers College Columbia University New York, N. Y.	Grades 1–8	Mispronunciation Speed of reading Oral reading Oral vocabulary and 17 other reading skills
Gates Reading Readiness Tests	Bureau of Publications Teachers College Columbia University New York, N. Y.	Grade 1	Following directions with pictures Word matching Matching words to words Rhyming Reading letters and numbers

			Interpretation of prose passages
	Columbia University New York, N. Y.		
S.R.A. Reading Record	Science Research Associates 57 West Grand Ave. Chicago 10, Ill.	Grades 8–12	Rate of reading Reading comprehension Paragraph meaning Using alphabetical directory Interpretation of map, diagram, etc. Reading advertisement Use of index Technical vocabulary Sentence meaning General vocabulary
Gates Primary Reading Test	Bureau of Publications Teachers College Columbia University New York, N. Y.	Grades 1–2.5	Word recognition Sentence reading Paragraph reading
Gates Advanced Primary Reading Test	Bureau of Publications Teachers College Columbia University New York, N. Y.	Grades 2.5–3	Word recognition Paragraph reading
Gates Basic Reading Tests	Bureau of Publications Teachers College Columbia University New York, N. Y.	Grades 3.5–8	Reading to appreciate general significance Reading to predict outcome of events Reading to understand precise directions Reading for details
Reading Comprehension: Cooperative English Test	Educational Testing Service Princeton, N. J.	Grades 7–12 Grades 13–16	Vocabulary Speed of reading Comprehension As above

among these three tests, one is making a choice between a test which provides a rather large sample of behavior in two limited aspects of reading and tests which provide smaller samples but of a greater number of reading functions.

Certain facts need to be considered in the evaluation of tests such as these. First, the fact that there is some agreement among the names given to the variable measured by different tests does not mean that useful diagnostic categories have been developed, and just how these categories are to be used in the diagnosis of reading difficulties remains obscure. Most of the manuals which accompany the tests leave the application of the results up to the imagination of the teacher. The analysis of reading difficulties during the last twenty years has shifted from an emphasis on the motor components to an emphasis on a full-scale clinical investigation of the causes of reading difficulties. The typical diagnostic reading test does not take into account the more recent trends in the diagnosis of reading difficulties.

The reader must learn to appraise tests in this area by applying the principles for test evaluation which were presented in the previous chapter. A list of reading tests is provided in Table 6.2 to help the student locate useful materials for review and criticism. The tests listed have not been selected on the basis of any criterion of merit; rather, they represent a collection of widely used instruments which the student may wish to study.

Newer Approaches to Evaluation

The evaluation movement, in contrast to the measurement movement, has emphasized that in most situations objective tests represent indirect methods of measurement and should be used only where more direct methods of measurement cannot be applied. A major change in evaluation procedures during the last fifteen years has been a tendency to appraise student development not so much in terms of paper-and-pencil tests, but in terms of the way in which the pupil handles other types of situations. The argument is that if education is to be considered as preparation for life as well as a sample of life itself, then the success of an educational project must be evaluated in terms of the subsequent behavior of the students outside the school.

For example, if one of the objectives of a course is the development of good speech habits, then it is much better to appraise the outcomes of that course in terms of the actual improvement in speech habits than in terms of a paper-and-pencil test of knowledge of good speech habits. In this case, as in most others, the objective paper-and-pencil test is a poor substitute for direct observation of behavior in common situations. Indeed, the educational value of objective tests would be much improved if they were generally regarded as substitutes for better and more direct methods of appraising pupil development.

An excellent example of this modern approach to educational problems is found in the eight-year study (25) of the Progressive Education Association. In this study an attempt was made to appraise not only those outcomes of English instruction which can be measured by paper-and-pencil tests but also the other outcomes which most teachers recognize as important but do not measure. For example, an attempt was made to appraise the extent to which instruction in English developed desirable interests in reading. An investigation was made to determine the extent to which the reading of students was abundant, varied as to type of content, appropriate to the needs of the reader, and increasingly mature through the high school years in terms of difficulty, complexity, and depth of insight. A careful record was kept of the books which each pupil read voluntarily and the extent to which the pupil enjoyed each book. The maturity of the student's reading interest was measured by means of a scale based on one developed by Jeanette H. Foster (9). The Foster Scale classified 250 authors into six different levels of maturity according to the characteristics of the readers who enjoy them most. By the use of this scale it was hoped to measure the maturity of each student's reading interest. In the eight-year study the Foster Reading Scale was extended to cover 1,000 authors.

An attempt was also made (8) to evaluate the reading of magazines undertaken by pupils. This was done only once or twice a year and did not form a continuous process of evaluation. The evaluation procedure involved giving the pupils a check list which included the hundred magazines covering about 94 per cent of the magazine reading done by high school pupils. In the check list they were asked to indicate how often they read each magazine, how thoroughly they read it, and where they obtained it. In addition they were asked to state which magazines they preferred to read. The maturity level of each magazine was determined.

An attempt was also made to appraise the pupils' reading of newspapers by determining what papers were read, the amount of time devoted to newspaper reading, and the sections of the paper which were read most regularly. An incidental and interesting outcome of this appraisal was that very few pupils could identify the political policy of the newspaper they read.

The eight-year study is also of interest to English teachers because it tended to develop new methods of appraising pupils' appreciation of literature. In this field as in other fields the evaluation committee attempted to obtain evidence of appreciation or lack of appreciation wherever it could be found. Formal examinations represented only a single and minor method of collecting evidence of student development in this field. The evaluation staff of the eight-year study attempted to make a careful analysis of what was meant by literary appreciation at the secondary school level and developed evaluation instruments on that basis.

The main method used to appraise pupil appreciation of literature was the use of a questionnaire for determining students' reactions to their reading. The questionnaire on voluntary reading attempted to assess seven major aspects of the pupils' reaction to the material which he had read on a voluntary basis in his leisure hours. These seven aspects were the satisfaction derived from reading, the desire to read more of the same kind of material, the desire to know more about the things read, the desire to make creative expressions, the desire of the student to identify himself with the situation described in the reading material, the desire to think more about what has been read, and the desire to make fair judgments about the reading material.

This approach to the appraisal of the outcome of instruction in English represents a healthy departure from the traditional type of essay examination in which the pupil is asked to discuss some aspect of his reading. It has been widely used both at the high school, general college, and college level (6, 7). This new approach, however, is possible only in the situation where the student and teacher are working closely together and where the student knows that appraisals of his work are made, not for the purpose of assigning a mark, but for the purpose of helping him to obtain all he can out of life. A similar approach was taken by Dora Smith in her study of the outcomes of English instruction in elementary schools in the state of New York (24) in which she investigated the out-of-school reading of the pupils. Her findings indicate the kinds of variables she tried to measure by means of questionnaires. These findings are broadly summarized in the following paragraph (24, p. 37):

> Pupils in the seven towns show a general lack of knowledge of good current books for children. Evidence indicates, that as pupils progress through the elementary grades, the schools are not conscious of the competition of inferior books suited to children's interests, which are read in increasingly greater numbers than are good wholesome books for children. . . . The books read by boys are inferior to those read by girls. . . . only one pupil in sixteen read a current-events magazine during the three weeks of the study.

The questionnaire techniques described above do not replace the traditional techniques for measuring outcomes in courses in literature, but there is no doubt that they do appraise the attainment of important objectives which have remained largely unappraised in the past.

Summary

The field of language arts has shown extensive development in recent years in techniques for appraising pupil growth. This has involved the improvement of methods of appraising the written products of the pupil and a focusing of attention on the communication value of the pupil's writings. Although it is important for the pupil to learn the mechanics of expression, these are of little value if the individual still has difficulty in transmitting his ideas. Appraisal of the pupil's writings must be in terms of both his facility with the mechanics and his communication skill. Techniques have also been evolved for studying the pupil's skill in writing poetry and other forms of aesthetic expression. However, these techniques must still be considered to be in the experimental stages and cannot be used for routine assessments.

The development of reading tests represents a major step in educational measurement, for there is good evidence that a pupil's ability to profit from typical school curricula depends to a great extent on his reading skill. Reading tests are widely used and measure the achievement of an objective to which most, if not all, teachers would subscribe. The writer considers that reading tests are much more useful as measures of achievement than as devices for *diagnosing* the reasons underlying a pupil's reading difficulties. Diagnostic tests are widely used, but, while many of them provide useful measures of achievement, their value in diagnosis may well be questioned.

The most recent innovations in the assessment of pupil development in the language arts involve attempts to appraise the extent to which the school program is effective in changing the reading habits and interests of the pupils. Evidence of such changes is obtained from records of what pupils choose to read in their leisure hours rather than from the more conventional type of instrument.

References

1. Abbott, Allan and Trabue, M. R., "A Measure of the Ability to Judge Poetry," *Teachers College Record,* 22, 1921, 101–126.
2. Beverly, C., "Standards in Oral Composition: Grade One," *Elementary English Review,* 1, 1925, 360–361.
3. Cook, Walter W., "Evaluation in the Language Arts Program," pp. 196–214 in *The Forty-Third Yearbook of the National Society for the Study of Education, Part II*: Teaching Language in the Elementary School, Chicago, Illinois, University of Chicago Press, 1944.
4. Dewey, John, *Art as Expression,* New York, Milton Balch and Company, 1934, pp. 355.
5. Dykema, K. W., "On the Validity of Standardized Tests of English Usage," *School and Society,* 50, 1939, 766–768.
6. Eckert, Ruth E., *Outcomes of General Education: An Appraisal of the General College Program,* Minneapolis, Minnesota, University of Minnesota Press, 1943, pp. 210 + XIV.
7. Eckert, Ruth E. and Marshall, Thomas O., *When Youth Leaves School,* New York, McGraw-Hill Book Company, Inc., 1939, pp. 360.
8. Eells, Walter C., *What Periodicals Do School Pupils Prefer?* Wilson Bulletin for Librarians (December, 1937), reprinted in Evaluation of Secondary Schools: Supplementary Reprints. 744

Jackson Place, Washington, D. C., Cooperative Study of Secondary School Standards.

9. Foster, Jeanette H., "An Approach to Fiction Through the Characteristics of Readers," *Library Quarterly*, 6, 1936, 124–174.

10. Fries, Charles C., "For Economy and Good English," *University of Michigan School of Education Bulletin*, 3, 1932, 118–120.

11. Goldstein, Harry, *Reading and Listening Comprehension at Various Levels*, New York, Bureau of Publications, Teachers College, Columbia University, 1940, pp. 69 + IV.

12. Greene, H. A., Jorgenson, A. N., and Kelley, V. H., *Iowa Silent Reading Tests, Advanced Test:* Form A (Revised), Yonkers, New York, World Book Company, 1927.

13. Harring, S., "A Scale for Judging Oral Composition," *Elementary English Review*, 5, 1928, 71–73.

14. Hartog, P. and others, "The Marking of English Essays," *A Report of An Investigation Carried Out by a Subcommittee of the International Institute of Examinations Enquiry Committee*, London, England, Macmillan, 1941, pp. 165 + XV.

15. Hosic, J. F., "The Chicago Standards in Oral Composition," *Elementary English Review*, 2, 1925, 170–177 and 255–261.

16. Hudelson, E., *Hudelson's Typical Composition Scale (Grades II-XII)*, Yonkers, New York, World Book Company.

17. Hudelson, E., *Hudelson's Maximal Composition Scale (Grades II-XII)*, Yonkers, New York, World Book Company.

18. Hudelson, E., *Hudelson's English Composition Scale (Grades IV-XII)*, Yonkers, New York, World Book Company.

19. Lewis, E. E., *Lewis's Scale for Measuring Special Types of English Composition (Grades IV-XII)*, Yonkers, New York, World Book Company.

20. Manicoff, Rose, *The Effects of Extensive Teacher Reading of Poetry: An Experimental Study with Junior High School Pupils.* Doctoral Dissertation in the Library of Fordham University, 1937, pp. 207.

21. Nelson, M. J. and Denny, E. C., *The Nelson-Denny Reading Test for Colleges and Senior High Schools*, Forms A and B, New York, Houghton Mifflin Company, 1929.

22. Netzer, R. F., "The Evaluation of a Technique for Measuring Improvement in Oral Composition," *Journal of Experimental Education*, 6, 1937, 35–39.

23. Smith, Dora V., *Evaluating Instruction in Secondary School English: A Report of the Regents Inquiry.* English Monograph No. 11, Chicago, National Council of Teachers of English, 1941, pp. 273 + XIX.

24. Smith, Dora V., *Evaluating Instruction in English in the Elementary Schools of New York: A Report of the Regents Inquiry.* Eighth Research Bulletin of the National Conference on Research in English, Chicago, Illinois, Scott, Foresman and Company, 1941, pp. 96.

25. Smith, Eugene R., Tyler, Ralph W., and the evaluation staff, *Appraising and Recording Student Progress,* New York, Harper and Brothers, 1942, pp. 550 + XXIII.

26. Smith, Gordon P., *A Psychological Study of Poetry Writing by Children.* Thesis Submitted for the Degree of D. Phil., Oxford University, 1940.

27. Stalnaker, John M., "Testing the Ability to Organize," *English Journal* (College Edition), 22, 1933, 361–367.

28. Stalnaker, John M., "Essay Examinations Reliably Read," *School and Society,* 46, 1937, 671–672.

29. Stalnaker, John M. and Stalnaker, R. C., "Reliable Reading of Essay Tests," *School Review,* 42, 1934, 599–605.

30. Thorndike, Edward L., "Handwriting," *Teachers College Record,* 11, 1910, 87–88.

31. Tiegs, Ernest W. and Clark, Willis W., *California Reading Test, Intermediate Form AA,* Los Angeles, California, California Test Bureau, 1950.

32. Trabue, M. R., Nassau County *Supplement to the Hillegas Scale (Grades IV-XII),* New York, Teachers College Bureau of Publications, Columbia University, 1916.

33. Traxler, Arthur E., "Value of Controlled Reading: Summary of Opinion and Research," *Journal of Experimental Education,* 11, 1943, 280–292.

34. Van Wagenen, M. J., *Van Wagenen English Composition Scale (Grades IV-XII),* Yonkers, New York, World Book Company.

35. Williams, E. D., Winter, L., and Woods, I. M., "Tests of Literary Appreciation," *British Journal of Educational Psyschology,* 8, 1938, 265–284.

CHAPTER 7

The Measurement of Work Skills

Introduction

One of the major achievements of individuals in our society is the acquisition of a work skill which enables them to earn a living in a complex industrial culture. A substantial part of the entire educational system is concerned with the development of work skills. All kinds of organizations devote a major part of their time to the assessment of the extent to which these work skills have been developed. Placement services such as those operated by the separate states and also private organizations are much concerned with the process of assessing the work skills of the individual so that he can be placed in a job which he can handle adequately. Business and governmental agencies which employ large numbers of individuals have also shown interest in this problem of the assessment of the work skills of those who apply for positions.

The importance of the skilled man to industry, coupled with the limited capacity of industry for training such individuals, has resulted in a great expansion of public education in this area. Large cities throughout the country have in recent years developed specialized vocational and technical high schools which are training individuals in a wide range of crafts from the simpler skills such as that of the welder to the more complex skills such as that of the engineering draftsman. In fact, the skills which may be learned in these schools vary in complexity all the way from a level just below that of the skill of the professional person down to those which are so simple that some would classify the corresponding occupation as unskilled.

Although it is possible to purchase instruments which measure a great many of the academic skills which the high schools attempt to develop, it is remarkable how few are the tests available which attempt to measure proficiency in the work skills for which training is commonly provided. Publishers and producers of tests have not for the most part found it either possible or profitable to produce such tests, though much has been done by the armed services in this area. The reasons for this apparent lack of enterprise are worth studying because they bring out the special problems of measurement in this area.

1. The behaviors to be developed in any training program which aims at producing skilled craftsmen are behaviors which involve the manipulation of objects and materials. The objectives involved in a course for electricians are defined in terms of the kinds of things which electricians have to *do*. These activities of the trained electrician involve the manipulation of tools and equipment in the solution of typical daily problems of the trade. Thus, achievement in a course for electricians is best measured in terms of the ability of the trainee to perform these tasks. If he can carry out the tasks assigned to electricians, then the course has provided a successful training program. Evidence of the ability of the trainee to work at the job for which he was trained is, at least in theory, best determined by observing his behavior after employment as an electrician. However, it is hardly ever practical to do this. It is not feasible to follow a man around after employment and make an objective record of his performance and evaluate his successes and failures, and even if it were otherwise feasible, the cost would be prohibitive. While the trained observer might be able to obtain evidence of achievement in this way, any attempt to use untrained observers such as the foreman in charge or employer provides little useful data. For all practical purposes, the ratings provided by on-the-job supervisors are unlikely to provide much in the way of useful evidence of the adequacy of a training program. The reasons for this are discussed in the section on ratings (pp. 213–215).

Another major disadvantage to the measurement of achievement by on-the-job observation appears when a man enters employment which calls for a very limited amount of his skill in some highly specialized area. An electrician leaving a training program for electricians may accept a job repairing electric motors, and for years he may do nothing except diagnose causes of failure and make repairs in this limited area. On a job of this kind, it would be quite impossible for him to demonstrate proficiency in the other areas of his trade. Indeed, observation on the job may seem at first sight to be the ideal method of assessing the outcomes of training, but a study of it reveals it to be one of the least adequate.

2. A much more desirable method of measuring achievement in a trade (or job proficiency, as it is called) is to present the individual with selected tasks to perform. These tasks, referred to as work samples, must have been carefully selected so as to be representative of the entire job for which the individual has been trained. Each task constitutes a performance test, once scoring methods have been developed for providing an appraisal of how well the individual has done on the task. The use of selected tasks for testing purposes overcomes many of the difficulties encountered in the previous method. Various aspects of the job can be properly represented in the appraisal, and the appraisal can be made under the supervision of a trained observer.

Nevertheless, there are difficulties which accompany this method of appraising achievement in a trade. Performance tests of this kind are extremely time-consuming both for the individual tested and for the person who supervises the test. The test usually requires quite complicated equipment and a considerable amount of space. Imagine the amount of space needed for administering a performance test to only ten men who have been trained as bricklayers! Since more than one man must usually be tested at a time, multiple sets of equipment are needed but are often not available for testing purposes. In addition, it rarely happens that a single person can administer a performance test to more than three or four persons; hence, if a group of any size is to be tested at one time, several test administrators are needed. Since these test supervisors must usually be skilled personnel, it generally happens either that money is not available to employ such individuals or that such individuals are not available.

Performance Tests of Achievement in Trades

For reasons which have just been mentioned, few performance tests of achievement, or job proficiency as it is called in reference to skilled trades, have been developed. Until the First World War, little was done in this area, but at that time the U. S. Army became interested in developing performance tests to measure the proficiency of enlisted men in certain skilled trades (3). It is probable that the Army was almost the only organization that at that time could afford to build performance tests and have the facilities for administering them. Some of these tests were later published in a book by Chapman (14) which represented a minor landmark in the history of measurement.

It is to the credit of Chapman and his associates, who included some of those who were to become the best-known members of the psychological profession, that they succeeded in identifying most of the difficulties involved in the measurement of occupational skill and developed tests comparable in quality with some of the best developed in more recent years. Refinements have been largely in minor matters rather than in matters of the general principles involved.

With the exception of stenography and typing, if these can be called skilled trades, little was done between the world wars to develop performance tests of achievement in skilled trade areas. In fact, it was not until the Second World War that interest was again aroused in this problem. While technical high schools and vocational high schools here and there may have developed performance tests of their own, little is to be learned about these tests from professional educational literature. It is also probable that industries developed performance tests of achievement in many areas of industrial skill, although relatively little was published concerning these devices, which ranged from the hopelessly inadequate to the professionally sound. A similar range of performance tests was developed and used by municipal, county, and state civil service commissions throughout the country, and many of these tests were readily exchanged among organizations of this kind, although they were rarely published. The published and standardized performance test of proficiency in a trade just did not exist between the world wars but remained an academic subject discussed at considerable length in every reputable textbook on psychological and educational measurement.

The Second World War brought a revival of interest in performance tests in areas of vocational skill as a result of the immense training programs undertaken by the armed services. In the armed services, however, as in civilian life, difficulties both financial and administrative hindered the widespread development and use of such measuring devices. While many service schools developed performance tests for local use and for appraising the extent to which the objectives of training had been achieved, such tests were seldom published for use on an army-wide or a navy-wide basis. At least one major reason for this was the absence of adequate job descriptions from which schools could find out the precise nature of the job for which men were being prepared. Thus several schools preparing men for a single given military occupation might differ substantially in the curriculum offered and in the expected outcomes of training. Under these circumstances, it would hardly be possible for several schools to use the same performance test of achievement for evaluating either the effectiveness of teaching or student progress.

There were certain notable exceptions in the matter of this lack of performance tests available for use throughout a branch or arm of the service. For example, the Bureau of Naval Personnel prepared a series of performance tests covering the operation of certain of the more common types of marine engine. Since the procedure for operating these engines was well defined, the matter of preparing tests to cover the procedure was *relatively* simple, though the preparation of even the simplest performance test is never an easy matter.

Teachers should acquire skill in the development of performance tests. Techniques for developing these instruments will be described later in this chapter after paper-and-pencil and oral techniques for assessing work skills have been discussed.

Performance Tests in Skills Developed in Business Education

A considerable number of proficiency tests have been developed in the general business area and particularly in stenography, typing, bookkeeping, and accounting. Many of these tests have been directed toward the measurement of the outcomes of specific high school courses rather than to the measurement of these skills as they are used in definite jobs. For example, the United States Armed Forces Institute tests in bookkeeping and accounting (16) are stated to be at the levels of first and second year high school, with one test at each level. There seems to have been a genuine attempt in this test to measure skills which might be considered to be practical outcomes of training in this field. The nature of the skill makes it appropriate to use paper and pencil as the basic materials required for a performance test.

Shorthand tests vary greatly in the extent to which they cover comprehensively the skills performed by the office stenographer. In some shorthand tests such as the Heitt Stenographic Test (7) for the Gregg System, the use of dictation has been limited to three minutes. In place of the usual dictation procedure, Part I of the test lists fifty printed words which are to be reproduced in shorthand, and in Part II words in shorthand are to be reproduced in regular script. Part III is a sentence completion type of test in shorthand, and Part IV requires the student to convert a continuous passage into shorthand. Part V is based on three minutes of dictation given at the beginning of the test. In contrast, the Seashore-Bennett Tests of Stenographic Proficiency (10) may be considered. These tests present five letters dictated through the medium of phonograph records. The records occupy twenty minutes of dictation and as many as fifty people may take dictation at the same time. The use of records eliminates a major source of variation in all dictation tests, namely, the variability of the speed of speech and the intonation of the voice of the person who does the dictating. It seems evident that the Seashore-Bennett test is much more closely related to the work of the stenographer than is the Heitt test. A stenographic test which does not give adequate emphasis or control to the matter of taking dictation is like a typewriting test which hardly requires the examinee to use the typewriter. Other new tests in this field, including one produced by Science Research Associates, show the proper emphasis in this matter.

Performance tests of typing are rather numerous and, in general, involve typing copy which may be presented in handwritten, printed, or typescript form. Some tests present copy on which corrections have been made. Usually typing tests provide a speed score as well as an accuracy score. This raises the problem of how speed scores and accuracy scores should be weighted and combined. The answer to this question is that the scores should be combined in such a way that they predict an ideal measure of proficiency with maximum accuracy, but the only difficulty is that there is often no ideal measure of proficiency, and none that approximates this ideal.

The student of this book who intends to teach commercial courses should study samples of available tests. In Table 7.1 many of the tests available for measuring the outcomes of courses in business education are listed, together with the source from which they can be obtained. The reader is reminded that it is usually necessary to order these materials through the teacher in the course on educational measurement or to obtain a note from him to the publisher authorizing the purchase.

Substitutes for Performance Tests of Vocational Skills

The difficulties involved in assessing the individual's skill in a trade, either by observing him on the job or on selected job problems which constitute a test, have resulted in psychologists looking for other methods of appraisal which might be cheaper to administer and require less space and equipment. The substitute usually attempted is that of presenting the problems not in terms of concrete situations with a full regalia of tools, equipment, and materials, but in terms of a situation described in some way either orally or in printed form.

There are three general types of attempts to solve this problem.

1. *Oral questioning* is one technique that has been used on an informal basis by occupational interviewers for generations, but the main deficiency of this system has been the informal, unplanned nature of these interviews. The first step which psychologists took in improving this procedure was to develop a set of questions which remained standard from one interview to the next. These standard questions referred to important aspects of the job and had to be worded in such a way that the skilled man would know exactly what was meant. Another necessary improvement was to develop a scoring system such that the replies to the oral questions could be scored with objectivity. Oral tests of this kind were developed in over a score of military occupations during 1917-18, but little was done to extend the work or to determine the adequacy of these instruments until the United States Employment Service nearly twenty years later began the systematic development of Oral Trade Questions designed to measure proficiency in a large number of skilled occupations. It may be said that the oral trade tests of the First World War were thoroughly inadequate in their scoring system, but that the Oral Trade Questions were much more adequate in this respect. The Oral Trade Questions (5) were improvements over their predecessors in many other ways. They were based on detailed job

TABLE 7.1
Some Tests of Work Skills in Business for the Student to Study

Title of Test	Publisher or Distributor	Level of Test	General Nature of Skills Which the Test Is Designed to Measure
Bookkeeping Test	National Office Management Association 2118 Lincoln Liberty Bldg. Philadelphia 7, Pa.	High school and adult	Correcting entries in Cash Book, Ledger, etc.
Examination in Gregg Shorthand	Educational Testing Service Princeton, N. J.	First year of training in high school	Transcription of written and spoken material into shorthand Transcription into longhand of shorthand passage
Examination in Typewriting	Educational Testing Service Princeton, N. J.	Level 1—First year typing Level 2—Second year typing	Various typing skills, including the setting up of a letter
Filing Test	National Office Management Association 2118 Lincoln Liberty Bldg. Philadelphia, Pa.	Intended for use in selection of employees	Filing skills
Heitt Stenographic Test	Bureau of Educational Measurement Kansas State Teachers College Emporia, Kansas	First and second semester of high school training	Skills in Gregg shorthand

Kauzer Typewriting Test	Bureau of Educational Measurement Kansas State Teachers College Emporia, Kansas	Level 1—first semester test Level 2—second semester test Level 3—fourth semester test	The series of three tests measures progressively more difficult typing skills
Machine Calculation Test	National Office Management Association 2118 Lincoln Liberty Bldg. Philadelphia, Pa.	Intended for use in the selection of employees	Skill in the performance of sustained work with calculating machines
Seashore-Bennett Stenographic Proficiency Tests *	The Psychological Corporation 522 Fifth Avenue New York 36, N. Y.	Intended for use in the selection of employees	Measures the ability to take down material dictated through a record played on a record player.
S. R. A. Dictation Skills *	Science Research Associates, Inc. 57 West Grand Ave. Chicago 10, Ill.	Grades 9–12 Adults	Measures the ability to take down material dictated through a record played on a record player.
S. R. A. Typing Skills	Science Research Associates, Inc. 57 West Grand Ave. Chicago 10, Ill.	High school students and adults	Common typing scales

157

* This test is not appropriate for the student who wishes to purchase a specimen set for a small sum of money. The test requires the use of a phonograph record, and for this reason costs a substantial sum. However, the adequate testing of shorthand requires the use of recorded materials.

analyses of what men actually did in the trades for which they had been prepared. On the basis of these job analyses, questions were prepared which covered important job elements. This long list of questions was eventually whittled down to a list of manageable proportions and evidence was collected to determine the extent to which the responses differentiated skilled, semiskilled, and unskilled men within the trade.

There are advantages as well as disadvantages in oral questioning. The administrative advantages are rather obvious, but in comparison with a written test they have the merit of not requiring reading skills in which a craftsman may not be practiced. On the other hand, not all examiners may speak clearly at all times, and even if examiners were selected for enunciation and their ability to speak "standard English," not all of the examinees may understand "standard English" as well as they understand some form of local dialect. The rate of speech may have an important effect on the outcome of the test and, in addition, defects of hearing must also be considered to be an important source of measurement, particularly in older people.

2. *Printed verbal tests.* These tests may present many of the tasks which appear in performance tests, but they must be presented and answered in a verbal form. They can ask questions concerning how aspects of jobs should be undertaken and what tools and materials should be used. They cannot, of course, determine whether the person has the manual skill and dexterity for performing these tasks. It is commonly said that paper-and-pencil tests measure knowledge of theory, while performance tests measure practical skills, but this statement is not true. A paper-and-pencil test may provide evidence of practical skill, and a performance test may provide evidence of a person's knowledge of theory.

The paper-and-pencil test situation for measuring skill in a trade is limited for three main reasons: (1) It cannot present problems which involve the manipulation of tools, equipment, and materials. (2) There are certain problems in many trades that cannot be presented at all through the medium of paper and pencil. One such problem is that encountered by the blacksmith in heating a piece of metal preparatory to working it. He will heat it until it is just the right color in terms of glow for his purpose. On a performance test, it is possible to ask a blacksmith to heat a piece of metal and to determine whether he heats it to the right degree before he starts working it. But since there are no suitable words to describe the changes in glow which occur as metal is heated, it is impossible to ask questions about this phenomenon on a paper-and-pencil test or to discuss it with a person who is being examined. (3) A problem presented in a paper-and-pencil form may not be the same problem to many individuals as the corresponding problem presented in the performance test situation. Individuals who have difficulty in reading may fail to understand a problem at all because of this handicap. Some may misread a problem presented in print and may therefore misunderstand it. Some may have difficulty in visualizing a problem presented in print, though they might recognize, understand, and solve the same problem if it were presented in concrete form.

Objective test items of the following type have been commonly used in paper-and-pencil attempts to measure job proficiency:

What tool should be used for tightening the bolts which hold the cylinder head onto the engine block of a gasoline engine?
   1. A torque wrench
   2. A socket wrench
   3. An adjustable-end wrench
   4. A ratchet wrench

What kind of saw should be used for cutting a 1-inch fir plank along the grain?
   1. A cross-cut saw
   2. A rip saw
   3. A hack saw
   4. A scroll saw

If the group to be examined is literate, and if the essential knowledge of the trade can be expressed in words, tests of this kind may provide a measure of the extent to which the individual possesses certain necessary knowledge. It should be noted that the possession of necessary knowledge is no guaranty of success in the occupation, since many other factors may be essential for success. It may be emphasized once more that paper-and-pencil tests do not measure the manipulative aspects of skill. These tests may measure a necessary but not a sufficient condition for proficiency. However, despite this limitation, tests of this kind may have value.

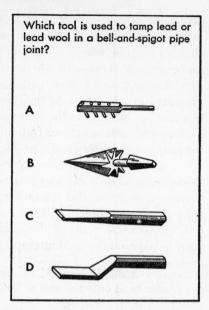

Each of the following pictures shows a mixing platform on which a 1-ton batch of concrete is to be hand-mixed. No turning or mixing has been done. Which job has been started right?

Which tool is used to tamp lead or lead wool in a bell-and-spigot pipe joint?

FIGURE 7.1

Illustration of test items for measuring knowledge of a work skill with the suggested answers in a pictorial form. Reproduced by permission of the Department of the Army from an official publication (1).

3. *Illustrated or pictorial tests* were used in both world wars for appraising the proficiency of men in certain skilled army trades (1). Examples of test questions of this type are shown in Figure 7.1.

In these items it is the suggested solution rather than the problem itself which is presented in pictorial form. In the problem in Figure 7.2 the reverse occurs, and it is the problem situation which is mainly presented in verbal terms. Note that the cooking range shown in the illustration is, or was, a standard piece of army equipment.*

While problems of this kind have much to recommend them, they present many difficulties from a test-construction point of view. First, there is the matter of cost. The work on such tests must be undertaken by competent artists whose services are necessarily expensive. Second, even though the illustrations are prepared by competent

* The author gratefully acknowledges the permission given by the Department of the Army to reproduce these materials.

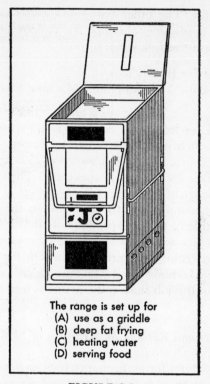

The range is set up for
(A) use as a griddle
(B) deep fat frying
(C) heating water
(D) serving food

FIGURE 7.2

Illustration of text item for measuring knowledge. The problem is presented partially in pictorial form. Reproduced by permission of the Department of the Army from an official publication (1).

persons, there is always the possibility that they may be ambiguous or fail to bring out certain essential details. Unless illustrations are well done, they are likely to produce more difficulties than they eliminate.

Published Tests of Proficiency in Skilled Trades

Tests of achievement in occupational skills, for reasons that have already been studied, have not attracted publishers. *The Third Mental Measurement Yearbook* (2) published in 1949, lists only two tests of this kind under the heading of tests in "Specific Vocations." The subsequent edition of the Yearbook, published in 1953, adds nothing to this list. The other tests listed under this category are instruments for appraising *aptitude* for various occupations. The two tests listed are the following:

Purdue Test for Electricians (8)
Purdue Test for Machinists and Machine Operators (9)

The Purdue Test for Electricians is an objective type of instrument which samples knowledge of electricity and its applications. This test might be a much better instrument for measuring achievement in a high school course in physics devoted to electricity than for appraising the knowledge of men in this trade. There is no emphasis placed on knowledge of how to handle the practical problems which the electrician encounters and there is little on the use and care of tools. Since the title of the test specifies only that it is to be given to electricians, and not what it is supposed to measure, no criticism can be made concerning misrepresentation. On the other hand, the Purdue Test for Machinists and Machine Operators is much more directly related to the job than is the previous test.

Check Lists and Ratings As Measures of Skill in Trades

Although substitutes for performance tests such as oral trade questions are designed to save time, labor, and the cost of large-scale facilities, it must be said that even these simple substitutes often present too many difficulties in their preparation and administration and even simpler assessment devices must often be used. In the employment agency, graduation from a given school and a transcript of grades is often accepted as evidence of skill. To this may be added some kind of check list on which the individual may indicate the extent to which he has had experience with the various aspects of the skill. If he has had experience with the more difficult aspects of the skill, it is assumed that he has greater proficiency than one who has had experience with only the simpler aspects. The validity of instruments of this kind depends upon the honesty of the individuals who fill them out, the degree to which the examinees interpret the directions in the way they are supposed to be interpreted, and the adequacy of the check list in covering the various aspects of the skill. Figure 7.3 illustrates a check list of this kind.

ARMY TRADE SCREENING TESTS
MACHINIST EXPERIENCE CHECK LIST
TC-17ar

NAME_____ ORGANIZATION_____
　　　(Last)　　　　(First)　　　　(Initial)

ARMY SERIAL NUMBER_____GRADE_____DATE_____

A. Below are lists of some of the operations which can be performed with various
tools and machines in the machine shop. If you have done the work with the
particular machine, and can still do it "on your own," make a check (✓) at
the left of the item. Leave blank those items with which you have had very
little or no experience.

1. OPERATIONS PERFORMED WITH A LATHE

( ) facing
( ) drilling
( ) undercutting
( ) counter boring
( ) spot facing
( ) straight facing
( ) taper boring
( ) tapping

( ) reaming of tapers
( ) external threading
( ) internal threading
( ) internal grinding (straight)
( ) external grinding (straight)
( ) internal taper grinding
( ) external taper grinding
( ) taper turning

( ) radius cutting
( ) relieving
( ) counter-sinking
( ) center drilling
( ) cutter grinding
( ) slotting
( ) line boring
( ) spring winding

DO NOT WRITE IN THIS SECTION

Name					
Army score on the Machinist Test ____					
Amount of previous experience as indicated by the check list (Check appropriate item below.)					
Extensive, covering the entire field ( )	More extensive than that of average man working as a MACHINIST ( )	About equal to that of average man working as a MACHINIST ( )	More limited than that of average man working as a MACHINIST ( )	Experience limited to few items ( )	
Soldier's preference	Interviewer's recommendation	Check if fully qualified	Major field of experience as a MACHINIST.........................( )	Check if fully qualified ....( )	
1....................	1....................	( )			
2....................	2....................	( )	Deficiencies in experience as a MACHINIST.............		
3....................	3....................	( )			
Interviewer's remarks....................			....		
Recommendations from Machinist Section					
....					
Final disposition					

FIGURE 7.3

Check list used for recording previous experience as a machinist. Reproduced
by permission of the Department of the Army from an official publication (1).

As a general rule, individuals filling out check lists are much more
honest than perhaps one might expect them to be, though the degree
of honesty will depend on the extent to which there are incentives to
falsify the record. Some years ago the writer had contact with a study
of the validity of check lists for differentiating between skilled and
unskilled men in particular trades. It was found that measures of

proficiency derived from check lists compared favorably in usefulness for this purpose with scores derived from paper-and-pencil tests of the work skills.

Rating Scales for Recording Student Progress in the Industrial Arts

The instructor in the industrial arts will often have to resort to the use of rating scales for recording student progress. It should be noted that the rating scale is not an appraisal instrument in itself but merely a device for recording appraisals that have already been made or for summarizing evidence that has already been collected. The rating scale shown in Figure 7.4 illustrates one such device for summarizing the observations of an instructor in a course in practical work. The sources of error in the use of such instruments are likely to be large because they inadequately summarize inadequate evidence. For a discussion of the difficulties in the preparation and use of rating scales of this kind, the reader is referred to Chapter 9.

FIGURE 7.4

Day-to-day System of Appraisal Developed for the Army Air Forces Technical Schools during the Second World War

Scale Value	Interpretation
5	Completed the job quickly and efficiently. Learned what to do, why to do it, and the relationship of this job to others being studied in the unit.
4	Completed the required job with little hesitancy. Understood what to do and understood generally the underlying principles.
3	Had a general idea of what was to be done. Finished the job with minor errors. Made false starts, changes and repetitions. Was not sure of himself or his product.
2	Was able with difficulty to complete parts of the job himself. Had an idea of what to do but lacked sufficient information or dexterity to complete all parts of the job.
1	Could not complete the job even with major assistance from the instructor. Did not know the parts of his job either by definition or by use. Had no understanding of why the job was to be done.

Although scales such as that illustrated in Figure 7.4 have uses, they also have serious limitations. It may be noted that the meaning of the scale values involves a number of quite distinct variables. This means that a man may show some of the qualifications for obtaining a given rating, but that some of his actions qualify him for one or more of the other categories. The fact that a man had no understanding of why a job was to be done would, by itself, give the man a rating of 1, but this same individual may have been able to complete the job with difficulty, a fact which would qualify him for a rating of 2. In which category should he be placed? Strictly speaking, he does not belong in any one category; consequently, those who use the rating scale must be instructed to place him in the category which, in general, most nearly describes him.

An alternative plan is to develop a series of rating scales in this area with each scale covering a specific aspect of the over-all characteristic to be rated. If this were done, there would be scales for rating the degree to which the individual sees the purpose of the job to be done, the degree to which he needs help in finishing the job, the degree to which he is able to carry through the job without fumbling or unnecessary activity, and so on. After the ratings are made on the separate scales, some formula is adopted for combining the ratings into a single over-all rating. This involves the assignment of weights to each of the elements.

The main argument against the use of a series of separate rating scales in place of the attempted over-all rating is the work and labor involved. In addition, there is serious question whether it is possible for an instructor to discriminate between the various aspects of proficiency. May there not be a tendency for instructors to make over-all evaluations in any case and then to justify these judgments by the specific ratings which they subsequently make? There is at least some evidence to show that this is a common pattern of behavior among raters. Further discussion of this problem may be found in Chapter 9.

Special Problems of Validating Work-Skill Tests

There are certain special problems connected with the validation of skill tests which need to be considered. If the test of skill includes all the elements which represent the full development of the skill, then the instrument is, by definition, valid. Under such circumstances there is no point in attempting validation studies and no method by which a validation study can be undertaken. On the other hand, if the performance test calls for only a few of the elements included in the fully developed skill, steps must be taken to demonstrate that proficiency in the skills measured is a satisfactory indication of all of the skills which should have been represented in the test. There is only one thoroughly satisfactory way in which this can be done and that is to validate scores on the performance test against scores on a test which includes all the problem situations that the person has been trained to handle. Except in relatively few situations this cannot be done, and indirect evidence of validity must be collected. Examples of such indirect evidence are those derived from a comparison of trained and untrained men, or a comparison of scores of those who are classified as skilled, semiskilled, and unskilled.

Figure 7.5 illustrates validation data of this kind gathered in an Army test for machinists (1). This test was strictly of the verbal type and included no illustrations.

It may be noted from this figure that some of the untrained men had considerable knowledge of this field although it is probable that few of these men would have had any proficiency as machinists. Also, it may be that some of the trained men obtained relatively low scores in relation to the trained group. Undoubtedly many of these men had more knowledge than is indicated by their scores, which may have been depressed by reading difficulties. This test might be used *in conjunction with other information* for the purpose of selection and placement, but it should not be used as the sole basis for selection or placement except when it is the only information available.

Research has established the value of oral and of paper-and-pencil devices for the measurement of work skills. In spite of all the limitations of these instruments, they have been demonstrated to have surprisingly good validity for predicting job proficiency, particularly in those occupations which require substantial knowledge and prolonged training. For this reason, a printed objective test of proficiency as a machinist is more likely to predict job proficiency than would such a test for a janitor, whose proficiency is probably determined much more by conscientiousness than by rigorous training.

The plan of validating tests against a measure of actual performance does present certain problems which are not evident on the surface. One of these is the weight to be assigned to each aspect of proficiency in the performance of the job. Not all aspects of pro-

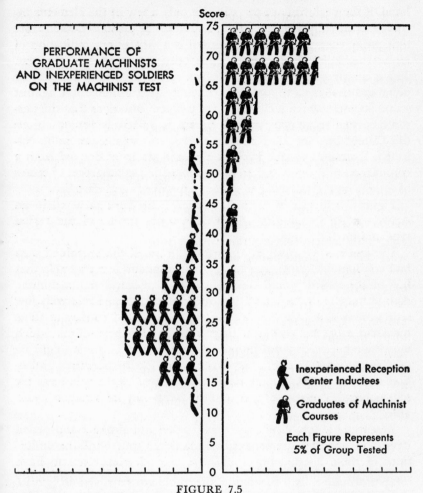

FIGURE 7.5

Distribution of scores of trained and untrained men on a machinist test.

ficiency are equally important. In the case of an auto mechanic, proficiency in the inflation of tires is probably much less important than the proficiency in adjusting the carburetor of the engine. Scores on different parts of any measure of performance need to be assigned different weights in proportion to the relative importance of the various aspects of the job. Difficulty arises in establishing an acceptable system for determining the weights to be assigned. In the final analysis, this is a matter of judgment, but whose judgment is to be accepted as final? The usual practice is to ask experts in the area to indicate by some numerical system the relative importance of each job aspect, and the numerical values assigned by the various experts are then averaged.

The Teacher's Program for Evaluating Work Skills

It has been pointed out that published tests of work skills are few. For this reason it is necessary for the teacher to develop his own program for measuring pupil progress and, although written tests without illustrations may be easily mimeographed and may measure the extent to which certain outcomes are achieved, it will still be desirable to implement this program with performance tests of the actual work skills in which training has been given. Since performance tests of work skills are developed on exactly the same basis as performance tests of other skills acquired in general education, the discussion here will be devoted to the general problem of developing performance measures. For this reason, the principles discussed will be applicable to the measurement of outcomes such as the ability to carry out a scientific experiment, the ability to conduct a meeting according to parliamentary procedure, and other skills in which individuals or materials must be manipulated.

The central difficulty in the development of performance tests of skills is the development of a scoring system which provides reliable scores from which valid inferences can be made concerning the ability of the pupil to undertake certain types of task. For this reason, it is desirable to begin the consideration of the development of tests of performance by considering the problems involved in scoring them.

There are three general methods of appraising an individual's performance in some practical task. These consist of (a) appraising the product, (b) appraising the procedure adopted to develop the product, and (c) measuring the time taken by the subject. From most standpoints it is the product that presents the most clear-cut evidence of what a person can do, and hence it is the appraisal of the product that should in most cases form the basis of the scoring procedure in the assessment of performance, but in the scoring of the product the following practices should be adopted as far it is possible:

1. Avoid over-all judgments of the product. If the task is to cut and finish a piece of wood to a certain specified size, do not rate the product in terms of the extent to which it generally meets the requirements set. The product should be appraised on as many specific characteristics as are relevant to its quality.

2. List aspects of the product that are to be evaluated. If the product is a typed letter, decide just what aspects of this finished product are to be scored. Are erasures to be scored if they are well done? Are spelling errors to be scored? Is the letter to be scored for layout and appearance, and should the student be penalized for failure to center the letter on the page, for failure to allow a sufficient margin, and for other mechanical features? If the task is that of cutting a piece of metal to size, the examiner must determine what dimensions of the product are to be scored and what departures from required dimensions are to be scored against the pupil.

3. While it is desirable to score the product in as many ways as are relevant in order to make the measures derived as reliable as possible, reliability should not be achieved by measuring aspects which have little significance. It is probably wise to avoid building performance tests around tasks which do not permit the scoring of various aspects of the product. The writer can recall the case of a radio repairman performance test which required the individual to diagnose the reason for failure of a piece of equipment and then to replace the part that had failed. Such a test classifies individuals into those that succeed and those that fail. It groups together in the same category those who succeed as a result of a systematic study of the equipment and those who succeed as a result of luck. It gives no credit to those who fail to repair the equipment although they check many aspects of it correctly. In summary, it is not suited as a task for use as a performance test from which a product score is to be derived.

4. Rules for scoring the product should be specified with the greatest precision possible. In some cases, only limited precision is possible; for example, when a product is rated for general appearance. Tasks for use as performance tests should be, as far as it is feasible, ones which result in a product that can be scored by precisely stated rules which do not require the scorer to use his own judgment.

Cases will arise in which agreement cannot be reached concerning which aspect of a product are the most important. In the case of handwriting, there are some who would feel that only legibility is important and that the assessment of all other characteristics is irrelevant. However, there are those who would feel that not only legibility but general elegance or evenness might be important enough to merit consideration. Judgment is involved in the selection of items for a check list for product evaluation, and the opinion of one person is usually insufficient for determining the selection. Groups of experts form a much safer basis.

5. Sometimes it is not possible to use a specific check list for recording the worth of a product. This is particularly true when the number of factors affecting a product are large and numerous minor details affect the quality. Such a condition exists in the evaluation of a welded joint or in the evaluation of handwriting. In such cases it is common practice to prepare a scale of work samples. In the case under discussion, a series of welds, graded in quality, might be prepared to form a scale. Samples to be graded would be matched with the weld in the series which it most resembled. This kind of a scale has been used extensively in the assessment of handwriting.

The second possible scoring procedure, which involves appraising the procedure for developing the product, has only limited applicability. It usually involves the observation of the examinee while he is taking the test, but in some cases, such as typing, the product shows unmistakable traces of every error made. If the examinee has to be observed during testing in order to score him for errors, it may require more time than the teacher can spare from other activities. Sometimes errors in executing a task can be checked at certain critical points when the student is stopped and his work checked before he goes on to the next steps. This procedure may make it possible for a teacher to administer a performance test to several students at one time and still score each step in the procedure for correctness. If this is done, the following points should be noted:

1. Each step which the pupil should take must be listed in a check list which also indicates what is to be considered a correct or an incorrect response. Illustrative items from various sources are, "Was the stock centered in the lathe chuck with the help of chalk?" "Was the microscope adjusted to the vertical position before using?" and

"Did the student inspect the radio receiver for loose or broken wires before testing it systematically?"

2. Only procedures that are strictly necessary for accomplishing the task should be scored. A procedure should not be included in a check list merely because it is *customary* to follow one particular procedure. It must be a *necessary* procedure in order to justify inclusion for scoring purposes.

3. Care should be taken in preparing a check list of procedures to avoid giving major emphasis to minor details. The items should represent a summary of the procedures essential for preparing the final product.

Finally, the problem of whether to score the individual for the amount of time which he takes on a particular task must be considered. As a general rule it may be said that the pupil should be penalized for using excessive time on a task only when speed is an important aspect of proficiency. Of course, the fact is that in most work areas, the acquisition of speed is considered extremely important. A typist must achieve a minimum speed to be employable. A machinist must be able to produce at a certain rate in order to retain his job, and, if in making a particular piece he takes six cuts where two would do, he is likely to be unemployable however excellent may be his final product. In such cases, the time taken by the pupil to complete a task should be one factor which enters into his score for the adequacy of his performance.

Turning from the scoring of performance tests, let us consider the selection of problems for performance tests. The chief difficulty encountered in the selection stems from the fact that only a few problems can be presented in any reasonable time in a performance situation. In contrast, in a multiple-choice paper-and-pencil test numerous problems can be presented which cover a great diversity of aspects of the subject matter. This fact must be kept in mind at all times in the construction of performance tests. The selection of problem situations must also involve the following considerations:

1. The problem situations chosen for inclusion in a performance test should represent problems of central importance in the field in which training has been given. They should not be problems of only fringe importance or represent situations which pupils are unlikely to encounter. Testing time is both brief and valuable and has to be

devoted to measurement of the achievement of the most important objectives.

2. If a problem requires the student to show only a very limited aspect of his knowledge or skill, it should not occupy a major part of the time to be devoted to testing.

3. The problems should not be trick problems which require the student to show a single flash of insight in order to obtain a solution. Such problems usually bear little relationship to the objectives in teaching and do not represent the kind of situation which the student has been trained to handle.

4. The problems insofar as possible should be realistic facsimiles of the problems to which the individual has been trained to respond. A performance test should be a reproduction of the life situation which is presented to the student under standardized and controlled conditions. If the student has been trained in the repair of ignition systems, it is inadequate to tests his skill by asking him to name the parts. If the student has taken a course in which he has attempted to learn effective speaking, it is not enough to examine him on his ability to criticize the speech of another. He should be tested on his own ability to speak effectively.

5. The way in which the problem is to be presented to the student must be carefully specified. If the task is to start a certain type of engine, then the type of engine must be specified and the exact condition in which it is to be presented to the examinee must also be specified. If he is to find it at operating temperature rather than at room temperature, then this must be specified in the directions for administering the test. All the adjustments of the engine that can be varied must be specified.

6. If any tools are required by the examinee during a performance test, then these must be specified, together with the way in which they are to be presented to the examinee. The usual practice is to lay out the tools on the bare surface of a table, but the arrangement should be identical for all examinees.

7. The instructions to be given to the examinee must be written out, and it must be indicated whether they are to be read to him or whether he is to read them. The instructions must tell the examinee exactly what he is to do. Sometimes it is necessary to indicate to the examinee the time he will be allowed for the test, and sometimes he

is allowed to work at his own speed. The way in which any questions asked by the examinee are to be answered must also be specified.

Summary

1. The development of work skills constitutes a central objective of major phases of education and it is most important that attempts be made to determine the effectiveness of vocational curricula in achieving their goals.

2. The armed services have been the most active agencies concerned with the development of methods of appraising proficiency in work skills, and, although the tests they have developed in this area would not be appropriate for use in schools, the experience gained in the development of these instruments is valuable to the teacher of vocational subjects.

3. Performance tests should be used as far it is feasible for measuring proficiency in work skills. Great care must be taken in the development of such tests to ensure that they sample the more important aspects of the skill. It is also necessary to develop a scoring system which involves precisely defined standards rather than judgments. Performance tests may be scored by appraising the product or by appraising the procedures which the examinee uses in the development of the product. It seems clear that product scoring is more feasible than procedure scoring for most performance tests developed by teachers of vocational courses. The procedures discussed for developing performance tests should be carefully studied by any teacher who intends to build a performance test.

4. The only major area of training in work skills for which performance tests can be purchased is the area of commercial education. Tests have been developed for typing, shorthand, and bookkeeping which meet adequate professional standards. However, the student should be cautioned that some tests of shorthand require the performance of activities which are remote from those that are performed in actual jobs.

5. Oral and printed tests which can be administered without cumbersome equipment have been developed as convenient substitutes for performance tests. Such devices have been successful in

predicting proficiency in those work skills which have some complexity. In the simpler work skills, written and oral tests are much less useful than performance tests. Another kind of device for assessing proficiency is a check list of the various operations which a person may have to perform on a particular job.

References

1. *Army Trade Screening Tests,* War Department Pamphlet No. 12–13. Washington, D. C., United States War Department, July, 1945, pp. 11.

2. Buros, Oscar K. (Editor), *Third Mental Measurement Yearbook,* New Brunswick, New Jersey, Rutgers University Press, 1949, pp. 1047 + XIV.

3. *C. C. P. Trade Tests.* Committee on Classification of Personnel in the Army, Trade Test Division, 1917–18.

4. Chapman, J. Crosby, *Trade Tests,* New York, Henry Holt and Company, 1921, pp. 435 + IX.

5. Division of Occupational Analysis, Washington, D. C. *Oral Trade Question,* U. S. Government Printing Office, 1945.

6. *Examination in Bookkeeping and Accounting,* Two Levels, First Year Secondary School, 1945; Second Year Secondary School, 1945; United States Armed Forces Institute. Published by American Council on Education. Distributed by Educational Testing Service, Princeton, New Jersey.

7. *Heitt Stenography Test,* Emporia, Kansas, Bureau of Educational Measurement, Kansas State Teachers College, 1938–39.

8. *Purdue Test for Electricians,* Chicago, Illinois, Science Research Associates, 1942.

9. *Purdue Tests for Machinists and Machine Operators,* Chicago, Illinois Science Research Associates, 1942.

10. *Seashore-Bennett Stenographic Proficiency Test:* A Standard Recorded Stenographic Work Sample. New York, The Psychological Corporation, 1946.

CHAPTER 8

The Construction of Paper-and-Pencil Tests and the Assignment of Grades

61
174
149
55
27
52

THE CONSTRUCTION OF CLASSROOM TESTS

Introduction

It was emphasized in Chapter 2 that the degree to which the objectives of most educational programs are achieved should be assessed in terms of the extent to which the individual manifests the appropriate responses to life situations which the program is designed to develop. However, many of these responses cannot be observed until after the individual leaves school, and thus direct evidence of the value of the school program becomes extremely difficult to obtain. In other words, the ultimate criterion of the effectiveness of teaching often cannot be used and it is necessary to appraise it in terms of proximate and more accessible criteria. The performance of the pupil on classroom tests represents the commonest proximate criterion used for this purpose.

Although the teacher may be able to purchase many useful tests of thinking skills, study skills, and work skills, classroom tests of knowledge and understanding of school subjects must be developed mainly by the teacher. For this reason, proficiency in the construction of tests is essential for all teachers.

The Selection of the Type of Test to be Used

The great variety of objectives which the teacher may attempt to achieve makes it difficult to provide generalizations concerning types of instruments that should be used for assessing pupil achievement. Before discussing measurement techniques in detail it may be well to state the few generalizations that the teacher can use in judging the merit of the various methods.

1. *The Form of the Test Problem*. The problems provided by the teacher's test should be within the general domain in which learning is believed to have occurred. This does not mean that the test problems should be precisely those which the pupil has learned to solve, for the teacher may have attempted to achieve transfer of training as part of the learning process, and the test problem may be a device to measure the extent to which transfer has occurred.

2. *The Context of the Test Problem*. By the context of the test problem is meant the general nature of all conditions which affect the pupil in solving the problem. It is essential that these conditions be as far as possible identical with those which prevail in the situation with which the pupil has been trained to cope. Differences in these conditions may invalidate the data obtained from the test. A test problem which has to be solved in a very limited amount of time may not provide useful information of how that person will perform when there is no time limit. A student may state in a test that he would handle a certain social problem in a specified way which the teacher may approve, but the pressures exerted by the teacher in the classroom situation may be an aspect of the context of the test problem which destroys its validity for predicting how the pupil would behave in other situations.

3. *The Form of the Response*. The student's response to the test problem has to be such that it provides evidence of the extent to which an objective has been achieved. This means that judgment must not play a major part in the interpretation of the results of the test problem. The usual method of eliminating as far as possible the process of judgment is to set up rigid rules for the interpretation of the response, so that there is no disagreement in assigning numbers to indicate the degree to which the response is desirable, or true, or adequate. The scoring system may vary in the degree to which it involves judgment, but as far as possible the scoring system should be objective; that is, the rules should be so well defined that persons capable of understanding them should be able to apply them and arrive at identical scores.

Objectivity of scoring, however, is not the only goal to be achieved.

Sometimes it may be necessary to sacrifice some objectivity of scoring in order to achieve validity. For example, at the college level it is common practice at the end of a course in freshman English to require students to write a composition in order to measure their ability to organize ideas, to express ideas, and to use written speech effectively. If these compositions are scored for spelling and punctuation, the scoring system will be completely objective, but objectivity will have been achieved at the expense of validity. In order to score these compositions for the characteristics concerning which evidence is sought, it is necessary to abandon rigid rules and to rate them for

TABLE 8.1

Appropriateness of Essay and Objective Tests for Appraising Various Outcomes *

Category of Outcomes	Free-Response Test and Essay Test	Objective Test
Knowledge or information	Does not usually permit extensive coverage of course content.	Well suited for extensive sampling of course content.

Written expression	Necessarily the most valid test for appraising writing abilities as such:
	    Organizing material
	    Writing correctly and effectively
	    Treating a topic logically and adequately
	    Style
	    Aesthetic expression; creativity
	Useful in advanced courses for evaluating ability to assimilate, organize, and evaluate critically a comprehensive array of ideas.
		Not appropriate for appraising writing abilities.
		Useful device for measuring mechanics of expression:
		    Grammatical usage
		    Punctuation, capitalization, spelling.

Reading abilities and skills	Can be used, but is usually not the most economical method.	Well suited for measuring reading comprehension, evaluation of what is read, appreciation of literature.

* From: Furst, Edward J., "Objectives Which Can Be Appraised by the Essay Examination" (unpublished).

TABLE 8.1 (*cont.*)

**Appropriateness of Essay and Objective Tests for Appraising
Various Outcomes**

Category of Outcomes	Free-Response Test and Essay Test	Objective Test

Other thinking skills and abilities; "higher mental processes"	Can furnish valuable evidence on the following:
	    Inductive thinking; making original interpretations of data
	    Deductive thinking; applying generalizations to new situations
	    Logical thinking; analyzing arguments, etc.
	Advantage lies in the emphasis upon originality rather than upon discrimination among already furnished statements or data. The student's "frame of reference" can often be inferred from his writing.
		Well-constructed exercises can furnish evidence of: discriminative thinking;
		    inductive thinking; interpreting data;
		    deductive thinking; applying generalizations to new situations;
		    logical thinking; analyzing arguments, etc.
		Main limitation is that student deals with data and products of thought already furnished. Main advantages lie in extensiveness of sampling and in the structuration of the test situation.

Mathematical skills and abilities	Chief value here again lies in emphasis upon methods of solution followed voluntarily. Can give valuable clues as to errors in thinking, etc.	Objective exercises can appraise computational skills and problem-solving abilities efficiently. Chief value lies in the extensiveness with which field can be sampled.

qualities which can be defined only in general terms. Such ratings can be undertaken only by experts, who may agree in general terms concerning the rules to be applied in scoring, but who would be hard put to it to write down these rules in such clear and simple words that they could be applied by the intelligent layman.

It is evident that the form of test item selected by the teacher will depend on the function to be served. In order to help the teacher in this task, Table 8.1 is presented, which summarizes the main uses of the objective and essay or free-response type of examination. However, for most purposes, at the elementary or high school level, the objective test is likely to be a more useful form for test questions than the essay question. Thus more extensive consideration will be given to the former type of test question than the latter.

A careful study of Table 8.1 will indicate that the free-answer and essay tests should not be used interchangeably. Each has its special uses and limitations. The selection of one or the other as a technique of measurement should depend on a consideration of which is most appropriate.

OBJECTIVE-TYPE TEST QUESTIONS ✓

The writer has summarized in another volume (1) the methods of construction of most of the commonly used types of objective test questions.* However, the merits of the multiple-choice (best-answer) type of test question are so great and the range of uses so extensive in comparison with other types of items that it will be the only type considered here. Mastery of the writing of multiple-choice types of questions alone would provide the teacher with a powerful and flexible technique for the assessment of many important outcomes of education.

The essential structure of a multiple-choice test question consists of a problem and a number of suggested solutions, of which one is usually correct. The first part—that is, the problem—is sometimes called the *lead,* or *stem.* The suggested solutions are sometimes called the *alternatives,* and the incorrect alternatives are sometimes called the *decoys,* or *distracters.* The test question as a whole is referred to as an *item.* Table 8.2 summarizes these terms for two items which measure a relatively simple and a relatively complex process.

The items in Table 8.2 also illustrate another point, namely, that the skill measured by an item may vary from one group to another. If children have been taught specifically that there is an increase in

* The author gratefully acknowledges permission given by The Odyssey Press to summarize these materials.

the sale of bread during depressions, then the test item will measure not reasoning but memory for information. The item on the left side of the table is likely to measure knowledge of vocabulary, but a person who does not know the meaning of the word *parturition* may reason that in derivation it is more closely associated with the word *birth* than with any of the other words. Thus a vocabulary-test question may at times function as a reasoning-test item. The fact is that it is never possible to be certain that a test question will measure what it is designed to measure unless the educational background of the pupils responding to the item is known.

TABLE 8.2

Names of the Parts of a Multiple-Choice Test Question

	Item for Measuring Vocabulary Knowledge	Item for Measuring Reasoning Skill in Social Studies
Stem or Lead	What is the meaning of the word *parturition*?	Which of the following products might be expected to be sold in greater volume in times of depression?
Correct Alternative	1. Birth	1. Bread
Incorrect Alternatives, Decoys, or Distracters	2. Cell division 3. Nutrition 4. Fertilization 5. Development	2. Cheap automobiles 3. Clothing 4. Shoes 5. Newspapers

It may also be noted that the difficulty of a multiple-choice test item may be varied in two ways. It may be varied by making the problem in the lead more or less difficult to solve. It may also be varied by adjusting the alternatives in such a way as to make it easier or harder for the pupil to discriminate among them. It is considered preferable for the difficulty of an item to depend more on the nature of the problem stated in the lead than on the choice of alternatives.

SUGGESTIONS FOR CONSTRUCTING
MULTIPLE-CHOICE ITEMS *

The present writer has already outlined in a previously published book procedures that are commonly suggested for developing objective classroom examinations, and the reader is referred to that volume for a fuller and more extensively illustrated treatment of the topic. The limited discussion which follows summarizes the major points that the classroom teacher should consider in the development of objective examinations.

General Rules

1. *The item as a whole should present a problem related to an identifiable objective of teaching.* When a teacher has finished constructing a classroom examination, it should be possible for him to make a tally of the number of test items which correspond to each objective. It is particularly desirable to do this, for it will enable him to determine which outcomes are being measured and which are not being measured by the test. Since a test appraises only a limited sample of the possible outcomes of teaching, it is desirable in the writing of tests to concentrate on the more important aspects of these outcomes.

2. *The item as a whole should be presented in a form which makes it easy for the pupil to understand the nature of the problem to be solved.* It is not uncommon to find test problems presented in language which is difficult in structure or vocabulary or which is inappropriate to the subject-matter field. Shop-work problems should be stated in the language of the shop and not in highly academic language. Another related error is that of presenting in verbal form problems which should be presented in pictorial form. Consider the following question: "What is usually found between the cylinder head and the block of a gasoline engine?" This question requires the pupil to visualize the relative locations of the cylinder block and the cylinder head before he can solve the problem. Some pupils may find it difficult to visualize objects, and hence it may be more desirable to

---

* The section on rules for constructing multiple-choice items is based on Travers (1). The author is greatly indebted to the Odyssey Press for permission to use this text as a source of basic ideas on test construction.

present a diagram which shows the cylinder head and the cylinder block and to ask the pupil to name the part which lies between them. The problem presented in this form may be solved by the pupil without performing complicated mental antics.

3. *One item in a test should not provide information needed in solving another item in the test.* It is not always easy to identify such overlapping items, and an independent reviewer is often required to read through a test in order to identify cues of this kind.

Rules for Stating a Problem

1. *The lead of the item must present a single central problem.* A good plan in building classroom examinations is to start by writing problems in the form of questions. These questions should be based on the objectives of teaching. Vague general questions should be omitted, since such questions are not likely to be clearly related to any set of well-defined objectives. Avoid writing leads to items such as "People are . . ." or "When Columbus landed . . ." and similar incomplete statements, for leads such as these do not permit control of what is being measured.

It is also important to avoid stating double problems such as "How does the presence of large masses of water and the absence of mountains affect the climate of the state of Michigan?" Such a question includes two problems, one related to the effect of large masses of water and the other to the effect of the absence of mountains on climate. The reliability of the test is likely to be improved by restating this question as two separate questions.

Not until the problems have been stated should consideration be given to the writing of correct answers and distractors.

2. *The problem stated in the lead must have a definite answer.* Many problems stated in the leads of poorly constructed multiple-choice items do not have a definite answer. Do not write problems such as "What was the cause of World War II?" A problem of this kind does not have a clear-cut answer, partly, at least, because of the complexity of the problems presented. Problems which are less comprehensive in scope, such as the following, provide better means of appraising the student's achievement:

What excuse did Hitler offer for the invasion of Czechoslovakia?
What was Hitler's main purpose in making a pact with Russia?

3. *The problem must be accurately stated and generally should not include irrelevant material.* Problems should be stated with precision, and all the material in the statement of the problem should be to the point. Do not expect the pupils to guess what you have in mind, and do not assume that the pupils will know what you are talking about because they have worked with you. Remember that even the best examinations are likely to include some ambiguous items, so eliminate as many of them as possible.

Teachers commonly dress up test problems in an attempt to make them more interesting to the pupils or to make them appear more closely related to daily life. Window dressing of this type is not usually appreciated by pupils. It adds to the amount of reading called for by the test and, unless reading ability is being measured, an irrelevant variable is introduced. In the following alternative statements of the same problem, the form of the second statement is preferable to the first:

> Johnny goes to the store to buy some potatoes. If the price of potatoes is 6¢ a pound, what does he pay for 12 pounds?
>
> What is the price of 12 pounds of potatoes at 6¢ a pound?

4. *The problem should be stated in a positive form.* It is desirable to avoid negative terms in the statement of problems. Do not ask questions such as

> Which one of the following economic factors does *not* contribute to inflation?
>
> Which one of the following foods includes the *least* amount of protein per gram?
>
> Which one of the following ways of organizing one's studies is most *un*desirable?

In reading problems such as these it is common for the reader to fail to notice the word or syllable that has been capitalized or italicized. For this reason, it is best to avoid the use of such words as *not, never, least,* and words which have prefixes such as *un*. Occasionally items may include such elements, but they must be either capitalized or italicized, as they are in the above example. It should be noted that pupils taking tests usually have a mental set toward finding positive solutions to positive problems. The use of a negative statement in the lead of an item produces a situation in conflict with this set.

Rules for Developing Suggested Answers

1. *The number of suggested answers for a problem will depend both on the nature of the problem and the level of development of the pupil.* Young pupils can handle fewer alternatives than older pupils because of limitations of their span of comprehension. For this reason, multiple-choice items included in work books for the second grade usually have only two alternatives, one of which is correct. In contrast, standardized tests given at the junior high school level usually consist of items containing four or five suggested answers. It is usually not profitable to attempt to develop items with more than five alternatives, since these additional alternatives are unlikely to function; that is, they will remain either unselected by pupils or selected only by those who are guessing blindly. Only those alternatives that serve some useful purpose should be included in the test. If the test is to have maximum reliability, it is important that each decoy be considered as an adequate solution to the problem by some members of the group to be tested. It is also important that those who choose the decoys should represent a lower level of the achievement to be measured than those who choose the correct answer.

2. *The suggested solutions should require the pupil to make discriminations of the kind which he has been trained to make.* Test items may be at fault in presenting the pupil with discriminations which are simpler or harder than those he is expected to be able to make. Usually the error is in making classroom tests which call for discriminations which are too difficult and go beyond the program of training.

3. *One answer should be beyond any question a correct answer to the problem. The incorrect alternatives should be incorrect answers to the problem.* It is always revealing to ask other teachers to take the tests made for one's own class. The result is usually that they fail to endorse some of the supposedly correct answers as correct and some of the decoys are strongly defended as representing correct answers. Such differences cannot be settled by dispute but by discarding the test item and building another about which there is no controversy. Unfortunately, many test writers feel bound to defend

their test items against all attacks. Such test writers are unlikely to produce satisfactory results.

4. *The distracters should distract.* There should be a rationale behind every incorrect alternative offered. The common practice of first writing a problem, then a correct answer, and then filling in the incorrect alternatives with whatever comes to mind is a practice which does not result in the development of good test items. Each wrong alternative should be the kind of solution which a student might arrive at on the basis of faulty reasoning or incorrect information. For example, in finding incorrect alternatives to the problem $\frac{1}{2} + \frac{3}{4} = \quad$, it might be reasonable to argue that some pupils would add the numerators and add the denominators and hence arrive at $\frac{4}{6}$ or $\frac{2}{3}$ as an answer. This reasoning process would provide one of the incorrect answers. If students of education at the end of their first course in educational psychology were asked why instruction in reading is commonly postponed until the second grade, a suitable distracter might be, "The curriculum of the first grade is too crowded with other matters." Those who did not understand the concept of maturation and its application in the postponement of reading until the second grade might find this distracter extremely attractive as a solution to the problem. In this case, the less the person knows, the more acceptable the distracter becomes as a solution to the problem.

5. *The suggested answers should be as brief as possible.* Long answers are cumbersome to read and difficult to compare one with another. All too often the suggested answers for items are unnecessarily long because material included in them should have been included in the lead of the item. The following item written in two versions illustrates unnecessary verbiage in the alternatives:

Poor Version with Long and Cumbersome Alternatives	*Improved Version with Shortened Alternatives*
The balance wheel of a watch is built to compensate for	The balance wheel of a watch is built to compensate for
1. day-to-day and momentary changes in temperature.	1. changes in temperature.
2. sudden movements as when a wrist-watch wearer swings his arm.	2. sudden movements.
3. shocks which occur if the watch is dropped.	3. shocks.
4. variations in barometric pressure as when the weather changes.	4. variations in barometric pressure.

It should be noted that nothing is lost by reducing the alternatives in length. In the writing of tests, as in any other form of writing, much is to be gained by the elimination of unnecessary words.

6. *Irrelevant cues should never help those who cannot solve the problem, though they may be used to mislead them.* There are certain common cues that teachers are likely to provide in their tests which enable the alert pupil to identify the correct answers to problems he would otherwise be unable to solve. The following rules will help to eliminate such cues:

(a) Avoid making the correct answer longer than the others, because the pupil who cannot solves the problem is likely to be attracted to the longest and most complete answer offered. A good plan is to make all answers approximately the same in length.

(b) Avoid including in the correct alternative a word which is a key word in the lead. It will make this alternative attractive to those who cannot solve the problem. The following item illustrates this point:

The basic unlearned element in the development of a conditioned *reflex* is a

1. reflex
2. learned method of response
3. glandular response
4. memory trace

(c) Avoid the use of absolute terms such as *never, always, all,* and so forth, in the incorrect answer. Pupils may know that such alternatives are likely to be wrong, while carefully worded alternatives which use guarded terms such as *sometimes* and *generally* are likely to be correct.

(d) Make sure that, when the lead of the item is an incorrect statement, all of the alternatives complete the statement in a grammatically correct manner. What often happens in the writing of multiple-choice items is that the lead and a correct answer are written first. Then the distracters are written, but by this time the test writer has forgotten the exact wording of the lead for which the alternatives provide endings. It is fairly obvious to the pupil that the alternative that does not fit grammatically is incorrect.

(e) Select alternatives that come from a closely related content area. An alternative which is out of line with the other alternatives in this respect is likely to be judged immediately by the pupil as being incorrect. The two items which follow illustrate this type of irrelevant cue:

What is the purpose of pasteurization of milk?	Which American scientist was mainly responsible for isolating heavy hydrogen?
1. To render bacteria harmless	1. Urey
2. To kill bacteria	2. Millikan
3. To destroy toxins produced by bacteria	3. Langmuir
4. To improve the nutritional value	4. Curie

In each of these two items the last alternative comes from a different domain than the others. In the item on the right, it is particularly serious because the problem itself calls for an American scientist but Madame Curie is well known as a Frenchwoman of Polish origin.

The Matching Test Item

The matching type of test item is a widely used variation of the multiple-choice problem, but it is not recommended for use since nearly all matching items can be reduced with resulting efficiency to a series of multiple-choice items. The writer can find no arguments which support the use of matching items.

The Assembly, Reproduction, and Scoring of Objective Tests

The writing of the test items is only one step in the preparation of a test. Once they have been written it is most desirable that they be checked to determine whether they are appropriate for measuring the particular objective which the teacher originally had in mind. They should also be reviewed for accuracy of the correct answer and for difficulty level. It is usually necessary to discard some test items because they are too difficult. The final selection of items should then be arranged in a suitable order, and, while there are many ways of doing this, the method which is most likely to be appropriate on the greatest number of occasions is that of arranging them in order from easy to hard. A more advanced discussion of this problem would present the relative merits of a considerable number of other methods of arranging test items, but these cannot be considered here. A final step in the assembly of items is to check on the position of the correct answer among the other alternatives to insure that it does not too frequently occupy one particular position. Once this has been done, directions for the administration of the test must be prepared. Suggestions for suitable directions can be found on the cover pages of most published tests of achievement. The materials are then ready for reproduction, and a system of scoring may be devised.

Reproduction of Tests. Objective test items should be reproduced in the same general form in which they are reproduced here. This permits the use of a double column of test items on the usual sheet of mimeographed paper. Under no circumstances should the items be read to pupils unless each pupil has before him a written version. The only type of item that can be administered with any success by oral methods is the true-false type of item, which is not recommended for most purposes.

Scoring. Answers should nearly always be marked on a separate answer sheet provided for that purpose, for this permits the use of a stencil key for scoring the test. As mentioned earlier, this scheme is essential for rapid and accurate scoring. In the case of objective test questions, it is recommended, unless there is some very compelling reason to do otherwise, that one point of credit be given for each item correctly answered. Unless the student has been instructed to answer every item, even if he does not know the answer, a fraction of his wrong answers should be subtracted from his score to prevent the student who guesses a great deal from obtaining an unduly high score. The fraction to be used is

$$\frac{1}{\text{no. of alternatives} - 1}$$

Should Test Items Be Given a Trial Run?

Teachers, like many others who administer examinations, are not usually able to give their test items an experimental tryout. Teacher-made tests usually have to be administered shortly after they are made. Consequently, such tests are likely to include some items that are misinterpreted, some that are ambiguous, and even a few that do not have a correct answer among the alternatives. These items reduce the efficiency of the test. They do not necessarily do much harm provided there are enough other items to compensate for the inclusion of some useless materials. A single test score should be based on a substantial number of functioning test items if it is to have reliability. For this reason, it may be necessary to add together the scores from a number of short objective tests in order to obtain a score sufficiently reliable for assigning a grade.

Of course, as the teacher becomes experienced, he will have in his files a growing collection of objective test items. Complaints by students and reviews by his colleagues will undoubtedly help him to eliminate the poorer ones. Then, if he makes an analysis of how many pupils answered each item correctly, he will also be able to eliminate those items that are too easy or too hard.

It may happen that the teacher will have opportunity to participate in a study conducted by the school as a whole or by a group of schools. Under such conditions, it may be possible to try out tests in advance of their use in the study of which they are to be a part. The items which have desirable properties as measuring instruments may then be separated from the others; thus the resulting final forms of the instruments will be more efficient than the trial ones on which they were based. Such refinement takes much time and labor and should not be embarked upon except when it is clearly feasible. When such is the case, the teacher should study a much fuller account of test construction such as that which is found in another book (1) by the present writer.

THE FREE-ANSWER EXAMINATION

Introduction

The essay examination has been for the last 150 years the major device used for the appraisal of achievement. Extensive use of this form of test has resulted in improved understanding of its uses and limitations and in a departure from its classical form which required the student to present a well-organized and readable article on an assigned topic. These changes in the form of the essay examination have resulted in the emergence of a great variety of examination forms which are collectively referred to as free-response types of test items. Most free-answer forms of examination differ from examinations which call for the writing of an essay in that they place con-

siderable restrictions and limitations on the response of the examinees, and sometimes may restrict his response to a single word. The
purpose of these restrictions is commonly to facilitate scoring, but a
more defensible purpose is to limit measurement to certain specified
attributes.

The special values of the free-response type of examination in
contrast to the objective type of question have already been enumerated. It may have been noted that this list of special uses does not
include the claim that free-response tests are superior to objective
tests because they require recall, while the latter are based on a
process of recognition. This is commonly claimed to be the main
advantage of the free-answer type of test, but the advantage is
mainly illusory.

After what has already been said, it hardly seems necessary to
stress the fact that the free-answer type of examination should be
designed to measure well-identified objectives. A basic criticism of
so many essay tests developed by teachers is that they attempt to
measure some vague variable called "general achievement." Such
tests usually attempt to do too much in too short a time. A sample
of the pupil's behavior based on only thirty or sixty minutes of work
can provide only a limited amount of information. Therefore, it is
better to design free-answer tests with a limited number of well-
defined objectives in view.

Restricting the Response

In order to make the responses of those examined measurable
in terms of a series of common dimensions, it is necessary to place
certain restrictions on the response of the examinee. A three-hour
essay examination for prospective teachers which required the candi-
date to "write an essay on theory of learning" restricts the response
only in terms of the general nature of the content to be included and
in terms of the time to be taken in writing the composition. Such
restrictions are insufficient to produce essays which can be scored
in useful ways. In general, it may be said that any examination
which requires the examinee to write an essay on some rather broad
topic is almost certain to prove inadequate as a measuring device.
The nature of the restrictions that can be imposed in order to im-

prove the free-response test as a measuring device will now be discussed.

Restrictions on Length. It has already been pointed out that the examiner should avoid asking the student to write general essays on general topics. Rather should he be asked to perform the more specific tasks of comparing, contrasting, demonstrating, listing events of a given class, and so on. It would be preferable to ask the examinee to compare the foreign policy of the Democratic and Republican parties in 1940 than to ask for a general account of American foreign policy prior to our entering World War II. The former places more restrictions on the response of the examinee than the latter, and thus makes it easier for the examiner to compare the responses of different candidates.

Many devices can be used to restrict the scope of the examinee's response. One of these is to describe a problem in some detail and to break it down into certain components, each of which must be treated separately in the written answer. The following is an example of a free-response type of question taken from an examination given to graduate students of education in which the problem has been broken down into a number of components:

You are a teacher in a rural high school which has a total faculty of fifteen. The principal has assigned to you the task of setting up a testing program in the school. He is a little vague about the purposes of this program, but feels that it is desirable and that somehow it should serve as a part of the guidance program. (1) What would be your initial step in relation to other faculty members in establishing this program? (2) What criteria would be used in the selection of testing devices? (3) What steps would you take to insure that the results of the tests were used?

In this type of problem a considerable amount of detail is given and as much as a thousand words or more may be used in outlining the problem. In addition, the response is limited to certain specified aspects of the problem; in this case three have been selected. By breaking down the response into several distinct aspects it becomes possible to score or otherwise evaluate these separate parts more easily.

Another technique used for restricting the response of the individual within scorable limits is to provide material to be criticized or to be commented on in some way. An English teacher preparing an examination of this type might reproduce a poem and ask the pupils questions concerning the meaning of the poem, what effect the writer of the poem was trying to create and how he was trying to create it, and so forth. A home-economics teacher might apply this examination technique by supplying the pupils with a sequence of menus and asking the pupils such questions as "What are the principal nutritional deficiencies in these menus?" "What foods would you add to provide a more complete diet?" "What substitutes would you make in order to reduce the cost of the diet without reducing its nutritional value?"

Restrictions on the Way in Which the Response Is to Be Organized. It is sometimes desirable to restrict the form of the response of the examinee. For example, it is sometimes useful to indicate that the response is to be given in outline form. This latter restriction is particularly desirable where the test is *not* measuring characteristics of language structure. Sometimes the form of the answer is restricted by the use of such questions as "Give three reasons . . ."

Restrictions Imposed by the Time Limits of the Examination. This is not a particularly desirable way of restricting the response of the subject, since the test then becomes in part a measure of a speed factor. As a general rule it may be said that the free-answer type of examination should allow most examinees to do all they can do, because speed is rarely a relevant variable. While it is administratively desirable to set time limits on most examinations, it is important that these limits be liberal. Free-answer tests which are speeded are likely to be almost unscorable in terms of any reasonably objective standard.

The Scoring of Free-Answer Examinations

Adequately designed free-answer examinations restrict responses so that they provide evidence of the achievement of the objective that is being studied and so that they can be reliably and validly scored. The best rules for scoring free-answer tests will be of little help in marking a poorly designed instrument. Hence, whatever suggestions are given here for the scoring of such devices can be applied only to properly designed tests. Of course, the reverse is also true. There is little point in developing a free-answer test with great care if no provision is made for proper scoring.

The procedure adopted for scoring free-answer tests is necessarily closely related to the purpose of the examination. A test designed to sample the information possessed by the pupil will be scored on a different basis from one designed to measure poetic talents. In addition, it is inevitable that different procedures will be adopted when three thousand essays are to be scored than when only thirty are to be scored. In the latter case, which is typical for the classroom teacher, it is unlikely that crucial decisions will depend on the score on that examination alone. On the other hand, in large-scale examining it is likely that important decisions may depend on the scores achieved. Furthermore, in the large-scale examination it may be reasonable to spend several hundred dollars on the establishment of scoring procedures, but in the scoring of classroom examinations such expenditures could not and would not be justified.

Scoring When the Objectives to Be Measured Are Informational in Character. It has already been pointed out that the free-answer examination is not particularly suitable for measuring informational objectives, but since it is widely used by teachers for that purpose, it is necessary to discuss scoring in this connection. Several methods of scoring have been developed. One method is for the scorer to write óut a complete, ideal answer to the question. Points are then assigned to each idea presented in the ideal answer, and the responses of pupils are scored according to the number of ideas which they mention and which are in the ideal answer. The difficulty with this system is that the teacher preparing the ideal answer may interpret the question differently from the way pupils do; thus the key produced cannot be properly applied to the responses of the pupils. Mainly for this reason an alternative procedure is sometimes adopted which requires the development of a key on the basis of the responses of the pupils. In the latter procedure, answers of pupils are read and the ideas contained in them are listed. This procedure is continued until the reading of further answers adds nothing to the list of relevant ideas mentioned. Points are then assigned to each idea listed and the entire list is used for scoring the answers of the pupils. The procedure is a little laborious, but the results are usually more reliable and more valid than those produced by a scoring method which relies upon the general impression the reader gains from the answer.

Scoring When the Objectives to Be Measured Are Complex Skills. It is generally considered that the free-answer type of test is most appropriately used in the measurement of the ability to perform complex psychological operations such as are included within the concepts of organizing, critically evaluating, and creating. The ability to perform various writing skills must also be considered under the present heading.

The main difficulty of scoring free-answer tests for the assessment of the adequacy of complex mental processes is that it is not usually possible to specify accurately just what is to be assessed. Consider for example the case in which themes written by pupils are to be scored for "adequacy of organization." Now adequacy of organization is a very complex concept and involves both the degree to which the ideas show some *logical sequence* and the extent to which the composition has the property of aesthetic unity. Neither the concept of *logical sequence* nor the concept of *aesthetic unity* can be defined with any precision, although much can be done to clarify the meaning of these concepts. Sometimes this is done by providing dictionary definitions. Sometimes it is done operationally by providing scorers with examples of writing which illustrate the presence or absence of these characteristics.

Where an examination has been given to a large number of individuals and many scorers are employed, it is essential that all scorers be thoroughly oriented in a preliminary conference. In addition, it is desirable to have a small group of papers scored by all scorers. This constitutes a trial run and is followed by a conference at which discrepancies in scores assigned to the same paper are studied and resolved. What this procedure does is to reduce differences among examiners in their concept of what is to be measured by providing identifiable operations through which the concept becomes defined.

In the measurement of complex processes through the free-answer test, it is sometimes possible to score by means of a check list which refers to certain general characteristics of the solution offered. If the student of chemistry were given the task of designing apparatus for carrying out a certain experiment, it might be possible to score the answer in terms of a check list of items such as the following:

1. Will the design permit the experiment to be undertaken?
2. Is the design more complex than is necessary?
3. Does the apparatus make use as far as possible of easily available materials and equipment?
4. Does the design of the apparatus introduce any major sources of error?

Such a check list may serve as a basis for scoring or be used more directly in the scoring process. Sometimes the items in the check list may each be extended to form a rating scale. In such a case, the second item in this check list would become a scale for recording the degree to which the apparatus was more complex than necessary and might vary from *grossly overelaborate* to *as simple as seems possible*.

CONVERTING SCORES INTO GRADES

Basic Problems of Recording Appraisals of Pupil Achievement

The problem of assigning grades is one which it would be logical to study after the measurement of every aspect of growth had been considered. Thus the reader may be surprised to find a discussion of grades presented here rather than at the end of the volume. However, the fact remains that the assignment of grades in school is an activity related largely to the intellectual achievements of children. Thus the consideration of the actual problems of grading faced by schools is appropriately placed immediately after the chapters which deal with the measurement of intellectual outcomes.

Every institution has the problem of establishing a grading system, and every thoughtful group of teachers agrees that no system now in use is fully satisfactory. This means that in introducing into a school any particular system of assigning and recording grades, it is necessary to weigh the advantages against the disadvantages of the proposed system.

Grades are means of transmitting information concerning the achievements of pupils. It is clearly important that they present the information in a form which is thoroughly understandable by the person who is to receive it and, since this is so, a form of grading which is satisfactory for transmitting information to parents, who have little specialized knowledge of measurement techniques, may be quite unsatisfactory for transmitting information to guidance workers, who have considerable specialized knowledge. Grades must be presented and recorded in a form which is as understandable as possible to the user. The central problem, then, in the assignment of grades is to transform scores derived from tests and other methods of assessing pupil achievement into a form which will tell someone else what he needs to know about the progress of the pupil. In order to acquire an understanding of the problems and methods of assigning grades it may be well to consider them from the points of view of what other teachers and guidance workers may want to know about the pupil, what the parents want to know, and what the pupil needs to know about himself.

Grades Recorded for Transmitting Information to Guidance Workers and Teachers

It is reasonable to assume that professional personnel in the school will have considerable technical knowledge and can, therefore, interpret grades which present information about the pupil in a technical form. The cumulative record is the usual source to which professional personnel are likely to turn if they wish to obtain information about the pupil, and it is the various forms in which grades may be entered on this record that will now be appraised.

The Per Cent Type of Grade. This is the commonest and usually the least interpretable type of grade. It is a system founded on a vague tradition. In order to interpret per cent grades, it is usually necessary to know something about the grading practices of the person who has assigned them, and such information is often unavailable. One teacher may rarely give a grade higher than 85, while another rarely gives a lower grade. The usual per cent grades transmit little information unless other factors are known.

The Letter Grade. This common system of recording grades presents most of the problems of per cent grades. However, since it involves only a few categories, these are more likely to be well defined than are those based on a 100-category system as is the per cent system. It is usual for a letter grade system, as is the case with a per cent system, to incorporate the idea of a cutoff point between those who pass and those who fail. The terms *pass* and *fail* are not usually well defined, but in most cases they imply that the failing student has acquired insufficient background in the area to profit immediately from work at the next higher level. A rigid line of demarcation between the passing and failing does not seem to be a very desirable feature of any grading system, for a distribution of grades is likely to distribute pupils from those at one end of the scale who will have little difficulty in mastering the next phase of the work down to those who will have great difficulty. There is no sharp break between those who should go on and those who should not.

Normalized Standard Scores. There is a growing movement in favor of converting scores on which grades are based into normalized standard scores before entering them on a cumulative record. This has certain advantages over most other forms of recording, since the system eliminates teacher differences in grading practices. The writer is in favor of this practice where the grades are to be used by professional school personnel only, and it is a simple matter for teachers to use this sytem with the help of Table 8.3. In order to use this table, it is first necessary to rank the children in order according to their achievement. Suppose that there are thirty children in the class that has been ranked. Find in the table the column which has 30 at the top of it. In this column the number immediately below 30 is 71. This is the normalized standard score of the top pupil. The next pupil scores 66, the next 64, the next 62, and so forth. The table makes it possible to do this for any size of class from five to forty-five pupils. Normalized standard scores may be averaged if it is convenient to do so.

Although normalized standard scores have many advantages over both letter grades and the usual per cent scores, there are certain objections to their use which come largely from college registrars and others who are outside of school systems but who use transcripts of grades. Such individuals prefer the older system to which they are accustomed.

School personnel who interpret cumulative records must remember that a single grade provides only a very small amount of information about a pupil. The reliability of the grades assigned by teachers to pupils after spending one hour a day with them over a semester is usually quite low. This means that pupils who have achieved identical levels of achievement at the end of the semester may be assigned

Number of Persons Ranked

Rank	5	6	7	8	9	10	11	12	13	14	15	16	17	18	19	20	21	22	23	24
1	63	64	65	65	66	66	67	67	68	68	68	69	69	69	69	70	70	70	70	70
2	55	57	58	59	60	60	61	62	62	62	63	63	64	64	64	64	65	65	65	65
3	50	52	54	55	56	57	57	58	59	59	60	60	60	61	61	62	62	62	62	63
4	45	48	50	52	53	54	55	55	56	57	57	58	58	59	59	59	60	60	60	61
5	37	43	46	48	50	51	52	53	54	55	55	56	56	57	57	58	58	58	59	59
6		36	42	45	47	49	50	51	52	53	53	54	55	55	56	56	56	57	57	57
7			35	41	44	46	48	49	50	51	52	52	53	54	54	55	55	55	56	56
8				35	40	43	45	47	48	49	50	51	51	52	53	53	54	54	55	55
9					34	40	43	45	46	47	48	49	50	51	51	52	52	53	53	54
10						34	39	42	44	45	47	48	49	49	50	51	51	52	52	53
11							33	38	41	43	45	46	47	48	49	49	50	51	51	52
12								33	38	41	43	44	45	46	47	48	49	49	50	51
13									32	38	40	42	44	45	46	47	48	48	49	49
14										32	37	40	42	43	44	45	46	47	48	48
15											32	37	40	41	43	44	45	46	47	47
16												31	36	39	41	42	44	45	45	46
17													31	36	39	41	42	43	44	45
18														31	36	38	40	42	43	44
19															31	36	38	40	41	43
20																30	35	38	40	41
21																	30	35	38	39
22																		30	35	37
23																			30	35
24																				30
25																				

TABLE 8.3

This table is to be used for converting rankings to normalized stand
scores which have a mean of 50 and a standard deviation of 10. The first s
in using the table is to rank in order all pupils in terms of the achievement
which scores are to be assigned. Next find the column in the table which re:
to the particular number of pupils to be ranked. If there were twenty-
pupils, find the column marked 22 at the top. This column shows that the p
who achieved the highest rank should be assigned a standard score of 70,
next highest 65, the next highest 62, and so forth.

Number of Persons Ranked

26	27	28	29	30	31	32	33	34	35	36	37	38	39	40	41	42	43	44	45	Rank
71	71	71	71	71	71	71	72	72	72	72	72	72	72	72	72	73	73	73	73	1
66	66	66	66	66	67	67	67	67	67	67	67	68	68	68	68	68	68	68	68	2
63	63	63	64	64	64	64	64	64	65	65	65	65	65	65	65	66	66	66	66	3
61	61	62	62	62	62	62	62	63	63	63	63	63	63	64	64	64	64	64	64	4
59	60	60	60	60	61	61	61	61	61	62	62	62	62	62	62	62	63	63	63	5
58	58	59	59	59	59	59	60	60	60	60	60	61	61	61	61	61	61	62	62	6
57	57	57	58	58	58	58	59	59	59	59	59	60	60	60	60	60	60	60	61	7
56	56	56	57	57	57	57	57	58	58	58	58	59	59	59	59	59	59	60	60	8
54	55	55	55	55	56	56	56	57	57	57	57	58	58	58	58	58	58	59	59	9
53	54	54	55	55	55	55	56	56	56	56	57	57	57	57	57	58	58	58	58	10
52	53	53	54	54	54	54	55	55	55	55	56	56	56	56	56	57	57	57	57	11
51	52	52	53	53	53	54	54	54	54	55	55	55	55	56	56	56	56	56	57	12
50	51	51	52	52	52	53	53	53	54	54	54	54	55	55	55	55	56	56	56	13
50	50	50	51	51	52	52	52	53	53	53	53	54	54	54	54	55	55	55	55	14
49	49	50	50	50	51	51	52	52	52	52	53	53	53	54	54	54	54	54	55	15
48	48	49	49	50	50	50	51	51	51	52	52	52	53	53	53	53	54	54	54	16
47	47	48	48	49	49	50	50	50	51	51	51	52	52	52	52	53	53	53	53	17
46	46	47	47	48	48	49	49	50	50	50	51	51	51	52	52	52	52	53	53	18
44	45	46	46	47	48	48	48	49	49	50	50	50	51	51	51	51	52	52	52	19
43	44	45	45	46	47	47	48	48	49	49	49	50	50	50	51	51	51	52	52	20
42	43	44	45	45	46	46	47	47	48	48	49	49	49	50	50	50	51	51	51	21
41	42	43	43	45	45	46	46	47	47	48	48	48	49	49	49	50	50	50	51	22
39	40	41	42	43	44	45	45	46	46	47	47	48	48	48	49	49	49	50	50	23
37	39	40	41	42	43	44	44	45	46	46	47	47	47	48	48	49	49	49	49	24
34	37	38	40	41	42	43	44	44	45	45	46	46	47	47	48	48	48	49	49	25
29	34	37	38	40	41	42	43	43	44	45	45	46	46	46	47	47	48	48	48	26
	29	34	36	38	39	41	41	42	43	44	44	45	45	46	46	47	47	47	48	27
		29	34	36	38	39	40	41	42	43	43	44	45	45	46	46	46	47	47	28
			29	34	36	38	39	40	41	42	43	43	44	44	45	45	46	46	47	29
				29	33	36	38	39	40	41	42	42	43	44	44	45	45	46	46	30
					29	33	36	37	39	40	41	41	42	43	44	44	44	45	45	31
						29	33	36	37	38	40	40	41	42	43	43	44	44	45	32
							28	33	35	37	38	39	40	41	42	42	43	44	44	33
								28	33	35	37	38	39	40	41	42	42	43	43	34
									28	33	35	37	38	39	40	41	42	42	43	35
										28	33	35	37	37	39	40	41	41	42	36
											28	32	35	36	38	39	40	40	41	37
												28	32	35	37	38	39	40	40	38
													28	32	35	36	37	38	39	39
														28	32	34	36	37	38	40
															28	32	34	36	37	41
																27	32	34	36	42
																	27	32	34	43
																		27	32	44
																			27	45

very different grades, although justice would demand that they all receive the same grade. The low reliability of single grades in courses at the high school and college level means that they have limited value for predictive purposes. On the other hand, the average grades which a high school pupil receives during three or four years of high school may provide a highly reliable measure of the general level of his achievement in high school. The average grade not only has sufficient reliability to be used for predicting future achievement, but it also has validity for that purpose.

Grades Recorded for Transmitting Information to Parents

The emphasis on the partnership of school and home in helping the child to develop to the limit of his potentialities makes it more than ever desirable that there be a mutual exchange of information. The report card has been the traditional means of informing the parent of the child's progress, but unfortunately it has often conveyed little information to the parent and has been used by some teachers as a threat for enforcing school discipline.

As a result of the recognition by teachers that report cards have not been satisfactory in the past for transmitting information to the parents, various attempts have been made to improve them and to find substitutes. One change has been in the direction of indicating on the report card only whether the pupil's progress is satisfactory or whether improvement is needed. Such simple information seems to have more meaning for the parent than the older practice of reporting detailed scores. These newer-type report cards do not draw attention to the competition among pupils but indicate only whether a minimum acceptable level has been achieved. Sometimes, the newer type of report card may indicate what the teacher believes to be the reason for the pupil's shortcomings, such as poor attitude.

Some schools have abolished the report card as a means of transmitting information to the parent and have attempted to develop other procedures. One of these is to write each parent a letter at the end of each semester. This procedure has merit, for the letter can be devoted mainly to those aspects of the pupil's development in which parent-teacher planning is most needed. Nevertheless the task of writing thirty or more letters is a formidable one. Any person who has read through a series of such letters is inevitably greatly disappointed because they provide little information, and the little that is given is for the most part presented in a dull, uninteresting form. The reader of these reports will also note that the same phrases and expressions are repeated with great monotony in letter after letter, indicating that the teacher is more impressed with the uniformity of pupil behavior than with the uniqueness of the individual pupil. The fact seems to be that most teachers do not have the literary talent or the observational acuity necessary for writing vital and meaningful accounts of pupil behavior. This is further substantiated by the fact that teachers who undertake this task report it to be one of tremendous difficulty and therefore it is looked upon as a burden. The writer believes that a letter to parents is an excellent method of providing the parent with information about his child, but it should be used only by those teachers who possess this type of communication skill.

Most who cannot communicate well in writing can communicate well in a face-to-face discussion. Hence it has often been proposed that teachers should transmit information to parents through regularly scheduled interviews. This method offers real promise, for it is likely not only to make for effective communication from teacher to parent, but also to permit communication in the reverse direction. The main difficulty of using the teacher-parent interview as a method of reporting is that it adds at least a half hour to the teacher's working day. This is a serious difficulty, for, in any case, the teacher's work day does not cease at the hour when school is out.

Grades Recorded for Transmitting Information to the Pupil

Not many years have passed since it was customary to report grades to pupils for the purpose of "rewarding the diligent and punishing the lazy." Those who were assigned *failing* grades were given them as a warning to mend their ways. It was also customary in schools to assign grades on a competitive basis so that a specified percentage of the pupils always failed on a graded assignment. These practices are fortunately largely on the way out.

The purpose of reporting a grade to a pupil should be to provide him with helpful information. Sometimes a grade may indicate whether his work has met an acceptable standard in cases where there is some standard of acceptability. Typing pupils may well be informed at the end of two years that a grade of F means that their typing skills are such that they could not retain commercial jobs as typists, or that a grade of C represents skill equal to that required by the average business typist. The same principle may be applied in reporting grades to pupils in other commercial and business courses. In general education, the problem is a different one, for there are not the same social standards by which a pupil can judge his achievements. Certainly, in most written assignments which pupils complete, the corrections made by the teacher should be the main basis of informing the student of his accomplishments, and to summarize these corrections in the form of a letter grade or a per cent adds no information. When an objective test of fifty multiple-choice items has been administered to a group of pupils and if this test can be considered to measure the extent to which an objective has been achieved, the information which the student needs most is how many of the items he answered correctly and which ones he was unable to answer correctly. The latter information will enable him to plan a review of the unit of work on which the test was based. It should be noted that in this situation the conversion of a score into a letter grade serves no useful purpose as far as imparting information to the pupil is concerned, although some type of conversion is necessary if the results of the test are to be entered on a cumulative record. Converting scores into letter grades which imply success or failure dooms many to consider themselves as failures without showing them how to succeed.

The Pupil's Own Evaluation of His Achievement

Since there are educators who believe that the most important appraisal of a pupil's achievement is his own appraisal, a few words must be said about self-appraisals. First, there is the problem of what standard the individual should use in making such personal evaluations. He may judge his own achievement in terms of his expectations—that is, in terms of what he expects to achieve. For an adult who takes up painting as a leisure-time pursuit, this may be an excellent standard in terms of which to make judgments, but if the individual expects eventually to earn his living by painting pictures, it may come as a rude shock to him to find that his own evaluation does not correspond to that of others. When the individual judges himself in terms of his own standards, his evaluation will depend upon his *level of aspiration*—that is, the level of performance which he sets for himself as a goal. Much experimentation has revealed that the level of aspiration of the individual is commonly quite unrealistic and set at a level higher than the individual can ever hope to attain. If such individuals are left to be evaluated only by themselves, they are doomed to a life of apparent failure, but evaluations by others in terms of the standards of others may help these individuals to make an adjustment.

Second, there is the problem of insight which involves the extent to which the individual knows his own performance and can match it with some standard set by himself or by others. One of the major discoveries of clinical psychology has been that individuals have, in general, very little insight or understanding into their own behavior. Individuals may not recognize reproductions of their own voices or descriptions of themselves. When they are asked to rate themselves, they tend to overrate themselves on desirable qualities and underrate themselves on undesirable qualities. Lack of insight seems to be the rule, and it may well be argued that the teacher may in the evaluation process serve the function of giving the individual insight into his own behavior. Clinicians seem to be agreed that the best method by which the individual may obtain insight into himself is through prolonged and personal contact with another in an atmosphere of permissiveness. It is of interest to note also that clinical psychology has accepted the position that the individual achieves insight not through being told the truth about himself (which he is likely to reject), but through his own explorations stimulated by the kind of relationship which the clinical psychologist provides.

Although the argument of the clinician does have applications to the evaluation process, it also has limitations. It is probably most applicable in cases where the teacher is concerned with personal characteristics of the type in which the clinician is most interested. It has limited application in the area of intellectual achievement and skill, where the weight of evidence, and often its objectivity, forces the individual to take a realistic position with respect to his own achievement.

It was pointed out at the beginning of this discussion that certain authorities in education have suggested that the only grades which matter in education are those which the individual assigns to himself. The difficulty here is that the individual's own evaluations of himself are important only to the individual. Society, on the other hand, is concerned with what a person can actually do in terms of some objective standard. At some point the pupil must face these social evaluations.

Amount of Growth Versus Level of Achievement as a Basis for Assigning Grades

Two teachers may have identical objectives, groups of pupils of equal ability, and may give the same percentage of A's, B's, and C's, and yet their grades may indicate entirely different kinds of attributes. One teacher may attempt to grade in terms of the amount of growth that has taken place in the direction of the desired objectives, while the other may grade in terms of the extent to which the desired objectives were achieved. These two systems of grading may produce different results, for the pupil who shows the greatest amount of growth toward a given objective may not be the one who shows the greatest final achievement with respect to the same objective. Teachers are familiar with the pupil who starts with little background but who makes substantial progress during the semester yet whose final achievement is far behind that of the more advanced pupils. Equally familiar is the pupil who comes to a program with a rich background and who is so far advanced that he can make little progress toward achieving the objectives of the program, since they are already largely achieved. If the teacher were to grade the latter type of pupil on the basis of growth, he would be given a low grade.

Even if there were strong arguments in favor of recording grades in terms of amount of growth in the desired direction, it is not a particularly practical procedure, since it involves basic theoretical difficulties which have already been touched upon and may be illustrated again in the context of grades. A certain teacher administered an achievement test in two equivalent forms, one at the beginning and one at the end of the semester. Assume that the test could be demonstrated to be a valid measure of the objectives of the course. In terms of raw scores on these tests, one pupil raised his score from 20 to 40 during the semester, while another raised his score from 70 to 90. In each case the increase in score was 20 points, and if the pupils were being graded in terms of amount of growth, the teacher might be inclined to give the two pupils the same grade. However, this involves the assumption that an increase in score from 20 to 40 is equal to an increase from 70 to 90. In other words, it assumes that these two intervals are equal, but this assumption can never be made. Even the interval from 20 to 40 cannot be considered equal for all pupils in at least one sense, for a dull pupil may find that it takes immense effort to raise his score 20 points over this interval, but for a bright child it may require little effort. Grades which attempt to indicate amount of improvement are simply not practical devices at the present time.

Any system of central records in a school or other type of educational institution provides usable material only insofar as the institutional staff agree whether grades are to indicate amount of growth or status. Too often, a combination of both systems is used within a single school which renders the records uninterpretable. Thus a grade of A assigned to a given student in a given course may mislead the guidance worker if it is taken to indicate a level of proficiency, when it was given to indicate substantial progress even if the final level of proficiency was only mediocre.

Summary

1. This chapter has presented procedures for the development of various forms of paper-and-pencil tests. The form selected for a test should be appropriate for measuring the particular outcome. A table was provided to help the teacher decide between using multiple-choice and free-answer tests.

2. If the teacher decides that a multiple-choice type of test is appropriate, it is desirable that test items be built in accordance with the general principles discussed. It is of special importance that each item have a central problem stated in the lead and that the alternatives present a series of suggested solutions from which the student must identify the correct solution.

3. Free-answer tests are difficult to build and to score, but in many types of appraisal they are more appropriate than so-called objective tests. They are particularly useful for measuring certain complex skills. In the construction of free-answer tests it is of critical importance to place restrictions on the response of the pupil who takes the test. Unless this is done, it may not be possible to develop a reliable method of scoring.

4. Performance on tests must ultimately be reported in some form. The reporting procedure is usually referred to as grading. The procedure adopted for reporting grades will depend on the purpose of reporting and the role of the person to whom the report is made. Parents, pupils, and professional school personnel require such reports, but the form of reporting should differ in the three cases.

5. The student of education should recognize that a single grade derived from a single course provides only the most limited information about a pupil. Not only does a single grade have rather poor reliability, but it also refers to a limited sample of behavior in a limited educational area. Guidance workers, if they are to make inferences from grades, should base these inferences on grades from many courses taken over a substantial period of time.

References

1. Travers, Robert M. W., *How to Make Achievement Tests*, New York, The Odyssey Press, 1950, pp. 180 + IX.

PART III

Measuring Personality Development

CHAPTER 9

The Assessment of Personality

THE ASSESSMENT OF PERSONALITY BASED ON A THEORY OF COMMON TRAITS

Introduction

One of the striking changes in education over the last half century is a growing belief among teachers that the school should produce desirable changes in personality. Just what is meant by "personality," what changes are to be made in it, and how these changes are to be accomplished usually remains obscure, but the general sentiment expressed in this viewpoint is considered today to be highly commendable, even though the ideas expressed are not clear. The implication is that whatever is to be changed is nonintellectual in character and that it is different from what the nineteenth-century educators referred to as "character." The latter term is usually accepted as referring to the ethical and moral characteristics of behavior. The famous McGuffy readers represented a genuine attempt to develop attributes of the latter kind, but little is known about the effects of these stories in which good always triumphed over evil and in which crime never paid.

No term has been so recklessly used in education as the term *personality*. There is common agreement that some of the most serious problems of adult living are a result of inadequacies in personality. This agreement, together with the accepted view that the social characteristics are mainly learned, has encouraged teachers to list among their goals "the development of personality." Programs at all levels from nursery school to college claim to produce, or at least attempt to produce, "well-rounded personalities." The appraisal of the extent to which this objective is achieved requires that careful thought be given to its content, scope, and boundaries. Differing viewpoints concerning the function of the teacher in developing pupil personality are described in the following paragraphs:

1. The interest of some teachers in the development of personality is limited to the acquisition of the social customs of the culture within which the individual lives. Teachers of home economics have stressed the teaching of how to behave as a host, as a guest, and in the numerous other types of role which every person must commonly play. These habits of behavior may be learned with or without insight into the purposes, contemporary or archaic, which they were designed to fulfill. The purpose of achieving this objective is to help the individual avoid embarrassment in a society in which conformity is demanded. In the learning that occurs at this level there need not be and probably is not much integration of the response learned with other aspects of the personality. The child may learn to say "thank you" with the same degree of automatism as that with which he walks. The fact that he says "thank you" may imply no more feeling of thankfulness than a knee-jerk reflex implies a desire to kick.

2. Other teachers are interested in developing less specific responses than those which are characteristic of social conventions developed in their simplest form. These teachers are concerned with the development of traits which influence a great variety of specific responses, such as a tendency for the child to demonstrate a friendly manner toward those who help him or who do things for him. In other words, the child should not only learn to say "thank you" but to do it in a way which shows some friendliness. In a similar way, in working in committees with other children, these teachers feel that it is not enough for the children to know parliamentary procedure, but it is also desirable for them to show a behavior tendency which might be called cooperativeness.

3. Still other teachers point out that characteristics vary in the *depth* to which they influence behavior. In any area of learning it is uneconomical in terms of time for the individual to learn a specific response which occurs only in one type of specific situation. The greater the range of responses modified by learning, the more effec-

tive is the learning process. As far as personality is concerned, if the school can produce deep-seated changes of a desirable nature, then learning with extensive consequences will have occurred. On the other hand, if only superficial responses are learned, the yield in relation to educational effort is poor. On this account, it is of advantage to produce deep-seated changes. However, there are reasons why it may not be possible for the school to make changes of this kind. These reasons will be discussed in the paragraph which follows.

4. There are also the guidance workers and school psychologists who are particularly concerned with developing an interrelationship between the various aspects of an individual's personality. Aspects of personality may be in conflict, operating independently, or may be integrated so that they function together. Conflicting elements may become integrated either temporarily or permanently. Much has been written by educators on the need for integrating the personalities of growing children, but how this is to be accomplished usually remains unspecified. Knowledge gained from psychotherapy in recent years would indicate that there is little likelihood that the teacher will be able to influence these integrative aspects of personality development to any marked degree. The kind of relationship developed between therapist and patient seems to be an essential factor in changing the personality of the patient. This personal relationship must exist over a long period, often years, and it is a fundamentally different relationship from that which exists between teacher and pupil. Those who claim that the school can make fundamental changes in personality are disregarding most of the facts known about the formation of personality.

Traditional Trait Theory

The traditional trait theory assumed that trait names such as honesty, friendliness, aggressiveness, and so forth, describe characteristics of behavior which have two properties:

1. They are alleged to be pervasive and enduring properties of behavior; that is, a person who has a high degree of honesty will be honest to a high degree in all situations that he encounters, and the

person who has little of the trait of honesty will show little of this characteristic of behavior in all situations.

2. They are alleged to exist to some degree in all individuals; that is, all individuals are in varying degrees honest, friendly, aggressive, and so on.

It is unfortunate that all behavior is not of this simple character. In the case of a few traits, most individuals tend to show consistency, but these traits seem to be the exception rather than the rule. Individuals who are highly intelligent in terms of intelligence-test scores tend to handle problems in a manner which is generally considered to be intelligent, but even in this case consistency is only moderate. The intelligent professor may show behavior on the level of a moron in handling his personal affairs. Much less consistent is a person with respect to behaviors which might be described as aggressive. The aggressive businessman may often achieve his ends by means of behavior which is suave and totally lacking in overt aggression. Traits which refer to social characteristics seem to be particularly unstable from one situation to another.

The deathblow to the traditional trait theory came through the epoch-making studies of Hartshorne and May (8). In these studies, certain attributes of character such as honesty and deceit were measured by a number of tests in a variety of situations. The data indicated a very low relationship between the degree of honesty shown by an individual in one situation and the degree of honesty shown by the same individual in another situation.

Allport and his students (1) some years later demonstrated that although the Hartshorne and May data showed that most individuals were inconsistent in the extent to which they handled various situations with honesty, it could be demonstrated that a minority of individuals did show a consistent degree of honesty and hence their behavior could be described in terms of such a trait. Social traits tend to have this characteristic of showing consistency in only a few individuals and are those which psychologists have most difficulty in measuring. The problems involved in the measurement of such traits, which characterize the behavior of only a few, are largely unsolved; thus the discussion of personality measurement presented here refers largely to the measurement of traits which are important characteristics of most individuals.

Nature of Rating Devices

Rating scales are commonly referred to as the oldest of psychological measuring devices, since they have been used for several hundred years. It is really not correct to refer to them as measuring devices, since they are used for recording observations rather than for making observations. The guidance counselor may rate the pupil on certain personal characteristics, but the scale itself is not used for making the observations in the same way in which a test of intelligence is administered to the individual in the assessment of his abilities. The intelligence test is used as a stimulus situation which makes it possible to study the responses of the individual whose abilities are being appraised. Rating scales do not perform this kind of function except under the unusual circumstance when they are used for self-ratings; that is, when the individual rates himself.

Rating scales are used in summarizing the same kind of data that are summarized in written characterizations. However, rating scales are not only useful as an aid in summarizing observations; they also serve the purpose of restricting observation to certain defined aspects of behavior. The effectiveness of rating scales will obviously depend on the degree to which they define accurately the category of behavior to be recorded and the extent to which it is possible for the rater to observe the kinds of behavior that are to be recorded on the rating sheet. Alas, it happens all too frequently that the rater is left in some doubt as to just what is to be recorded and has difficulty in making all of the observations that he needs to make.

The fact that in such situations the rater must to some extent exercise his own good judgment shows that rating is a subjective process. The occurrence of subjective judgment merely means that the observing and recording process lacks definiteness. Although rating scales may be considered primarily as devices for recording observations, it is common for them to require the rater to interpret what is observed. It is this aspect of rating scales which accounts for most of their unsatisfactory features for it is usually not clear just what the rater is required to do in the interpretation of his observations. Also, it must be kept in mind that there is no rigid line of demarcation between observation and interpretation, and much of what is ordinarily called observation involves extensive interpretation.

It has been emphasized throughout this volume that, wherever possible, observation of behavior should be made under conditions which permit the maximum amount of control. Test situations are merely attempts to provide individuals with a standardized environment in which their responses can be recorded with objectivity; that is, so that independent observers can agree on the score assigned. Whenever possible, ratings should be used for recording observations in standardized situations where conditions have been arranged so that the standard stimulus situation will produce the general category of responses to be observed. Rating devices will be most satisfactory when they are used in situations that are standardized and least when they are based on general, or what one might better call, casual observation. A common type of situation in which ratings are used is the one in which there is some, but only very limited, control over the situation. The rating of teachers by supervisors in classroom situations is typical of a procedure in which there is some control but far from complete control of all elements involved. While all the teachers to be rated are confronted with classes, these may represent a wide range of grades, of number of pupils, and of types of pupils which they include. If some of the classes include only children who are behavior problems, while others include only bright children, the behavior to be expected of the teachers may vary markedly, since teaching in two situations may require different patterns of response. A parallel situation arises in the rating of the social characteristics of children in free-play situations in school. The situation may be different for different children, as when children differ in the length of time that they have been in the group. Thus a child may appear to be withdrawn and unsociable just because he is a new member of the class.

The Prognostic Type of Rating

In some situations a rating is used for predicting how an individual will behave in some situation in the future. An example of this is a practice adopted for many years at a large university where the officer who studied the applications for admission made a prediction of the future academic performance of the applicant. This assessment was an over-all judgment based on all the information available. This information included high school records, a statement by the principal of the high shool, a mass of miscellaneous information provided by the applicant, and a statement written by the applicant himself. Over a period of years these ratings were found to be comparable in accuracy with the predictions made by the most valid tests for the purpose. It may be noted that in making these ratings, the admissions officer was able to take into account information which is not ordinarily available, namely, the standard of marking used in the particular high school from which the student came, and was able to make some correction for this in the appraisal of the high school transcript.

There are a great many situations in which prognostic ratings are unsatisfactory, not because of the kind of information they are designed to produce, but because of the vagueness of the behavior to be predicted or the unidentified nature of the situation within which behavior is to be predicted. For example, if ratings by teachers were used for predicting how a child would behave in an out-of-school social situation, the predictions would almost certainly have no value, because social behavior lacks apparent consistency.

METHODS OF RATING

Introduction

Considerable ingenuity has been devoted to the development of rating scales, but it is probable that the resulting improvement is small in comparison with the amount of ingenuity which has been applied. Rating methods vary in two respects. First, they vary in the kind of process which is suggested for summarizing or interpreting the observations on which the ratings are based. Second, they vary in the way in which the final judgments are recorded. These various methods must now be reviewed, keeping in mind that ratings are used only in the absence of better and more objective methods of assessment.

Ranking Methods

Ranking methods are best adapted to the problem of selecting the top individuals in a group. The teacher is not usually interested in the problem of ranking children according to the degree to which they possess some given characteristic. Acceptable educational philosophy stresses the point that each child should be evaluated in terms of what he *himself* can do and not in terms of what others can do. Despite this philosophy, schools still continue to use ranking methods, and eventually on graduation from high school the young men and women are indelibly stamped with their *rank* in their graduating class. Therefore, ranking systems will be considered, keeping in mind the fact that they have limited value.

One of the first systematic attempts to use ranking procedures in judging the characteristics of men took place during the First World War, when the so-called man-to-man rating system was first developed. In this system, as in all others, the initial step is that of defining the continuum to be measured. It is not sufficient to state that the continuum is to measure "leadership" or "cooperativeness." The continuum must be defined according to the principles discussed in Chapter 2 of this volume. In the *use* of the man-to-man type of rating scale, the first step is to select from the group of individuals who are to be rated that individual who has the greatest amount and that individual who has the least amount of the characteristic on which they are to be rated. The second step is to select individuals at intermediate points along the scale. The individuals thus selected are used to identify points along the scale. Usually five individuals, including the two in the extreme positions, are used in this step. The third step involves matching the remainder of the individuals in the group with those who have been selected to identify positions on the scale.

The man-to-man method is a system for ranking individuals. The rationale seems to be that in any group some persons can be more easily assessed than others in terms of a given variable, and hence these should be chosen for identifying positions on a scale. The argument is carried one step further by assuming that, in general, it is easier to match individuals with individuals than it is to match individuals with scale positions that are described in words. As far as the writer knows the soundness of this rationale has never been adequately established. It seems quite possible that merely ranking the individuals in order by choosing the highest, then the lowest, then the next highest, and next lowest, and so on, might be just as satisfactory.

An inconvenient aspect of the man-to-man type of rating scale is that ratings based on different groups are not comparable. This is a basic weakness of all ranking methods. Groups may differ so much in range on a given characteristic that there may be practically no overlap between them. Thus the individual who receives the highest rank in one group may have less of the particular characteristic than the person who ranks lowest in the other group.

Descriptive Rating Scales

The common type of descriptive rating device provides a series of definitions of points on the continuum on which appraisals are to be made. Sometimes only the extremes of the scale are specified, but the percentage of the individuals falling within each value on the scale may or may not be indicated, as in the example given in Figure 9.1.

FIGURE 9.1

Graphic Rating Scale with Only the Ends of the Continuum Defined

Meaning of scale value	Sits quietly in place, fidgets little			Restless most of the time, leaves seat for the slightest excuse, has difficulty in getting down to work.	
Scale value	1	2	3	4	5
Percentage of sixth grade boys falling in each scale value	5	25	40	25	5

It should be noted that in the type of scale given in Figure 9.1 it is possible to specify the percentage of individuals who are to fall into each one of the categories only after this has been experimentally determined.

Sometimes several positions on the rating scale may be defined by verbal description, as in the rating scale shown in Figure 9.2.

FIGURE 9.2

Rating Scale in Which a Number of Scale Values Are Defined

1	2	3
Never participates in class discussion even when invited to do so by teacher	Participates in class discussion only when drawn in by the action of the teacher	Occasionally volunteers to participate in class discussion when the topic seems to be of special interest

4	5	6
Participates quite frequently in class discussion and does at least his share of keeping the discussion going	Participates with great frequency in class discussion and does much to keep discussion going	Participates in class discussion to such an extent that it interferes with the participation of others

Acceptable Practices in the Construction of Descriptive Rating Scales

In the construction of rating scales it seems desirable to follow certain practices and avoid certain common errors, which are outlined as follows:

1. *A rating scale should describe a single limited aspect of behavior.* Many rating scales manifest the fault of including too many variables. For example, a single rating scale, instead of dealing only with the amount of physical activity shown by a child, also included reference to the extent of his interests. One end of the scale was defined by the statement that "the child is physically very active, constantly leaves his seat, and seems interested in everything that

happens around him." This scale includes too many elements and should have been drawn up as at least two separate scales. A rating scale previously discussed on page 164 and used in the assessment of the performance of men in practical work in technical schools suffers to some extent from this same defect.

2. *Scale points should be defined in terms of descriptions of identifiable behavior.* Rating scales frequently suffer from the defect of using general terms which have very little meaning. Consider the following *ill-constructed* rating device:

Rating Scale of Physique

Very Inferior	Poor	Average	Good	Excellent

Nearly every aspect of this scale is inadequate. The series of terms from *very inferior* to *excellent* have little meaning. The implication that everybody below average is either *poor* or *very inferior* is quite ridiculous. The term *physique* is not properly defined. It is not clear whether this term refers to physical strength, degree to which the individual is healthy, general type of body build, or something else. Scales of this type should never be used.

3. *The number of positions on the scale must be related to the accuracy with which assessments can be made.* This same principle applies in all fields of measurement. If appraisal is so rough that individuals can be divided into only two categories, there is little point in using three or more categories. The use of an excessive number of scale positions is analogous to the person using a scale marked off in inches but who tries to measure to the nearest one-tenth or one-hundredth of an inch. In psychological and educational assessment there rarely seems to be much point in using more than five categories on a rating scale, and there are certainly few scales of demonstrated utility which use more than this number.

Conditions for Using Rating Scales

The value of assessments recorded on a rating scale will vary according to the extent to which the scale is adequately constructed and according to the conditions under which it is used. A rating scale which may yield useful assessments in one situation may yield nothing of value in another. The conditions of use which affect the value of ratings are discussed in the paragraphs which follow in so far as these scales are used for recording the present characteristics of the individual rated. Scales used for prognostic purposes present other special problems, some of which have already been considered.

1. *It must be possible for the rater to observe the behavior described on the rating scale.* The writer can recall cases in which employers have requested him to make ratings of his former students on such characteristics as cooperativeness when he has never had an opportunity of observing in these students manifest cooperative behavior of the type that occurs in a typical office situation. Even if this characteristic had been observed in a limited situation, there is a question as to whether ratings of it have any predictive value in other situations. Rating forms sent by employers suffer rather commonly from this defect.

2. *Ratings should be undertaken under conditions which do not result in some general tendency to overrate or underrate.* An example of this type of situation is that which exists in many schools where the supervisor feels obliged to give high merit ratings to all teachers because low ratings would reflect on the apparent efficiency of the school.

3. *Ratings should not call for more work and effort than the rater can be expected to undertake.* Sometimes teachers may be required to rate every pupil in the class on each of a number of characteristics. Certain pupils may have been observed with respect to these characteristics, while others may not have been. The procedure may call for the rating of all pupils regardless of whether the teacher feels she can or cannot undertake the task. It does not have to be pointed out that under such conditions little is accomplished. Rating forms are devices for recording observations, but what if there are no observations to record?

4. *Raters should be aware of the halo effect.* When ratings are made for a number of characteristics on a number of individuals, the intercorrelations between the ratings are higher than one might expect them to be. This has generally been attributed to what is known as the halo effect; that is, a tendency for raters to note outstanding characteristics which tend to influence ratings on all other

characteristics in the same individual. A person with an outstanding desirable characteristic tends to appear generally in a good light and his weaknesses may be overlooked. The reverse may occur in the case of a person who has some undesirable characteristic to a marked degree. This undesirable trait may make it difficult for raters to see any desirable characteristic that the individual may show.

5. *Ratings from several observers should be averaged if reliability of ratings is to be achieved.* There seem to be considerable advantages in many situations in averaging the ratings of several observers. If children of high school age are to be rated, it may be desirable to obtain ratings from several of the teachers with whom they have some contact. The average of these ratings is likely to have more value than the ratings of any one teacher. The purpose of averaging the ratings is to eliminate certain types of random error. It may help to reduce the effect which special aversions or likings of the individual observers may have on the ratings that are thus produced.

6. *When individuals are to be rated on several scales, the scales should be set up so that the desirable ends of the scales are not consistently to the right or to the left of the rating sheet.* This rule has been stated in every discussion of rating scales published in the last twenty-five years. The supposed purpose of this practice is to make the rater think about each scale, and it prevents him from simply marking the same position on the scale all the way down the list. How effective it is in achieving this purpose does not seem to have been established.

Forced-Choice Rating Scales

Various attempts have been made to develop rating scales which are free from the rater biases and errors which have been discussed. A recent attempt in this connection is the forced-choice rating scale which, in its most common form, presents characteristics in groups of four. The following might be such a group:

> Tires easily
> Orderly in work
> Volunteers to help other pupils
> Lacks initiative

The task of the rater is to read through each group of characteristics and to select the one which is most typical and the one which is least typical of the person rated. The responses of the rater can then be scored with a key which has been prepared by an elaborate statistical technique on the basis of data collected in the construction of the scale.

The procedure of developing forced-choice scales is complicated, costly, and outside the scope of the activities of most teachers. In addition, although the technique is interesting as an experimental device, its value has not yet been definitely established.

An Overview of Rating Scales

The vast amount of work which has been devoted to the improvement of rating scales has not resulted in a corresponding amount of progress, and it may be well to pause and consider the possible reasons for this. Of central importance seems to be the fact that the data to be recorded in most rating scales are extremely meager in quantity. A teacher who is required to rate thirty children for some aspect of social adjustment after he has had the opportunity to observe them for only a few weeks may have little information on which to base these ratings. It is in a similar context of impoverished information that most ratings are made, and it is inevitable that, in some situations, ratings recorded on the best type of rating sheet that can be devised will supply relatively little information. No rating scale can be more valid than the data on which it is based.

THE EVOLUTION OF THE PERSONALITY INVENTORY

Introduction

The traditional approach to the problem of assessing the relations of the individual to the society in which he lives has been that of recording observations in the form of ratings. The difficulty of making ratings has resulted in attempts to abandon this approach in favor of procedures which involve the more direct measurement of the variables involved. The development of measuring instruments has, in general, paralleled the development of theory in the area, and some of the early devices were particularly deficient because of the inadequacies of the theory on which they were based. The early instruments were of the inventory type and presented lists of statements to which the individual responded in some way. The development of the nonverbal type of personality test occurred at a much later date and to a considerable extent as a protest against the inadequacies of the verbal inventory approach.

One of the earliest inventories was that developed by Woodworth (31) in 1917 and given the deliberately harmless name of "Personal Data Sheet." This inventory listed 116 items of behavior which psychiatrists had included in their description of "neurotic" patients. The individual taking the inventory had to decide in the case of each item whether it was, or was not, descriptive of him. The basic concept on which this inventory was based, and on which many subsequent inventories were based, was that individuals varied with respect to a variable called neuroticism, which usually remained undefined. This measurement process is analogous to measuring the degree to which individuals are sick but without specifying the type of sickness from which they are suffering. The concept of a single over-all factor of mental health dominated much of the early work in the measurement of personality and was still a dominant concept when Thurstone (29) developed his Personality Schedule in 1930, which was designed to measure the degree to which the individual was generally maladjusted or neurotic. The following are illustrative items from this test, which borrowed much from Woodworth's original inventory:

> Do you get stage fright?
> As a child, did you like to play alone?
> Do you daydream frequently?
> Are your feelings easily hurt?
> Do you consider yourself a rather nervous person?
> Do you laugh easily?

This type of inventory, which attempted to measure over-all personality, was the precursor of two general developments in this area of psychological measurement. On the one hand there developed a series of instruments which attempted to measure differences in personality unrelated to the dimension of adjustment-maladjustment, and on the other hand there appeared a number of inventories which attempted to diagnose specific types of maladjustment. The inventories which represent attempts to measure differences in personality characteristics that are not ordinarily considered to have pathological significance will be discussed first.

Inventories for Measuring Nonpathological Traits

These types of inventories are intended mainly for the adult and late adolescent level. Little has been done to develop the inventory approach for younger persons.

The Bernreuter Personality Inventory (3), first published in 1931, deserves mention only because of its widespread use over a period of at least two decades. This instrument is a typical inventory of 125 items to which the individual responds "Yes," "No," or "Unable to answer with yes or no." The original test provided four scales, but later these were extended to six, entitled neurotic tendency (B_1-N), self-sufficiency (B_2-S), introversion (B_3-1), social dominance (B_4-D), self-consciousness (F_1-C), and solitariness (F_2-S). For all practical purposes the three scales of neurotic tendency, introversion, and self-consciousness measure the same variable, which reflects the fallacy of judging a scale by its name. Later Flanagan (6) used a factor analysis to demonstrate that the interrelations between the scales were such that they seemed to be measuring only two factors, which he named tentatively self-confidence and sociability.

Published studies on the value of the Bernreuter Personality Inventory up to 1942 have been reviewed by Super (24), who points out that the inventory provides a greater number of scales than the items warrant. He also refers to the instrument as not only the most widely used (at that time) but also the most widely abused instrument for the appraisal of personality. In summarizing the results of the 147 studies included in his review, Super concludes that the inventory is of questionable value in sorting out individuals who manifest behavior problems.

The unsatisfactory interrelationships among the scales on the Bernreuter Personality Inventory led subsequent makers of inventories in the area of personality measurement to pay special attention to the whole problem of preparing instruments which would measure independent (uncorrelated) variables. The problem of finding uncorrelated variables in this area is one which has occupied the attention of many psychologists in recent years. The main technique is one known as factor analysis, which cannot be elaborated upon at this time except to say that it is designed to produce measures of separate and fundamentally distinct characteristics of individuals. The student who is interested in the products of this approach is referred to the studies of Cattell (4).

In order that the reader may appreciate the great variety of characteristics which psychologists have *attempted* to measure with inventories designed for non-clinical use, it is suggested that he examine the material presented in Table 9.3. However, the reader must also keep in mind that the personality inventories listed might perhaps be likened to samples brought back by explorers. The value of these samples is still a matter for speculation.

It is the opinion of the writer that inventories as yet available for measuring the personality characteristics of normal individuals are of use only for experimental purposes. They do not provide a satisfactory basis for discovering the characteristics of pupils in the higher grades. The direct observation of the pupil must remain the teacher's primary source of information about pupil development, and rating scales will remain useful devices for focusing attention on what is to be observed and for providing uniform methods of recording. However, the teacher should acquire some facility in judging the merits of inventory measuring devices for possible experimental use, and in this connection should be aware of the following facts:

1. The method used in developing the inventories is simply a device for sorting out the items into categories which are, so far as possible, uncorrelated. The mathematical sorting process does not guarantee that the items measure important variables in personality any more than a complex procedure for sorting out merchandise in a department store would ensure that the merchandise was of good quality or of utility.

2. There is no evidence yet that the various measures provided by these inventories measure what they are supposed to measure. The process of naming the factors is quite unsatisfactory and subjective. For example, the factors measured by the Guilford-Martin

TABLE 9.3

Some Inventories Designed to Measure Personality Traits

Name of Inventory	Publisher	Names Given to Traits Which the Inventory Is Designed to Measure
Guilford-Martin Inventory of Factors GAMIN. Abridged Edition	Sheridan Supply Company P.O. Box 837 Beverly Hills, California	Pressure for overt activity Lack of inferiority feeling Ascendancy in social situations Lack of nervousness Masculinity
Guilford-Martin Personnel Inventory I	Sheridan Supply Company P.O. Box 837 Beverly Hills, California	Objectivity Agreeableness Cooperativeness
Inventory of Factors STRDC	Sheridan Supply Company P.O. Box 837 Beverly Hills, California	Social introversion Depression Thinking introversion Tendency to cycloid behavior Carefree disposition Cyclothymia vs. schizothymia General mental capacity vs. mental defect Emotionally stable character vs. general emotionality Dominance vs. submissiveness Surgency vs. desurgency Positive character vs. dependent character Adventurous cyclothymia vs. withdrawn schizothymia Infantile imaginative emotionality vs. mature, tough poise Trustful cyclothymia vs. paranoid schizothymia Bohemian unconcern vs. conventional practicality Worrying suspiciousness vs. calm trustfulness Radicalism vs. conservatism Independent self-sufficiency vs. lack of resolution Will control and character stability
16 PF Test	Institute for Personality Testing Champaign, Illinois	Nervous tension
Thurstone Temperament Schedule	Science Research Associates, Inc. 57 West Grand Ave.	Active Stable Vigorous Sociable Impulsive Reflective

226

Personnel Inventory I (7) might collectively be descriptive of paranoia, but Guilford and Martin prefer to call them objectivity, agreeableness, and cooperativeness.

3. Although the method of developing the inventories represents an attempt to find a series of measures to appraise certain fundamental and independent components, there are often high correlations between the various scales. This means that the scores on different scales do not tell different things about a person.

4. Inventories pertain to the verbal behavior of individuals. It must be remembered that what a person says he would do if placed in a particular situation is often different from what he would actually do.

Table 9.3 lists a number of inventories and the names given by the authors to the traits which the inventory attempts to measure. A worth-while experience for the student is to obtain a sample set of materials for one of these instruments and then to review the evidence provided concerning its utility.

THE DIAGNOSTIC INVENTORY

Early Attempts to Develop Diagnostic Inventories

A second group of descendants of the neurotic inventory of the type developed by Woodworth is the diagnostic type of inventory designed to measure types of pathological deviation.* These inventories were designed to indicate not just whether the individual is sick or healthy but the type of sickness from which he might be suffering. Three difficulties immediately faced the ambitious psychologists who attempted to handle this problem. First there was the fact that psychiatrists and clinical psychologists could not all agree on a fundamental classification of pathological deviations. Second, the overlapping and combination of the numerous types of mental maladies made it difficult to identify specific behavioral characteristics typical of each deviate category. Third, the fact that an adequate classification system of abnormalities had not yet been achieved

---

* What is said here should not be taken to imply that any rigid line can be drawn between characteristics that are commonly considered as pathological and those that are not conventionally so classified.

meant that major difficulties were encountered in identifying group known definitely to deviate in a given way to whom the test can be administered for validation purposes.

The earliest diagnostic inventory for clinical purposes seems to be that developed by Doncaster G. Humm and Guy W. Wadsworth (13) and published under the name of the Humm-Wadsworth Temperament Scale. It was first published in 1934, but was later revised. The inventory itself consists of 318 questions, but only 165 of these are scored, the remaining ones being included to provide "atmosphere." The inventory provided the following seven scales: (1) normal, (2) hysterical, (3) manic, (4) depressive, (5) autistic, (6) paranoid, and (7) epileptoid. These categories do not represent a widely accepted system for classifying the deviant individual and probably represent the favorite system of classification of the authors of the test. One special feature of this test is the "no count," which is simply the number of *no* answers given. An excessively high or low "no count" is said to be an indication of the invalidity of the test. This "no count" may be said to be a precursor of a series of attempts to develop indicators of the extent to which a given test score represents honest responses of the particular subject who took it. The test seems to have been mainly notable for this feature, but, like many pioneering efforts, failed to achieve wide acceptability. Those who developed later diagnostic instruments undoubtedly benefited from the technical weaknesses and limitations of the device, particularly with reference to lack of an adequate basis for selecting and validating the items.

The Minnesota Multiphasic Personality Inventory

A more recent type of inventory of the diagnostic type, and more conventional than the Humm-Wadsworth Inventory in the categories used, is that known as the Minnesota Multiphasic Personality Inventory (12). The basic work on the development and construction of the instrument is described in four papers by Hathaway and McKinley (9, 10, 16, 17), who are the authors of the instrument. The device consists of 550 statements drawn from a pool of items used in previous inventories. The following examples illustrate the great variety of items that are included:

I am inclined to take things hard.
I believe my sins are unpardonable.
I was a slow learner in school.
I have a good appetite.
I loved my father.

The final collection of items included in the test covers a great range of topics. The subject responds to the items by indicating whether they apply to him, do not apply to him, or that he is not sure. The inventory is scored in terms of the following nine scales: (1) hypochondriasis, (2) depression, (3) hysteria, (4) psychopathic deviate, (5) masculinity-femininity, (6) psychasthenia, (7) paranoia, (8) schizophrenia, and (9) hypomania.

In addition to the scores on these nine scales, three additional scores are also computed from the schedule. These are as follows:

1. A so-called "lie scale" which is claimed to indicate any tendency to falsify responses. It includes items such as "I have never defrauded any one." The assumption is that any person who indicates that such a statement applies to him is not telling the truth.

2. An F scale, which is supposed to indicate whether the individual understands the question. The nature of the score on this scale does not seem clear.

3. A ? scale, which is a count of the number of items which the examinee responds to by marking the question-mark sign on the answer sheet to indicate that he cannot give either a *yes* or a *no* response. A high score on this scale indicates that the other scores are probably invalid.

These scores are referred to as *validating scores*. This implies that unless the individual obtains scores within certain limits on these variables, scores on the other variables cannot be considered to be valid. Of course, the converse of this is not true, for even if the scores do fall within certain intervals on these scales, there is still no guarantee that the scores actually are valid. Hathaway and McKinley (11) also point out that certain individuals may display unusually high scores on the F scale and still have valid scores on the other scales in the series. This seems true of certain psychotic groups.

The procedure for developing the scale was strictly empirical and involved the administration of the entire group of 550 items to groups of individuals showing clear cases of hypochondriasis, depression, hysteria, and the rest, and this was followed by a comparison of the responses of these individuals with the responses of a group of seven hundred "normal" individuals. Items were then selected which discriminated between hypochondriacal patients and normals, depressive patients and normals, and so on. Hathaway and McKinley imply that the "normal" group represents a cross section of the Minnesota population between the ages of sixteen and fifty-five, but since they were all cases applying for treatment at the University Hospital, Minneapolis, Minnesota, they must to some extent represent a selected group. In obtaining the groups with specific abnormalities, considerable effort was made to insure that the cases selected actually suffered from these abnormalities. However, the care with which the groups were selected does not entirely compensate for the fact that some of them were relatively small. Despite this deficiency, the claim is made that a high score on a scale is found to predict the presence of the corresponding symptom in 60 per cent of the cases.

Satisfactory validation of the Minnesota Multiphasic Personality Inventory for the purpose for which it was developed still needs to be undertaken. While there are numerous studies which describe relationships of measures on the inventory with measures derived from other tests and questionnaires, the evaluation of the instrument as a clinical device does not seem to provide consistent answers to the same question. The clinician may interpret each score as a separate entity or he may attempt to analyze the profile as a whole, taking into account the relationship among scores. The latter procedure seems to be preferred by those who have used the instrument in clinical practice, and Meehl (18), following this procedure, attempted to carry out a validating experiment. By inspecting the profiles and then sorting them into categories, he was able to diagnose correctly about two-thirds of the patients included in the study. When an attempt was made to classify patients into the two categories of normal and abnormal on the basis of fairly well-defined criteria, he found that only 9 per cent of the normals were classified as abnormal and 36 per cent of the abnormals were classified as normal.

Somewhat contradictory results were achieved by Hunt (14) and his associates in making blind diagnoses on mental patients in a veterans' hospital. In this study 30 per cent of the 110 profiles were excluded as being unclassifiable, which should have increased the chances of the remainder being correctly classified, but the degree to which correct classifications were made was not superior to what might be expected to occur on a chance basis.

The difficulty in the evaluation of these experiments is that no information is provided, nor can be available, on the validity of the diagnoses of the patients. It seems to be a common opinion held by psychiatrists that psychiatric diagnosis is far from perfect, and two psychiatrists will not show satisfactory agreement when a large number of hospital cases are to be classified. It is possible that differences in the validity of the so-called criterion may account for differences in the results of various studies. If this is the case, as it probably is, the instrument must be considered as one of considerable promise.

Diagnostic Inventories for Lower Age Levels

The inventory approach to the appraisal of personality has been very largely a venture related to the study of the adult. The language difficulties involved in the adaptation of verbal instruments for use with children have discouraged many from developing personality inventories for use with children. Another aspect of the development of these devices at the adult level is that much more is known about the structure of adult personality than is known about the personality of the child. The majority of studies of the structure and pathology of personality have been undertaken with adult groups.

However, at least one ambitious though perhaps ill-advised attempt has been made to develop a personality inventory for use with children.* This device, known as the California Test of Personality (27, 28), provides forms at five levels from kindergarten up to adult. Before an evaluation of the series is made, it is desirable to give a brief description of the kindergarten to third grade level of the tests which illustrates the problems of measurement involved in the most acute form. The latter test is organized in the following manner, with *eight items* in each subtest.

---

* At the time of publication a new personality inventory for the 11–17 year old group has been announced by Raymond B. Cattell and his associates at the University of Illinois. Evidence concerning the usefulness of this instrument is still lacking and it can be regarded only as an experimental device.

Part I.   Self-adjustment: Based on feelings of personal security.

     A.   Self-reliance
     B.   Sense of personal worth
     C.   Sense of personal freedom
     D.   Feeling of belonging
     E.   Freedom from withdrawing tendencies
     F.   Freedom from nervous symptoms

Part II.   Social adjustment: Based on feelings of social security.

     A.   Social standards
     B.   Social skills
     C.   Freedom from antisocial tendencies
     D.   Family relations
     E.   School relations
     F.   Community relations

It is quite obvious that subtest scores based on only eight items could not have much significance. The length of each subtest would be too short to provide adequate reliability, let alone validity, and yet the suggestion seems to be made that a profile of all scores on all subtests should be prepared. Reliability coefficients are given only for the two major parts of the inventory and both of these coefficients seem to be fairly adequate. However, evidence of validity is lacking almost entirely, since the section of the manual devoted to validity is concerned largely with a general discussion of the problem of validity. The major purposes of the inventory are to determine the extent to which the pupil is adjusting to the world, but the degree to which it is achieving this end is unknown.

Criticism of this type of instrument is not entirely fair unless some recognition is given to the difficulty of validating an instrument of this kind. The ultimate validation of the instrument requires that the scores on each scale be compared with evidence of the degree of existence or absence of the characteristic that the inventory is claimed to measure. The practical difficulties involved in this may seem to be almost insuperable. For example, the collection of evidence concerning the individual's "sense of personal freedom" can be undertaken only in a clinical interview situation, and the validity of the evidence collected in this situation may be most inadequate, for the subject may not be willing to provide the necessary evidence. Similar difficulties apply to other categories.

There are, in addition, the limitations produced by the inventory approach itself. An inventory of this type is likely to measure a general factor which in the literature has generally been called "neuroticism" for lack of a more definite name.

Finally, there is one powerful argument against the use of the inventory approach at the lower age levels which seems almost strong enough to eliminate such devices for consideration as potential measuring instruments. The argument is that to a very considerable degree the child has not yet learned to attach language symbols to his emotional states. Dollard and Miller (5) have been largely responsible for pointing out the significance of this fact, and an important aspect of the therapeutic system which they advocate involves the naming and identifying of internal states. For these writers, a part of the process of growing up and developing mature response systems involves the development of a language system for describing inner states. From the standpoint of Dollard and Miller, it would be quite unfeasible to study the emotional problems of a child in terms of his language responses to a language stimulus. For this reason alone, the California Test of Personality for use at the lower age levels must be considered as of very doubtful value even for experimental purposes.

ALTERNATIVES TO THE INVENTORY APPROACH

Introduction

In most of the measures of personality which have been described in this chapter, measurements are made by subjecting the individual to a standard stimulus situation and then restricting his response to a few verbal categories such as "Yes" and "No." Some psychologists have felt that such an approach is unsatisfactory and have proposed the alternative one which requires that individuals be presented with standard stimulus situations and then be permitted a wide range of responses. Illustrations of this approach are presented by instruments in which a person is shown an ink blot and is asked what it resembles, or read part of a story and is asked to finish it. Tasks such as these permit great freedom of response and perhaps permit the individual to reveal his salient characteristics in a way which is not possible with an inventory approach. Of particular importance in this group of instruments are those which involve not only freedom of response but also the mechanism known as projection.

Projective Techniques

The term *projection* was first used by Freud in a technical sense to refer to a common *defense mechanism*. An illustration of this defense mechanism is seen when an individual ascribes to another an undesirable trait which is characteristic of himself but which he refuses to recognize in himself because recognition of it would arouse anxiety. It is as if the individual *projected* his own traits into the other individual. At the present time the term *projection* includes a much greater range of phenomena than Freud included within its scope, for it is recognized that a person may attribute to others his own good characteristics as well as those which he considers undesirable. He may also project his characteristics into inanimate objects.

The term *projection* is also used with reference to a large number of perceptual processes, as when an individual projects meaning into a stimulus situation which is so unstructured that different observers cannot agree upon the meaning of the situation. As a matter of fact, the essential feaure of most projective techniques used in assessment seems to be the presentation of a stimulus pattern which can be interpreted in a great variety of ways. The stimulus pattern may be an ink blot, an incomplete sentence or story, a sequence of sounds which resemble speech, a picture of some event, and so forth. Ingenuity can proliferate these stimulus patterns indefinitely. These indefinite stimulus patterns are interpreted by observers in a great variety of ways, and it is presumed that the particular interpretation selected depends upon the latent structure underlying the personality of the observer.

In another type of projective technique, the subject is asked to perform some action or series of actions and, since he is given considerable freedom in deciding on the task which he is to perform, his actions must be determined largely by events within himself. Illustrations of this kind of technique are seen in tests which involve drawings, handwriting, making designs with blocks, and so on.

In the latter tasks, as in the former, the instructions given are not sufficient to guide the subject's actions completely, and hence the course of action which he pursues must be partly determined by his own characteristics. For example, a person is instructed to "draw a man" and is given a sheet of paper and a pencil with which to execute the task. The person assigned this task must supply all the details. He must decide whether to draw the man either large or small, thin or fat, standing or sitting, with clothes drawn in detail or in hazy outline, or not at all, and so forth.

It is assumed that the decision he makes in these and in all other matters related to the task have determinants and are not arbitrary. It is also assumed in the use of these projective devices that the determinants of the behavior of the individual taking a projective instrument are significant elements in the structure of his personality. This assumption cannot always be justified. A person asked to "draw a man" may simply reproduce the sketch he has just observed in a magazine, or he may be an artist and make a sketch of another person in the room. A person asked to complete a story may use a story he read in the paper that morning. The determinants of behavior in taking a projective instrument are not necessarily significant aspects of personality.

When projective techniques are used, there may be powerful forces operating which prevent the individual from revealing important aspects of his behavior. A student to whom a projective instrument is being administered which is to determine whether he is to be admitted to a particular training program may be very reticent. His responses in this situation are likely to be commonplace and limited in number or length. The situation is threatening to the subject, who defends himself by playing safe and by not giving away much information about himself.

Some examples of projective techniques must now be considered so that problems of quantification can be given closer consideration.

Highly Unstructured Stimulus Situations

Stimulus situations used in projective techniques vary in the extent to which they are structured. If the stimulus is a picture which the subject is asked to interpret, the stimulus situation would be said to possess considerable structure. On the other hand, if an ink blot is the object to be interpreted, or if the stimulus object is a sequence of meaningless sounds similar to speech only in intonation, then the stimulus situation would be said to be highly unstructured. In the latter situation, it is impossible for the person being examined to use many cues in deciding on the organization to impose or the meaning to project into the stimulus situation The best-developed projective technique which makes use of a highly unstructured situation is the Rorschach, which is of much greater interest to the clinician than to the educator. However, since our understanding of projective techniques is derived to a tremendous extent from knowledge accumulated in the use of the Rorschach, a brief discussion of this instrument seems appropriate.

The Rorschach technique was originally developed by a Swiss psychiatrist by whose name the test is known (23). It consists of a sequence of ten cards, each one of which presents an ink blot which may be in black and white or have colors in addition. The blots themselves were originally selected by Hermann Rorschach himself from thousands which he tried out. The significance of the series of blots lies not only in the fact that each blot has been selected on the basis of sound reasons, but also because the blots have been selected to form a definite sequence. They should not be used in just any sequence, since it is important, for example, that card 2 follow card 1, and not the reverse.

One of Rorschach's major discoveries was that features other than content are important in interpreting what a person sees in a blot. Psychologists prior to Rorschach had made extensive analyses of the responses of individuals to ink blots, but the emphasis was on _what_ they saw. Rorschach realized that the most significant aspects of a response might be discovered by a study of factors other than content. Rorschach developed a system of classifying the responses according to what he considered were the most important features. The basic essential of Rorschach's system is to give each response a twofold classification in terms of its "location" and in terms of the apparent determinants of the response. By location is meant whether a response names some object represented by the blot as a whole or whether it refers to some major or minor detail. By the determinant of a response is meant whether the response is to the outline of the blot (form), to the color, to the shading, to movement (as when a person states that he sees a running dog), or to some other aspect of the blot.

Certain categories of content are also given special emphasis in the interpretation of the report, such as the meaning of human or animal objects. At the present time there are several recording systems in use. These systems show agreement in terms of the general nature of the categories used but differ to some extent in the symbols used for shorthand purposes in recording and describing the responses. They also differ in the extent to which they involve detail in the system of classification. The general approach which the individual may have to the task as a whole may also have significance. For example, contrast the approach of the following pair of individuals:

Individual A. This individual approaches the task of interpreting each blot in a systematic manner. He first interprets the blot as a whole. He then breaks down the blot into major sections and gives an interpretation to each section. Finally he interprets some of the smaller elements.

Individual B. This individual seems to have no system in his approach. He takes quite a time in settling down to the task and then spends his time interpreting minor details.

Unfortunately, Rorschach did not live long enough to see his work acclaimed by the world as a major development in psychological assessment, but he must be credited with having evolved every major idea on which present Rorschach technique is based. The subsequent work of Beck, Hertz, Klopfer, and others must be considered as that of refining the techniques developed by Rorschach rather than of introducing major innovations.

The emphasis on noncontent factors does not mean that content should be disregarded. The competent Rorschach administrator uses every possible source of information, and in recent times there has been a renewed emphasis on content, particularly with reference to the symbolism which the content manifests.

At the present time the administration of the Rorschach requires the services of a competent clinician who has had special training in the technique. This is a consequence of the kind of psychological theory of behavior on which the instrument is based. The fact that the response of the subject is not rigidly controlled to a few categories makes it possible for the individual to manifest a great variety of behaviors. In the final analysis of the Rorschach record, which usually consists of a written interpretation, the individual is described in terms of whatever characteristics are appropriate in describing his personality. These characteristics may not be appropriate in describing any other person. In the ultimate analysis, the administration of a Rorschach is a study of how the individual responds to an unusual situation. The detailed record of this study can be used sometimes to make generalizations concerning the individual's behavior in other situations.

It is quite beyond the scope of this book to summarize the procedures that are followed in the interpretation of the record of a person's responses to the blots. The method of interpretation is extremely difficult to teach, because scores derived, such as the number of movement responses, will be interpreted differently as other scores vary. The interpretation of a score depends upon the pattern of scores as a whole. However, in order to illustrate the kind of information that is found in a report of a Rorschach administration, the following interpretations of the responses of an individual are given:

Report of a Rorschach Administered to a Girl Aged Seventeen

A. *Intellectual aspects.* High average or better. She has good abilities but is not working up to capacity. Almost everything she said had to be pulled out of her. She is apathetic and her productivity is low but she is definitely capable of doing more. She is concrete in her mental approach and her capacity to do abstract thinking is limited. Her thinking is commonplace but shows common sense and adequate contact with reality. She is also quite careful and shows some concern about doing well.

B. *Emotional aspects.* She shows a very passive, constricted, and withdrawn personality. She lacks spontaneity and vitality, and functions well only when pushed. There is no evidence of any acute anxiety state. Neither is there evidence of marked depression or of psychotic or neurotic breakdown. Her performance provides more a picture of depersonalization; that is to say, there is a lack of adequate ego development which carries with it little capacity for establishing emotional relationships.

Although at the present time she shows little self-assertion and practically no emotional spontaneity, she has capacities for developing both her inner life and warm human relationships. It is probable that she defends herself against outside stimulation because she is not ready to accept the concomitant responsibilities. She is a sensitive girl and fearful of being hurt. Also she feels very insecure and needs affection and warmth. Another reason for her difficulty in handling emotional relationship is her limited experience along these lines.

C. *Summary.* Emotionally she is very withdrawn and restricted. If encouragement and understanding is offered her she could develop adequate human relationships. The test indicates that if such opportunities are not provided she may withdraw even further.

The reader should not assume that the information given in such a report is necessarily correct. Indeed, one can be sure that only a limited amount of it is sound, and at the present time there is no way of separating the correct from the incorrect information. There is also no way of knowing the extent to which the individual's responses to the Rorschach were determined by such irrelevant factors as his attitude toward the person administering the technique. The reader would do well to study carefully an article by Miller (19), which discusses the numerous ways in which responses to the Rorschach cards can be influenced by irrelevant aspects of the situation.

The Validation of the Rorschach Technique

Hermann Rorschach made his technique available as an experimental instrument which still had to be systematically studied. The kind of developmental research which Rorschach envisaged has never been fully undertaken, not so much because of an unwillingness on the part of clinicians to develop such studies, but because of the almost insuperable difficulties which such studies entail. If it were possible to interpret single scores meaningfully, without reference to other scores, the problem of validation would be a relatively simple one. It would involve the comparison of scores such as number of movement responses with the type of behavior which the score is supposed to predict. However, this simple situation does not exist, and validation must consist of demonstrating the relationship between the total behavior pattern manifested in the test situation and the pattern manifested in other situations. Limited attempts have been made to do this by making a comparison between the interpretations given to Rorschach records by persons who had never known the persons examined and some other record of the behavior of these persons. On this basis some agreement has been found between blind diagnosis made in this way and diagnosis made on other bases. Of course, the fact that the instrument has been shown to have value in diagnosing mental disease does not justify the conclusion that it is of value for making other types of predictions.

Although the evidence concerning the validity of the instrument is still most inadequate, a promising fact to be considered is that some of the hypotheses which have been tested concerning the value of the technique have been substantiated. Whether this will be true of the future remains to be seen, and although some of the hypotheses developed in clinical situations will later be rejected, it nevertheless seems to be one of the most promising clinical instruments yet developed. A serious difficulty in the use of the instrument stems from the fact that responses are influenced by such uncontrolled factors as the attitudes of the person who administers it.

The Picture-Interpretation Type of Assessment

Another projective device for the assessment of personality grew out of an attempt by Morgan and Murray (20) to develop a picture-interpretation instrument. A first description of the test, known as the Thematic Apperception Test, was given in the literature in 1935, and in 1938 in Murray's *Explorations in Personality* (21), an attempt was made to interpret the results of the technique in terms of a general theory of personality. The essential feature of this technique is that the individual is shown a picture and is asked to tell a story about it. It is hypothesized that phantasies thus reported are in some ways reflections of important factors which influence the individual's behavior in other situations. In general, it is held that an instrument of this kind may reveal the wishes, hopes, fears—that is, motives—as they are expressed in phantasies. There are substantial difficulties involved in the use of the data derived from devices of this kind, and although ingenious attempts have been made to develop scoring systems, as that developed by Tomkins (25), the main practical value of the instrument seems to be in the way in which the material may be used to enrich characterizations based on other information. Many clinicians *feel* that the data derived from the Thematic Apperception Test enable them to give fuller and more precise descriptions of individuals than would be possible from an interview alone. In the last sentence, the word *feel* was deliberately italicized to indicate that clear-cut evidence is largely lacking to show that this use of the instrument is justified. On the other hand, there are a large number of related facts which all point in the same direction and which indicate that phantasies are revealing forms of behavior. The Thematic Apperception Test seems to have had very limited application in education largely because it was developed for use with adults. However, other instruments have been developed which can be applied to younger groups.

Symonds (26), taking his cues from the Thematic Apperception Test, prepared a series of pictures designed primarily to elicit characteristic phantasies in adolescents. These pictures were developed according to criteria which Symonds (25) himself developed as a result of a preliminary study.

According to these criteria the pictures should lack detail in their background, should be vague in theme and content, and should portray characters with whom the subjects might identify themselves. Thus the pictures developed by Symonds represent almost an impressionistic type of art, in which the main characters are adolescents who are shown in various situations which involve either other adolescents or adults. A few of the pictures include no human characters. In spite of the attempt to make the pictures relatively unstructured, it is generally agreed by those who inspect them that they embody what artists refer to as "a great deal of feeling"; that is, there is some uniformity of response toward them.

Symonds collected 1,680 stories told by forty adolescents about the series of forty-two pictures. These stories provide a rich addition to the chronicles of the phantasy life of adolescents. In order to demonstrate how this type of assessment procedure may provide useful information for the educator, two quotations from Symonds (26) are given here:*

* By permission from *Adolescent Fantasy,* by Percival M. Symonds. Copyright, 1949, Columbia University Press.

From the stories collected in this study it can be assumed that adolescents dream of success and achievement, but rather unrealistically. Getting a job and money were persistent concerns, but many stories were built around the theme of making one's way in the world. The Horatio Alger theme of starting at the bottom of the ladder in a lowly position, rising gradually through hard work (and luck) and eventually becoming manager of the business or head of the firm was not at all uncommon, with the additional possibility of marrying the boss's daughter. *Ambition,* with eventual success, less frequently was directed towards a school or college career. Many of the stories were unrealistic about money. It came easily and in large quantities. If it could not be earned, there was always the possibility of robbing a bank or inheriting a legacy. There seem to be no brakes to financial speculation in this area. [26, p. 221.]

*   *   *

Educators need to be aware of the fantasies that adolescents have with regard to *school*. School, instead of being a happy place, is to them a place which arouses anxiety. Punishment and the threat of failure hang over many of these adolescent storytellers. To them school was a place of assigned tasks, a challenge to success, and the dread of failure. If one wanted to be and was successful, there might be the faraway and shadowy bliss of college in prospect. Teachers were almost always stern, threatening, and avenging figures—seldom was any affection shown by or for them. Homework became a burden and was a further source of conflict with parents. [26, p. 223.]

These quotations illustrate the kinds of uses of picture-interpretation techniques in education. They are primarily of use in diagnosing the difficulties and problems with which the individual is faced, but probably have limited value in assessing the level of development of the individual with respect to certain social characteristics. There is, however, one recent development in the use of picture-interpretation tests which still needs to be considered.

McClelland and a group of scientists (15) have developed a method of scoring picture-interpretation tests for certain aspects of motivation. For example, it is possible to score an interpretation of a picture for the extent to which it reflects need for achievement or need to belong to a group. McClelland has developed a scoring system of substantial reliability which can be applied, and the scores have been demonstrated to be related to motivational conditions. For example, when the test is administered at times when the individual's need for achievement is aroused, scores will be higher than when he is tested under apathetic circumstances. It can also be shown that at times when he is well motivated and his output is high in performing certain simple tasks, his achievement-need score is also high. The approach appears to be most promising.

The importance of McClelland's work seems to stem from the fact that he has succeeded in developing a projective technique which can be used to measure a single variable. Once this has been done the task of validating inferences based on scores becomes greatly simplified and it is extremely encouraging that McClelland has been able to demonstrate that scores on his instrument can be reasonably interpreted as measures of achievement motivation.

Other Projective Devices

Numerous other projective instruments have been developed for the study of personality. Play techniques, in which the child is given the opportunity of manipulating dolls and other equipment, have had a long history of development, but mainly as therapeutic techniques rather than as potential measuring instruments. Drawings have also been used extensively in connection with therapy, but in recent years there have been attempts to use drawings as assessment devices for the diagnosis of mental disease and for the prediction of behavior.

The most carefully studied of drawing techniques is based on the simple administrative procedure of providing the individual with a blank sheet of paper and pencil and asking him to "draw a person." The tendency for individuals to project their own body image into their drawings is seen in the simple fact that males tend to draw males and females tend to draw females. As a matter of fact there are few exceptions to this rule. Undoubtedly some individuals much more than others base their drawings on their own image of themselves, but in any case the process is largely unconscious.

For further information about projective techniques, the reader is referred to a comprehensive book on the subject by Anderson and Anderson (2).

Other Types of Test with Limited Restrictions on the Response

Other types of test situations, in addition to projective techniques, have been developed which place few restrictions on the response of the individual who is tested. Most of these other instruments present tasks which are essentially intellectual in nature, but two other conditions are also introduced into the situation. First, the individual is frustrated in some way from achieving the goal which is set. Second, it is arranged so that the individual is highly ego-involved in the task. The outcome of the test is a description of how the individual behaved in undertaking this task under these special conditions.

Some of the most interesting examples of this approach to the assessment of personality are provided by the wartime work of the Office of Strategic Services. To some extent the devices used in that program were adaptations of those which had been developed previously in Europe, but it seems to have been one of the first attempts to use such devices on a systematic basis.

The Assessment Program of the Office of Strategic Services

The assessment program of the Office of Strategic Services (22) represents one of the most interesting and colorful approaches to the study of personality. Although the program has been widely criticized because of the lack of evidence of the validity of the devices which it included, its importance must not be minimized because as an imaginative venture it has been a significant source of ideas. The assessment program was developed for the purpose of attempting to predict the service careers of men and women recruited for the Office of Strategic Services. Altogether 5,391 recruits underwent a three-day program of intensive study at an assessment center, and a small number passed through a shorter one-day program. The term "assessment" seems to have acquired widespread use through this program and was used in preference to the term "measurement" to indicate that judgments, characterizations, and descriptions were used in the making of predictions. While some traditional-type tests were used which yielded scores, the most interesting of the test situations developed provided only qualitative data about how the individual reacted in the given situation.

In describing the procedures used, the authors of the volume which describes the program indicate that one of the most important features of the testing procedure was the fact that the personnel examined and the assessment staff lived together during the three-day period, and the examinees, referred to as the students, were under constant scrutiny from the moment of arriving at the assessment center to the moment of departure. It was, therefore, possible to observe the students in a great variety of situations both planned and unplanned.

A major difficulty in the development of the entire assessment program was the great variety of jobs to which the students were to be assigned. Often the nature of these jobs was known only in the vaguest terms, and there must have been occasions when it was impossible to know in advance the tasks which a person might have to undertake on his assignment. If a man was sent into enemy territory for the purpose of obtaining certain information, he might have no way of knowing just what situations he might have to handle in order to obtain the necessary information. The fact that the nature of the job was largely unpredictable may have made it almost impossible to predict individual success or failure on a given assignment. This is a point of considerable importance, because psychologists know that predictions will be most successful when full information is available concerning the nature of the situations in which predictions are to be made.

A striking example of the devices developed in this program is the Construction Test. The essential materials for this test consisted of a number of poles and some blocks into which the poles could be fitted and then pegged in position. These materials resembled a large-scale Tinker Toy outfit, with poles up to seven feet in length. The student was assigned the task of building a structure in the form of a cube with diagonals across each of the four sides. In order to handle this construction problem, the student was given the help of two assistants who were, in reality, stooges of the assessment staff. The task was so arranged that it could not be completed by a single person in the time allowed.

The essential feature of the Construction Test does not lie in the mechanical nature of the task but in the relationship of the individual tested to his two helpers. One of these played a passive role and did absolutely nothing unless ordered to do so. The other played an aggressive role of offering impractical suggestions, criticizing the subject and his plans, objecting to the way in which directions were given, making personal comments about the subject, engaging in irrelevant discussion, distracting him from the task, and in general interfering with the effective completion of the project. With all this needling, the stooges were, nevertheless, supposed to obey actual orders.

In this type of situation, it did not seem feasible to score the subject for his performance on the task. More important was it to classify the kind of solution which he selected for the problem. Some subjects faced with this situation would give up. Others would dismiss the helpers and attempt to do the task alone, which was an impossible goal to accomplish in the time allotted. Still others became authoritarian toward the helpers. A few became angry, and the report records that more than one lost his temper to the extent of striking one of the helpers with his fist. Some offered more acceptable solutions, such as first giving the men a proper orientation and then handling them in a kid-gloves manner, and laughing off their criticism. Although the assessment staff is right in saying that "Just what was measured in this situation is difficult to state exactly" (22, p. 111), the concept of making assessments in terms of the kind of solution which an individual selects in a frustrating situation is a concept of considerable importance.

The subjects in this situation knew that they were being tested and that they were being observed by the assessment staff; hence it is reasonable to wonder whether this fact may not have modified the student's behavior and enabled him to take a more detached and objective view of the situation than would have been the case otherwise. One very surprising item of information in the report of the administration of the test is that the majority of the students entered fully into the situation and became thoroughly ego-involved in its outcome. This seems clear from the number of cases who showed emotional disturbances of a fairly severe nature during the test. The same tendency to become deeply involved in an assigned role was also noticeable in another situation in which the subject was mercilessly cross-questioned about an alibi which he had concocted to cover up an imaginary offense he was told he had committed. Although he was aware of the fact that the role he was playing was fictitious and that the cross-questioning was no more real than a stage play, many showed severe emotional strain which was of such a degree that they were unable to complete the three days of testing. It is quite possible that some individuals reveal salient characteristics in situations of this kind because they fall easily into the roles assigned to them; others may not because they may play roles from which they remain emotionally detached in the testing situation. Most cases will probably fall in between these two extremes.

It is not the intention here to discuss the validation of the tests developed in the project, because the value of the work it encompassed lies in the ideas developed and not in the validity of the instruments.

Summary

1. In this chapter it has been pointed out that psychologists have devoted their attention in the field of personality mainly to the problem of identifying and measuring traits which have wide applicability in the description of the behavior of most individuals. Traits which are descriptive of the behavior of only a small minority of individuals have received little attention, although such traits would have to be measured in any battery capable of describing the salient behavior characteristics of all individuals.

2. Three major approaches to the development of systems for describing personality were discussed. These involved ratings, inventories, and free responses to standardized situations. The merits and limitations of each one of these approaches may be summarized as follows:

a. *Ratings*. The value of rating scales lies in the fact that they serve the purpose of indicating which aspects of behavior are to be observed and how the observations are to be recorded. Since ratings have extensive use in schools, procedures for developing rating scales were considered in detail. It must always be kept in mind that the value of a rating can never be more than the value of the observation on which it is based.

b. *Inventories*. The types of inventories considered have little immediate application in school situations because little is known about what they can be used to predict. This judgment does not apply to interest inventories, which will be considered in a separate chapter and which have extensive educational applications.

c. *Free Responses to Standardized Situations*. The instruments considered in this category have great promise but require special skill for their application and interpretation. School psychologists with specialized training may be expected to make use of projective techniques and interpret the results to the teacher, who should have some familiarity with their uses and limitations.

3. Finally, it should be noted that the instruments discussed in this chapter refer mainly to social aspects of personality where measurement procedures are least adequately developed. Greater practical success has been achieved in measuring attitudes and interests which are personality characteristics that the teacher can not only measure but also change. It is these latter characteristics which are of great educational significance to which the following two chapters will be devoted.

References

1. Allport, Gordon W., *Personality; a Psychological Interpretation*, New York, Henry Holt and Company, 1937, pp. 588 + XIV.

2. Anderson, Harold H. and Anderson, Gladys L., *An Introduction to Projective Techniques*, New York, Prentice-Hall, Inc. 1951, pp. 720 + XXIV.

3. Bernreuter, R. G., *Personality Inventory*, Stanford, California, Stanford University Press, 1931.

4. Cattell, Raymond B., *Personality*, New York, McGraw-Hill Book Company, Inc., 1950, pp. 689 + XII.

5. Dollard, John and Miller, Neal E., *Personality and Psychotherapy*, New York, McGraw-Hill Book Company, Inc., pp. 488 + XIII.

6. Flanagan, John C., *Factor Analysis in the Study of Personality*, Stanford, California, Stanford University Press, 1935, pp. 103 + X.

7. Guilford, J. P. and Martin, H. G., *Personal Inventory* I, Beverly Hills, California, Sheridan Supply Company, 1943.

8. Hartshorne, Hugh and May, Mark A., *Studies in the Nature of Character*. I. *Studies in Deceit*, New York, The Macmillan Company, 1928, pp. 306 + XXI.

9. Hathaway, S. R. and McKinley, J. C., "A Multiphasic Personality Schedule (Minnesota) : I. Construction of the Schedule," *Journal of Psychology*, 10, 1940, 249–254.

10. Hathaway, S. R. and McKinley, J. C., "A Multiphasic Personality Schedule" (Minnesota) : III. The Measurement of Symptomatic Depression." *Journal of Psychology*, 14, 1942, 63–84.

11. Hathaway, S. R. and McKinley, J. C., *Manual for the Minnesota Multiphasic Personality Inventory*, New York, The Psychological Corporation, 1951, pp. 16.

12. Hathaway, S. R. and McKinley, J. C., *Minnesota Multiphasic Personality Inventory*, Revised Edition, New York, The Psychological Corporation, 1947.

13. Humm, Doncaster G. A. and Wadsworth, Guy W., *Humm-Wadsworth Temperament Scale*, Los Angeles, California, Humm Personnel Service, 1940.

14. Hunt, Howard F., Carp, Abraham, Cass, William A., Winder, C. L., and Kantor, Robert, "A Study of the Differential Diagnostic Efficiency of the Minnesota Multiphasic Personality Inventory," *Journal of Consulting Psychology*, 12, 1948, 331–336.

15. McClelland, David C., Atkinson, John W., Clark, Russell A., and Lowell, Edgar L., *The Achievement Motive*, New York, Appleton-Century-Crofts, Inc., 1953, pp. 384.

16. McKinley, J. C. and Hathaway, S. R., "A Multiphasic Personality Schedule" (Minnesota) : II. A Differential Study of Hypochondriasis," *Journal of Applied Psychology*, 10, 1940, 255–268.

17. McKinley, J. C. and Hathaway, S. R., "A Multiphasic Personality Schedule (Minnesota) : IV. Psychasthenia," *Journal of Applied Psychology*, 26, 1942, 614–624.

18. Meehl, P. E. and Hathaway, S. R., "Profile Analysis of the Minnesota Multiphasic Personality Inventory," *Journal of Applied Psychology*, 30, 1946, 525–564.

19. Miller, Daniel R., "Prediction of Behavior by Means of the Rorschach Test," *Journal of Abnormal and Social Psychology*, 1953 48, 367–375.

20. Morgan, C. D. and Murray, H. A., "A Method for Investigating Phantasies: The Thematic Apperception Test," *Archives of Neurology and Psychiatry*, 34, 1935, 289–306.

21. Murray, H. A., *Explorations in Personality*, New York, Oxford University Press, 1938, pp. 761 + XIV.

22. Office of Strategic Services, Assessment Staff, *Assessment of Men*, New York, Rinehart and Company, 1948, pp. 541 + XV.

23. Rorschach, Hermann, *Psychodiagnostics,* New York, Grune and Stratton, 1942, pp. 226.

24. Super, Donald E., "The Bernreuter Personality Inventory," *Psychological Bulletin,* 39, 1942, 94–125.

25. Symonds, Percival M., "Criteria for the Selection of Pictures for the Investigation of Adolescent Fantasies," *Journal of Abnormal and Social Psychology,* 34, 1939, 271–274.

26. Symonds, Percival M., *Adolescent Fantasy,* New York, Columbia University Press, 1949, pp. 397 + XII.

27. Thorpe, Louis P., Clark, Willis W., and Tiegs, Ernest W., "Manual of Directions," *California Test of Personality* (Primary Series), 1954.

28. Thorpe, Louis P., Clark, Willis W., and Tiegs, Ernest W., *California Test of Personality* (Kindergarten to Third Grade), California Test Bureau, 1954.

29. Thurstone, L. L., "A Neurotic Inventory," *Journal of Social Psychology,* 1, 1930, 3–31.

30. Tomkins, Silvan S., *The Thematic Apperception Test,* New York, Grune and Stratton, 1946, pp. 297 + IX.

31. Woodworth, Robert S., *Personal Data Sheet,* Chicago, Illinois, C. H. Stoelting and Company, 1917.

CHAPTER 10

The Measurement of Attitudes

THE CONSTRUCTION OF VERBAL ATTITUDE SCALES

Introduction

The previous chapter presented a discussion of procedures for measuring those personality traits which are believed to permeate a wide range of behavior. Among the traits considered were social traits which, it was pointed out, are not particularly amenable to measurement. A much more promising area both for producing pupil change and for measuring the changes produced is that of attitudes. In this area, it is possible for the teacher who has limited knowledge of statistics to build instruments of quality and to measure the extent to which experimental curricula are achieving specific objectives.

The Concept of Attitude

Murphy (13, p. 279) has pointed out that a study of the early development of the individual child reveals that attitudes are first manifested in simple postural responses of acceptance or rejection. Afterreactions, similar to those which accompany these early responses, eventually become characteristic of the individual's orientation to almost every situation he encounters. The child acquires a multitude of positive and negative responses to situations and symbols which color and to a considerable extent determine his relationship to the culture in which he lives. These positive and negative responses do not develop merely as a result of a maturational process, for they seem to be to a considerable extent learned responses to situations, learned as a result of satisfying or frustrating experiences. Some of these experiences are deliberately planned by the adults with whom the child comes into contact, while others are incidental, unplanned experiences which may be only coincidental in character.

The early childhood patterns, with their apparent simplicity, seem to become increasingly complex as the child grows, until the effective experiences of the individual may be so complex that neither he nor any clinical psychologist can ever disentangle all the elements involved. Consider, for example, the common attitude of the adult toward his parents. On the surface it is friendly and even protective, but as every clinical psychologist knows, it is often underneath extremely hostile and aggressive. An individual may have, at one and the same time, opposing attitudes toward the same object. In the case of the individual's attitude toward his parents, it is hardly surprising that it should always contain both negative and positive elements, since they are rooted in the innumerable satisfying and frustrating experiences which parents provide for their children.

The study of attitudes is also complicated by the fact that a person may reveal different attitudes when exposed to different situations. Imagine a situation in which a teacher is being visited in her classroom by the local superintendent of schools. In discussing his observations with the principal, he comments on the fact that the teacher seemed to have such a *friendly attitude* toward the children in her class. The principal says that this is not the teacher's *real* attitude toward the children, because in the ordinary way she becomes very hostile in class when provoked, and shows a high frequency of aggressive behavior in conducting her class. What the principal means by *real* attitude is the habitual mode of reaction of the teacher toward children in the classroom situation. This attitude manifested by the teacher toward children in the ordinary course of events is no more real, nor less real, than the attitude manifested in the presence of the supervisor. It is simply that the one type of behavior is characteristic of the teacher under one set of circumstances, while the other type of behavior is characteristic under other circumstances. If it is desired to measure the attitude of the teacher toward the children on a continuum of hostility-friendliness, it is important to specify the circumstances that prevail when the measurement is undertaken. If the attitude of the teacher is appraised in some way under circumstances in which she is highly motivated to show a friendly attitude, the measured attitude will be at the friendly end of the scale, while under other circumstances the measured attitude might be at the other end of the scale. In most cases, what is desired is to measure the attitude of the teacher as it is inferred from the characteristic classroom behavior and uninfluenced by the presence of a supervisor.

In the measurement of pupil attitudes exactly the same problem occurs. The goals of education aim at developing attitudes which will prevail in situations outside of the school. However, pupil attitudes are commonly measured in a situation in which pressures to conform to the attitudes approved by the school authorities are important influences in the situation. This does not mean that merely removing the children to a room outside of the school and measuring their attitudes in these new surroundings will provide measures of the out-of-school attitudes that it is desired to measure. The influence of the school and the faculty may be as great in the new surroundings as in the school itself.

Although the concept of attitude still needs clarification, there is also a need for defining more carefully the objects toward which attitudes are directed. Too often attempts are made to measure attitudes before the object of reference is properly defined; for example, when an attempt is made to measure "attitude toward democracy" when the concept of democracy is complex and differs in significant respects from one person to another.

It is convenient to follow Allport and make a distinction between a trait and an attitude. Allport (1) states that while both an attitude and a trait represent forms of *readiness for response*, an attitude is directed toward a specific object of reference. A person may have an attitude toward communism but be impulsive in a general way. The type of responses he makes toward various aspects of communism represent an attitude, but impulsiveness because it is a general characteristic and is not directed toward a particular object of reference is therefore called a trait. As attitudes become more and more general in the stimuli that arouse them, they become traits.

Opinions and Attitudes

Opinions are verbal statements hypothesized to be symptomatic of attitude. When individuals express opinions, their statements can be considered to reflect their position on a scale which represents all degrees from a very favorable attitude to a very unfavorable attitude. A single opinion may provide very limited evidence concerning a person's attitude, or it may supply enough to locate his position on a scale with considerable precision. When the opinion expressed represents an extreme viewpoint, it is more likely to place him correctly than when it represents a position nearer the middle of the scale.

Attitude scales represent attempts to place individuals on a single continuum on the basis of some expression of opinion which is accepted as evidence of the individual's position on that continuum. In the following sections, the various methods of constructing attitude scales that are commonly used are described and discussed with reference to their use and limitation in the assessment of attitude changes in pupils.

METHODS OF PREPARING ATTITUDE SCALES

The Social Distance Method of Attitude Scale Construction

The grandfather of all devices for the systematic measurement of attitude was developed by Bogardus (2), a sociologist who became interested in the problem of social distance between people of different races, different nationalities, and different religions. The Bogardus method of measurement was extremely simple and involved no complicated procedure for assigning scale values. He simply asked his subjects whether they would accept members of a given group in any of the following categories:

1. to close kinship by marriage
2. to my club as personal chums
3. to my street as a neighbor
4. to employment in my occupation
5. to citizenship in my country

6. to be visitors to my country only
7. would exclude from my country

This type of scale does have certain advantages over the Thurstone type of scale, which will be considered later. It attempts to measure attitude in terms of the action a person may be expected to take rather than in terms of the verbal stereotypes or expressed opinions which may not be too closely related to the actions an individual might take. Of course, there is no guaranty that what a person says he will do corresponds to what he will actually do in a given situation.

The Thurstone and Chave Method of Attitude-Scale Construction

It is evident that statements representing a range of opinions concerning some matter may be collected and arranged in order according to the extent to which they represent a favorable or unfavorable attitude. A person could then read these statements and select the one most nearly representative of his own attitude, and the position of the statement thus selected would represent a crude measure of the person's attitude. The instrument developed by this procedure would be unsatisfactory in many respects. There would be no assurance that the statements actually represented the full range of opinion, and neither would one be sure that the statements were properly distributed over the range of opinion covered. Adequate criteria for the selection of the statements included in the scale are needed, and psychologists who have worked on this problem have suggested a number of different criteria that might be used. The earliest systematic attempt to establish and use criteria for this purpose was due to the efforts of L. L. Thurstone and E. J. Chave (21). The method which these workers developed must now be considered, because it is still widely used for the construction of attitude scales.

A typical Thurstone and Chave type of attitude scale is shown in Figure 10.1 (6). This scale was designed to measure a variable which might be named "attitudes toward teaching." The numbers to the extreme left of the scale are the scale values which indicate the extent to which an item reflects a favorable or unfavorable attitude. When the scale is presented to the subject, there are no scale values indicated opposite each item. The score on the scale is the average scale value of the items to which the response of "Yes" is given. The scale values indicate the degree to which each statement was considered by a series of judges to represent a desirable or an undesirable attitude toward teaching as a profession.

FIGURE 10.1

Scale of Attitudes Toward Teaching

Below are a number of statements about teaching as a profession. Consider each statement carefully and write *yes* in the space before each statement with which you are in complete agreement and *no* before all other statements.

Scale Values

34_____ A good teacher should be an inspiration, a leader, and an adviser.

26_____ Teachers can teach parents to help their children.

0_____ The teaching profession does not need very bright people entering it.

33_____ The social prestige of teachers should be the same as that of lawyers, doctors, and ministers.

30_____ There is opportunity to grow and learn in the teaching profession.

4_____ The routine nature of teaching makes it unattractive to imaginative people.

7_____ The main attraction of teaching is that it offers financial security.

24_____ The financial rewards of teaching are a secondary matter in choosing it as a profession.

5_____ Teaching probably becomes monotonous after a few years.

1_____ Teaching is an occupation requiring relatively little skill.

35_____ The teacher plays a vital role in the development of good citizenship.

31_____ The work of teachers gives opportunity for expression—the work is creative, builds for the future.

18_____ A person whose main interest in teaching is that it provides a secure job should not be permitted to teach.

12_____ A teacher has to put up with many minor irritations in her work.

23_____ Students will inevitably have a high regard for good teachers.

2_____ Very able people would be wasting their time in teaching.

32_____ There are many personal rewards of the teaching profession—self-respect, personal worth, professional competence, sense of creative power.

Score = Sum of weighted "Yes" answers divided by number of "Yes" answers.

The scale also illustrates some of the limitations inherent in this type of scale. It is evident that it could not be usefully administered to college seniors enrolled in a teacher-education program because these students might be working under pressures which might make them feel compelled to endorse statements only at the favorable end of the scale. As a matter of fact, when this questionnaire was administered to a group of seniors in the school of education of a large university, the scores were bunched at the numerically high end of the scale and no score fell below twenty. While there was no way of determining with certainty whether these scores were influenced by the pressures of the situation, the personal knowledge which the writer had of the students indicated that not all of them thought so highly of teaching as a profession, and some probably did not have any properly crystallized attitude at all.

An examination of the attitude scale shown in Figure 10.1 reveals that the scale values are not assigned on the simple basis of arranging the statements in order and then numbering them. The entire Thurstone and Chave procedure for selecting statements is closely related to the procedure for assigning scale values, and hence it is necessary at this point to examine the steps which are prescribed by this method of attitude-scale construction.

The method of constructing a scale of attitudes toward any particular object, institution, or idea involves the following steps:

1. Several diverse groups are asked to write opinions about the particular object, institution, or idea. These statements should be brief and should be such that they can be endorsed or rejected in accordance with the attitude of the individual. Each statement must also supply evidence of a person's attitude. Statements should be neither ambiguous nor double barreled. Irrelevant statements should be discouraged by giving clear directions to the individuals expressing opinion. It should be noted that at this stage the written statements should cover the total range of opinion that it is desired to measure. A selection of these statements ultimately forms the attitude scale. Sometimes the statements are written by the person who is constructing the attitude scale. A psychologist interested in developing a scale of attitudes toward teaching as an occupation might start by writing a hundred statements representing a great variety of opinions over the total range for which it was desired to develop a measuring scale. Usually the individual who attempts to develop a range of expressions of opinions out of his own head will produce a less satisfactory series of statements than would be obtained from a group.

2. The statements are typed either on small slips of paper or on

small file cards. The cards are then given to subjects who are asked to sort them into a number of piles. In Thurstone's original demonstration of the method, individuals were asked to sort the statement into eleven piles, the series of piles representing an evenly graduated series of attitudes. The piles should not be described by phrases of the type used in graphic rating scales. This is important in order that the piles may *appear to represent a scale of equal intervals* according to the judgment of the individuals who sort the statements. The differences in attitude from one pile to the other should always appear equal.* It should be observed that the assumption is made that the sorting process does not involve the attitude of the sorter. Sorters who have fundamentally different attitudes should still be able to agree on whether one statement expresses a more or less favorable attitude than another.

3. In order to explain the next step, let it be assumed that one hundred individuals were used to sort the statements and that pile 1 represented the least favorable attitude and pile 11 the most favorable attitude. A table similar to that shown in Table 10.1 is then prepared for each item.

TABLE 10.1

Data Concerning Statement No. 6

Scale Value ——— Q ———	Pile 1	Pile 2	Pile 3	Pile 4	Pile 5	Pile 6	Pile 7	Pile 8	Pile 9	Pile 10	Pile 11
Number of times item was placed in each pile					5	8	13	17	34	23	
Cumulative frequency					5	13	26	43	77	100	

The above table is interpreted in the following way: For statement No. 6 there were five judges who placed it in pile 5, eight who placed it in pile 8, thirteen who placed it in pile 9, and so on. These frequencies are then accumulated from left to right in the lowest

---

* It should be noted that for this reason the method is commonly called the method of equal-appearing intervals. Suitable instructions for the judges who are to sort the statements are found in Thurstone and Chave (21, p. 31).

row on the table. The number 13 is obtained by adding 5 and 8, and 26 is obtained by adding 5, 8, and 13, and so forth.

The scale value for the item is the value which corresponds to a cumulative frequency of 50. In the case of the above statement, it would lie between 9 and 10 and is best determined graphically. This is done by plotting the data on a graph with the pile number on one axis and the cumulative frequency on the other, and the assumption is made that the pile number is the scale value for the mid-point of the pile. The graph shown in Figure 10.2 has been drawn from the data in the above table to show how this is done.

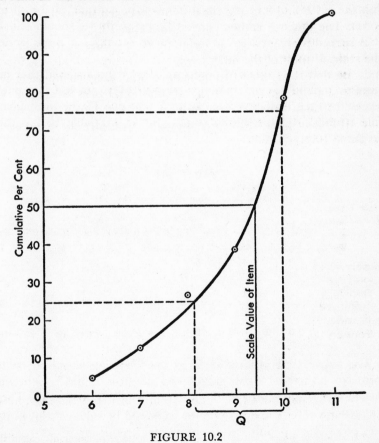

FIGURE 10.2

Graphical method of determining the scale value of the attitude item for which data are presented in Table 10.1.

From this graph, it is easy to read off the scale value corresponding to a cumulative frequency of 50, and this value is the scale value for the item.

The reader will have noticed that a space was left in Table 10.1 for a value indicated by the letter Q. The Q-value indicates the extent to which the statement represents a clearly defined point of view. Statements with high Q-values will be ambiguous or have other major defects. The Q-value is obtained from the graph by marking off the scale values which correspond to the 25 per cent and 50 per cent cumulative totals. In the graph then, the two values are 7.9 and 9.2, and the distance between them, the Q-value, is 1.3. The Q-value is then entered in Table 10.1.

A special problem arises in assigning scale values near the ends of the scale. If most of the judges assign a statement to pile 11, it may indicate that the statement might have been assigned by some subjects to a point beyond that pile if additional piles had been provided. In such cases the scale value is estimated from the data in pile 10 and in piles with lower numbers. Consider the data shown in Table 10.2.

TABLE 10.2

Data Concerning Statement No. 52

Scale Value _____

Q _____

	Pile 1	Pile 2	Pile 3	Pile 4	Pile 5	Pile 6	Pile 7	Pile 8	Pile 9	Pile 10	Pile 11
Number of times item was placed in each pile	0	0	0	0	0	0	2	6	9	22	61
Cumulative frequency							2	8	17	39	100

The data from piles 7, 8, 9, and 10 for this item would be plotted on a graph. The graph thus produced would be extrapolated to find the point corresponding to a cumulative frequency of 50 (50 per cent).

This procedure is illustrated in the graph shown in Figure 10.3.

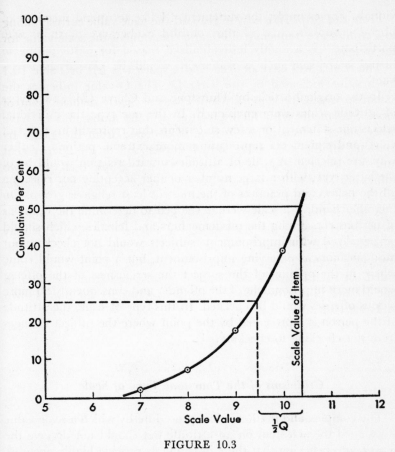

FIGURE 10.3

Graphical method of determining scale value of an attitude item for which data are presented in Table 10.2.

The value of Q in this case is found by taking the difference between the scale values corresponding to cumulative frequencies of 25 and 50 and then doubling this value.

4. From the data thus collected the final scale is built. The statements selected should have low Q-values and be well distributed over the entire range of scale values. In addition, Thurstone and Chave in their original study used a third criterion for selecting statements—that of relevance. The latter criterion is necessary because some of the statements apply only to a very small group of indi-

viduals. For example, the statement, "I like to attend meetings of liberal groups because of the youthful exuberance of those who participate," is a highly individualized reason for participating in liberal activities. Such a statement would be classed as irrelevant.

In the original article by Thurstone and Chave (21), two types of attitude scales were envisioned. In the one type the individual selects one statement or a few statements that represent his point of view, and statements representing more extreme positions, either way, are rejected. A scale of attitudes toward religion would be of the latter type, with a large number neither accepting nor rejecting all the beliefs and practices of the most or least religious group. On the other hand, if a scale were developed to determine the opinions of persons concerning the misdemeanors and felonies which should be penalized with imprisonment, subjects would not check minor misdemeanors as deserving imprisonment, but a point would come where in the opinion of the subject the seriousness of the offense would merit imprisonment of the offender and consequently all more serious offenses would be checked. In this type of scale, the attitude of the person is represented by the point where the subject changes from not checking to checking.

Criticisms of the Thurstone Type of Scale

The complex and mathematical procedure by which a scale value is assigned to each item on an attitude test should not deceive the reader into believing that these instruments provide highly accurate measures of attitudes. These scales are only devices for describing on a numerical scale the opinions which individuals express. It is evident that these attempts to describe opinions in such simple terms are often most inadequate. A person's opinions do not usually show the high degree of organization which the builders of scales must assume them to have.

In addition, it must be kept in mind that verbal attitude scales sample only a limited range of behavior, namely, verbal behavior. It is common knowledge that verbal behavior does not always bear a simple relationship to other forms of behavior.

These cautions, which must be kept in mind in using and interpreting the Thurstone type of scale, apply also to other types of verbal scales which must now be considered.

Other Methods of Constructing Attitude Scales

The Thurstone and Chave method of constructing attitude scales is one of several methods of developing such devices. It is probably the one that the teacher is most likely to use if he begins to adventure into this domain. However, some brief reference must be made to some of the other methods.

Likert (10) has developed a method which produces a scale rather different in form from that produced by the Thurstone and Chave method. The method of responding to a Likert scale is not that of selecting a "Yes" or a "No," but that of selecting one of a series of alternatives. The type of multiple response which Likert used in his original presentation of the technique involved the following alternative responses to each statement:

Strongly Approve   Approve   Undecided   Disapprove   Strongly Disapprove

This is not the only type of multiple response which Likert uses. Another type is illustrated by the following attitude-test item:

How far in the educational system (aside from trade education) should the most intelligent Negroes be allowed to go?

1. Grade school
2. Junior high school
3. High school
4. College
5. Graduate and professional school

Each question thus constitutes a short attitude scale in itself. This is an advantage, for it means that each item yields more information than do items to which there is only a Yes-No response. However, since the teacher will probably not be sufficiently familiar with the statistical techniques needed for developing a Likert-type scale, it will not be further elaborated upon here.

A still more complex procedure for developing attitude scales is that suggested by Guttman (8), who was impressed by the fact that, on attitude scales of the Thurstone type, individuals do not usually show a consistent set of opinions.

A person responding to a scale of attitudes toward the church might endorse statements at the opposite end of the scale such as "I like to go to church on Sunday" and "I believe that the churches have done much more harm than good." Sometimes the tendency of subjects to endorse statements at opposing ends of an attitude scale may mean that the person does not have an integrated attitude but merely a set of unrelated beliefs. Sometimes, however, a person may have a psychologically well-integrated attitude and still endorse statements characteristic of different points along the attitude continuum. In the example cited in this paragraph, the individual concerned might have a well-integrated and consistent attitude toward churches and, while he feels that churches have done more harm than good, still believes that it is an institution which, with some changes, may be the salvation of mankind.

Guttman has attempted to build attitude scales on which individuals show only consistent responses. Such scales on which individuals are always consistent are referred to as scales with perfect reproducibility, but the fact is that such perfect scales do not usually result even from the most elaborate attitude-construction procedures. Even on the best scales in this respect that have been built, individuals show themselves to have somewhat inconsistent attitudes.

The impression of the present writer is that the complicated procedure developed by Guttman does not have sufficient advantages for the teacher to need more than passing familiarity with it. The teacher may encounter published scales of attitude which have been prepared by the Guttman method, but in his own work he will undoubtedly stay with the Thurstone and Chave approach. Before passing on to other topics, the student may be interested in examining examples of attitude scales prepared by Guttman and his associates. Many examples of such scales may be found in a volume by Hovland et al. (9).

Discussion of Verbal Attitude Scales

The devices discussed in this chapter provide procedures for studying the opinions of individuals. Nothing that has been said about them should be taken to indicate that they provide anything more than a record of a person's expressed opinion. It must be emphasized that it is dangerous to attempt to predict from a person's expressed opinion how he will behave in other situations. Sometimes predictions of this kind can be made, but only after it has been well established that there is a relationship between behavior in the particular situation and behavior in the test situations. In some cases, the relationship has been well established. For example, it has usually been found that there is a close relationship between a person's expressed political opinion and how he will vote at an election. Voting behavior is highly predictable from expressions of opinion. However, even in this case the relationship is not perfect, for there are always a few who change their minds once they are in the voting booth. Verbal scales measuring attitudes toward labor organizations, religion, communism, or other major institutions or objects have also been shown to have value in predicting related behavior. For example, labor organizers obtain different average scores from business owners on the first of these scales. Similarly, churchgoers obtain different average attitude scores from non-churchgoers on scales of attitudes toward religion. The relationship between a person's expression of opinion and his attitude as evidenced by his behavior in other situations is rarely perfect but it is nevertheless quite commonly a close one. It is for this reason that the verbal attitude scale has been widely used in studies of the effectiveness of various educational practices in producing changes in attitude.

SOME APPLICATIONS OF ATTITUDE SCALES

Introduction

Studies designed to collect evidence of attitude change resulting from events in educational programs have been conducted by numerous investigators during the last twenty years. Studies have usually been restricted to the investigation of the results of a specific type of educational experience such as an excursion, a movie, or a particular classroom experience. The author is not aware of the existence of a single study in which an attempt has been made to assess attitude change in a situation in which a total educational program is designed to change a particular aspect of attitude. The fact is that the situations in which attitude changes have been measured have been unfavorable from the educational point of view because they refer to rather isolated incidents, and yet substantial attitude changes have been demonstrated to occur even under these conditions.

Attitude change that is likely to be relatively permanent must be based on an educational program in which there is consistent reward of the behavior which is symptomatic of the attitude that is to be changed. In the world in which we live today, it seems inevitable that attitude education must be piecemeal in nature, but the result is that individuals grow up with a miscellaneous and often unrelated set of opinions which usually show striking inconsistencies and which represent a patchwork rather than a design.

The general plan of school studies of attitudes is to select a scale designed to measure an attitude that a particular school experience is designed to change and to administer this scale to a large group of children. Half the children are then exposed to the experience designed to change attitudes, then the entire group is retested on the attitude scale. The purpose of this procedure is to determine whether the children who have the special experience show on the average greater attitude change than the others.

Very large numbers of studies of attitude change in school children have been made. Most of these were made over a decade ago and served the purpose of demonstrating that attitude changes produced by schools could be measured. This fact seems well established, but a few studies will be presented here, since they suggest to the student of education studies of the kind he may undertake later in the school in which he teaches.

The Effect of Reading Material on Attitudes

Bateman and Remmers (3) demonstrated in a series of experiments that attitudes toward social problems measured by verbal scales could be shifted in either direction through the use of printed material, while a general discussion in the classroom of the same topic in which both sides of the picture were presented left attitudes unchanged. The general nature of the experiments was as follows:

Experiment I. During a two-week classroom unit on the topic of divorce, special reports were prepared by individual students and reference readings were suggested. A teacher gave a lecture on the subject, and each student was required to write a paper on the topic. This unit was not designed specifically with a view to changing the attitudes of the students.

Experiment II. An attempt was made to develop more favorable attitudes toward social security (it was a relatively new venture at that time). Students were assigned the task of reading an article by the secretary of labor entitled "Should We Plan for Social Security?"

Experiment III. An attempt was made to develop a more favorable attitude toward social security by reading to the students an article on the subject.

Experiment IV. An attempt was made to change the attitudes of a group of students who felt favorably inclined toward labor unions to a less favorable attitude by means of reading them a somewhat biased paper on the subject.

In every case the attitudes of the students toward the institution or practice was measured both before and after the students were exposed to the material. In every case it was found that the material produced the change in the average measured attitude that had been anticipated, but in the case of the divorce question measured attitudes remain unchanged.

Another study by Remmers and Whisler (18) demonstrated the cumulative effect that a *series* of readings may have on the attitude of seventh, eighth, and ninth grade students. However, although a series of readings did increase the total effect, there was a progressive decrease in the contribution that successive readings made to the total attitude shift. The first reading in the series has the greatest effect in changing attitudes, provided all the readings are equally effective in propaganda.

It should be noted that these results do not mean that every child in the group changed his attitude in the way desired. The changes reported are for the average attitude change of the group involved. No doubt some of the children showed practically no change at all in the direction anticipated. It must also be remembered that although the average changes in attitudes were statistically significant, they were small, and their importance lies not so much in their actual magnitude as in the fact that they show that attitudes can be changed even through reading material that requires only a few minutes to read. It suggests that if reading material is properly directed through the school years, socially significant changes in attitudes could be produced.

Motion Pictures and Attitude Education

With the rise of the motion picture as a popular form of entertainment, many individuals and especially members of religious groups began to feel concern for the effect of such entertainment on the attitudes, standards of conduct, and behavior of youth. In the early thirties it was felt that children, as a result of attending movies, acquired undesirable attitudes and forms of behavior manifested by the screen villain. The effect of protests on the part of individuals concerned with the welfare of youth was to stimulate a whole series of researches into the actual effect that the movies had on the boys and girls who attended them. These researches have considerable significance for schools as well as for organizations more directly concerned with the provision of recreational facilities for youth. Since the movie is becoming more and more a part of the general school program, it is important to discover whether it is an effective device for changing attitudes in desirable directions and in modifying behavior.

A study of Peterson and Thurstone (16) supplies valuable information concerning the degree to which popular movies are effective in changing attitudes in youth. In this study, children of varying ages were shown popular movies which were likely to alter their attitudes. For example, 240 children in grades 9 through 12 in a school in a small town were shown the movie "Street of Chance." This movie portrays the life of a gambler in such a way that individuals who see it may conceivably be influenced in their attitude toward gambling. The attitudes of the children were measured before and after the experiment by determining the severity of punishment which they thought was merited by various crimes including gambling. Before seeing the film the children felt that the pickpocket and the petty thief deserved more severe punishment than the gambler, but the reverse was the case after they had seen the movie.

In another experiment it was found that the attitude of children toward the Chinese was materially altered by seeing either of the films "Sons of the Gods" or "Welcome Danger." In the case of the former film, the attitudes of the children changed in the direction of becoming more favorable to the Chinese, for the film describes the upbringing of a Chinese man, Sam Lee, who is in every way an excellent character and possesses many of the good qualities that people admire. Not only are the main characters of the movie good people but the whole picture of Chinese life as portrayed in the film is attractive.

The fact that movies may produce changes in attitude does not necessarily imply that such changes are permanent. The significance of such changes will depend largely on their permanence. Consequently, Peterson and Thurstone considered it an important matter to determine the degree to which such changes were permanent and not the transitory effect of exciting entertainment. In order to further this part of the study, a sample of the children on whom the effects of movies had been measured were retested on the attitude scales after periods ranging from two up to nineteen months. Typical results derived from this retesting program are shown in Table 10.3. It is evident from an examination of this table that whatever attitude changes are produced by movies are likely to be lasting. There is a tendency for the effects of movies to be slightly diminished through the passage of time, but an appreciable part of the attitude change remains.

It must be remembered that the permanence of such attitude changes is due mainly to the fact that the children in the experiment did not encounter any propaganda likely to change their attitudes in the opposite direction between seeing the movie and having their attitudes retested. It is not of any great importance to those children what their attitudes are in the matters under consideration. It is probable that this is the main reason why their attitudes are so easily changed by relatively short film narratives. Here as elsewhere it may be said that the more easily an attitude is changed the more likely it is that it makes little difference to the individual what attitude he holds.

TABLE 10.3

The Amount of Attitude Change, Resulting from Moving Pictures,
That Persisted for Varying Intervals of Time.
From Peterson and Thurstone (16)

Film	No. in Experimental Group	Interval between Seeing the Film and Retesting	Percentage of Attitude Change Due to Film That Remained after Interval	Direction of Attitude Change
The Criminal Code	257	2½ months	87	Less favorable attitudes toward present methods of punishing criminals
	195	9 months	78	
Sons of the Gods	117	5 months	62	More favorable attitudes toward the Chinese
	76	19 months	60	
The Big House	559	2 months	100	Less favorable attitudes toward present methods of punishing criminals
Numbered Men	549	4 months	111	
The Criminal Code				

A Recent Study of the Effect of Movies on Attitude Change

One of the most comprehensive studies yet undertaken of the effect of movies on attitudes was a product of the Second World War when the U. S. Army developed a series of films entitled "Why We Fight," for the purpose of giving newly inducted soldiers a clearer understanding of the events leading up to the entry of America into the war. The Information and Education Division of the Army, which was assigned the task of evaluating these films, planned and executed the series of experiments (9).

The investigators began by attempting to determine the educational objectives of the films, but since it was soon found that those who had produced the films had only rather vague general purposes in mind, it was necessary to infer objectives from a study of the materials. Questions of factual information and opinion items were formulated and these items were tried out in a preliminary experiment. After the revision of the instruments, two groups of subjects were selected, one of which was shown the film and the other constituted a control group.

A noteworthy aspect of the entire procedure was that every effort was made to convince the subjects that the questionnaires had nothing to do with the showing of the film. In the considered judgment of the experimenters this was felt to be an important matter, since, if the men knew that the effects of the film were being studied, they might have felt that they were expected to give certain stereotyped answers. Even the questionnaire given one week after the showing of the film was dissociated from it by many ingenious devices. It is believed that this aspect of the experimental method of testing the effects of films is a considerable improvement over previously developed experimental methods.

The general results of the experiments are summarized in the following words of the investigators (9, pp. 254–255):

The films had marked effects on the men's knowledge of factual material concerning the events leading up to the war. The fact that the upper limit of effects was so large—as for example in the cases where the correct answer was learned and remembered a week later by the majority of the men—indicates that highly effective presentation methods are possible with this type of film.

The films also had some marked effects on opinion when they specifically covered the factors involved in a particular interpretation, that is, where the opinion test item was prepared on the basis of film-content analysis and anticipated opinion change from such an analysis. Such opinion changes were, however, less frequent and, in general, less marked than changes in factual knowledge.

The film had only very few effects on opinion items of a more general nature that had been prepared independently of film content, but which were considered the criteria for determining the effectiveness of the films in achieving their orientation objectives.

The films had no effects on items prepared for the purpose of measuring effects on the men's motivation to serve as soldiers, which was considered the ultimate objective of the orientation program.*

The authors of the study rightly point out that the ultimate criteria of the effectiveness of the film are to be found in the behavior

* By permission from *Experiments in Mass Communication*, by Hovland, Lumsdaine, and Sheffield. Copyright, 1949, by Princeton University Press.

of the soldier in combat, but for obvious reasons combat data could not be obtained on the control and experimental group. However, it is perhaps a little overoptimistic to hope that a fifty-minute film or even several such films would have marked and lasting effects on the behavior of the individual.

THE SINGLE QUESTION FOR ASSESSING ATTITUDES: THE PUBLIC OPINION POLL

Introduction

The public opinion poll is a method of measuring attitudes. It is not usually used for the assessment of individual attitudes, but must be considered to be a technique for assessing the attitudes of groups. Single-question methods of determining attitudes have been extensively used, and often misused, in education, and recently, through the work of H. H. Remmers, a public opinion poll of considerable interest has been introduced into the high schools of the nation. An understanding of this approach to the study of attitudes is therefore important for the teacher. The discussion presented here is perhaps enough to help the teacher develop questionnaires for studying the attitudes of children in his own classes. The teacher who is interested in a more extended discussion of the technique is referred to a book by Parten (15).

Problems in the Framing of Questions

It has been pointed out by administrators of public opinion polls that the clarity and lack of ambiguity of the questions are crucial to the validity of any poll. If the questions do not convey the meaning they are supposed to convey, the results of the poll will be valueless. It need hardly be pointed out that it is extremely difficult to prepare a statement which conveys precisely the meaning intended and nothing else. The difficulties which lawyers have had in this respect bear witness to the truth of this statement, and even the development of a special type of legal language for the purpose of avoiding ambiguity has hardly solved the problem. The fact seems to be that very few individuals are capable of writing clearly, and a recognition of this fact should place us on our guard when we attempt to formulate a questionnaire.

Cantril (5) has studied with great care the defects that commonly appear in questions used in public opinion polls and for detailed information the reader is referred to his excellent book on the subject. The main points of advice which this authority has to give on question writing may be summarized as follows:

1. *Questions must have clearly identifiable meaning and must be sufficiently limited in scope.* Questions such as "Do you favor America's present foreign policy?" are practically valueless for obtaining interpretable expressions of opinion. Except in broad terms, even the political experts do not agree on what America stands for in her relations with other nations. Most persons are likely to endorse some aspects and reject others. The question is much too broad in scope and needs to be broken down into a series of questions which refer to much more limited aspects. For similar reasons, there is no value in asking teachers in New York the question "Do you consider teacher education in the New York state teachers colleges adequate or inadequate?" The question is too broad to permit a simple answer in terms of "Yes" or "No."

An example of how easy it is for a question which seems clear to be misinterpreted is cited by McNemar (11). Gallup asked the following question in one of his regular polls during the war: "After the war, would you like to see many changes or reforms made in the United States or would you rather have the country remain pretty much the way it was before the war?" This same question was asked by the Department of Agriculture's program surveys, but was also followed by a further question on how the question was interpreted. This additional question brought to light the astounding fact that only 60 per cent of the respondents understood the question to refer to general domestic conditions. The remaining 40 per cent of those interviewed were either unable to explain what the question meant to them or ascribed to it a meaning other than the intended one. Of the total group interviewed, 47 per cent voted for changes or reforms, but if only those who interpreted the question correctly were considered, then 60 per cent were in favor of change. It is facts of this kind which should caution the reader against using broad, general questions.

2. *Questions have little value if they call for a stereotyped answer.* A familiar question which has appeared in numerous public opinion polls is the following: "Are you in favor of labor unions?" A very large percentage of the adult population of the country responds "Yes" to the question, but the surprising element in the situation is that individuals who are commonly considered antilabor are included among the "Yes" respondents. What is happening is that the latter group are giving a stereotyped response, for in our society there is a certain respectability attached to the support of labor organizations. When this same group is asked about specific aspects of labor unions, they withdraw their endorsement. For related reasons almost all educators are in favor of providing a liberal education, although what one endorses as a liberal education another would reject as lacking in liberalism.

3. *Questions should not raise unfamiliar issues.* There would be little point in conducting a poll among teachers asking whether they endorsed or did not endorse Senator X's position on federal aid for education. The chances are that most teachers would be quite unfamiliar with Senator X's position.

4. *Questions designed to measure public opinion must be concerned with issues about which persons have formulated opinions.* There would be little value in conducting a poll in a community related to the issue of whether the local board of education should be given power to raise money by taxation unless this issue had been intensively discussed and studied by the population to be polled. Until individuals had time to think through the issue, the results of a public opinion poll would be meaningless. Do not ask pupils questions about social issues they have never considered.

5. *Questions asked must be such that the results of the poll will provide interpretable information.* Many questions asked in studies of opinion yield little information. The writer can recall one ill-planned study in which elementary school principals were asked "What percentage of the student teachers in your school will eventually become good teachers?" The answers to such a question are uninterpretable. One principal answers 20 per cent because he thinks few teachers are "good"; another gives the same answer because he believes that present trainees are much less adequate than those of previous years. Even if such difficulties were removed, there would

still be serious doubt as to whether a question of this kind has any value at all.

6. *Questions should use only words with which the respondents are familiar, and the structure of the question should be, as far as possible, simple and straightforward.*

7. *If the questions are to be answered by choosing one of several alternatives, it is important that the alternatives provided be exhaustive. However, the alternatives must not be too many or too long.*

Cantril (5) collected evidence on the extent to which questions suffered from these deficiencies by administering certain questions to a group of individuals and then interviewing each to see how the questions were interpreted. To illustrate the general character of his results, it may be noted that in the case of one question only four persons out of forty interviewed were found to have interpreted it correctly.

The single question, by forcing people into extreme positions where they do not belong, often obscures the truth. This is well brought out in a study reported by Cantril in which it was found that "interventionist sentiment" measured by various questions from May to September, 1941, varied from 78 per cent down to 8 per cent, depending on the form of the question used. In this series of questions for measuring public opinion about the same topic, it would appear that different questions forced the subjects into taking positions at different ends of the scale, sometimes feeling that their position was nearer to the one end and sometimes that it was nearer to the other.

The careful study of a question by its author will rarely reveal all of the ambiguities that probably exist. This is because the author of a question has a certain *set* in writing it which enables him to see it in only one way. He must have his questions reviewed by others, but even this procedure may let some defects slip by. It is desirable to try out questions on individual subjects who are personally interviewed to give their interpretation. It seems to be inevitable that almost any question will be misinterpreted by somebody at some time. The case may be recalled of a certain registrar of a large university who stated that he had never in his entire career been able to phrase directions which every student would interpret in the same way. Public opinion polls present the same kind of problem. All that can be done, at best, is to phrase questions in such a way that they will be misinterpreted by a minimum of those who are confronted with them.

Reliability and Validity of Single Questions

It is all too common to assume that single questions have perfect reliability and validity. Administrators, teachers, and workers in educational research distribute questionnaires, collect and tabulate the data, and report on the results as if the same results would certainly be achieved if the questionnaires were administered a second time. It is also commonly assumed that the results can be taken at their face value, that all respondents understand the questions in the way they are supposed to understand them, and that they give in their answers exactly the information they are supposed to provide. Such assumptions are known to be far from reality.

Mosteller (12) collected information on the reliability of data collected by means of single questions in interview situations. Two interviewers met with the same group of persons twice at an intervening interval of three weeks. When they asked questions concerning car ownership, agreement to the extent of 96.5 per cent was achieved between the data obtained in the first interview and the data obtained in the second. No reasons were given for the 3.5 per cent discrepancy. A part of it may have been due to genuine changes in car ownership, but at least a part may have been due to errors made by interviewers in recording the data and misunderstandings on the part of those who were answering the questions. More disturbing are the results achieved when questions were administered which called for opinions rather than facts. When the interviewers asked the question "Do you think Roosevelt is doing a good job, only a fair job, or a bad job in running the country?", much lower reliability was achieved, with identical responses in only 79 per cent of the cases from one interview to the other, and yet this question was one about which the public had formed a fairly definite opinion at the time it was asked.

The evidence suggests that the more factual a question happens to be, the more likely it is to show stability from one interview to the next. Questions calling for opinion will have lower reliability than questions calling for facts. Considerable variation may be expected in the reliability of opinion questions. If these questions refer to matters where opinion has been well crystallized, where people have come to the point of taking definite sides, then the answers may be expected to have relatively high reliability. If the question refers to matters which are relatively new, where the population questioned has not yet thought through the matter with any care, and where the implications of any particular opinion with respect to the issue have not been properly considered, then respondents cannot be expected to be consistent in the opinions they give.

The Sample in Public Opinion Polls

It is well recognized that in public opinion polls the selection of a sample to be interviewed is crucial in determining the accuracy of the final outcome. If opinion with respect to a specific issue is to be estimated for a large population such that all members cannot be interviewed, it is necessary to interview a sample which has been selected so that it is representative of the larger population. It is evident that it is quite impossible to select a group which is representative in every way of the population of which it is a sample, for in a sense each and every individual is unique. A sample is representative with respect to certain characteristics only. It is customary practice in public opinion polls to select the sample so that it is representative with respect to geographical and urban-rural distribution, color, and economic status. Sometimes the factors of age and sex are also used. The sample is selected in such a way that the percentage of persons in each category in the sample is the same as that in the parent population. The public opinion analyst may compare the distribution of each one of these factors in the sample with that in the total population by referring to the figures given in the census.

While the procedure for selecting a representative sample may seem simple enough on the surface, it is full of pitfalls. Those who remember the presidential elections of 1948 will recall how many of the polls failed to predict the outcome and at least part of their failure seems to be a result of methods used in selecting the sample on the basis of which public opinion was estimated. One major deficiency in the system commonly used at that time apparently is that when interviewers are free to select the persons they are to interview, they show definite preferences in those they select. In order to overcome these difficulties of sampling, Likert has developed an area-sampling technique in which individuals to be interviewed are identified for the interviewer by a systematic method.

The Purdue Opinion Panel

A development of note in educational measurement has been the application of public opinion polling techniques to the identification of problems and problem areas in the lives of high school students. This opinion poll is operated by the Division of Educational Reference, Purdue University, under the direction of H. H. Remmers. It has been used to measure the attitudes of high school students on personal and social problems such as dating, drinking, smoking, relations with parents, labor and management relations, uses of atomic energy, causes and areas of inflation, and foreign affairs. The diversity of the appraisals made by this technique is evident from the titles of some of the reports that have been published, for these include "Youth's Philosophy of Education: Functional or Traditional?", and "The Citizenship Attitudes of High School Youth."

The polls are conducted three times a year in the participating schools, which pay a small sum for each student included in the poll. The cost to the school is extremely small, and in return it is sent an individual school report showing how the students answered the questions, and in addition it receives a report showing the nationwide results, with special breakdowns of the votes according to the grade in school, sex, religion, political party preference, socioeconomic status, amount of education of the parents, and geographical region of the students.

The organizers of the poll, in order to obtain a properly balanced sample, request schools to poll ninth and tenth grade students as well as their juniors and seniors. In one such poll reported in November, 1944, fifteen thousand pupils were included in the poll. From these it was necessary to select a smaller sample which would be representative of high school students. This sample is shown in

Table 10.4, divided according to sex, grade, school size, religion, income, and place of residence.

TABLE 10.4

Composition of Stratified Sample of High School Students Used in Making Analysis (19)

Classifications of Students	Number of Students
Total	2,610
Boys	1,285
Girls	1,325
Ninth grade	712
Tenth grade	684
Eleventh grade	600
Twelfth grade	614
Rural (under 2,500)	1,313
Urban (over 2,500)	1,297
Protestant	1,524
Catholic	571
Jewish	139
Other or none	376
Low income	1,911
High income	699
East	696
Midwest	935
South	639
Mt. Pacific	340

It may be observed that in comparison with the country as a whole an unduly large number come from the larger schools and from the Midwest. While an effort was made to select from the fifteen thousand pupils included in the poll a group which would be as nearly as possible representative of the total population of the nation's high schools, at that stage of the project there were inevitable difficulties involved in obtaining a thoroughly representative sample. These difficulties have since been largely resolved.

Inadequacies in the selection of the sample for reporting results have much less serious consequences in the high school poll than in the typical public opinion poll, since schools are mainly interested in their own local results.

In the particular poll for which the breakdown of the sample is given in Table 10.4,* the following items are quoted from a summary of the highlights of the results:

31 per cent indicate that what happens on dates should never be discussed with parents.

24 per cent feel that parents hardly ever understand the problems of modern youth.

59 per cent would never justify whipping or slapping as punishment.

39 per cent say young people should seldom be punished by being made to stay at home.

81 per cent say that petting or necking is at least sometimes all right when out on dates.

74 per cent say that parents allow their children enough spending money.

44 per cent approve of "going steady" as a usual occurrence.

These results are given in order to demonstrate the kind of findings which the high school poll may produce.

Although the primary purpose of the Purdue high school poll seems to be to provide teachers with information useful in planning the curriculum, there is no doubt that the report of the results can provide material for constructive discussion in the classroom. There are also possibilities that the poll might be used on occasions as a basis for assessing the effectiveness of new programs introduced to handle some of the problems which the poll reveals.

The Future of Opinion Polls in Education

The techniques used in public opinion polls have considerable value as measuring devices in an educational context provided they are applied by persons who have training in the use of these techniques. This does not mean that the writer endorses the present proliferation of ill-planned and ill-conceived educational studies which make use of questionnaire techniques. Most of the energy devoted to such studies is wasted, but need not be wasted. The teacher must appreciate the fact that questionnaire studies appear

* Data presented in this table and in the text are reproduced by kind permission of Dr. H. H. Remmers, Director, Division of Educational Reference, Purdue University.

deceptively simple, but when great care is exercised in their development, they can provide valuable information.

DISGUISED METHODS OF MEASURING ATTITUDES

Introduction

A criticism of the verbal attitude scale is that the purpose of the scale is evident to those who read it, and this makes it possible for the individual to mark the scale to indicate any particular attitude position that he wishes. Attempts have been made to develop attitude measures which are such that individuals cannot identify the purpose for which they are administered and cannot know the way in which his responses are to be interpreted.

Projective Techniques as Indirect Methods of Measuring Attitudes

Proshansky (17) developed a projective device for measuring attitude toward labor by adapting the method used by Murray in the Thematic Apperception Test. Proshansky searched through magazines and newspapers and collected pictures which illustrated some aspect of social conflict. The pictures were then sorted by subjects to select those which were ambiguous with respect to the outcome of the social conflict portrayed. Other pictures which had nothing to do with social conflict were added to the series to disguise the purposes of measurement. The pictures finally selected were reproduced on lantern slides and the following instructions were prepared for subjects:*

You will be shown a number of slides exposed for a short period of time. Examine each one carefully, and then give a detailed account of what you think the picture represents. If you wish, make up a story about each picture. You will be allowed only 2½ minutes to write your response, so answer as fast as you can. Although the exposure of each picture will be short, do your best and try to remember as much of the picture as you can. In any event, whether you give your impression or tell a story, be brief, be accurate, and don't lag.

* Permission to quote from the Proshansky study was generously granted by the American Psychological Association.

The slides were presented to two groups of college students which differed in their attitude toward labor. At the same time an attitude scale developed by Newcomb (14) to investigate attitudes toward organized labor was also administered. As far as one can judge from the description of the experiment, attitudes were assessed by judging the stories written by the subjects. For example, the following description of a picture would be given a high antilabor rating:

Picture of one room, very messy, stove in the center, woman on the left, man standing next to the stove, couple of children near them. This is a room of what we call "poor people." They seem to be messy, sloppy people, who seem to enjoy dwelling in their own trash.

The ratings of the pictures for evidence of attitude were found to show substantial coefficients of correlations with the Newcomb attitude scale. The results led Proshansky to conclude that there was considerable imaginative distortion of the subject's original perception of the picture, subsequent falsification in attempting to recall, and elaboration of the meaning. All of these three factors made the situation a useful one for the appraisal of attitudes.

Another study by Fromme (7) attempted further exploration of the use of projective techniques in the appraisal of attitudes. He used, as did Proshansky, a modified version of the Thematic Apperception Test. As an illustration of the kind of themes written in describing the pictures, the following example is presented, although Fromme admits that his illustration is much richer in material than the average theme written by his subjects (7, p. 468):*

Here is a man who was brought up to be sincere, honest and uprighteous. He becomes a clergyman after long training in the church and practices well. One day, as he is out walking, he accidentally comes upon a violent strike. He never before saw people handled this way and is immediately disillusioned. His eyes are now opened to reality, however, and he intervenes in order to quell the violence. He is then manhandled and is thrown into jail along with several workers. He is, of course, released because of his position but vows to dedicate the rest of his life, even at the risk of his position to change things in order to establish greater freedom for the laboring class.

From data such as the above, attitudes are appraised by inspection, and since the appraisal is subjective, it is probable that the

* This material is reproduced by kind permission of The Journal Press.

derived measures of attitude have rather low reliabilities, at least lower than are usually found with the conventional types of attitude scale. A particularly interesting indirect measure of attitudes was developed by Brown (4), who adopted the basic idea of the Rosenzweig Picture-Frustration Test to his purpose. The Rosenzweig test consists of twenty-four cartoonlike pictures, each one of which represents a common type of situation in which an individual feels frustration. The individual in the picture who is the cause of the other's frustration is shown saying certain words which help to explain the situation to the subject. The words are shown in captions in the style used in comic books. The other figure in the picture is shown with a blank caption box above his head. The features of the persons in the pictures are drawn with little or no expression in order to facilitate the projection of the subject's own emotional responses through his identification with the situation. The task of the subject in the test situation is to write a caption for the person who is being frustrated. In the original instrument by Rosenzweig two types of situations are presented. The one situation is termed ego-blocking and is one in which a person is interrupted, disappointed, or deprived of something by some distance. The second type of situation is termed super-ego blocking and involves an accusation or charge made by one person against another.

Brown's instrument consists of twenty-four pictures in each of which a person is frustrated. The pictures represent the following types of situations:

A. Three pictures in which a Negro is the source of a white person's frustration.
B. Three pictures in which a white person is a source of frustration to a Negro.
C. Six pictures in which a person identifiable through the situation as a Jew is subject to a frustration or aggression against him.
D. Six pictures in which a person recognizable as Jewish is the source of frustration to someone who is obviously Gentile.
E. Six pictures in which the frustrations are independent of racial or religious issues.

The last six pictures listed were included in order to obtain a measure of the individual's reaction to frustration independent of the racial issues involved. These pictures also, it was hoped, might disguise in part the purposes of the test.

The results reported by Brown (4) do not represent the results of a detailed validation of the instrument, since the project of which it was a part was terminated before a careful study of the instrument was completed. However, the technique seems to be of sufficient interest to report it here together with some of the preliminary findings.

Illustrative of the use of the technique is the following example of the reaction of a subject to one of the pictures which shows a man holding a pen in front of a book marked at the top "Register Here." Beside the man is a suitcase and a hat, and on the other side of the counter is another man who is saying, "We take no Jews here— Sorry." The responses of three subjects, A, B, and C, were as follows in completing the caption:

A. "So this is America!"
B. "A room please with a bath. I thought America a free country."
C. "Oh, pardon me."

Brown's interpretation of these comments is as follows: "A's comment indicates an active protest against anti-Semitism. C virtually demonstrates an acceptance of anti-Semitism and does everything short of directly endorsing it."

While little data are presented on the subject, Brown reported that individuals who showed racial prejudice on a questionnaire also showed the same prejudice in responding to the Picture-Frustration Test.

Summary of Methods for Measuring Attitudes

1. The best-developed methods of measuring attitudes are those which involve the listing of opinions and which then require the individual to check those which he endorses. Such lists of opinions, when they are methodically prepared, are referred to as attitude scales.

2. The Thurstone and Chave method seems to be the one which the teacher can best apply, since it calls for little specialized mathematical knowledge. Other methods require substantially greater knowledge of statistics.

3. Attitude scales have been used with success to demonstrate the effect of particular aspects of the curriculum on pupil attitudes,

even when precautions were taken to dissociate the administration of the attitude test from the experience designed to change attitude.

4. The opinion poll represents a method of measuring attitude in which single questions are used as short attitude scales. The method is used for the assessment and comparison of the attitudes of groups rather than individuals.

5. Special precaution must be taken in the development of questions for polling opinions to insure that ambiguities are eliminated and that the questions are easily interpreted and answered.

6. If only a sample of the group whose opinion is to be assessed can be administered the question, great care must be exercised in the selection of the sample.

7. Public opinion polls have been introduced into high schools on a nationwide basis. Such polls make it possible for school faculties to obtain a great deal of information concerning pupil attitudes toward problems that affect them personally.

8. Attempts have been made to develop measuring instruments for the assessment of attitudes which do not reveal to individuals tested the purpose of the test. Such disguised methods of measuring attitudes are in only the earliest stages of development.

References

1. Allport, Gordon W., *Personality; a Psychological Interpretation,* New York, Henry Holt and Company, 1937, pp. 588 + XIV.

2. Bogardus, Emory S., *Immigration and Race Attitudes,* New York, D. C. Heath and Company, 1928, pp. 268 + XI.

3. Bateman, Richard M. and Remmers, H. H., *The Relationship of Pupil Attitudes Towards Social Topics Before and After Studying the Subject.* Bulletin of Purdue University, 37, No. 4, Series 2, 1936, 27–51.

4. Brown, J. F., "A Modification of the Rosenzweig Picture-Frustration Test to Study Hostile Inter-Racial Attitudes," *Journal of Psychology,* 24, 1947, 247–272.

5. Cantril, Hadley, *Gauging Public Opinion,* Princeton, New Jersey, Princeton University Press, 1944, pp. 318 + XIV.

6. Coombs, C. H. and Travers, R. M. W., *Study of Attitudes Towards Teaching,* Ann Arbor, Michigan, University of Michigan Press, 1947.

7. Fromme, Allan, "On the Use of Certain Qualitative Methods of

Attitude Research. A Study of Opinions on Methods of Preventing War," *Journal of Social Psychology,* 13, 1941, 429–459.

8. Guttman, Louis, "A Basis for Scaling Quantitative Data," *American Sociological Review,* 9, 1944, 139–150.

9. Hovland, Carl, Lumsdaine, Arthur I., and Sheffield, Fred D., *Experiments on Mass Communication,* Volume III, Princeton, New Jersey, Princeton University Press, 1949, pp. 345 + X.

10. Likert, Rensis, *A Technique for the Measurement of Attitudes,* Archives of Psychology, No. 140, 1932, pp. 55.

11. McNemar, Quinn, "Opinion-Attitude Methodology," *Psychological Bulletin,* 43, 1946, 289–374.

12. Mosteller, Frederick, in Cantril, Hadley, *Gauging Public Opinion,* Princeton, New Jersey, Princeton University Press, 1944, pp. 318 + XIV.

13. Murphy, Gardner, *Personality, A Biosocial Approach to Origins and Structure,* New York, Harper and Brothers, 1947, pp. 999 + XIII.

14. Newcomb, Theodore M., "Labor Unions as Seen by Their Members: An Attempt to Measure Attitudes," *Industrial Conflict,* edited by Hartman, G. W. and Newcomb, Theodore M., New York, Gordon, 1939, pp. 313–318.

15. Parten, Mildred, *Surveys, Polls, and Samples,* New York, Harper and Brothers, 1950, pp. 624 + XIII.

16. Peterson, Ruth C. and Thurstone, L. L., "Motion Pictures and the Social Attitudes of Children," *Motion Pictures and Youth,* New York, The Macmillan Company, 1933, pp. 75.

17. Proshansky, Harold M., "A Projective Method for the Study of Attitudes," *Journal of Abnormal and Social Psychology,* 38, 1943, 393–395.

18. Remmers, H. H. and Whisler, L. D., *The Effects of Instruction on Pupils' Attitudes Towards Agricultural Policies,* Purdue Studies in Higher Education, 34, Series 3, 1938, 83–99.

19. Remmers, H. H., Drucker, A. J., and Hackett, C. G., *Youth Looks at the Parent Problems,* Report No. 23, Purdue Public Opinion Panel, Lafayette, Indiana, Division of Educational Reference, Purdue University, 9, No. 1, 1949 (mimeographed).

20. Stouffer, Samuel A., Guttman, Louis, Suchman, Edward A., Lazarsfeld, Paul F., Star, Shirley A., and Clausen, John A., *Measurement and Prediction,* Princeton, New Jersey, Princeton University Press, 1950, pp. 756 + X.

21. Thurstone, L. L. and Chave, E. J., *The Measurement of Attitude,* Chicago, Illinois, University of Chicago Press, 1929, pp. 96 + XII.

CHAPTER II

Studies of the Assessment of Interests

Introduction

The term *interest* refers to a multiplicity of different phenomena, and a part of the difficulty of presenting a coherent and well-organized account of the assessment of interests stems from the great range of meanings which the term *interest* may assume. Recent writers (19) tend to give three rather distinct meanings to the term and speak of (1) expressed interest, (2) manifest interest, and (3) inventoried interest. The three terms refer to three different methods of determining a person's interests. A person's *expressed interests* are determined by his response to a question such as "What do you like doing best in your spare time?" *Manifest interests* are determined by observing what the individual does in his spare time or perhaps at work. *Inventoried interests* are determined by presenting the individual with a long list of activities and then asking him either to check those he enjoys or to check whether he likes, dislikes, or feels indifferent about each. *Expressed vocational interest* is indicated by the occupation a person says he would like to be in, while *manifest vocational interest* is indicated by the occupation he is in or is preparing to enter.

It is assumed by many writers that the three methods of measuring interests which have been described are attempts to measure the same basic variable but with varying degrees of contamination with other variables. Oddly enough, it is not known at the present time the extent to which this assumption is reasonable. It is clear that the three methods of measuring interests should produce results that are related, but the relationship may turn out to be a very complex one when the facts have been determined.

Difference between Values and Interests

A problem of central importance in this area is the relation of interests to values, but little has been done to clarify the relationship. It seems true that certain individuals seem motivated primarily by a lust for personal power, others seek wealth, other religious experiences, and so forth. Persons seeking power may have varied interests, some attempting to build an industrial empire, others attempting to control the affairs of state, and similar endeavors. In terms of current usage it is not customary to refer to an interest in power, but rather to refer to the desire for power as a central value within which motives are organized. Interests, on the other hand, refer to likes or dislikes for specific objects or situations. As Murphy (12) points out, interests may change, but the value system of an individual may remain unaltered. This may be illustrated by the case of a man who has only moderate success in building an industrial enterprise, and too little to satisfy his desire for power. He may then lose all interest in his industrial enterprise and become interested in politics, which he may view as a more promising field for his aspirations. Interests in activities persist only as long as they satisfy some of the needs of the individual. When they cease to satisfy needs, interests change to new fields, but the needs and value systems of the individual may remain unchanged.

Distinction between Attitudes and Interests

There is no strict division between the meaning of the term *attitude* and the meaning of the term *interest*. Both concepts involve feelings of liking-disliking and acceptance-rejection. The difference lies more in the fact that interests are likings or dislikings for activities, while attitudes are likings or dislikings for objects or ideas.

The confusion between liking for an activity and liking for objects is seen in many interest inventories in which the subject is asked to indicate the extent to which he likes various kinds of people. It must be pointed out here that when we say we like people of a certain type, we usually mean that we like *being* with people of that type. The liking refers to the activity and not to the people, who are merely part of the situation which produces inwardly satisfying feelings. In the same way, when we say we like modern art, we really mean that we like looking at or studying or producing modern art. It is our inaccurate language which confuses attitudes and interests.

Specific and General Interests

Frequent reference is made in technical literature to specific and general interests. By a specific interest is usually meant a liking or disliking for a specific activity, while a general interest refers to a liking or disliking for a class of activities. The concept of general interest is useful only in so far as it is based on the established fact that liking one of the activities is positively correlated with liking for the other activities within the general interest area. It is useful to think in terms of a general interest in mechanical things, since a liking for certain specific mechanical activities can be taken as a symptom of liking for other mechanical activities. It would be meaningless to discuss a general interest in watching athletic events if it were shown that a liking for watching one type of sport was unrelated to a liking for watching another, as in the case of individuals who may like to watch baseball but who have little interest in watching boxing. The grouping of likes and dislikes must be based on statistical studies of the way in which they are grouped and not on opinions of how they are grouped. There is little point in developing an interest inventory to measure pupils' interest in improving their community unless there is evidence to show that interests in this area can be demonstrated to have positive statistical interrelationships.

Measures of Expressed Interests

If measures of children's expressed interest are collected, they should be collected systematically. This can be done by means of questionnaires, which should be prepared with great care according to the principles outlined in the last chapter. The potentialities of this approach can be seen by examining a study by Jersild and

Tasch (7). This study was executed in grades 1–12 of the public schools of Springfield, Missouri, and called upon each child to fill out a questionnaire covering the following items:

My three wishes
What I'd like to learn more about at school
What I don't care to study about
What I like best in school
What I like best outside school (that is, away from school, when I am not at school)
What I like least at school
What I like least outside school (that is, away from school, when I am not at school)
What I want to be or do when I grow up
The most interesting thing I have done at school during the past week or so
One of the places I especially like to go to
One of the happiest days of my life

The approach illustrated by these items is a refreshing departure from the kind of approach taken in most interest inventories in which the individual is required to express a preference for one of several activities in which he has never participated and about which he has little knowledge. It should be noted that some of the items represent indirect approaches to the assessment of interests, as in the case of the first item, which asks the child to write down three wishes. These may provide no information at all concerning the child's interests, since the answer may refer to the personal problems the child faces, but the same question may in many instances provide useful information concerning interests.

The following summary of the results of this study indicate the kind of findings that may be derived from a simple instrument of this type:

First, the wishes of children tend to be concrete and for specific things that affect them personally. The frequent mention of gifts in answer to the question on gifts is interpreted by Jersild and Tasch to indicate that children value highly material rewards and that perhaps the schools should make greater use of this fact.

Second, children's interests vary substantially from school to school and from class to class. This is consistent with the belief that interests are learned and suggests that teachers might do well to concern themselves with the building of interests rather than in using those that already exist.

Third, there is a steady decline in interests in school work as the children grow older.

Fourth, in grades 4–12 the social studies were mentioned more often favorably than unfavorably. The reverse was true in the case of activities related to mathematics and English.

Fifth, the expressions of interest had little to do with the basic problems faced by the children in their lives. Jersild and Tasch point out that since expressed interests provide little indication of the needs of the children, they do not provide satisfactory clues as to what the educational program should include.

Sixth, there were great variations between schools in the amount of hostility expressed by the children toward one another.

Seventh, of considerable educational importance is the fact that children may fail to develop interests at home because of the restricted range of the interests of the parents. Also, the interests demonstrated by children may develop the same interests in the parents; for example, a child who becomes interested in an art or craft may encourage the parents to participate.

The main suggestion provided by this study would seem to be that the schools would do well to concern themselves with the development of interests rather than with the determination of interests as starting points of the learning process.

In a "last thought" on the last page of the report, Jersild and Tasch agree that the hundreds of studies of children's interests have had "limited educational significance." These writers go on to point out that the study of children's expressed interests should not be undertaken from the point of view of discovering likes and dislikes so that a curriculum can be built around them, but rather for the purpose of determining the function of specific interests in the total life of the child.

The Rationale of the Interest Inventory

Research points to the conclusion that, among adolescents and younger children, expressed interests tend to be transitory, and thus the fact that an activity is described today by such an individual as

liked provides little basis for predicting whether it will be liked to
morrow. This is hardly surprising, because much of the activity c
the adolescent might be described as exploratory. The immedia
result of this fact is to limit the kinds of predictions that can be mac
from expressed interest. However, this does not mean that the stud
of the expressed interests, and particularly expressed vocational in
terests, of young persons is valueless, for it does have value in th
study of the kinds of explorations which are being made and of th
general nature of the interests of groups.

If expressions of specific early-adolescent interests have limite
worth for predictive purposes, it is still possible that a study of th
general nature of the activities for which an individual expresse
liking or disliking may provide a basis for predicting future prefer
ences. It is this type of question which interest inventories have bee
designed to answer. In the interest inventory the individual is aske
to indicate in some way his liking or preference for a large numbe
of activities. These expressions of liking or preference are in som
way grouped together to indicate the general nature of the person'
interests. The anticipation, which has been at least partly justifiec
is that such a procedure may show up trends in interests which ar
not apparent in transitory expressed interests. Attempts to develo
inventory methods of measuring interests have been largely directe
toward the measurement of vocational interests, and it is these at
tempts which will be considered now.

The Measurement of Vocational Interest

The extensive work which has been devoted to the developmen
of measures of vocational interest gives recognition to the educationa
importance of the area. There have been two main approaches t
this problem, the one designed to determine the general types o
activity which the individual prefers and the other to estimate th
degree to which the pattern of interests of the individual correspond
to the pattern of interests found among individuals successful i
given occupations.

The argument in favor of the second of these two approaches i
that a person will find work congenial if he has the same patter
of likes and dislikes as those who are successful in the same job

ince this approach to the study of vocational interests is the one
hich has been most extensively studied, it will be discussed first.
'he work in this area has been the major life enterprise of Edward
. Strong Jr. of Stanford University, whose Vocational Interest Blank
14, 15) has now become world famous. Strong and his associates,
s well as numerous independent individuals, have carried out
tudies on the Vocational Interest Blank. These have been summar-
zed in a large volume prepared by Strong (16).

Strong's Vocational Interest Blank (14, 15) consists of lists of
.musements, occupations, school subjects, peculiarities of people,
.obbies, and activities, The individual indicates his like, dislike, or
ndifference for each of the activities or kinds of individuals described.
'urther lists ask the individual to choose between such matters as
lealing with things or dealing with people, and for his preferences
.mong famous people. A final part asks the individual to make an
:stimate of his own characteristics; for example, whether he wins
'riends easily. The assumption seems to be implicit in this final part
hat a person likes to do the things he does best.

TABLE 11.1

Occupations for Which Keys are Available for Form M (Men) of the Vocational Interest Blank (14)

Group I
Artist
Architect
Psychologist
Physician
Dentist

Group II
Mathematician
Engineer
Chemist

Group III
Production manager

Group IV
Aviator
Farmer
Printer
Mathematics-science
teacher
Policeman
Forest Service

Group V
Y.M.C.A. physical direc-
tor
Personnel manager
Y.M.C.A. secretary
Social science teacher
City school superintend-
ent
Minister

Group VI
Musician

Group VII
Certified public account-
ant

Group VIII
Accountant
Office worker
Purchasing agent
Banker

Group IX
Sales manager
Real estate salesman
Life insurance salesman

Group X
Advertising man
Lawyer
Author-journalist

Group XI
President of manufactur-
ing concern

Occupational Level

Masculinity-Femininity

Interest-Maturity

Separate blanks have been built for men and for women. The inventory has undergone substantial revision since the form for men was first published in 1927. Form M, for men, which is in use at the time of writing, was published in October, 1938, and the revised Form W, for women, in 1943.

The Blank is scored for the resemblance of the pattern of choices marked by the subject to the pattern of markings shown by successful individuals in each one of a series of occupational groups. The scale can be scored for each one of the occupational scales listed in Table 11.1. Each score indicates the extent to which the individual's pattern of likes and dislikes is more similar to that of successful individuals in that occupation than it is to that of people in general.

The scales available for the form for women are shown in Table 11.2.

TABLE 11.2

Occupations for Which Keys are Available for Form W (Women) of the Vocational Interest Blank (15)

Artist	Physician
Author	Social worker
Dentist	Stenographer-secretary
Femininity-masculinity	Teacher of English
General office worker	Teacher of mathematics and physical sciences
Housewife	
Lawyer	Teacher of social sciences
Librarian	Y.W.C.A. secretary
Life insurance saleswoman	Physical education teacher
Nurse	Elementary school teacher

Group scales are also available for groups I, II, V, VIII, IX, and X, shown in Table 11.1. These group scales are prepared by combining the persons in the occupations included in the group, and then the patterns of responses of individuals taking the inventory are compared with typical responses for these consolidated groups.* Strong developed these group scales in the belief that it would simplify the scoring procedure and because he felt that the

---

* The procedure for developing keys is actually more complicated than is indicated here. The procedure involves the comparison of the responses of successful individuals in particular occupations with the responses of a mixed group of individuals. When an item shows marked differences between the responses of the two groups, it is weighted heavily in the final key.

esults were more useful than the detailed breakdown of scores in he guidance of young men still in high school.

The reliability of the scales seems in most cases to be satisfactory. On the form for men, only one scale has a coefficient of reliability below 0.80. On the form for women, three of the scales have reliability coefficients below 0.80. These reliabilities were estimated by he split-half method, grouping odd-numbered and even-numbered tems, and correcting for the reduced length of the test which this echnique involves.

What is measured by scores on the Vocational Interest Blank? Although research on the device has assumed gigantic proportions, his simple question cannot be answered in a simple way. Strong imself (16) describes the scales as measures of vocational interest, but the writer can see no evidence to substantiate this claim. It can be said without making unwarranted assumptions that scores on the test indicate the degree of resemblance between the responses of the individual who takes the test and the pattern of responses of successful practitioners in various occupational groups. If one wishes, one may refer to this measure of resemblance as a measure of vocational interest, but it is good to keep in mind that it is only a measure of resemblance. Strong does not discuss validity in terms of what the inventory measures, but in terms of two criteria: (1) the extent to which scores differentiate successful from unsuccessful individuals in various occupations, and (2) the ability of the instrument to predict the success of individuals in occupations to which they are assigned on the basis of their scores. The Blank might be valid in terms of each of these criteria and still fail to measure the extent to which an individual is interested in a given vocation. Strong is concerned mainly in validity determined on the basis of statistical relationships.

Strong's inventory also includes scales for occupational level, masculinity-femininity, and interest-maturity, which require some special comment. The occupational level scale contrasts the interests of men in unskilled occupations with those in the income bracket which includes the top one-seventh. The score on the scale is designed to indicate the extent to which the likes and dislikes of the individual resemble those of the one group or of the other.

The masculinity-femininity scale contrasts the characteristic pattern of likes, dislikes, and performances of men with the corresponding pattern for women. The score on the scale indicates the exter to which the pattern of likes, dislikes, and preferences of the indivi ual resembles that of men or that of women. It does not measur masculinity-femininity in terms of the psychological characteristi which are commonly stressed as differentiating men from womer From the point of view of interpreting scores, the name of the sca is misleading, for the scale seems to discriminate between those wh have an interest in outdoor activities, tools and mechanical oper; tions, and hard physical work on the one hand and those who hav an interest in sedentary activities, aesthetic objects, and domesti affairs on the other. Thus the individual who has a preference fc sedentary activities is likely to have a score toward the feminine en of the scale, regardless of sex. Much of the difference between me and women in their responses to the Vocational Interest Blank re flects differences in the roles that the American culture imposes upo the life of men and women. It certainly cannot be assumed to repre sent any more fundamental difference.

The interest-maturity scale has had a long history of development The original scale was mainly related to differences in education type of occupation as well as differences in age. This complicatio rendered the original scale largely useless. For this reason, Berman Darley, and Paterson (2) described the scale as a combined meas ure of age and occupational level. At a later date Strong developec two scales, one of which contrasted the interests of fifteen-year-olc boys and twenty-five-year-old men, and the other of which con trasted twenty-five-year-old men and fifty-five-year-old men. Late the fifteen-to-twenty-five-year interest-maturity scale was again re vised, and it is this revised scale which has been most widely used This revised scale correlated 0.45 with age in the case of a grou whose ages ranged from fifteen to thirty, but just what it does meas ure remains in doubt. Strong spends a whole chapter of his book discussing the scale and presents data on the correlation between scores on the scale and scores on innumerable other variables, but with all this array of factual material the reader finds it impossible to attach any clear meaning to the scale.

The procedures for scoring the inventories developed by Strong are, at best, complicated. It is not usually practical to score the inventories by hand, and especially since various organizations pro-

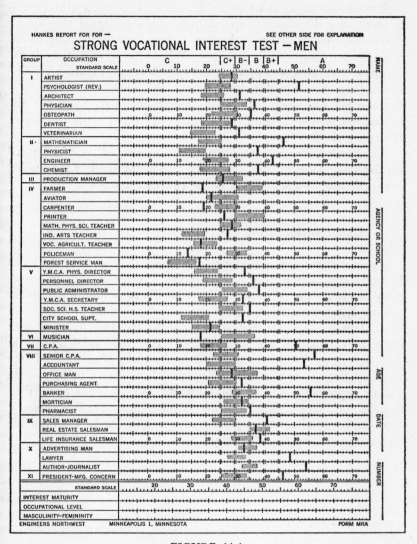

FIGURE 11.1

Profile sheet used by Testscor for reporting scores on the Strong Vocational Interest Test. The marks indicate the scores of an individual who took the test. Reproduced by kind permission of Testscor.

vide machine scoring at a reasonable charge. Testscor, a Minneapolis concern, has developed a special machine for scoring the Strong inventories which makes it possible to score the instrument on all scales at an exceptionally low cost. When this service is used, the results are reported on a profile sheet (6), shown in Figure 11.1. The heavy lines on this profile sheet indicate the scores on each occupational scale. The scores marked along each one of the scales are raw scores, but standard scores for all scales are given along the top of the rating sheet.

The shaded area indicates the range of scores of men in general on the scale. Thus the higher a score falls to the right of the shaded area, the more meaningful it is for guidance purposes.

Homogeneity of the Pattern of Responses of Women

There seems to be considerable evidence that women are more homogeneous than men in their interests. This means that an instrument such as the Vocational Interest Blank would differentiate among fewer occupations in the case of women than in the case of men. This is to be expected, if only for the fact that many women enter an occupation not because they have any special interest in that type of work but because it is a stopgap way of earning a living until marriage comes their way. Vocational choices for many women do not represent a selection of a lifetime pursuit but a convenient activity for filling in time until marriage. Another possible reason is that the range of activities permitted girls tends to be less than the range of activities permitted boys.

The Kuder Preference Record—Vocational

A second approach to the measurement of vocational interests is provided by the Kuder Preference Record—Vocational, (8, 9) which has evolved through a number of different forms. This inventory presents activities in groups of three, and the person taking the test selects from each group the activity he likes best and the activity he likes least. The illustrative item presented in the manual (9) is the thirteenth in the inventory and is as follows:

Build bird houses
Write articles about birds
Draw sketches of birds

On the basis of the preferences expressed the individual is given a score for his interest in each one of the following areas of activity:

0. Outdoor
1. Mechanical
2. Computational
3. Scientific
4. Persuasive

5. Artistic
6. Literary
7. Musical
8. Social Service
9. Clerical

The inventory is claimed to be suitable for high school students and for adults. However, the present writer feels that there is little point in administering the inventory to pupils below the tenth grade, if only for the fact that many of the words and phrases are too difficult for them to understand. Recognizing this fact, the publishers provide a glossary of difficult words, but this does not overcome the additional criticism that the inventory calls for expression of preferences for activities which are outside the range of experience of even children in the upper grades of high school. The common practice of administering the Kuder to every child in a high school is to be avoided, because the results will almost certainly be not used. Mass programs of this type have only one outcome; namely, the filling of the files with unused scores because the task of interpreting the profiles is delegated to the teachers and not to specialized guidance workers. As a general rule it may be said that instruments of this kind should be administered only when the results can be used by professional guidance workers in the counseling of individual students. As a mass testing enterprise it is a waste both of student time and of school funds.

It should be mentioned that the inventory not only ranks interests in order but also indicates the strength of each of the interests. The usual intention is to determine the interest which is most likely to be dominant when several possible activities compete for the attention of the individual. Some help can be obtained in the interpretation of scores by examining the average profiles for individuals in a large number of different occupations. These typical profiles are provided separately for men and for women and at first inspection seem to provide an excellent basis for interpreting the scores. However, when it is observed that some of the groups include only seven cases, it is realized that considerable caution is necessary in the use of the data for the interpretation of profiles.

The Kuder Preference Record—Personal

An extension of the Kuder Preference Record to other areas of preference is found in a relatively new instrument known as the Kuder Preference Record—Personal (10, 11). According to the manual for this instrument, it is designed to measure preferences in the following areas:

1. *Sociable*—expressed preferences for personal activities of a sociable nature—a preference for taking the lead and being in the center of activities involving people.
2. *Practical*—expressed preference for personal activities of a practical nature—a preference for dealing with practical problems and everyday affairs rather than interest in imaginary or glamorous activities.
3. *Theoretical*—expressed preference for personal activities of a theoretical nature—a preference for thinking, philosophizing, and speculating.
4. *Agreeable*—expressed preferences for personal activities of an agreeble nature—a preference for pleasant and smooth personal relations which are free from conflict.
5. *Dominant*—expressed preferences for personal activities involving the use of authority and power.

The inventory presents activities in groups of three, and the person taking it must choose the one which he likes most and the one which he likes least.

At the time of writing it is too early to say whether the instrument will have value. The evidence provided on validity in the preliminary edition of the Examiner's Manual is not particularly striking. While a group of farmers achieved highest scores on the "practical" scale, a finding which seems reasonable, a group of eighty-five insurance salesmen showed highest scores on the "sociable" scale, which seems much less according to expectation.

This extension of the Kuder Preference Record may eventually prove to be of some worth. It is much more a measure of values than of interests as these characteristics have been defined here, and, consequently, it is likely to be more an indicator of the motives operating in the individual rather than the specific types of activities to which he will devote his energies.

An unusual feature of the two types of the Kuder Preference Record is the so-called verification scale, which is designed to identify those who have answered the items carelessly or who have failed to follow the directions. This validity score needs to be validated; that is, evidence must be collected to show that it does identify those whose scores are in some way distorted. The idea is ingenious, though not novel, since a similar device had already been used in the Minnesota Multiphasic Personality Inventory and the Humm-Wadsworth Temperament Scale.

Special Problems in the Validation of the Preference Record

There are difficulties involved in the validation of instruments such as the Kuder Preference Record. The clarification of the meaning of the term *validation* is in itself a major problem in this area, for the term may have many different meanings.

First, the problem of validation may be simply that of determining the extent to which the responses made in answering the test are the expressed preferences of the individual. In other words, does the individual record his characteristic preferences or is he motivated by irrelevant factors in making his choices? On this basis it is commonly assumed that the inventory is valid largely because the difficulties of obtaining evidence of validity, in this sense of the term, seem to be unsurmountable. The only obvious approach would be to follow the administration of the Preference Record with interviews in an attempt to establish whether the preferences expressed in answering the Record were typical expressions of preference or whether there was some reason for falsification of responses. But if the data collected in the interview do not correspond to the data given in the Preference Record, which set of data is to be considered the most authentic and most valid?

The assumption that expressions of preference on an inventory represent typical expressions of preference is not entirely satisfactory. It has already been pointed out that in the design of questionnaires it is important to limit the questions to areas in which the individual has a clearly formulated and well-crystallized viewpoint. Little value can come of the process of asking persons whether they would prefer to be secretary of state, or secretary of defense. The fact that they had never considered this problem before is likely to make the decision arbitrary, and the examinee may give different answers when the question is repeated at a later date. To what extent the questions in the Kuder Preference Records are subject to this criticism is hard to determine, but caution should be exercised in assuming that the responses to the items represent typical responses.

Second, the problem of validation may refer to the extent to which the responses given in the Record correspond to the individual's actual choices of activities. In other words, does the individual who, for example, has a highest preference score in the mechanical area actually select activities which involve mechanical skills if he has opportunities of making such choices? It is unreasonable to expect a perfect relationship between expressed preferences and preferences as they are actually manifested, since few are able to engage freely in the activities which they prefer because the hard realities of life may force participation in activities for which the individual has little relish. If it is unreasonable to expect a perfect relationship between expressed preferences and manifest preferences, what degree of relationship may be expected? Nobody knows the answer to this question, but many would take the view that any positive correlation between preferences expressed on an inventory and so-called manifest preferences is evidence of validity. Much needs to be discovered yet about these matters and also about the relation of measures of interest with satisfaction derived later from vocational and avocational interests.

Other Interest Inventories

The interest inventories that have been discussed are only a few of the many that have been published. They have been selected mainly because they are the ones about which the greatest amount of information has been collected. Numerous others have been published which may be as useful as those described. If the reader wishes to obtain further information concerning other inventories, he i referred to Buros' *Third Mental Measurement Yearbook* (3) and *Fourth Mental Measurement Yearbook* (4).

Basic Dimensions of Interests

The selection of dimensions of interest for inclusion in measuring instruments has depended to a large extent on the judgment of the psychologist building the device. It is true that some attempt has been made to select dimensions which are as far as possible independent of one another, but this goal has been only to a limited extent attained. Some research has been undertaken in an attempt to identify clearly distinct dimensions of interest. Travers (18) in a review of recent research in this area concludes that the difficulties of establishing fundamental interest variables are such that they cannot be overcome by the techniques that are at present available. Such research as has been done has served mainly the function of identifying the difficulties involved. However, despite this limitation of the instruments at present available, they have had substantial uses in the study of practical educational problems.

THE MEASUREMENT OF READING INTERESTS

Introduction

One of the few areas in the curriculum in which instruments have been developed for the specific purpose of appraising pupil interest is the area of reading. The assessment of reading interests has been attacked from two standpoints, namely, from the standpoint of what children choose to read (manifest reading interests) and from the standpoint of what they say they prefer to read (expressed reading interests). The weaknesses of each one of these two methods of assessing interests has already been discussed.

In a summary of studies of manifest reading interests of children Rankin (13) points out that there seems considerable uniformity among studies in the finding that children show a steady increase in the number of books read up to the seventh grade, but that during the high school period there is a decline in reading interest measured in this way. Just what this measure of reading interest—the number of books read—means is not entirely clear, and its meaning will vary from one situation to another. Although it is a measure of reading interest, it must also be influenced substantially by the opportunities provided for borrowing books, the types of books that are available, and pressures exerted by the immediate classroom situation on the pupil.

The Fictitious Annotated Titles Technique

A technique developed by Thorndike (17) for studying the reading interests of children is based on the use of a list of fictitious titles of books, each one of which is followed by a brief description of the supposed content of the imaginary book. The child is asked to respond to each of the titles by marking "Yes" if he thinks he would like to read the story, by "No" if he thinks he would not like to read the story even if he had nothing to do, and by encircling a question mark if he cannot make up his mind whether he would or would not like to read it. The children were warned that they were not to indicate what they thought they ought to read but rather what they would really like to read. The list included altogether eighty-eight annotated titles.

In order to provide a check on the honesty and care with which the questionnaire was executed, six titles were included which Thorndike felt confident would not interest children in the ten-to-fifteen-year-old group, with which he was mainly concerned. In choosing such titles as "Famous Sermons by Famous Preachers," Thorndike could be fairly sure that he was listing titles outside of the ordinary range of interest of these youngsters. In the study proper, any child who expressed an interest in four or more of these titles was excluded from the group on whom the analysis of the data was based on the assumption that carelessness or other irrelevant factors were influencing his responses. Justification for this procedure is found in the fact that the duller and younger children were the ones who tended to mark these six selected titles, and it is these two groups of all groups who might be expected to avoid them as reading material. The procedure is similar to that of using validating scores, a practice commonly adopted by the makers of several personality inventories.

From this type of device, it is possible to group the titles into areas such as animal stories, wild life, adventure, child life in other lands, and so on, and to study the relative interest of various age groups in each of these general topics. It is also possible to compare the reading interests of boys with those of girls and those of brighter children with those of duller children. On the basis of the analysis of the responses of about three thousand children, Thorndike came to the following conclusions concerning the patterns of interest expressed through this specific device:

1. In either sex, there is considerable uniformity of interests over the age range of ten to fifteen and over a range of intelligence quotients of as much as 30 points. There is, so to speak, a typical pattern of reading interests for boys, and another typical reading interest pattern for girls. Of course, in interpreting these results, it must be taken into account that the group included in the study covered an age range of only six years.

2. Boys and girls have distinct patterns of reading interests, and so different are these patterns that if the extent to which boys like a specific topic is known, no prediction can be made concerning the extent to which girls will like it. Sex seems to be the most important single determiner of reading interest, but no inference can be made concerning the basis for this difference. Society may force a difference in the pattern of reading interests of boys and girls.

3. With respect to reading interests as appraised by the fictitious titles device, bright children (with a median I.Q. of 123) resemble a mentally duller group (with a median I.Q. of 92) who are two or three years older. It is not that the bright children show a different pattern of reading interest from the duller children, but that they reach each stage of interest development at a slightly earlier age. Contrary to common belief, the brighter children are not more academic in their reading interests than the duller children. Also, it may be noted that any differences between the brighter and the duller in reading interests are small in comparison with the differences between boys and girls.

While Thorndike's "fictitious titles" technique may be used and applied by individual teachers, as with all measuring techniques, it should be used with caution and the results must be interpreted with care and discrimination.

THE APPRAISAL OF VALUES

Little has been done to determine whether motives can be usefully classified in terms of the values toward which they are directed, and hence little is known about the measurement of the strength of motives grouped in such terms. Discussion of values in technical literature has been very largely on a theoretical rather than on an experimental basis, and little has been done to determine by careful scientific study the number of values that it is convenient to hypothesize. One of the few instruments which has been devised for measurement in this area is called the Study of Values. The original edition of this test was used in numerous studies scattered over a twenty-year period and was then revised in 1951. Many of these studies are both listed and described in the Manual of Directions (1) for the revised edition.

The Study of Values includes two types of items, of which the following are illustrative: *

The main object of scientific research should be the discovery of pure truth rather than its practical applications. (a) Yes; (b) No.

To what extent do the following famous persons interest or attract you? (a) Florence Nightingale; (b) Napoleon; (c) Henry Ford; (d) Charles Darwin.

In each case the choice made by the person in answering the questions is hypothesized to reflect his basic value system.

The Study of Values is necessarily based on an a priori analysis of the basic values in human motivation. The analysis was made by Eduard Spranger, a German philosopher, who in 1928 published a speculative volume entitled *Lebensformen*. In this volume, which represents one of the more brilliant examples of armchair psychology, an attempt is made to justify the idea that men can best be understood in terms of the values toward which their dominant

---

* By permission from *A Study of Values* by Allport, Vernon and Gardner. Copyright, 1951, by Houghton Mifflin Co.

motives are directed. Spranger's system is essentially a method of classifying men in terms of the values on the basis of which their behavior seems to be organized. It must be noted that no experimental evidence is supplied to justify the classification, nor is there any evidence to show that the personality of individuals tends to be dominated by one or the other of the values which Spranger describes. There is also no evidence to show that the values described are unrelated or independent of one another in some way statistically or psychologically. But with all of these shortcomings, one can say that Spranger did try to offer a thoroughgoing rationale for his typology and his work shows brillance even if it lacks an adequate factual basis.

Just as Alfred Binet produced a useful test on the basis of a more or less speculative study of intelligence, so too does the instrument based on Spranger's speculations have merit as an experimental instrument even though the rationale on which it is based lacks an adequate experimental background. Spranger's system classifies men according to whether their lives tend to be dominated by one of the following values:

1. The Theoretical
2. The Economic
3. The Aesthetic
4. The Social
5. The Political
6. The Religious

A detailed description of the nature of these values is given in Spranger's book, and a more general account in the Manual of the Study of Values.

Since the purpose of the scale is to determine the value or values which are dominant in the behavior patterns of the individual, the scores derived from the scale show the relative strength of the various values within the individual. For example, a high score on the religious scale does not mean that the individual is highly motivated by religious values. It means only that religious values have greater motivational force than the other value systems included in the study. Scores made by an individual on one of the scales cannot be compared directly with the score of another individual on the same scale.

Since the purpose of the scale is to rank the six values described in terms of the extent to which they are effective in directing the behavior of the individual, it is logical that the scoring system is such that a high score on one scale necessarily depresses the scores on the other scales. It is not possible to obtain a high score on all of the six scales. If some of the scores are high, then others must be low.

Considerable evidence has been collected concerning the validity of the Study of Values. The general approach has been to identify certain groups concerning whom the dominant value would be widely agreed upon, and then to determine whether the scores on the scales are in agreement with expectation. Some agreement has been found in studies of this type between these scores and expectations.

A major difficulty of developing measuring instruments in the domain of values stems partly from the difficulty of developing a classification of value systems. This is reflected in the fact that the Study of Values remained the only instrument available for measurement in this area for over twenty years. However, there has recently been developed a new instrument which attempts to appraise the individual's "general goals of life." This instrument (5), developed as part of a major research study in education, requires the individual to scrutinize a series of 190 pairs of statements of the following general type:

> Fine relations with other persons.
> Self-sacrifice for the sake of a better world.

The person to whom the inventory is administered reads each pair of statements and decides which one expresses more adequately his main goal in life. On the basis of his decisions on the 190 pairs of items, he is given a score for the degree to which his preferences reflect each one of the following as a goal in life:

A. Serving God, doing God's will.
B. Achieving personal mortality in heaven.
C. Self-discipline—overcoming my irrational emotions and sensuous ideas.
D. Self-sacrifice for the sake of a better world.
E. Doing my duty.
F. Peace of mind, contentment, stillness of spirit.
G. Serving the community of which I am a part.

H. Fine relations with other persons.
I. Self-development—becoming a real, genuine person.
J. Finding my place in life and accepting it.
K. Living for the pleasure of the moment.
L. Getting as many deep and lasting pleasures as I can.
M. Promoting the most deep and lasting pleasures for the greatest number of people.
N. Making a place for myself in the world; getting ahead.
O. Power; control over people and things.
P. Security—protecting my way of life against adverse changes.
Q. Being able to "take it"; brave and uncomplaining acceptance of what circumstances bring.
R. Realizing that I cannot change the bad features of the world and doing the best I can for myself and those dear to me.
S. Survival, continued existence.
T. Handling the specific problems of life as they arise.

The difficulties of obtaining evidence of the validity of this type of instrument cannot be fully discussed here, but the major problems must be mentioned. First, the possibility must be considered that many individuals do not have a major goal in life which they can describe in words. Goals which the individual is unable to describe in words are familiar to the clinician, and these have to be disregarded by the inventory approach. Second, there is real difficulty in determining whether the inventory taps anything more than verbal stereotypes which reflect how the individual likes to think of himself. The inventory may possibly provide more information about the individual's "idealized" self rather than about the self which he manifests to the world.

Summary

This chapter has attempted to present the problems of measuring interests and the types of instruments that have been developed to solve some of these problems. If interest inventories are administered in carefully selected situations, there is no doubt that they can be of value, but mass administration can rarely be justified. This is in accordance with the viewpoint that scores on such inventories should not be interpreted by any rule-of-thumb method but should be considered only as one item of evidence pertaining to the individual's responses to life. Scores from interest inventories can be of value only when they are derived from individuals whose interest patterns have achieved some stability. At present, it requires skilled judgment to determine whether such stability of interests probably exists in a particular individual.

Measures of inventoried interests may also serve the purpose of summarizing the vague and varied likes and dislikes so that the individual can see for himself the pattern which his interests assume. It may thus help the individual acquire a clearer concept of himself and the kinds of situations from which he is likely to derive satisfaction.

Measurement in the domain of values offers considerable promise, for here one may expect to find variables which permeate a wide range of the individual's activities. However, the measurement of values is still in the early stages of development.

References

1. Allport, Gordon W., Vernon, Philip E. and Lindzey, G., *A Study of Values*. Revised Edition. *Manual of Directions,* New York, Houghton Mifflin Company, 1951, pp. 11.

2. Berman, I. R., Darley, J. G., and Paterson, D. G., *Vocational Interest Scales,* Minneapolis, Minnesota, University of Minnesota Employment Stabilization Research Unit 3, No. 5, 1934, pp. 22.

3. Buros, Oscar K. (Editor), *The Third Mental Measurement Yearbook,* New Brunswick, New Jersey, Rutgers University Press, 1949, pp. 1246 + XIV.

4. Buros, Oscar K. (Editor), *The Fourth Mental Measurement Yearbook,* New Brunswick, New Jersey, Rutgers University Press, 1953, pp. 1163 + XXIV.

5. *General Goals of Life Inventory,* Princeton, New Jersey, Cooperative Test Division, Educational Testing Service, 1950.

6. *Hankes Report Form for Strong Vocational Interest Test,* Form M, Minneapolis, Minnesota, Testscor.

7. Jersild, Arthur T. and Tasch, Ruth J., *Children's Interests and What They Suggest for Education,* New York, Teachers College Bureau of Publications, Columbia University, 1949, pp. 173 + XIII.

8. Kuder, G. Frederic, *Preference Record—Vocational,* Form C, Chicago, Illinois, Science Research Associates, 1949.

9. Kuder, G. Frederic, *Examiner's Manual, Preference Record—Vocational*, Form C, Chicago, Illinois, Science Research Associates, 1949, pp. 24.

10. Kuder, G. Frederic, *Examiner's Manual for Preference Record—Personal*. Chicago, Illinois, Science Research Associates, 1949.

11. Kuder, G. Frederic, *Preference Record—Personal*, Chicago, Illinois, Science Research Associates, Form BI, 1948.

12. Murphy, Gardner, *Personality, A Biosocial Approach to Origins and Structure*, New York, Harper and Brothers, 1947, pp. 999 + XIII.

13. Rankin, Marie, *Children's Interests in Library Books of Fiction*, Teachers College Contributions to Education No. 906, New York, Teachers College Bureau of Publications, Columbia University, 1944, pp. 146 + IX.

14. Strong, Edward K. Jr., *Vocational Interest Blank*, Form M (Men), Revised, Stanford, California, Stanford University Press, 1938.

15. Strong, Edward K. Jr., *Vocational Interest Blank*, Form W (Women), Stanford, California, Stanford University Press, 1947.

16. Strong, Edward K. Jr., *Vocational Interests of Men and Women*, Stanford, California, Stanford University Press, 1943, pp. 746 + XXIX.

17. Thorndike, Robert L., *A Comparative Study of Children's Interests*, New York, Teachers College Bureau of Publications, Columbia University, 1941, pp. 48 + V.

18. Travers, R. M. W., "Individual Differences." In Calvin Stone (Ed.) *Annual Review of Psychology*, Vol. VI, 1955 (in press).

19. Wallace, Wimburn L., *The Relationship of Certain Variables to Discrepancy Between Expressed and Inventoried Vocational Interest*. Manuscript in the library of the University of Michigan, 1949, pp. 99.

CHAPTER 12

Some Approaches to the Assessment of Social Development

Introduction

In the chapter on the assessment of personality, some reference was made to the measurement of certain aspects of social development. It was indicated that social behavior associated with trait names such as honesty, sociability, leadership, social dominance, and so forth, tends to be highly variable from situation to situation. If a person's behavior is honest in one situation, there is little basis for predicting that his behavior will be honest in another. The concept that social behavior can be predicted from a knowledge of the degree to which a person is characterized by certain traits is not a particularly useful one. For this reason, some psychologists have suggested that the pupil's social development should be studied not by methods which attempt to assess his traits but by methods which measure his actual social participation. The latter methods provide *limited* but sometimes useful information about pupil development. The data derived from these methods should always be interpreted with the greatest of caution.

Sociometric Techniques

One of the simplest and most interesting techniques for the appraisal of the social adjustment of the pupil in the classroom group is the sociometric technique developed by Jacob L. Moreno, a Viennese psychiatrist who emigrated to America. The technique (8) was first used in a New York City school and consisted of the simple device of asking each child to write down the name of the child that he would like best to sit near. From the data thus collected, it was possible to make a diagram showing preferences expressed by children in any class. Sociograms such as are illustrated in Figure 12.1 may be drawn from data such as these. In this table, eleven children

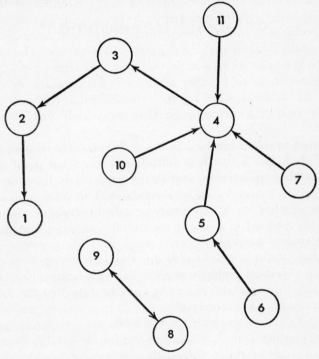

FIGURE 12.1

A sociogram representing an aspect of the relationships between eleven pupils.

are represented by the nine numbered points. The arrow pointing away from one of these points toward another point indicates the child whom this particular child prefers. Thus child 7 prefers child 4, and child 8 chooses child 9, while child 9 chooses child 8. The most popular child in terms of the question asked is child 4, who was selected as a preferred seating companion by three other children. In contrast, no child chose either child 6 or 7 as a preferred seating partner. The children who are not selected by any of the other as preferred companions are commonly called social rejects. This type of diagram is known as a sociogram.

In the common form of sociometric measure each child names another as a preferred companion for one specific type of activity, but the sociometric technique may also call upon the individual to name two or three or more who would be preferred as companions. There are certain difficulties involved in the handling of the data when the latter type of sociometric device is used, and one of them is the problem of how to present first, second, and third choices on a sociogram without making it excessively complex. The common practice is to plot all choices in the same way without making any discrimination as to whether a choice is first, second, or a third. When this is done, a social reject on the sociogram represents a more extreme case of social rejection than when only first choices are plotted.

Another problem involved in the differential use of first, second, and third choices is that it is difficult to know what significance to attach to these differences, and this is particularly true when each child is given a score for sociometric status. The latter is an attempt to measure what would commonly be called popularity and is most commonly assessed in terms of the number of times that the child was selected as the preferred companion for a given activity. When sociometric status is measured in this way, it is common practice to count all expressed preferences regardless of whether they are first, second, or third choices. Attention may be called to the fact that the number of choices received by a child may be different from the number of children expressing a preference for him, since one child may list another as first, second, and third choice. However, after a careful study of this problem, Bronfenbrenner (2) came to the conclusion that the number of choices received represented a reliable index of sociometric status.

In sociometric studies, subjects may be asked to choose companions for various purposes. In the Brofenbrenner study and in another by Gronlund (4) the children were asked first to choose those they liked best to work with, those they liked best to play with, and those they liked best as seating companions. The sociograms based on these three reasons for choice showed some differences as well as substantial resemblances. Whatever sociometric status may indicate in this type of situation, it does seem to have acceptable reliability and, as a matter of fact, in one experiment by Bonney (1), was found to have reliability comparable to that of intelligence tests. The latter result is particularly surprising when it is considered that Bonney made his measures over three consecutive school years.

How to Make a Sociogram

Detailed procedures for constructing a sociogram have been well described in a pamphlet prepared by the Horace Mann-Lincoln Institute of School Experimentation of Teachers College, Columbia University (5). This publication should be considered as a basic guide for those teachers who wish to use this technique. A less detailed account is given here.

Step I. The individuals in the group are asked to choose other members of the group either as companions for specific activities or in terms of whether they like them, admire them, wish to be like them, and so forth. It is usually preferable for each person to choose at least three others on each basis.

Step II. The expressed preferences are then plotted on paper. The usual practice is to start with the individual who seems to be the most popular. Thus in the initial stage of plotting the intra-group relationships the type of diagram shown in Figure 12.2 might emerge.

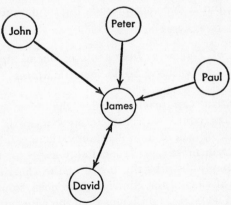

FIGURE 12.2
Initial step in the preparation of a sociogram.

This diagram indicates that four individuals, John, David, Peter, and Paul, expressed a preference for James and that James expressed a preference for David. The direction of the arrow indicates the direction of choice. The next step is to plot out in a similar way the relations of any other individuals representing focal points in the final sociogram. Finally, these various groupings are brought together on one chart.

Various elaborations may be made of this simple procedure. First, second, and third choices may be plotted separately by using different types of lines—dotted, continuous, and broken lines. However, little seems to be achieved by this refinement, and the common practice seems to be to plot sociograms without making any distinctions between first, second, and third choices.

Another refinement in the plotting of sociograms is to draw them in such a way that specific groups can be identified. Boys may be represented by circles and girls by squares. Sometimes it may be profitable to plot members of different social groups in some way so that they can be differentiated in the final sociogram. From diagrams of the latter type it may be possible to diagnose special social problems resulting from racial prejudices.

A final word of caution needs to be given with respect to the use of the sociogram. The device represents social relationships within a class and does not indicate the sources and causes of these relationships. It is a device for pointing out important facts which need to be interpreted, but it does not provide interpretations.

Accuracy of Teachers' Judgments of Social Adjustment as Measured by Sociometric Status

To what extent can teachers judge the social adjustment of pupils in the classroom? No complete answer can be given to this question because of lack of data. Certainly, there can be little doubt that the teacher in most cases is inevitably aware of the aggressive child who probably disturbs the peace of the classroom, although from the point of view of the clinician these noisy troublemakers are likely to present less serious problems than the withdrawn child who, because he assumes a background position, is less easily noticed.

One of the few studies designed to investigate the extent to which the teacher is aware of the problems of adjustment of individual students was undertaken by Gronlund (4). This study undertook to determine the accuracy of teachers' judgments concerning the extent to which sixth grade pupils were accepted by their classmates as work companions, seating companions, and play companions. The study was undertaken in forty sixth grade classes in which each pupil was asked to name five others with whom he would like best to work, to play, and to sit. On this basis each pupil was given a score of sociometric status in terms of the number of times he was selected as a companion. Each teacher was requested to make judgments concerning the extent to which each child was selected by the others as a companion for each of these three activities. This was accomplished by ranking the children in order of sociometric status. In addition, the teacher was asked to list the three boys and three girls that she liked most and three of each sex that she liked least. The study was undertaken toward the close of the school year when the teachers probably knew as much about their pupils as they would be ever likely to know.

The study showed important differences in the ability of teachers to judge the sociometric status of individual pupils. Coefficients of correlations between teacher judgments of sociometric status varied from 0.268 up to 0.838, with a mean of 0.595. The judgments of the teachers poorest in this respect would be quite worthless for the purpose of individual guidance. As might be expected, teacher judgments of sociometric status with respect to choosing companions for play were less accurate than judgments with respect to choosing companions for work or for seating. Teachers have less opportunity to observe play groupings than they have to observe seating and work groupings.

The ability to judge sociometric status bore no relationship to the age of the teacher, the length of her teaching experience, recency of college training, size of class, or whether the teacher had been with the class for one or for two semesters.

Gronlund's study also brought to light the interesting fact that teachers tend to judge too favorably the sociometric status of the boys and girls they prefer and too unfavorably the sociometric status of those they like least. The bias in judgment is in the direction expected. Another interesting fact revealed by the study was that the ability of the teacher to judge sociometric status seemed to be independent of the amount of freedom enjoyed by pupils during class hours. It is possible that this apparent lack of relationship may be due to the inadequacy of Gronlund's instrument for measuring classroom freedom, which consisted of a questionnaire filled in by pupils concerning their activities in class.

Specificity of Sociometric Status as a Measure of Social Adjustment

The technique of sociometry may seem to provide a simple basis for assessing social adjustment, but great caution should be exercised in interpreting the data thus collected. The fact that a child is classified as a social reject on the basis of a sociometric test does not necessarily imply general social maladjustment but perhaps merely a local maladjustment. Undesirable sociometric status should be interpreted as a symptom rather than as a disease in itself. The relation of this symptom to the total life of the individual needs to be understood.

Correlates of Sociometric Status

Sociometric studies have been designed largely to demonstrate group structure and its relationship to other variables. Little has been done to study the characteristics of members of groups who have highest sociometric status or who are rejects in specific situations. Such data are obviously necessary for teachers who wish to obtain fuller understanding of sociometric techniques. A teacher may observe from the study of the sociogram of her class that it is organized in an undesirable way, but the full significance of a measure such as sociometric status needs to be understood.

Jennings (7) attempted to find some of the correlates of sociometric status in a study conducted in the New York State Training School for Girls. This institution represents a closed community of four hundred girls ranging in age from twelve to sixteen. These girls come from underprivileged homes, are within the so-called normal

range of intelligence, and are committed for various offenses classified as sexual delinquency. The sociometric test was conducted
twice over a period of eight months, and each girl could choose or
reject as many as she desired as living companions, work companions, recreation companions, and study companions.

Jennings then selected three groups, one consisting of girls chosen
least frequently as companions, one including girls chosen about as
frequently as the average girl, and one group of girls chosen with
exceptionally high frequency as companions. The behaviors com-
plained of by housemothers were then tabulated for these three
groups of girls. The underchosen group were more often described
as having characteristics which might interfere with group activities
or upset morale. In this category are behaviors such as aggressiveness, dominance, and quarrelsomeness. On the other hand, and
inconsistent with this conclusion, is the fact that "rebelliousness" and
"retaliatory behavior" is more characteristic of the overchosen girls
than of the underchosen. Facts such as these do not assist materially
in understanding differences in sociometric status, and even if they
did provide distinctively different pictures of individuals at opposite
ends of the sociometric scale, caution would have to be exercised in
interpreting the difference for two main reasons.

First, it would not be clear whether these discriminating characteristics were causes or consequences of sociometric status. The child
rejected by the group may be expected to show many undesirable
characteristics as a result of this rejection. The feelings of insecurity
resulting from rejection may result in the manifestation of aggres-
sions and other unfriendly acts which might not occur in a more
favorable social situation. In this area, a field theory of personality
has real application, for the characteristic responses of the individual
may be expected to be related to his social status in a group.

Second, it seems probable that the kinds of characteristics included in the Jennings study cannot be accurately assessed. A judgment that an individual is rebellious is a very subjective judgment.
It is quite probable that the judgments of the housemothers were
influenced by the halo effect; that is, they tended to attribute a wide
range of undesirable qualities to the rejected girls because they themselves had feelings of aversion toward them.

The study of aspects of the personality of the individual that result
in social rejection in a given group and characteristics which result

from being rejected could be separated from one another only by clinical case studies of rejected individuals. Superficial questioning of the type that can be undertaken through questionnaires would probably yield little if anything, since a careful probing and study of the individual personality would be necessary. A complication is also introduced into studies of this kind by the fact that a person who is a social reject in one group may have the highest sociometric status in another. Rejection may not be a sign of general social maladjustment but merely an indication that the individual is trying to assimilate himself in a social group unsuitable for him.

The Social Distance Scale—A Refined Sociometric Technique

The Horace Mann-Lincoln Institute of School Experimentation has adapted the Bogardus Social Distance Scale for use in the study of the social structure of classrooms. The instrument thus produced is called the Classroom Social Distance Scale (6). By means of this device each child in a classroom expresses his like or dislike for every other child by indicating whether

1. He would like to have him as one of his best friends.
2. He would like to have him in his group but not as a close friend.
3. He would like to be with him once in a while but not often for a long time.
4. He did not mind him being in the same room but did not want to have anything to do with him.
5. He wished he were not in the same room.

The purposes of this instrument are roughly the same as those of the sociometric device. It enables the teacher to identify children who have special difficulties in getting along with others in the group, and also, to some extent, the data can be used for identifying the nature of the groupings within the classroom. From this device, a score can be obtained for each child indicating the degree to which he is accepted by the other children in the room.

The publication describing this device emphasizes the importance of using it only in situations where the teacher can be sure that the responses of the children will be given honestly, for unless there is honesty there cannot be validity.

Social Development Measured in Terms of Group Participation

Another approach to the appraisal of the social development of the individual is illustrated by a follow-up study of certain selected students observed during the Eight Year Study. It may be recalled that in 1932, some three hundred colleges and universities agreed to free a group of thirty schools from formal college entrance requirements for their graduates in order that these schools might be able to experiment with changes in the curriculum. The recommendation of the principal of the school was to be accepted in lieu of the usual admission requirements. By 1936 about two thousand graduates of these schools had entered college under the conditions of the agreement.

Under a grant from the General Education Board, the Commission on the Relation of School and College of the Progressive Education Association set up a study to evaluate the college experience of the graduates from the thirty schools in which a new experimental program had been introduced. The general procedure of this follow-up study (3) was to compare the college behavior of students from the experimental schools with significant aspects of the behavior of a comparable (control) group of students from other schools. This comparison group was matched with the experimental group (from the thirty schools) with reference to scholastic aptitude, sex, race, age, religious affiliation, size and type of secondary school from which students came (public or private), size, type, and geographic location of home community, socioeconomic status of the family, extracurricular activity in secondary school, and vocational objectives.

The data collected in this study were used to compare the amount of group participation demonstrated by the experimental group with the amount shown by the control group. For this purpose, a tabulation was made of the percentage of students in each group that participated in each of a number of social activities. Data were collected on frequency of participation in each one of the following group activities:

1. Organized sports
2. Art, dramatics, and musical groups

3. Social clubs
4. Religious groups on campus
5. Publications
6. Special interest clubs
7. Student government
8. Departmental clubs
9. Social service groups
10. Forensics
11. Political and social action groups

Differences between the two groups were found to be extremely small, but one wonders just how differences would have been interpreted if they had been larger. It is implied in the study that a high score in terms of social participation would be considered more acceptable than a low score, a viewpoint which reflects the current concept of the goals of the individual's social development. Not everybody would endorse this viewpoint.

Intellectualistic Aspects of Social Development

Until recent times, there has been a considerable emphasis on intellectualistic aspects of social development; that is, on those aspects which are based on the student's knowledge of how to behave in certain given situations. One of the most careful analyses of these intellectual aspects of social behavior was made by the evaluation staff of the Eight Year Study. In considering this area under the general heading of "social sensitivity" the Committee on Evaluation of the Eight Year Study identified six major aspects as follows:

1. Social thinking such as occurs in interpreting social facts and in applying them to new problems and in understanding agreements concerning social problems.
2. Social attitudes, beliefs, and values.
3. Social awareness such as occurs when the individual perceives a social problem or expresses concern over it.
4. Participation in socially worth-while activity.
5. Social information such as is evidenced by knowledge of social events and generalizations.
6. Skill in social action, by which was meant effective participation in groups concerned with social action.

It may be observed that apart from the second and fourth of these objectives, which involve attitudes and interests, respectively, these goals are to a considerable extent intellectualistic in character and place little emphasis on the personal relation between the individual and his society. The measurement of most of the objectives of this type have been considered previously in chapters which deal with the intellectualistic aspects of education. The measurements of outcomes listed under the second objective has been considered in the chapters on attitude measurement, and the fourth received attention in the chapters on the measurement of interests.

It may be noted in passing that the major attempt in the Eight Year Study to measure the intellectualistic outcomes of social development was an instrument to measure the ability to apply social facts and generalizations to social problems. This test involved three aspects of this problem: (1) The ability to see the relationship between general principles and facts and social issues inherent in various problems. (2) The ability to evaluate arguments concerning various aspects of a social problem. (3) The ability to determine the effectiveness of certain social policies in achieving certain goals. In the test, each section consisted of the statement of a social problem followed by a single suggested situation. This is followed by a series of statements concerning the suggested solution. Some of these statements support the solution, others indicate it is worthless, and still others are merely irrelevant. The student is asked to classify each statement as supporting, contradictory to, or irrelevant to the suggested solution. He is then asked to go back and re-examine the statements and determine whether each can be proved to be either true or false.

This instrument, as in the case of most of the other tests developed in the Eight Year Study, has a rather complex scoring system which is designed to enable the teacher to diagnose difficulties in the thinking of the student. However, it is not clear whether a brief measure can yield this amount of information, and part scores may be too unreliable and therefore lack validity to the point where this diagnostic aspect of the test cannot be actually used.

Another intellectualistic approach to the problem of measuring social adjustment is presented by tests which attempt to measure the pupil's knowledge of social customs or etiquette. A number of these have been published. One by Rowland and Dreese (9) is designed to measure information of this kind in grades 10 to 16, while another by Strang, Brown, and Stratton (11) is claimed suitable for grades 7 to 12. Instruments such as these measure certain knowledge desirable for social adjustment.

It hardly seems necessary to point out the criticisms that can be made of the intellectualistic approach to the evaluation of social development. Such evaluations are made out of context; that is, they exclude elements which are essential determinants of the response that will actually occur in social situations. Thus the response given in the test situation may not correspond to any response that occurs outside of the test situation, and the dimension measured by such a test may be a product of the test situation.

The intellectualistic approach is blind to the fact that social responses are extremely complex phenomena and are not determined on an intellectualistic basis alone, but are influenced by tendencies acquired as far back as early infancy. These tendencies seem to be largely outside of the conscious control of the individual.

Summary

This chapter has presented a review of sociometric and other techniques for assessing social development. The immediate product of sociometry is a sociogram which is a diagrammatic representation of the preferences which the members of a group show for one another in choosing partners for participating in a particular activity. The sociogram does not indicate the reasons for a person's popularity or rejection, and therefore great caution must be used in the interpretation of a sociogram. The reader should also be on guard against committing the error of assuming that the undesirable traits of a pupil may be the cause of his rejection by the group. It is probable that in many cases the undesirable traits of a person rejected by a group may be a *result of* rather than a *cause of* his rejection. The excellent study by Jennings (7) was presented mainly to illustrate the problems and difficulties of interpreting sociometric data. Nevertheless, sociometric techniques have uses when cautiously applied.

Other approaches to the study of social development through the measurement of amount of participation in various social activities have been used. If social participation of this type is considered a desirable educational goal, then the method is a reasonable approach to the measurement of the extent to which this objective is achieved. However, many teachers might not subscribe to this objective but would look upon the joining of organized social activities as only one source of satisfaction of social needs.

Finally, consideration was given to the appraisal of the intellectualistic aspects of social development which have been measured through paper-and-pencil tests. These seem to be the least promising of those techniques considered.

References

1. Bonney, Merl E., "The Relative Stability of Social, Intellectual, and Academic Status in Grades II to IV, and the Interrelationship Between These Various Forms of Growth," *Journal of Educational Psychology,* 34, 1943, 88–102.

2. Bronfenbrenner, Urie, "A Constant of Reference for Sociometric Research: Part II Experiment and Inference," *Sociometry,* 7, 1944, 40–75.

3. Chamberlin, Dean, Chamberlin, Enid, Drought, Neal E., and Scott, William E., *Did They Succeed in College?* New York, Harper and Brothers, 1942, pp. 291 + XXIV.

4. Gronlund, Norman E., *The Accuracy of Teachers' Judgments Concerning the Sociometric Status of Sixth Grade Pupils,* Sociometry Monographs, No. 25, pp. 62.

5. Horace Mann-Lincoln Institute of School Experimentation, *How to Construct a Sociogram,* New York, Teachers College Bureau of Publications, Columbia University, 1950, pp. 37.

6. Horace Mann-Lincoln Institute of School Experimentation, *Classroom Social Distance Scale,* New York, Teachers College Bureau of Publications, Columbia University, New York, 1950.

7. Jennings, Helen H., *Leadership and Isolation* (Second Edition), New York, Longmans, Green, and Company, 1950, pp. 349 + XVII.

8. Moreno, Jacob L., *Who Shall Survive?* New York, Beacon House, 1953, pp. 763 + CXIV.

9. Rowland, Creelman and Dreese, Mitchell, *Tests of Etiquette,* George Washington University Series, Washington, D. C., Center for Psychological Services, George Washington University, 1941.

10. Smith, Eugene R., Tyler, Ralph W., and the Evaluation Staff, *Appraising and Recording Student Progress,* New York, Harper and Brothers, 1942, pp. 55 + XXIII.
11. Strang, Ruth, Brown, Marion A., and Stratton, Dorothy C., *Test of Knowledge of Social Usage,* New York, Teachers College Bureau of Publications, Columbia University, 1933.

PART IV

Predicting Pupil Progress

CHAPTER 13

Techniques Used in the Prediction of the Progress of Learning

Predicting the Progress of Learning

Previous chapters have been devoted principally to the problem of assessing the outcomes of learning, although it has been necessary to some extent to consider problems of learning along with problems of assessment. The pages that follow are concerned primarily with a different problem, namely, that of predicting the extent to which an individual can learn successfully in a given area. *The problem may be stated in broad terms as that of predicting the extent to which given objectives can be achieved in given individuals.*

In this chapter, it is proposed to discuss the types of intruments used for estimating the aptitude of students for particular types of educational programs and the thinking upon which these instruments are based. In the next chapter, a review will be presented of studies in which the actual predictive value of these instruments has been assessed.

The Problem of Prediction

The ultimate purpose of psychology is to discover the laws of human behavior. These laws would enable the scientist to predict the response of an individual to a stimulus situation.

It is evident that the discovery of these laws involves more than the study of relationships between stimulus and response, for common observation indicates that individuals vary greatly in the responses which they show to the same stimulus situation. Individuals respond differently to the same situation because they have different characteristics. These characteristics, which produce differences in responses, have been named *intervening variables* by Tolman because they intervene between the stimulus and the response. These intervening variables, according to Tolman (19), "interconnect between the initiating causes of behavior on the one hand, and the final resulting behavior itself, on the other. Thus, the prediction of the response to a stimulus situation requires that the intervening variables be known."

Consider the problem of predicting the high school pupil's response to a first course in French. Let us assume that we know the nature of the teaching which is to occur in this particular class, but from this knowledge alone the student's response cannot be predicted. His response may later be summarized by the teacher by a letter grade of A or by a letter grade of F, but what the response will be cannot be determined from a knowledge of the stimulus situation alone. In order to make the prediction it is necessary to be able to measure certain intervening variables which determine what his response to a given stimulus situation will be. Thus the laws of behavior must be formulated in terms of a relationship which may be represented in the following way:

Stimulus→ Intervening Variables→ Responses

Tests of aptitude are attempts to measure some of the intervening variables which relate the learning situation to the responses in that situation. Thus, in the case of the high school pupil who is learning French, the relationship represented above may be rewritten as:

The classroom situation→Aptitude for learning →Achievement
(stimulus)   a foreign language   demonstrated in
                    (an intervening variable)   some performance
                              +   (response)
                    other unidentified inter-
                    vening variables

Intervening variables such as that represented in this relationship are best defined in terms of the devices through which they are measured. There is little value in postulating an intervening variable unless it is possible to measure it, and until such a measure has been developed no definition of it is likely to be satisfactory.

This chapter is devoted largely to a study of attempts which psychologists have made to develop measures of intervening variables which determine the pupil's response to a learning situation.

It must be noted that it is rarely if ever possible to identify or measure all the intervening variables that relate the stimulus to the response. These are invariably numerous and complex, and only a few can be identified, let alone measured. However, even if tests were available which measured all the intervening variables, the data obtained from such instruments would not be adequate alone for predicting responses unless the stimulus situation were known. This is the major difficulty in predicting achievement from aptitude-test scores, for in making such predictions only vague general information is available concerning the stimulus situation in which the person is to be placed. It is not known whether the teacher will be friendly or aloof, demanding or *laissez faire*, well organized or poorly organized, and so forth. In addition, no information will be available concerning other aspects of the learning situation, such as whether conditions for study outside of school will be favorable or unfavorable. Thus, it can hardly be expected that the prediction of the pupil's behavior will be accurate from a measurement of the intervening variables alone because there are other important determinants of behavior.

If it were possible to hold the stimulus situation constant for all individuals whose behavior is to be predicted, it might be expected that the predictive power of measures of the intervening variables would be greatly increased. For this reason, an aptitude test designed for predicting behavior in a particular course of instruction which varies but little from section to section might be expected to have greater predictive power than one designed for similar courses in a large number of different schools.

The purpose of this chapter is to describe the general characteristics of the types of instrument most commonly used for predicting achievement. Emphasis will be placed on those which have become well established rather than upon the numerous instruments which appear each year and which usually have a short life span. Since the prediction of achievement must be made at the present time largely in terms of tests of intellectual skill, this chapter is devoted to the description of such tests. The use of personality variables in predicting achievement has already been touched upon in previous chapters and cannot be discussed at further length here.

EARLY APPROACHES TO THE PROBLEM

The problem of predicting achievement is an old one, and until the turn of the century was solved on the basis of the general principle that the best criterion of how an individual will perform in the future is how he has performed in the past. On this basis, the University of the State of New York introduced the Regents' examinations in 1864 as a device for selecting the scholastically more adept for admission to the limited facilities for secondary education. These early examinations were designed to predict the future achievement of pupils in elementary schools and were tests of the type of content which characterized education at the elementary school level. Later, when secondary education became a requirement for all, the early type of Regents' examinations was moved up to the end of the secondary school, where it still exists. The pattern of the early Regents' examinations is the typical pattern of measuring educational aptitude that dominated education throughout the nineteenth century. It is the pattern of predicting future achievement on the basis of past achievement measured by a more or less standard achievement examination. It is the traditional pattern adopted by most European universities for admitting students.

Another approach to this problem was opened by Alfred Binet, a physician by training, who had become interested in problems of psychology early in his adult life. He published a volume entitled *The Psychology of Reasoning* in 1886 when he was only in his twenty-ninth year. He was a man of the broadest interests, and from 1886 until his death in 1911 published numerous books and monographs with such various titles as *Hypnotism* (1887), *Changes in Personality* (1892), *Introduction to Experimental Psychology* (1894), *Psychology of Great Calculators and Players of Chess* (1894), and numerous others. Binet's stature as a scientist and thinker places him among the great men of his age. Apart from Binet's position of prestige among his contemporaries, the fact that he published in 1903 a volume entitled *Experimental Study of Intelligence* made him a natural choice for undertaking in 1904 a special study for the minister of public instruction in Paris, who was concerned with the problem of identifying those children who could not profit from the ordinary instruction provided in the schools because of their inadequacies in intelligence. It was recognized by the French school authorities that certain children in the schools failed to make adequate progress for two main reasons. On the one hand, there were those who had the necessary abilities but who were somehow unmotivated. On the other hand, there were those who seemed to lack the necessary abilities and who, however hard they might try, could not learn what they were expected to learn in the ordinary school situation. Binet was assigned the task of developing procedures which would enable the authorities to identify these least able children.

Binet's problem was one which French psychiatrists had been considering for years, and they had developed various questionnaires for the purpose of identifying children of limited mental capacity. Binet was fully familiar with the merits of these questionnaires and also with their limitations. He noted many cases in which children had been classified as feeble minded on the basis of their responses to these questionnaires and yet had demonstrated later that they were at least average in ability. He observed that one reason for this state of affairs was that the questions were given in a nonstandard manner and that the answers to the questions were scored in an arbitrary and subjective way according to the whims of the physician who administered the test. Binet did not discard the ideas of contemporary workers; rather, he revised and systematized their ideas, and in his writing he acknowledges the extent to which he felt indebted to others—particularly to two fellow physicians, Drs. Blin and Dumaye, from whose questionnaires he borrowed extensively.

For Binet, the core of his problem of assessment of the child's "intelligence" and his central concept of intelligence was that it is the basic capacity for making "judgments." His measuring device had to be one which measured the ability of the individual to exercise judgment, but he also specified that the situations presented should not be influenced by the kinds of experiences that occur in school, otherwise the pupils who were bright but unmotivated would obtain a low ranking on the test. For this reason, he decided that the problems included should be drawn from out-of-school situations and that they should be of a type familiar to every child. These commonplace problems included in the test called for "judgment" on the part of the child, and in addition they were to be objectively scorable; that is, the scoring system should not depend upon the judgment of the person administering the test, but upon rules which could be followed easily.

Binet recognized almost every major problem of psychological measurement. He recognized that his scale could not be considered a measuring instrument in the sense in which the physicist develops measuring instruments. He designed his instrument for the purpose of ranking children in order. He noted that his scale did not have a true zero and that intervals on the scale could not be assumed to be equally spaced, but he felt that these matters were unimportant and of purely academic interest; for his immediate problem could be adequately handled if he were able to rank children with respect to their ability to profit from the teaching in schools. As a matter of fact, Binet was convinced that psychological measuring scales could never be built so that they would have the properties of physical measuring devices.

The scale which Binet eventually developed consisted of a series of problems at each one of a series of age levels. The problems were mainly of a type which might be encountered outside of the schoolroom, at least such was the intention. They were all, according to Binet's estimates, problems which involved judgment. Through experimentation the difficulty of the problems at each age level was adjusted so that the average child could pass the items up to his level. In addition, a system of scoring was developed which would eliminate much of the subjectivity which might be involved in the scoring of the scale.

Binet also validated the scale by studying the relationship of scores on the test to the judgments of teachers concerning the level of intelligence of their pupils. This technique has been used commonly for the purposes of validating tests of intelligence. The weaknesses of the method are obvious, for even if tests of intelligence were perfected far beyond the point where they are now, correlations between these tests and teachers' judgments would be of only moderate size. The Binet type of intelligence test may be expected to correlate about 0.7 with the judgments of teachers when circumstances are favorable; that is, when the teachers have been able to observe children over a wide range of situations. Correlations higher than this value may not be anticipated except through accidental variation.

Binet recognized the fact that the problems selected for his scale should be such that they would be familiar to most children. This ideal was not and could not be realized, but since he was concerned mainly with the children of the city of Paris, his problem was less difficult to handle than that of later psychologists who attempted to develop scales which could be given with equal success to children from a great diversity of backgrounds. One of the first problems which had to be handled in adapting the test for use in other countries was to adjust the content in such a way that it would be familiar to the children to whom it was given. It must be recalled that Binet was interested in the mental processes involved in the handling of the materials and not in a knowledge of content as such, though he did not follow this practice in all of his tests.

Binet must be given credit for having introduced the concept of *mental age*. The concept was a simple one. For each test passed in the series the child was given credit for a certain number of months of mental development. The sum of the months for which the individual receives credit gives a score for his mental age which is supposed to be equal to the mental development of the average child who has that particular age. If a child on the test has a mental age of six years it means that his performance is equivalent to that of an average six-year-old.

Although there are many values inherent in the concept of mental age, and it was certainly a major psychological invention, it has many unsatisfactory aspects. It involves the assumption that a twelve-year-old who has a mental age of eight resembles an average eight-year-old. This is probably not true, for it is becoming increasingly evident that a mental age of eight in the case of the twelve-year-old is in many ways a different phenomenon from that of a mental age of eight in a six-year-old. The retarded child may obtain the same score as a much younger but more precocious youngster and yet the two children may differ intellectually to a marked degree. It is becoming apparent that it is much more meaningful to compare a child with others of his own age than with average children over a wide range of ages. The more detailed consideration of this problem must await until certain other concepts in this area have been carefully considered.

The concept of the *intelligence quotient* * was developed at a much later time than Binet's original work. The concept seems to have been introduced by Stern, who noted the need for developing some measure of general intelligence which was such that the ability of children of one age could be compared with the ability of those of another age. The interpretation of a child's mental age can be undertaken only in relation to his chronological age. The intelligence quotient attempts to provide an index of ability which will remain more or lesss constant for a given child from one age to another. One condition necessary for constancy of the I.Q. is that growth continue at a more or less uniform rate, but as soon as there is a slowing down or cessation of growth, then the intelligence quotient becomes quite meaningless. If an adult were to achieve a maximum mental age of sixteen, the ratio of mental age divided by chronological age would steadily decline as he became older. This is a serious deficiency of the concept of the intelligence quotient, and simply means that it cannot be applied to adults in any direct manner. However, many tests of intelligence for adults also provide intelligence quotients as the final stage in the scoring process. These intelligence quotients obviously cannot have the same kind of meaning as intelligence quotients computed for children on the basis of a mental-age scale.

It would be of advantage if the intelligence quotient based on a mental-age concept were abandoned in favor of more useful measures of intelligence. This step has been urged for a long time by competent psychologists, but the use of the intelligence quotient has become deeply embedded in educational practices and attempts to abandon its use might be met with considerable resistance. What, then, are the practical alternatives to the intelligence quotient?

Alternative systems are all based upon the idea that norms for intelligence tests should be based on the same concepts as norms for all other types of test. This means that the score derived from these tests should indicate how an individual compares with other members of a specified group. In the case of intelligence tests, the most meaningful comparison group consists of those individuals who are

* The intelligence quotient is calculated by substituting values in the following formula:

$$\text{Intelligence quotient} = \frac{\text{mental age}}{\text{chronological age}} \times 100, \quad \text{or} \quad \text{I.Q.} = \frac{\text{M. A.}}{\text{C. A.}} \times 100.$$

of the same age as the person tested. For this purpose, standard scores may be used, or even percentile ranks may provide a useful system of recording scores. The latter have the advantage of being the simplest of all scores to interpret.

The advantages of the suggested alternative over the conventional type of intelligence quotient are considerable. Is it not more meaningful to state that the performance of a child is at the 98th percentile of his own age group than that he has an intelligence quotient of 130? The intelligence quotient can indicate the standing of the individual within his age group only if the standard deviation is known and if certain tables showing the area by certain sections of the normal curve are available. On the other hand, the percentile rank indicates directly the fraction of pupils of comparable age who achieved poorer or better scores, and the standing of the individual in the group can be assessed directly. Another advantage of the percentile rank or standard score over the intelligence quotient is that the former can be used equally well with adults as with children. No special tour de force is needed to apply the system to the higher levels.

TESTS IN USE TODAY

The Descendant of the Binet Test

The present descendant of the Binet test is the New Revised Stanford-Binet Test of Intelligence (18), which was published in its present form in 1937. The original scale derived by Binet included 54 tests, and the original Stanford revision of the scale expanded this number to 90. In the 1937 revision, this number has been expanded to 129. At the lower levels, 6 tests are assigned to each half year of growth, but at higher levels this number is assigned to a whole year. The latest revision provides two forms, L and M, which have little overlap in content but which provide comparable scores. Many of the tasks included in the scale are very similar to those used by Binet. The following illustrate some of the problems in the scale:

Identifying names of objects in pictures	Year 3–6
Copying a bead chain from memory	Year 6

Identifying similarities in objects (for example, wood
   and coal)   Year 7
Identifying why statements are absurd   Year 9
Copying designs from memory   Year 9
Repeating digits reversed   Year 9
Identifying absurdities in pictures   Year 10
Filling in blanks in sentences   Year 12

The year listed above is the year at which the item is first admin-istered, but it may also appear at the higher levels in the test.

It is evident from the description of the problems listed above that the scoring system cannot be entirely objective, but Terman and Merrill (18) have made every effort to make it so. Examples are given of correct and incorrect responses and an attempt is made to lay down definite principles which can be applied in determining how a response is to be classified in the selection of test problems. Many experimental test problems were eliminated because of the difficulty in scoring the responses to them.

The new revision, compared with the older one, includes a greater number of nonverbal tests at the lower level, and an attempt has been made to make the lower-level tests more interesting to the children. The new scale is also an age scale, and although Terman and Merrill concede that research workers prefer to use standard scores rather than the mental age or the intelligence quotient, the old systems of units are retained because of the familiarity of educa-tional personnel with these units. As a concession to the research worker, Terman and Merrill provide tables which make it possible to convert scores on the test into standard scores. As a matter of fact, the intelligence quotients which the test yields provide an approxi-mation to a series of standard scores with a mean at 100 and with a standard deviation of 16.

The retention of the mental-age scale and the intelligence quotient result in certain difficulties in the use of this scale for the assessment of the intelligence of the adult. First, there is the problem determin-ing the age at which intellectual growth can be said to cease. Terman and Merrill conclude that the age of sixteen can be taken to be that point, but there is little evidence presented to show that this is so. A major difficulty in determining the age of maximum growth arises from the fact that it becomes increasingly difficult to obtain a representative sample of the population as age increases, because there is an increasing number of children who drop out of school and it is almost impossible to trace these dropouts for testing purposes. Second, a scale developed largely for administration to children may not be entirely suitable for administration to adults.

Wechsler's Individual Tests of Intelligence

Two major criticisms of the Binet test and its adaptations and revisions have been considered. One of these is that the system of reporting scores is tied to a mental-age scale, and the other is that the problems have been selected to interest children rather than adults. Both of these criticisms pertain to matters which limit the value of the test for use by adults, and it was mainly these considerations which Wechsler had in mind in the preparation of the Bellevue Scale (23). In addition, Wechsler introduced certain improvements over the Binet type of scale in the method of administration and scoring and opened the way to the development of individually administered tests which provide a profile rather than a single score.

The names and descriptions of the subtests which form the Wechsler-Bellevue Intelligence Scale are shown in Table 13.1.

The scores on the parts are converted into standard scores before they are combined. Separate intelligence quotients are given for the verbal section, for the performance section, and for the test as a whole.

Each test in the series is administered as a unit so that the directions have to be given only once. In contrast, the Binet-type test requires that new directions be given for each problem, since the test problems are grouped according to level of difficulty, while in the Wechsler type of scale all problems of the same type are grouped together regardless of difficulty. The Wechsler type of scale makes for simplicity of administration.

Although Wechsler does not use the concept of mental age, he does paradoxically retain the concept of intelligence quotient. The latter is obtained by comparing the individual with others of comparable age. A given deviation from the mean in terms of standard

TABLE 13.1 *

Description of the Content of the Wechsler-Bellevue Intelligence Scale (23)

Name of Test	Illustrative Test Question or Description of the Test
1. General information	Where is London? (and other items of general information).
2. General comprehension	Why should we keep away from bad company? (Most of the questions ask for the rationale underlying common practices.)
3. Arithmetic reasoning	How many oranges can you buy for 34 cents if oranges cost 4 cents each?
4. Digits backwards and forwards	The series of digits provided vary in length from series of 3 to series of 9.
5. Similarities	In what way are wood and alcohol the same?
6. Picture completion	Each picture shows an object with a part missing. The missing part must be named.
7. Picture arrangement	Groups of pictures are provided. In each group the pictures must be arranged in order to tell a story.
8. Object assembly	The materials for this test consist of jigsaw puzzles.
9. Block designs	Designs must be copied by arranging small wooden blocks.
10. Digit symbol	Examiner shows how each number has a symbol paired with it. Examinee must then indicate the symbols which go with each one of a set of numbers.
11. Vocabulary	Examinee is asked the meaning of a number of words.

* A revised version of this scale is now in preparation and should be available in 1955. The illustrative test questions are reproduced by kind permission of the Psychological Corporation.

scores always corresponds to the same intelligence quotient. The latter thus represents the relative intelligence rating of the individual at his age and does not compare him with persons of other ages.

The use of the concept of an intelligence quotient without the use of the concept of mental age is paradoxical, for the intelligence quotient necessarily refers to a *quotient,* which is commonly the ratio of mental age to chronological age. This apparent inconsistency is explained by the fact that Wechsler has used the term *intelligence quotient* because it is a term commonly used to refer to an index of general intelligence which has been corrected for the age of the individual, but in retaining this measure he no longer implies that the mental age of an adult can be compared to a mental age of a child.

In scoring the test, the score on each part is converted into a standard score which has a mean value of 100 and a standard deviation of 15. The average of these standard scores on the various parts gives the intelligence quotient for the test as a whole. In a similar manner it is possible to obtain separate intelligence quotients for the verbal tests and the performance tests, each taken as a group.

Much has been written about the possible value of studying the profile of scores derived from the Wechsler-Bellevue Scale, but a large part of this writing is based on unwarranted optimism rather than on rational expectation. In the first place, the test does not seem to have been assembled on the basis of the kind of psychological theory which makes the study of a profile particularly profitable. In the construction of a test to achieve the latter objective it is important to select the tests so that they measure as far as possible independent—that is, uncorrelated—abilities. This does not seem to have been done in the development of the Bellevue Scale. Second, the test lacks an adequate theoretical basis of any kind. The Binet test was at least based on a rationale which is obviously lacking in the case of the Bellevue Scale. Third, the reliability of the scores derived from each part is too low for practical use in individual guidance.

Many have hoped that a study of the profile of the scores on the Bellevue Scale would provide a basis for diagnosing mental disease. Although numerous studies have been undertaken of this matter the results have not given too much support to such hopes. Rapaport (12) studied the profiles of scores of various groups in a mental hospital in order to determine whether particular types of mental illness were characterized by particular profile forms. In addition, the typical profile of each one of these groups was compared with a "normal" group which consisted of fifty members of the highway patrol. The validity of this study has been questioned on many grounds, but particularly with reference to the group selected as normal, and certainly it would be dangerous to draw extensive conclusions from it. While Rapaport did find differences between the profiles of different psychotic groups, many would question whether these differences would be found again if the experiment were repeated.

The original Bellevue Scale was developed for adults, but more recently a similar test for children has been developed under the name of the Wechsler Intelligence Scale for Children (22). This test is essentially the same in structure as the Bellevue Scale.

The Wechsler Intelligence Scale for Children, commonly known as W I S C, is claimed in the manual to be suitable for administration to children of ages five through fifteen years. The subtests in the battery are divided into two series which form the *verbal* and the *performance* sections of the battery. The subtests are as follows:

Verbal Subtests	*Peformance Subtests*
1. General information	6. Picture completion
2. General comprehension	7. Picture arrangement
3. Arithmetic	8. Block design
4. Similarities	9. Object assembly
5. Vocabulary	10. Coding

There are, in addition, two subtests which are referred to as *supplementary*. These are tests of *digit span* and *mazes,* and may be used either as additional tests when time allows or as substitutes for subtests in which the score has been in some way invalidated. Caution must be exercised in making a substitution. This must not be done merely because an individual has made a low score on one of the subtests. There must be good reason for believing that a score is invalid before another is substituted.

The merits of the W I S C are similar to those of the Bellevue Scale. It is convenient and simple to administer. Scoring is relatively objective. The measure of intelligence is a standard score which has a mean of 100 and a standard deviation of 15 and is based on individuals of the same age and sex. Norms are based on groups of a hundred boys and a hundred girls at each age level from 5 through

15 years, and each group was within 1½ months of the midyear. This means that those tested in the 8-year-old group were all between 8 years 4½ months and 8 years 7½ months. Some attempt was made to control the sample tested by selecting the group for proper representation of geographic area, urban-rural distribution, and parental occupation. Quotas in terms of each of these factors were set in terms of the 1940 United States Census.

What Do Intelligence Tests Really Measure?

The question is often asked "Do these tests really measure intelligence?" The question is based on a misunderstanding of the nature of psychological measurement, but needs to be considered because of the frequency with which it occurs. In answering the question it is first necessary to note that intelligence cannot be observed. It is an intervening variable which is postulated to account for the fact that individuals differ in the adequacy of their responses to certain problem situations. As is the case with all intervening variables, intelligence is defined in terms of the stimulus (problem) situations through which it is measured. Thus intelligence is defined as the variable measured by an intelligence test. The fact that scores from different intelligence tests administered to the same group do not show agreement merely means that each one of the tests defines intelligence in a different way. No person can say that one test defines intelligence better than another, although it is reasonable to conclude on the basis of studies that one definition of intelligence is more useful than another.

According to the modern conception of psychological measurement, the process of discovering the relationship between scores on an intelligence test and other variables such as academic achievement is not a process of discovering whether the test measures intelligence but one of discovering whether the intervening variable measured by the test operates in certain situations such as learning situations in the classroom.

The accuracy of the predictions which can be made with instruments of this type will be considered in the next chapter. It is sufficient at this time to limit discussion to the types of predictor variables that are defined by tests.

The Nature-Nurture Controversy

A textbook written on measurement in education twenty years ago would have devoted a section of considerable length to the problem of the degree to which tests of intelligence measure innate intellectual potentiality (nature) or the results of learning (nurture). Most of the questions that have been posed in this connection are probably not answerable, and it seems unlikely that research will permit the psychologist to make the statement that a certain percentage of differences in measured intelligence can be ascribed to innate characteristics. The problem is much more complex than such a statement implies. In recent years controversy in this area has been largely avoided, partly because of the difficulty of the problems involved and partly because for most practical purposes the value of intelligence tests lies in the accuracy of the predictions that can be made from them.

The Group Test of Intelligence

The Binet type of instrument was developed originally for use by the psychiatrist in making individual diagnosis and for selecting children for special programs of education in schools. It is still used to some extent for this purpose by city school systems that offer special education for children of retarded mental development. The increased recognition of the importance of individual differences among children in ordinary school programs has resulted in a need for measuring instruments which would provide assessments of the "intelligence" of all or most children. The step from an individually administered test to one which could be administered to groups of individuals was a major one with deep educational consequences. Fable tells that the group intelligence test came into being as a result of the ingenuity of a harassed student who had somehow forgotten to administer the twenty-five individual Binet tests which a certain class assignment required. The rest of the story is that the student selected those test items which could be administered to an entire group, and was able to finish his class assignment on time.

Be this as it may, the impetus to the development of group tests of intelligence came from the success which the individual test of intelligence had achieved during a decade of use. Coupled with this fact was the need for a group test for the purpose of classifying and assigning men to specific duties in the vastly expanded U. S. Army of the First World War. The latter was an event of tremendous importance in the development of psychological tests because it represented the first widespread acceptance of psychological techniques of measurement.

The group test of intelligence developed by the U. S. Army and known as the Army Alpha Examination became the model for developing many of the subsequent group tests of intelligence. However, it is not unfair to say that most of these group tests of intelligence were not based on a well-thought-out rationale as was the case of the original test developed by Binet. There are a few exceptions to this, one of the most notable of which is the case of the tests of intelligence developed by Thorndike, who attempted to build them on the basis of a carefully considered rationale. Many group tests of intelligence give the impression of including a variety of problems which the psychologist happened to have at hand. The content of a recent revision of the Army Alpha Examination (24) is worth examining because it is not too different from many other group tests of intelligence. Table 13.2 provides a description of a revision of the Army Alpha which is still available and in current use. This revision does not differ in major respects from the original version except for subtest G, which in the original might be described as a test of common sense.

The Army Alpha Examination, like most group tests of intelligence, presented a limited range of problems. Group tests are necessarily limited to paper-and-pencil situations with a resulting restriction in the range of problems that can be presented. In such a test it is obviously impractical to present problems which require the manipulation of materials other than those which can be presented in a paper-and-pencil form. The result has been that group tests of intelligence have often tended to present rather academic problems similar to those which might be given in a school situation. They have also tended to favor verbal materials rather than perceptual materials.

TABLE 13.2

Description of the Content of the Modified Alpha Examination, Form 9

Test A. The examinee must add two numbers varying from 1 to 4 digits.

Test B. The examinee is asked to follow complicated directions as, for example in the questions "Write the letter of the alphabet that is as far beyond E as M is beyond H."

Test C. Arithmetic reasoning—"How many pencils can you buy for 30 cents at the rate of 2 for 5 cents?"

Test D. The examinee is asked to complete an analogy such as: sky is to blue, as grass is to _____. The word which best fits in the blank space must be selected from the following four words: table, green, warm, big.

Test E. Numbers which form a series are provided. The examinee must write down the next two numbers in the series. For example, what are the next two numbers in the series 1, 2, 4, 8, 16, 32 . . .

Test F. Sentences are provided with the words mixed up. The examinee must put the words together in the right order and must then decide whether the statement is true or false.

Test G. Three numbers are given. The person must find the largest number that will go evenly into the three numbers.

Test H. Forty pairs of words are given. If the words in a pair mean nearly the same thing, the examinee writes S; if the words have opposite meanings, the examinee writes 0.

Another major disadvantage of the group test is that it does not permit the close observation of the child to whom it is being administered. Thus it is not possible to identify the child who is poorly motivated in the test situation or who in some way is so poorly adjusted to the situation that the score derived from it has little meaning.

The proliferation of group tests of intelligence has been immense, and out of all proportion to the amount of thought which has been given to the study of the nature of intellectual activity. Among this vast array of materials there is little uniformity in the type of content or in the meaning of the intelligence quotients which are derived from them.

The fact that group intelligence tests vary in content may not have serious consequences insofar as making predictions is concerned. However, variations in the psychological process involved, and the varying emphasis on numerical, perceptual, and verbal material, may seriously affect the uses to which the scores may be put.

Table 13.3 presents a description of the subtests in two widely used tests of intelligence.

TABLE 13.3
Analysis of Content of Two Group Tests of Intelligence

Kuhlmann-Anderson Tests (7) Grade II	New California Short-Form Test of Mental Maturity (17) Grades I–III
Making as many dots are there are boxes, crosses, stars, etc.	Identifying right and left side of objects.
Making as many dots as there are taps.	Identifying a diagram that has been turned around into an unfamiliar position.
Copying simple designs.	Identifying objects that go together such as coat and pants.
Placing a dot on the picture of the object that "has legs but cannot walk, has hands but cannot sleep, etc."	Identifying pictures that present ideas such as "the sun shining."
Finishing a series of diagrams that form a series.	Solving simple verbal reasoning problems.
Finding an object that is like three other objects.	Identifying "the one that moves fastest," "the plate that has the most pie on it," etc.
Writing down the number of dots counted.	Counting, subtraction, addition.
Matching figures and copying numbers in the figures that match.	Identifying pictures of objects named.
Following directions such as "making a dot under the smallest circle."	
Finding two figures that can be combined to make a given shape.	

The common practice of recording an intelligence quotient of a child on a cumulative record without indicating the test on which it is based points up the widespread unwarranted use of intelligence quotients. Intelligence quotients from different group tests may measure somewhat different aspects of intelligence. They may also present different distributions, so that an intelligence quotient of

160 on one test may be equivalent to an intelligence quotient of 145 on another. In addition, on some tests of general intelligence, the population on which standardization was undertaken was not adequately representative of the school population as a whole, and thus, for one test with which the author is acquainted, the child who is average on most other tests of general intelligence (and who, therefore, on these other tests will achieve an intelligence quotient of 100) may on this specific test achieve an intelligence quotient of 85.

INTELLIGENCE OR INTELLIGENCES

It has been a subject of dispute among philosophers for many centuries as to whether there is a single ability called intelligence which individuals possess to varying degrees or whether there are a number of independent abilities each of which might be considered to be one aspect of intelligence. The traditional method of handling this problem was that of general observation and introspection, but because of its very nature this procedure resulted in controversy rather than in a solution to the problem. It was not until the advent of psychological measuring instruments that steps could be taken to determine whether or not intelligence could be considered to be a unitary trait.

There are two kinds of processes which may be used in grouping together test problems into separate tests designed to measure separate aspects of intelligence. Test items may be grouped according to the extent to which they are successful in making certain given types of predictions. Intelligence test items may be grouped into categories according to the extent to which they are effective in predicting success in schools of law, medicine, and engineering. This would result in three tests measuring the particular aspects of intelligence important in these three fields of study. On a similar basis, tests for measuring the type of intelligence required for learning in any particular field can be built. The test known as the American Council on Education Psychological Examination (ACE) was built on just this kind of basis by selecting through experimentation those test problems that correlated highest with actual performance in college.

The process of developing tests which predict the ability to learn in specific situations results in the production of many effective measuring instruments. As a matter of fact, some of the most effective psychological measuring instruments available were built on this basis. Criticism of this procedure for grouping together test items cannot be made in terms of the ineffectiveness of the procedure because it is effective. Rather must it be made in terms of the great proliferation of tests which this system produces, for the inevitable outcome is a test for predicting learning in each type of situation in which learning occurs. Prognosis tests, which are considered later in this chapter, are also examples of attempts to build tests which measure the particular aspect of intelligence required for success in specific academic fields.

The grouping of tests of intelligence in terms of the extent to which they correlate with external criteria such as success in various learning situations does not seem to be the ultimate solution to this problem. An alternative procedure is to group tests in terms of the extent to which they are correlated among themselves. The process of grouping tests and items in terms of their relationships to one another is known as *factor analysis*. Usually it is not practical to study single items by this process, and it is more common to study the interrelationship of small groups of items which form brief tests which are highly homogeneous in content. The ultimate aim of this process, however, is usually to group together tests on which the scores are highly correlated with one another and yet which show low correlations with scores from other groups of tests.

The development of tests alone was not a sufficient condition for the study of the composition of intellectual traits. It required also the development of the mathematical techniques associated with factor analysis to make this possible. In this type of mathematical approach, the basic device is the correlation coefficient, which is given a special interpretation. If the scores derived from two tests are correlated, then it is assumed that the degree to which they are correlated is related to the degree to which they measure a common factor. It is easy on this basis to determine whether two tests measure a common factor. The difficulty comes in identifying the nature of the common factor. An example from the domain of physical measurement may serve to clarify this point.

It is a well-known fact that measures of height and weight will be interrelated to the extent of 0.7, even when age is held constant. This means, according to the customary methods of interpretation, that these two measures have an underlying common factor. What can be identified as the common factor which underlies these variables? Height and weight are distinct characteristics of the human organism. They are measured in different units. They are measures made completely independent of one another, and yet they are correlated measures, which implies that there is a common factor underlying the two variables. The point to note is that it is extremely difficult to identify a common factor even when one is dealing with physical measures, and it is even harder to do so when the variables are psychological. In the case of the example under consideration the common factor might be considered to be a general factor of bodily size or bulkiness which influences nearly all measures of size including that of weight. However, the concept of general size or bulkiness is a vague one and is merely an attempt, and a rather poor attempt, to represent in common language the fact that physical measures of height and weight are positively correlated.

Even more unsatisfactory are attempts to describe common factors underlying psychological tests. A test of vocabulary provides scores which correlate 0.6 with a test of reasoning. The student of psychology is likely to respond immediately to this situation by saying that the common factor is *general intelligence* or G, but all this does is to name an unknown rather than to describe or to understand it. To some extent this must be so because the psychological factors derived from a study of the intercorrelations between test scores are semantic abstractions rather than realities in the sense in which the test scores from which they are derived are realities.

Early Theories of Intelligence

The earliest development of factor analysis was due to the work of Spearman and his students in London in the twenties. Spearman had observed, just as the elder Thorndike and others had observed, that all tests of intellectual ability are positively correlated, which indicates that all of them could be considered to be measures of a common ability or factor of general intelligence. There was nothing novel at that time in postulating a factor of general intelligence, for such a postulate was made by workers in the time of Binet or even earlier. The question which Spearman asked was whether a *single* general factor could account for all of the inter-correlations between tests of intellectual ability. He observed that, when all the intercorrelations between the tests in a battery measuring intellectual operations were worked out, they could be arranged in a table to form a hierarchy, with the largest ones at the top right-hand corner and the smallest ones at the lower left-hand corner. He went on to deduce that the correlation coefficients should show certain relationships to one another within this hierarchy if a single common factor were to account for all of the intercorrelations among tests. He went on to demonstrate that in the case of his own battery of tests these intercorrelations between the tests could be interpreted in terms of the presence of a single general factor and only one common factor. He interpreted his data to mean that there was a single major intellective factor, which he called G, but that each test also had a specific factor which was so specific that it appeared in that test and in only that test. The specific factors (referred to as s) were believed to be so specific that there was little point in measuring them, for they appeared only in the specific test situations.

It may be noted that, from the point of view of guidance, the Spearman theory of intelligence presents a very simple situation, for it leaves the guidance worker with only a single intellective factor to be measured. No other intellective factor, apart from this general factor, has any predictive value.

Multiple-Factor Theories

The two-factor theory of Spearman we now know to be a grossly oversimplified theory of the interrelationship of mental abilities. His data substantiated this theory because it was based on a battery of tests of closely related mental processes. They were all verbal tests, and they all involved reasoning of a type which Spearman conceived to be the very core of intelligence. If all the tests in a battery involve the same kind of mental process and are similar in content, it is hardly surprising that they will be found to be highly intercorrelated and that the interrelationships can be accounted for on the basis of a *single* common factor. Spearman was right in drawing the conclusions he did draw on the basis of his data. What he failed to recognize in the early stages of his thinking was that his conclusions were sound only because his data were restricted to certain types of test. The extension of his test battery to include a greater variety of instruments resulted in data to which the original two-factor theory of G and s did not apply.

More extensive data showed that all tests of intellectual skill tended to be positively intercorrelated. However, the interrelationships among certain groups of tests tended to be such that although the general factor underlying all tests might account for part of the interrelationship, yet it was necessary to postulate other factors which were common only to certain groups of tests alone and which were not common to all tests in the battery. These factors, which only certain tests of intellective functions have in common, are known as *group factors*. If a battery of tests of reasoning includes some tests that are perceptual and involve diagrams rather than words, the correlation among the test scores will show a group factor common to the perceptual tests. This means that the perceptual tests will have something in common which does not pertain to the other tests in the battery. Whatever those perceptual tests have in common which characterizes them alone is known as a group factor.

The simple techniques of Spearman were not adequate for handling the problem of identifying and isolating group factors. New arithmetical methods were needed for this purpose, and these were provided by later workers, of whom Holzinger followed closely in the footsteps of Spearman, while Thurstone made substantial departures from earlier concepts. The Thurstone system is marked by the fact that it does not produce a general factor. By a procedure which almost resembles the sleight of hand of a magician the general factor is apparently spirited away. In actual fact, there is no way in which a general factor among tests of intellectual ability can be made to vanish. It is inevitably there because all tests of intellectualistic functions tend to be positively intercorrelated. In practice, the technique of Thurstone does not dispose of the general factor, but hides it in the group factors. Thus each measure of one of the group factors is contaminated to some extent with the general factor of which it is also a partial measure. The result is that scores from tests which measure the factors which Thurstone derives from his analysis tend to be positively intercorrelated.

The purposes of factor analysis are several. For Spearman it provided evidence of the soundness of a psychological theory of the nature of intelligence. For Thurstone also it is closely linked to the building of a psychological theory concerning the nature and structure of human abilities. It is considered as a basis for discovering what for practical purposes can be regarded as the basic abilities of man. It does provide a rational approach to the problem and one which is well rooted in data, and this is to be contrasted with the speculative approach of the earlier faculty psychologists. Related to this purpose is also a second one that must be considered, which is to reduce the number of variables that must be measured in a comprehensive survey of human abilities. The number of apparently different tests which can be developed has no limit, but it is evident that many of these devices must overlap in the abilities that they measure. Factor analysis can be of great value in reducing batteries which contain numerous tests to batteries of a few selected tests that measure relatively distinct abilities.

Many have stated that the process of factor analysis is similar to that of the chemist's search for the basic elements of which the physical universe is made. However, as Cronbach (5) has pointed out, the analogy is not a good one, for the process of factor analysis is in many respects not a process of finding basic psychological elements at all. He notes that the answers provided by factor analysis are not unique, and from the same battery of tests an unlimited number of different sets of factors may be derived, and different methods of factor analysis provide different answers to the problem. The methods of the chemist provide a single, unique, solution to the problem, and no new method will discover a different set of elements from those already discovered. The elements of the chemist have a reality which the factors of the psychologist do not have, for the latter are mathematical abstractions or convenient semantic devices. Factor analysis provides convenient classifications of behavior, but like all classifications it is only a useful method of handling observations and does not necessarily imply any profound theory concerning the nature of the observations.

Outcomes of Thurstone's work include a series of tests of the so-called primary mental abilities derived from his analysis. It must be pointed out once more that any number of different sets of primary mental abilities could be derived by his method from a given battery of tests and he has to make certain additional assumptions in selecting one set of variables as his primary abilities rather than another. How this is done need not be considered here.

The Thurstone test of Primary Mental Abilities have been published by Science Research Associates for the two levels of seven to eleven (19) years and eleven to seventeen (20). As an example of the content of these series it may be noted that the series known as the Chicago Tests of Primary Mental Abilities (for ages eleven to seventeen) is designed to measure six factors which have been named *verbal meaning, word fluency, reasoning, memory, number, and space* (20).

The success of this battery as a guidance instrument needs to be evaluated, but since there seems to be no careful studies of the use of the Thurstone Tests of Primary Mental Abilities in a guidance program, evaluation must be based here on the general experience of the author.

Guidance workers with whom the writer has discussed this matter generally express the opinion that test batteries based on factor analysis are difficult to interpret in counseling because of the lack of evidence of the predictive value of these factors. There also seems to be a general lack of evidence concerning the way in which scores should be combined in order to make predictions in specific fields. Success in law school may involve factors X, Y, and Z, but this fact is probably not available to the guidance worker, and even if it were available it would be necessary to know the extent to which each one of these factors should be weighted in making a prediction. It is much easier for the guidance worker to use a test which has been built specifically for a practical purpose and has a known predictive value in this respect.

The same applies in the case of making prediction in academic work either in specific subject-matter fields or in terms of average grades over a given period. It is much simpler and more useful to administer the American Council on Education Psychological Examination (known as the ACE) to a group of high school seniors and to use the information for assessing their potentialities as college students than it is to administer a battery of tests developed on the basis of factor analysis of the type in which Thurstone has engaged and to make the same kind of predictions. The ACE was built specifically for the purpose of predicting academic success in college. Its validity for this purpose is known not only in general terms but also in terms of specific types of institutions. Batteries of tests based strictly on factor analysis do not generally have data such as these to assist the guidance worker in interpreting the results.

These criticisms of the application of factor analysis may not represent permanent deficiencies of the approach. It is the lack of data concerning the predictive value of tests developed on the basis of it that is the cause of present difficulties. It may be assumed that eventually the time will come when a battery of tests of intellectual functions will be developed and validated for a great variety of uses. It will then be possible to refer to tables to determine which factors are to be used in making a specific type of prediction, how scores from the tests corresponding to the various factors are to be combined in making a specific prediction, and the expected accuracy of the prediction. It may be another fifty years before acceptable data of this kind are available on a specific battery. The main reason for this rather pessimistic outlook is the vast amount of time and money that must be expended in order to collect data of the type needed. These data must be collected over a period of years and will involve the labors of a large team of experts.

SPECIAL PREDICTION PROBLEMS

The Prognosis Type of Tests

In academic areas of study in which there are large numbers of failures there has been a real and persistent need to develop tests for eliminating those who are likely to have substantial difficulties in achieving the academic goals of teaching. It is in areas of this nature where successful predictions have been made from tests which sample directly the individual's ability to learn by testing him in miniature learning situations. Algebra is one such area in which the subject matter seems to have intrinsic difficulty such that relatively few pupils seem to gain much from a course given in it at the ninth grade. Foreign languages also present substantial difficulties for many students who otherwise have relatively little difficulty with their academic work.

With few exceptions the development of tests of this kind are based on some kind of analysis of the nature of the learning task. The Iowa Foreign Language Aptitude Test is a typical example of a test based on this kind of approach. In this latter test, emphasis is placed on the student's ability to learn miniature sample lessons in a foreign language which is strange to the student. In the case of this test, the foreign language to be learned is Esperanto, a language with which only a very rare student would have any acquaintance. Other parts of the test measure the student's ability to learn grammatical rules by learning to apply rules of grammar to a foreign language. Experience with this and other tests shows that it seems to be generally sound to hypothesize that the individual's learning rate in a test situation is a good indication of his learning rate in similar tasks over a longer period.

Although prognosis tests usually correlate highest with the criteria which they are designed to predict, they will usually show good predictions in closely related areas.

Aptitude for Music and Art

Two areas of aptitude which are clearly differentiated from the aptitudes required for academic work are those of music and art. Tests have been developed in each of these areas which have had at least some small success in predicting the ability of persons to profit from related training. In both art and music the principle applied in the development of aptitude tests is that a person must be capable of making certain discriminations before he can be expected to learn successfully. For example, it seems reasonable to suppose that a person who has difficulty in distinguishing one simple melody from another will be faced with great difficulties if he attempts to study music. Students of education and teachers who are interested in the problem of identifying musical talent are referred to the chapters which discuss this topic in a volume by Lundin (8). Since the Seashore Measures of Musical Talent, the first developed in the field, still seem to be superior to others that have been recently developed, they will be the only ones described here in detail. Readers interested in reviewing other tests are referred to Lundin's book on music, which summarizes the merits and weaknesses of various batteries.

The Seashore Measures of Musical Talent were published first in 1919. A revised edition (13) was produced in 1939. Other tests in the area have been patterned after the Seashore tests, which consist of a series of pairs of recorded sounds. The individual taking the test must decide in the case of each pair whether the first sound is the same or different from the second. In the first test, the sounds, if they differ, differ in pitch. The discriminations called for in subsequent tests are related to loudness, timbre, time, rhythm, and tonal memory. In the last test, pairs of sequences of tones are presented and the person must decide which tone in the second sequence differs from the corresponding tone in the first. These tests measure the ability to make certain sensory discriminations and do not involve aesthetic judgments. Despite this fact, the Seashore tests are more successful in predicting achievement in music than are subsequently developed tests which measure the ability to make aesthetic judgment. The predictive value of the tests is somewhat limited, and yet it is probably sufficient for identifying the few who have so little talent that they cannot profit from a program of general music education, or for selecting the few who have outstanding talent. However, even when such extreme groups are to be identified, only limited accuracy of prediction will be achieved.

It is of interest to note that critics of Seashore, who have pointed out that the tests do not measure aesthetic judgment, have attempted to build devices which measure such aspects of musical talent. Herbert D. Wing, one of Seashore's major critics and probably the one who is musically best informed, developed a battery of tests of musical aptitude (25) which included these additional aspects. However, research seems to indicate that these newer tests are no more effective in identifying musical talent than are the simpler Seashore tests.

The history of the development of tests of art aptitude parallels closely the history of the development of tests of musical talent, for the field has been dominated by a single test developed by Norman C. Meier. This test was originally developed in 1929, was subsequently revised in 1942, and was published under the name of The Meier Art Tests: I, Art Judgment (10). In this test, pairs of drawings are presented, but the design of one has been altered to make it less pleasing according to the judgment of critics. The person taking the test must decide which drawing of each pair is the more pleasing and is scored for whether his judgment corresponds with that of the critics. Although the test measures only one aspect of aptitude for art training, there is some evidence to show that it is useful as an aid in the identification of artistic talent.

The difficulty of producing tests of artistic judgment probably accounts for the fact that Meier's test has had over the years only one major competitior—The McAdory Art Test (14). The latter test has also been studied over a period of nearly two decades and there is some relatively recent evidence to show that it measures a somewhat different aspect of art aptitude than is measured by the Meier test.

Prediction of Success in Mechanical and Clerical Areas of Learning

The tendency for education to be academic in character and to be based on a tradition which emphasizes scholastic achievement as the major goal to be achieved has resulted in an emphasis in predictive studies on the prediction of academic achievements. The extensive development of vocational education in the last quarter of a century has produced a need for the development of devices which will predict success in learning in vocational subjects. However, it is possible that even if well-developed instruments were available for predicting success in vocational subjects, these instruments would not be used properly because of the social pressures which encourage students to enter academic courses because of the social prestige which these courses carry. Thus, the present tendency is for vocational high school programs to attract mainly those who cannot succeed in academic high school programs. While teachers in vocational programs emphasize the need for able students in their programs and the possibility of rapid advancement for these students after they have finished with training, this propaganda, which is probably true, has little effect on the quality of the student body.

It is likely that if a survey were made it would be found that it is in the areas of mechanical learning that tests of vocational aptitude are most commonly used. The tests which have achieved greatest success for this purpose are those which measure the extent to which the person has acquired mechanical knowledge. An example of this type of test is the Bennett Test of Mechanical Comprehension (3), a typical item of which is reproduced in Figure 13.1 by kind permission of the publisher.

This test has been developed in a number of forms for use at various levels, and a similar test is included in a well-known guidance battery of tests known as the Differential Aptitude Tests (3). Items of the same type were also used extensively in the Second World War in tests prepared by the Army and Navy. Although many of the problems might be described as problems in elementary physics, there is little correlation between performance on the test and amount of training in elementary physics. It is possible that this may

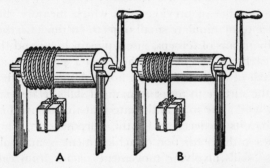

With which windlass can a man lift the heavier weight?

FIGURE 13.1

Illustration of the type of test item used in the Bennett Test of Mechanical Comprehension. Reproduced by kind permission of the Psychological Corporation.

be a reflection on the academic nature of teaching in physics which fails to help the student solve common problems which he encounters. Many of the items included might be considered to be excellent measures of important outcomes of teaching in physics, but those outcomes are often little stressed by instructors who emphasize the use and application of mathematical formulas. The Bennett-type test has had a long history of succesful prediction.

Other types of test which have been shown to predict with some success the ability to learn mechanical subjects involve questions requiring the examinee to name tools shown in pictures or to indicate their functions.

In the early days of the development of aptitude tests, considerable hope was expressed that tests of manual dexterity would provide useful predictions of success, for was not the craftsman usually described as one who "could use his hands"? These anticipations were not realized, for tests of manual skill have had almost negligible success. An example of such a test which requires the use of only paper-and-pencil materials is the MacQuarrie Test of Mechanical Ability (9), which asks the examinee to perform such tasks as placing dots as rapidly as possible inside small circles.

Tests of motor skill which require the manipulation of other than paper-and-pencil materials are quite numerous. One example of such a test is the Small Parts Dexterity Test (4), which is closely similar to a number of previous tests which measure the ability of the examinee to manipulate small objects. In this test, the examinee must first, by means of forceps, insert pins in holes and then place a collar over each pin, and he must then start a series of small threaded screws in each of a set of threaded holes. Although such a test may appear on the surface to measure manual skills related to success in mechanical work, one may anticipate that this test will be no more successful than its predecessors for this purpose.

Difficulties in the prediction of achievement in manual and other motor skills (skills involving movement) stems from the fact that such skills represent highly specific abilities. By this is meant that the ability to perform one of these skills can be predicted only to a very slight extent from the ability to perform another.

The field of vocational education in which the most work has been undertaken for the purpose of developing aptitude tests is probably the commercial field. Tests have been developed for predicting the achievement of pupils in shorthand courses. Most of these tests measure aspects of language skills which seem to be important in the successful taking and transcribing of shorthand. Tests of aptitude for typing have met with very little success.

Aptitude for Study in Professional Schools

Some of the largest testing programs in existence at the present time have to do with the problem of screening applicants for admission to professional schools. Testing programs of this type have a history which goes back over twenty years. These programs are not of direct interest to the teacher or school guidance worker, but they are of interest here as examples of the application of measurement techniques to broad problems of selection for specialized education. One of the first of these programs was the Graduate Record Examination, which, it will be remembered from an earlier chapter, was an outgrowth of the Pennsylvania Study and represented an attempt to provide graduate schools with measures of the extent to which applicants for admission had achieved the objectives of a four-year liberal arts program. The Graduate Record Examination consisted mainly of a battery of achievement tests, although it did include a "verbal factor" test which measured a combination of vocabulary and verbal reasoning. This battery of tests has been widely administered to applicants for admission to professional schools, but it is doubtful whether the results have been used extensively for the actual selection of students. As in the case of many selection devices, it is probable that it has had more value in discouraging applications for admission from the unqualified than in selecting the best qualified of those that apply. Since there are serious questions concerning the validity of the assumptions on which this test is based, its value for the selection of graduate students cannot be said to be established. However, it is possible that the new revision of these tests, published in 1955, may provide a sound basis for the selection of graduate students.

The early development of testing programs in the areas of medicine, law, and engineering have been summarized by Kandel (6) in an interesting work published in 1940, but much has happened since that time.

In the case of medicine, the earliest efforts to develop tests for the selection of medical students were initiated by F. A. Moss, who interested the Association of American Colleges of Medicine in the possibility of using objective tests for the improvement of procedures for selecting students. Moss pointed out that a substantial percentage of those admitted to medical schools failed to graduate for reasons of scholarship, and that this resulted in waste of the limited resources available for training physicians. The arguments were compelling and the Association established an experimental testing program under the direction of Dr. Moss. The early tests were experimental in character, but later forms were widely used in admitting students to medical schools. These later forms, which were prepared new for each year's testing, might well be described as intelligence tests given in a biological context. Some of the items called for the interpretation of biological charts. Others tested memory for biological materials. Still others measured knowledge of technical vocabulary. In short, the items were closely similar to those found in general intelligence tests except for the type of content on which they were based.

The Moss test seems to have had considerable success as a predictive device, but this program was abandoned in 1947 in favor of another test. This new test was referred to as the Medical Aptitude Test, but it would be better described as a battery than as a test. Later it was taken over by the Educational Testing Service, which changed its name to the Medical College Admission Test and revised it to a considerable extent. Its purpose seems to be more that of selecting educated citizens than that of selecting those most likely to succeed in medical school.

In the case of the selection of students for medicine, the development of a widely used aptitude test was a consequence of the fact that there existed a powerful and active organization of medical schools which were interested in sponsoring such an enterprise. In the case of other areas of professional training, there has not existed such a powerful organization interested in problems of student personnel and hence the sponsorship of special aptitude tests has been a much more recent development.

It is only since 1948 that the major law schools have attempted to sponsor an admission test which would measure any special aptitude that the completion of a law degree may require. As a matter of fact, the initiative seems to have come not from the law schools themselves but from the Educational Testing Service, which elicited the cooperation of law schools in this endeavor. It is too early to make any appraisal of this test, but it can be said that an earlier attempt by two independent workers, G. D. Stoddard and M. F. Ferson (15), indicated that an aptitude test of this kind should not be too difficult to construct. The test built by the latter workers seems to have been a useful predictor of law school success and, encouraged by this fact, three researchers, M. Adams, L. K. Funk, and D. B. Stuit, built a similar test with the help of several law schools.

In engineering a special project was developed in 1944 by the Graduate Record Office for the purpose of developing an admission test for engineering schools. This test, known as the Pre-Engineering

Inventory, was sponsored by the professional organizations concerned with engineering education, but it seems never to have become widely accepted as an admission test. It has also been taken over by the Educational Testing Service and has undergone progressive change. A test of engineering aptitude which has potential value for the counseling of young persons interested in engineering training is the Engineering and Physical Science Aptitude Test (11). The early data collected on this test indicate that it may prove to have substantial value for predicting success in introductory engineering subjects.

In the case of schools of dentistry, the problem of selection has become of significance only recently. Until the Second World War, schools of dentistry found it extremely difficult to fill their classes, but since then the number of applicants has greatly exceeded the number of places to be filled. In order to handle this problem, the Association of Schools of Dentistry has introduced a testing program to improve selection procedures. Most of the tests used in this program are devices published by other organizations, but a few have been developed especially for this program. One of the latter which has been used from time to time is a carving test in which a piece of chalk is whittled down to a given shape and size with a jackknife.

There is no point in consuming more of the reader's time with an enumeration of similar programs in other professional areas. However, certain trends in the nature of these programs need to be understood. Two general types of approaches have been taken in the selection of students for professional schools. The first of these approaches is that of developing what amounts to an intelligence test which measures the intellectual process needed for learning in the particular professional area. In this approach, a high correlation is sought between scores on the test and measures of achievement. The second approach is that of attempting to measure those characteristics which may contribute to the person's professional success after training. An example of this might be the use of a social studies test for the selection of students of medicine. It might be argued that a person who scored high on such a test might be a more respected member of the medical profession than one who had little background in this area. In this case, little correlation would be expected between test scores and measures of achievement in medical school.

SPECIAL PROBLEMS IN PREDICTION

The Guidance Battery

The administration of a single test for the purposes of making predictions and of helping the individual to make decisions concerning his future is becoming more and more a practice of the past. The tendency is toward the development of batteries of tests of abilities. These batteries are administered as units in their entirety. One of the most widely used of these is the Differential Aptitude Tests (3).

Most of the batteries do not contain anything particularly novel insofar as the tests they contain are concerned, but their advantage lies in the fact that uniform norms can be provided for all of the tests. The difficulty of purchasing similar tests from a number of different publishers is that each one of these independently developed tests is likely to have norms based on a different population. This makes it virtually impossible to present the results of these independent tests in the form of a profile. The advantage of basing all tests in a battery on similar norms is substantial, for it is then possible to study the strong points and weak points of the individual.

The Differential Aptitude Tests attempt to bring together in a single aptitude battery a number of types of tests which have been found to have useful predictive value in the past. The series of tests in the Differential Aptitude Tests consists of the following:

> Verbal reasoning
> Numerical ability
> Abstract reasoning
> Space relations
> Mechanical reasoning
> Clerical speed and accuracy
> Language usage: I Spelling, II Sentences

The tests in this series are new tests in the sense that they were developed for publication in this series, but similar tests have been published by a number of different publishers. The tests show substantial intercorrelation except for the clerical speed and accuracy test, which seems to measure a factor largely independent of the other tests. However, each represents a type of test which has had a long history of predictive value, and on that basis its inclusion in the battery is justified. The predictive value of these tests will be considered in the next chapter.

It must be noted that the tests are referred to as aptitude tests; that is, tests which measure potentiality for success. They were not developed to measure the extent to which certain objectives have been achieved, but rather are they designed to predict success in learning in a number of areas. The fact that some of these tests such as the Language Usage Tests resemble certain traditional achievement tests is irrelevant to the purposes of the battery. The distinction between an achievement test and an aptitude test is not in terms of the content of the tests but in terms of the purpose for which they are used.

The main advantage of the Differential Aptitude Tests over similar separately published tests lies in the fact that the latter were all standardized on the same population. The resulting norms make it possible to prepare for each student who takes the test a profile in which the relationship of one score to another can be inspected. The fact that separate norms are provided for boys and for girls is an additional advantage since on some of the tests, and particularly on those involving mechanical knowledge and to a lesser extent space relations, boys and girls show marked differences in average scores.

The difficulty with the use of these batteries is the limited amount of information available on their value. This is at least partly due to the fact that they are relatively new developments in the field of educational measurement and it takes time to collect the observations necessary for the adequate use of the battery. For some of the tests in these batteries there is already substantial evidence concerning their value for making various predictions. The mechanical reasoning test in the Differential Aptitude Battery is an example of a test which is based on material included in the Bennett Mechanical Comprehension Test, and the latter has a long list of validation studies to support its use. On the other hand, the space relations test in this battery does not present a type of test for which there is a well established validity. In fairness to the Psychological Corporation, it may be said that substantial efforts are being made to remedy this deficiency of the Differential Aptitude Battery and already some evidence has been collected concerning the predictive value of each test. Some of these data will be presented in the next chapter. However, more is needed than a mere compilation of masses of data of a type that are presented in the 1951 edition of the Manual (3) and which the present writer finds confusing because of their voluminousness. What are needed are concise and useful generalizations derived from such data which guidance workers can use.

The Biographical Record as a Predictive Device

The main biographical material used in making educational predictions is the individual's scholastic record. It has already been stated that the best evidence of how an individual will behave in specific situations in the future is how he has behaved in similar situations in the past. Previous grades in English are better predictors of future grades in English than are scores on tests regardless of whether the tests have or have not been specifically designed for that purpose. At least part of the correlation between previous grades in English and future grades in English is due to the fact that both are affected by similar influences. The grades of the student may have been raised spuriously in the past by apple polishing, and if that has been the case it is probable that they will continue to be raised by the same means in the future, and the reverse applies to the student who rubs the teacher the wrong way. These elements of personality lower the validity of grades but increase the accuracy with which future performance can be predicted from past performance.

The more similar is the previous educational situation to the future educational situation, the more accurate will be the predictions that can be made. The prediction of grades in English can be made more accurately from previous grades in English than from grades in social studies, but grades in English can be most satisfactorily predicted from previous grades in English when all teachers of English approach the subject from the same viewpoint and have the same attitudes toward pupils.

While these generalities are sound, they should be made with some qualifications. Single grades in individual courses may lack reliability to the point where little can be predicted from them. Arbitrary elements which influence the teacher in the assignment of grades may be such that the grades in a single course have little meaning, and thus it may be possible only to predict an *average* of several grades in the future from an *average* of several grades in the past.

In the last decade considerable interest has been shown in the extension of the idea of the systematic use of biographical material other than grades for prediction in education and in other areas. All three of the major branches of the armed services have developed and used instruments of this type. The general form of the biographical record as a measuring instrument is a series of items such as the following:

How many living brothers and sisters do you have?
(Do not count half brothers or half sisters.)

A. 0
B. 1
C. 2
D. 3
E. More than 3

In what surroundings did you spend most of your childhood

A. Country
B. Town with fewer than 500 inhabitants
C. Town between 500 and 5,000 inhabitants
D. Town between 5,000 and 20,000 inhabitants
E. City with more than 20,000 inhabitants

Items such as these may cover a vast range of material related to the background of the individual, and there is almost no limit to the possible length of a device of this kind. The problem has been to develop some system of scoring the items in such a way that the mass of responses becomes meaningful. The usual procedure of doing this has been an empirical one which has not been based on any adequate rationale. The common practice is to determine the correlation between each item and the performance that it is desired to predict and to score the items according to whether they show significant correlations. The early results achieved with this procedure have been promising, although the accuracy of the predictions that it has been possible to make has been very limited.

More recently, a technique has been developed, referred to as the homogeneous keying technique, which is a systematic method of sorting out biographical and other types of test items into groups.

For each group a score is derived which measures a particular aspect of the individual's background. Measures of the various aspects may show considerable independence one from another.

Measures of Nonintellectual Functions in Predicting Academic Achievement

Data will be presented in the next chapter to show the extent to which tests of intellectual functions predict achievement in programs of education. It will be shown that the maximum correlation usually found between scores on such tests and measures or ratings of achievement in a given course is usually about 0.7. This value can be interpreted by saying that when differences among pupils in academic achievement are considered, approximately 50 per cent of these differences can be interpreted in terms of differences in the intellectual functions measured by the tests. This also means that about 50 per cent of the differences among pupils in achievement are not measured by these tests but must be due to other factors which need to be identified.

A part of the present unpredictability of achievment is due to variations in the situation in which predictions are to be made. A part is due to the influence of unmeasured personality variables. In previous chapters, the problem of measuring such variables and the major instruments now used were discussed, but such instruments must still be considered to be in the experimental stage as far as the prediction of achievement is concerned.

Summary

1. The purpose of this chapter has been to describe the major instruments used in the prediction of the pupil's ability to achieve the varied objectives which may be achieved within the framework of contemporary education.

2. Aptitudes were considered as intervening variables relating stimuli to responses in educational situations. Aptitude research seeks to discover those variables that must characterize an individual before he can learn successfully in a particular situation.

3. Even if all of a person's aptitudes could be accurately measured, it would not be possible to predict accurately his success in achieving a particular educational objective unless learning conditions were known. This may be stated in another way; in order to predict a person's response to a situation, it is necessary to know the exact nature of the situation. One cannot predict the student's response to teaching without knowing the characteristics of the teaching situation.

4. Binet's early systematic attempt to predict educability laid the foundation for much later work. An idea of central importance to his conception of measurement of intelligence was that of mental age, on the basis of which others later developed the concept of the intelligence quotient. These concepts do not seem to be as useful as the concept that a child's intelligence should be reported in terms of his relative position within his own age group. The WISC is based on the latter concept.

5. Group tests of intelligence are much more economical to administer, but necessarily sample fewer of the person's abilities. This is a disadvantage if it is desired to inspect a broad range of abilities. It is also necessary for group intelligence tests to place emphasis on the person's ability to handle paper-and-pencil situations.

6. It has become increasingly evident that there are substantial advantages attached to measuring component aspects of intelligence which are sometimes described as factors. Of special importance in educational prediction are factors related to the use of words, the use of numbers, and knowledge of mechanics, which have become known as verbal, numerical, and mechanical factors. However, predictions of success in particular fields of study can best be made with prognosis tests, which are usually sample learning situations. This type of procedure has been adapted to the problem of predicting success in professional schools through aptitude batteries.

7. In recent years, the tendency has been for aptitude tests to be produced and administered in batteries. This permits the measurement of various aspects of intelligence and the conversion of the measures into scores which can be compared with one another. This permits the guidance counselor to determine the strong and weak points in a pupil's profile of aptitudes.

8. Biographical information should have value in predicting pupil

progress, but systematic methods of scoring and using such information are only in the experimental stages.

9. Tests of nonintellectual functions may eventually be expected to predict achievement. Some of these tests were considered in earlier chapters, but their use in predicting achievement is much less well established than is the value of measures of aspects of intelligence.

References

1. Anderson, Rose G., "A Note on the McAdory and Meier Art Tests in Counseling," *Educational and Psychological Measurement,* 11, 1951, 81–86.

2. Bennett, George K. and Fry, Dinah E., *Test of Mechanical Comprehension,* New York, The Psychological Corporation, 1951.

3. Bennett, George K., Seashore, Harold G., and Wesman, Alexander G., *Manual Differential Aptitude Tests,* New York, The Psychological Corporation, 1951.

4. Crawford, John E. and Crawford, Dorothy M., *Small Parts Dexterity Test,* New York, The Psychological Corporation, 1949.

5. Cronbach, Lee J., *Essentials of Psychological Testing,* New York, Harper and Brothers, 1949, pp. 45 + XIII.

6. Kandel, I. L., *Professional Aptitude Tests in Medicine, Law, and Engineering,* New York, Teachers College Bureau of Publications, Columbia University, 1940, pp. 78 + X.

7. Kuhlmann, F. and Anderson, Rose G., *Kuhlmann-Anderson Tests, Directions for Administering and Scoring,* Princeton, New Jersey, Personnel Press, Inc., 1952, pp. 89.

8. Lundin, Robert W., *An Objective Psychology of Music,* New York, The Ronald Press Company, 1953, pp. 303 + VI.

9. MacQuarrie, T. M., *MacQuarrie Test for Mechanical Ability,* Los Angeles, California, California Test Bureau, 1943.

10. Meier, Norman C., *Meier Art Tests: I, Art Judgment,* Iowa City, Iowa, Bureau of Educational Research and Service of the State University of Iowa, 1942.

11. Moore, Bruce V., Lapp, C. J., and Griffin, Charles H., *Engineering and Physical Science Aptitude Test,* New York, The Psychological Corporation, 1951, pp. 15.

12. Rapaport, David, *Diagnostic Psychological Testing,* The Menninger Clinic Monograph Series No. 3, Chicago, Illinois, The Yearbook Publishers, 1945, pp. 573 + XI.

13. Seashore, C. E., Lewis D., and Saetveit, J. G., *Seashore Measures of Musical Talents* (Revised Edition), Camden, New Jersey, Department of Education, R.C.A. Manufacturing Company, 1939.

14. Siceloff, Margaret McAdory and Woodyard, Ella, *Revised McAdory Art Test,* New York, Bureau of Publications, Teachers College, Columbia University, 1933.

15. Stoddard, G. D. and Ferson, M. F., *Ferson-Stoddard Law Aptitude Examination,* St. Paul, Minnesota, West Publishing Company, 1926.

16. Stoddard, G. D. and Vander Beke, G. E., *Iowa Foreign Language Aptitude Test,* Iowa City, Iowa, Bureau of Educational Research and Service of the State University of Iowa, 1944.

17. Sullivan, Elizabeth T., Clark, Willis W., and Tiegs, Ernest W., *New California Short Form Test of Mental Maturity,* Intermediate S-Form, Manual of Directions, California Test Bureau, 1951, pp. 16.

18. Terman, Lewis M. and Merrill, Maude A., *Measuring Intelligence,* New York, Houghton Mifflin Company, 1937, pp. 461 + XII.

19. Thurstone, L. L. and Thurstone, Thelma Gwinn, *SRA Primary Mental Abilities*—Elementary for Ages 7–11, Chicago, Illinois, Science Research Associates, 1954.

20. Thurstone, L. L. and Thurstone, Thelma Gwinn, *SRA Primary Mental Abilities*—Intermediate for Ages 11–17, Chicago, Illinois, Science Research Associates, 1954.

21. Tolman, E. C., "Determiners of Behavior at a Choice Point," *Psychological Review,* 45, 1938, 1–41.

22. Wechsler, David, *Wechsler Intelligence Scale for Children, Manual of Directions,* New York, The Psychological Corporation, 1949, pp. 89 + V.

23. Wechsler, David, *The Measurement of Adult Intelligence* (Third Edition), Baltimore, Maryland, The Williams and Wilkins Company, 1944, pp. 258 + XI.

24. Wells, F. L., *Modified Army Alpha, Form 9,* New York, The Psychological Corporation, 1951.

25. Wing, Herbert D., *Wing Standardized Tests of Musical Intelligence: A Test of Musical Ability on 10 Records,* Sheffield City Training College, Sheffield, England, 1948.

26. Yoakum, Clarence S. and Yerkes, Robert M., *Army Mental Tests,* New York, Henry Holt and Company, 1920, pp. 303 + XIII.

CHAPTER 14

The Prediction of the Progress
of Learning*

Introduction

The purpose of the previous chapter was to familiarize the student with some of the instruments that are commonly used for predicting the capacity of the pupil for learning in various situations. Most of these instruments were presented as attempts to measure intervening variables which affect the response of the pupil to the learning situation.

The value of these instruments lies in their usefulness for making predictions, and most of the predictions that are made from them relate to how the pupil will behave in school situations. Since some of the important responses of the pupil to the school situation are summarized and described in the form of grades, it is hardly surprising that numerous studies have been undertaken which demonstrate the value of various tests for predicting grades. The fact that grades have been so widely used in prediction studies should not be taken to imply that grades summarize all the significant responses of the pupil to the school situation. It is obvious that they do not, but, nevertheless, they represent one aspect of the pupil's response which it is valuable to predict if this can be done.

* This chapter represents a revision and extension of an article written by the author which is listed among the references. Permission to do this was generously granted by the University of Michigan Press. (First printed as "Significant Research on the Prediction of Academic Sucess," in *The Measurement of Student Adjustment and Achievement,* edited by Donahue, Coombs, and Travers. Copyright, 1949, University of Michigan Press.)

It has already been indicated that the predictive value of a test is commonly stated in terms of a correlation coefficient. In order to give the reader a clearer conception of the meaning of a correlation coefficient, it is necessary to provide some illustrations of the degree of relationship between two variables represented by correlations of various magnitudes. Figure 14.1 presents data showing the relationship between the scores on a test of scholastic aptitude and average grades during two years of college. In this figure, each dot, represents

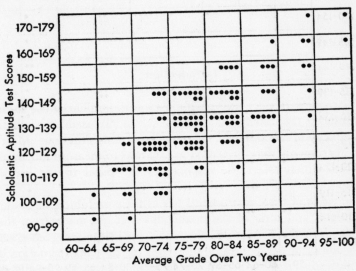

FIGURE 14.1

Diagram showing the relationship between average grades for a 2-year period of college and scholastic aptitude test scores for a particular group of students. The relationship can be represented by a correlation coefficient of 0.72.

one individual. It can be seen that there is a substantial relationship between scores on the test and average grades, and this relationship can be stated in terms of the correlation between these two variables, which, computed on the basis of these data, is 0.72. Figure 14.2 shows the relationship between scores on a predictor variable, the American Council on Educational Psychological Examination, and grades in freshman English in a certain university. In this case, the numerical value of the correlation coefficient between the two measures is 0.43. These two charts are presented in order to indicate the degree of relationship represented by correlation coefficients of various sizes.

Another concept must also be introduced to the student. This is the concept of multiple correlation. If two tests have predictive value of a person's performance, then it is possible that a combination of

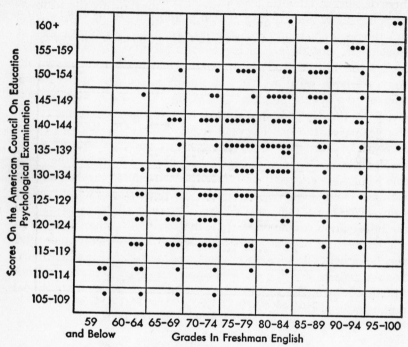

FIGURE 14.2

Diagram showing the relationship between scores on the American Council on Education Psychological Examination and grades in freshman English for a particular group of students. The relationship can be represented by a correlation coefficient of 0.43.

the scores from these two tests may produce an even better prediction than is provided by either test alone. In combining the test scores, one score may be given greater emphasis than the other. The correlation between such a combination of scores and a variable to be predicted will vary as the emphasis given to each component is varied. When the combination is such that it provides a maximum correlation, then the latter is referred to as a multiple correlation.

Sources of Information Concerning the Prediction of Achievement

Many hundreds of studies have been conducted during the last three decades in attempts to discover methods of predicting achievement in schools and colleges. Those conducted during the twenties and thirties were concerned mainly with predictions from tests of intellectual aptitude and achievement. More recent studies have been devoted to the study of personality in relation to achievement. For a comprehensive overview of studies in the field the reader is referred to a review prepared by Harris (17) in 1940 and a later review by Travers (37) in 1947. An excellent synthesis of the results of research on the prediction of achievement in college has been prepared by Garrett (14) and by Crawford and Burnham (8). The student who wishes to refer back to the primary sources of information will find that these reviews contain excellent bibliographies. Test manuals should also be consulted for data concerning the predictive value of tests. All that can be given here is a general summary of the information contained in these materials with some illustrations selected because of their appropriateness. A final general point must also be noted. This chapter is concerned with prediction in educational situations. For the problem of predicting performance in work situations, the reader should consult a reference work on vocational prediction.

Prediction of Scholastic Success in Elementary Schools

The prediction of academic achievement is of importance in two main situations. First, when an educational program is such that only a limited group can profit by it, predictions of the probable success of those who wish to take the program are important. Second, the prediction of academic achievement is important in the guidance of the individual student. In addition, discrepancies between predicted achievement and actual achievement are often significant symptoms of maladjustment.

We cannot discuss here the complex clinical procedure which has replaced Binet's relatively simple method of selecting those who needed special education at the elementary school level. However, the widespread use of the intelligence quotient for appraising the potential level of academic accomplishment of the elementary school child makes it desirable to evaluate the validity of intelligence quotients for this purpose.

Various studies report correlations between objective measures of elementary school achievement and intelligence measured by such tests as the Kuhlman-Anderson, the Revised Stanford Binet, and the National Intelligence. Correlations between intelligence quotients and elementary school achievement range from 0.30 to 0.80 for pupils of similar age. Rather small correlations have also been found between year-to-year gains made by pupils and intelligence quotients. There seems little evidence to show that the value of intelligence tests for predicting school grades changes much through the elementary school years.

The most recent emphasis in testing children of elementary school age has been upon diagnosing the causes of difficulties in specific aspects of learning. The development of diagnostic tests in various subject-matter fields has shifted attention from the problem of predicting over-all academic success to the problem of determining specific academic difficulties such as reading difficulties. The shift in emphasis is a fortunate one, since it is doubtful whether over-all predictions of achievement in elementary school are particularly useful except where extreme deviates are being considered. Additional research is needed into the organization of abilities at various educational levels and the relation of these abilities to learning in various areas, since research already undertaken in that area seems particularly promising.

Long-Range Predictions

Studies of long-range predictions of achievement in elementary school from intelligence-test scores indicate that such predictions have limited value. Intelligence quotients measured in the sixth grade were found to correlate 0.57 with grade level attained (1). Allen (1) found that intelligence quotients derived from Kuhlman-Anderson Intelligence Tests given in the first grade correlated with various aspects of achievement in the third grade to the extent of

0.32 to 0.53, and with fourth grade achievement from 0.30 to 0.53.

It has been generally established that a greater number of those elementary school children with intelligence quotients above 100 will enter college than those who are below, though there are relatively few investigations which have established the relationship between intelligence quotients measured at an early age and subsequent college success. Rosenfeld and Nemzek (31) found a correlation of 0.21 (N = 200) between intelligence quotients in the first grade and honor point ratio in college. Keys (22) found a correlation of 0.35 (N = 279) between college grades and intelligence quotients measured before the age of fifteen. Billhartz (5) found similar results. These are the results of but a few typical studies. From these data it may be concluded that measures of intelligence obtained before the ninth grade have limited value for individual predictions of academic success in college. This conclusion is contrary to a belief commonly held by school teachers that the intelligence quotient of a child is a sufficient basis for predicting academic success later in life.

While there are reasons why most tests have only limited value as predictors of behavior in specific situations, and these reasons will be considered later in this chapter, certain problems related to the making of long-term predictions need special consideration.

Any long-term prediction made during the period of growth makes certain assumptions about the future course of growth. Studies of the physical development of children over a period of many years indicate that all individuals do not grow at the same rate and that some children may continue to grow until a later date than others. Consider how this would affect predictions of the final physical height of individuals. Suppose that a ten-year-old child were tall for his age and were in the 90th percentile in relation to the height of other members of his age and sex. The prediction of the adult height of this individual is likely to be contaminated with large errors because of many unknown factors in his future development. He may reach maximum growth at an early age, or perhaps continue to grow until he is twenty-five or even thirty years of age. The age at which growth ceases is one of the many variables that must be known before accurate predictions of final adult status can be made. In addition, it is necessary to know the rate at which the individual will continue to grow. This cannot be predicted entirely from the rate of growth in previous years, since individuals may show spurts and also periods when development is depressed. Thus the number of unknown factors which influence the individual's final status in height are so numerous that it may be possible to make predictions at the age of ten which are only slightly better than predictions made on the basis of guessing.

The same problems must be taken into consideration when predictions of adult mental ability are to be made. The intellectual abilities of a child of ten cannot be expected to be a good indicator of adult intellectual status unless the future rate of mental growth of the individual is known and unless the length of the growing period is also known. General observation seems to indicate that some individuals are intellectually "late bloomers"; that is, they do not achieve the peak of their mental development until perhaps the mid-twenties or even later. Such individuals are supposedly among those who do not shine during youth in spite of a brilliant later performance in life. The tendency in the past has been for psychologists to assume that these individuals were for some emotional reasons unable to show their true level of mental ability early in life, but this hypothesis is becoming progressively less sound as knowledge is accumulated in the area.

If the hypothesis that there are such individuals as "late bloomers" is sound, then it is also necessary to hypothesize that there are also individuals who are "early bloomers"; that is, those whose mental growth stops at a fairly early age. It is presumed that eventually it will be possible to predict which children will be early and which ones will be late in achieving maximum adult status. When this is done, the problem of predicting adult intellectual status from childhood intellectual status will be greatly simplified.

Predictions of Academic Success in Secondary Schools

The prediction of academic achievement in secondary schools is a problem which has concerned the European educator much more than it has the American. Few European countries have yet adopted the principle of universal secondary education, and limited facilities for secondary education have made the problem of selecting students a major one.

In American schools, particular interest has been shown by investigators in measuring the academic aptitudes of pupils in the eighth, ninth, and tenth grades, since it is during this period that differentiation in education becomes of importance. Correlations between intelligence tests and achievement in academic subjects are between 0.4 and 0.6 during this period.

Other studies have shown that intelligence tests correlate to a significantly greater extent with achievement in some subject-matter areas than in others. Predictions from intelligence quotients are particularly poor in arts and music. Tests such as the Stanford-Binet are rather better predictors of English usage, literary acquaintance, reading, comprehension, and reading vocabulary than they are of geometry or map reading, which require a specialized understanding of space relations. Tests of reading comprehension and reading vocabulary are about as useful as intelligence tests in predicting tenth grade scholastic achievement, and one author (6) concludes that "measures of reading comprehension, reading vocabulary, the ability to locate information, reading, speech, and intelligence can be used together to make a 'fairly reliable judgment' of scholastic success in the tenth grade."

Certain academic fields in secondary school education such as algebra and geometry, which are noted for causing difficulty to many students, have been the subject of investigations into the possibility of forecasting success and failure. In eight studies reviewed by the writer (37), the median correlation between success in these fields and score on a prognosis test was 0.66.

It may be noted that once high school is reached, there is evidence that a student's grade in a particular subject-matter field can be best predicted from his previous grade in the same or related fields. Relative performance in the same subject is quite stable from year to year, so that tenth grade scores are in general about as good as eleventh grade scores for predicting twelfth grade scores in the same subject.

Differential Predictions at the Secondary School Level

Apart from the trend in recent years toward the development of prognostic tests for specific subject-matter fields, there has also been a trend toward the breakdown of measures of intelligence into various components. In general, it is believed that these components have greater predictive value than an over-all measure of ability. Examples of this trend are found in the breakdown of the scores of the California Test of Mental Maturity into a language and a nonlanguage intelligence quotient, the division of the Scholastic Aptitude Test of the College Entrance Examination Board to provide separate measures of verbal and mathematical ability, and the American Council on Education Psychological Examination to provide a linguistic and a quantitative ability score. This trend parallels the trend in the measurement of aptitude for higher education.

The differential prediction of academic success which can be made from tests such as the Differential Aptitude Test parallels those which can be made at the college level from the American Council on Education Psychological Examination. At the high-school level, the correlations of the verbal scores with English marks and with marks in foreign languages tend to be rather high, and so also are the correlations between the numerical scores with mathematical marks. As one would expect, the correlations of the verbal scores with mathematical marks and the numerical scores with languages tend to be somewhat lower, although they are not always substantially lower.

The Predictive Value of the Differential Aptitude Tests

The previous chapter mentioned that the present tendency in aptitude testing is to administer a battery of tests developed as a unity. It is therefore of considerable interest to examine the predictive value of one of these batteries. Considerable data is now available concerning the value of the Differential Aptitude Test (3) for predicting achievement in grades 8 through 12. Most of the data collected has been for academic subjects, in which areas not all of the tests were selected for predictive purposes. However, the data are still of considerable interest in spite of this limitation, and a summary is presented in Table 14.1, which is based on many thousand cases.

One of the interesting features of the table is the fact that the performance of the girls is generally more predictable than that of the boys. The evidence is in keeping with other data and with the

TABLE 14.1

Summary of Validity Coefficients between Differential Aptitude Test Scores and Grades in Years 8 through 12 *

The coefficients given are median values, since separate coefficients were computed for each school in the sample.

Subject	Verbal Reasoning Test I	Numerical Ability Test II	Abstract Reasoning Test III	Space Relations Test IV	Mechanical Reasoning Test V	Clerical Speed and Accuracy Test VI	Language Usage— Spelling Test VII	Language Usage— Sentence Test VIII
English (boys)	.48	.49	.32	.26	.20	.28	.45	.51
English (girls)	.54	.53	.42	.30	.26	.28	.45	.57
Mathematics (boys)	.32	.48	.33	.24	.19	.19	.28	.32
Mathematics (girls)	.39	.56	.39	.34	.26	.23	.26	.38
Science (boys)	.55	.50	.42	.34	.37	.18	.34	.48
Science (girls)	.58	.58	.45	.38	.38	.29	.36	.54
Social Studies and History (boys)	.45	.46	.32	.24	.21	.23	.33	.40
Social Studies and History (girls)	.50	.49	.36	.24	.22	.23	.35	.50

* The data presented here are derived from the 1947 edition of the manual. They are presented in preference to material from the later edition of the manual which is listed in the references because it is easier for the student to understand.

widely held belief that girls are more conscientious in their studies and that as a result their performance is more closely related to their abilities than in the case of boys for whom distractions interfere greatly with their academic studies.

Another interesting fact is that in English and social studies, the verbal reasoning test and the numerical reasoning test have approximately equal predictive value, which suggests that differential prediction may not be as practical as guidance personnel commonly assume it to be. Only in the area of mathematics does there seem to be any real difference in the predictive value of these two tests. Of course, it is not known whether this condition is due to factors which contaminate grades or whether it is inherent in the nature of the test.

It may be noted that the English usage test, which measures knowledge of sentence structure, is almost as good a predictor as the verbal reasoning test. One may well speculate on the reason for this. It is possible that grades in most courses are affected by the student's command of the English language. Hence the correlations with the English usage test may represent what is virtually a common factor in the educational situation.

Current guidance practice tends to use only the verbal reasoning and the numerical reasoning types of test for predicting academic success. The American Council on Education Psychological Examination is built and used on this basis. Consequently, it is not fair to evaluate tests IV through VIII shown in Table 14.1 on this basis. The value of the latter tests must be determined very largely in terms of the extent to which they predict success in commercial and shop areas. The space relations test seems to measure a highly specific ability and thus will probably provide good predictions in a few limited situations. The clerical speed and accuracy test is unlikely to provide useful predictions in an academic setting, since the operations called for in the test do not correspond to the operations called for in commercial courses. On the other hand, it is probable that the test will have good predictive value of the effectiveness of workers in certain simple jobs involving rapid filing, alphabetizing, checking, and so on, for past experience with similar tests has shown this to be the case. Tests useful for vocational guidance may not be useful for educational guidance, to some extent because training for a job is often only remotely related to the job itself and also because the abilities required for learning a job may be different from the abilities required for performing satisfactorily on the job.

Another feature of the Differential Aptitude Test is the presentation of data to be used for predictive purposes in terms of expectancy tables, which have now become fashionable again, though they were commonly used years before many people knew how to compute correlation coefficients. The expectancy tables presented in the manual at the time of writing are for those cases in which relatively close relationships were found between the tests and the criterion data. Fairly typical of these expectancy tables is that reproduced in Table 14.2.

The table is simple to read. Of those who obtained scores of 26 and up, one pupil received a grade of D, five received a grade of C, eight a grade of B, and five a grade of A. The same data are presented in the form of percentages on the right-hand side of the table.

TABLE 14.2

Expectancy Table Showing Relationship between Scores on the Verbal
Reasoning Test in the Differential Aptitude Tests and Grades
in Social Sudies of 191 Eighth Grade Boys

Number Receiving Each Grade					Raw Score	Per Cent Receiving Each Grade				
F&E	D	C	B	A		F&E	D	C	B	A
	1	5	8	5	26 and up		6	26	42	26
2	5	17	23	2	18–25	4	10	35	47	4
5	17	22	15	1	10–17	8	28	37	25	2
12	34	16	1		2–9	19	54	25	2	

Predicting Learning in Clerical Fields

Performance in shorthand courses seems to be much more predictable than performance in typewriting, probably because achievement in the former is less dependent upon motor skills than achievement in the latter. Most writers who have reviewed devices for prediction in shorthand together with the evidence of validity of these instruments have concluded that these devices should be considered as experimental in character and of limited value in predicting achievement in shorthand courses. While this conclusion is correct, it should not be taken to imply that instruments for predicting achievement in shorthand are any less adequate than instruments for predicting achievement in other school subjects. Osborne (29) reviewed studies made in this area up to 1943, and in eleven studies using tests of intelligence for the prediction of achievement in shorthand, the median correlation with the criterion was 0.34, which is comparable to the correlations found between tests of intelligence and achievement measured by grades in other high school subjects. Correlations between grades in shorthand and grades in other school subjects tend to be considerably less than correlations with tests of intelligence.

Various attempts have been made to build tests which will have specific predictive value for achievement in courses in shorthand. Bennett (3) developed a test measuring symbol writing, symbol transcribing, and spelling and found a correlation of 0.275, with subsequent achievement in shorthand in the case of the symbol writing and symbol transcribing test, and 0.475 for the spelling test. These correlations were based on five hundred cases.

Probably the prognosis test in this area which is based on the most careful and extensive study of the problem is that developed by Deemer and Rulon (10) as a result of a study of the relative merits of two systems of shorthand. This test involves five sections: (1) spelling, (2) speed of writing, (3) dictation, (4) word discrimination, and (5) vocabulary. The total test was found to correlate in different groups from 0.54 to 0.70, with a measure of achievement in a course in shorthand and at least five hundred cases were involved in these studies. It should be noted that these values do not differ to any great extent from the coefficients of validity found for prognostic tests for other school subjects. The validity of the test developed by Deemer and Rulon is comparable to that found for the Turse Shorthand Aptitude Test (38) in a study in which achievement was measured over a two-year period. Prognostic tests produced earlier than the two just considered seem to have had substantially lower validity. These last tests seem to have greater predictive value in the area for which they are intended to be used than tests of intelligence or tests of general academic aptitude, but the apparent improvement of recent shorthand prognosis tests over earlier tests may be due to a spurious factor. This factor is the inadequate and probably unreliable measure of achievement which was used in earlier studies. Achievement tests in shorthand are still inadequate, but substantial gains have been made and recent studies have measured shorthand achievement with instruments that are at least reliable even if all would not agree on every aspect of the validity of their content.

Prediction of success in typewriting has been less successful than prediction of success in shorthand. It is probable that typewriting may be considered to be a simple skill which all who can read and write can learn unless they suffer from some major defect in muscle control such as cerebral palsy. If this is true, it would follow that motivational factors would be more important in determining difference in rate of learning typing than would be other characteristics of the individual. One difficulty in studies of predicting typewriting has been that it is difficult to separate typing skills from other related skills. If a pupil is given the task of reproducing a letter on the typewriter, the reproduction may include the word *garantee*, which was correctly spelled in the original. Should this be included as a typewriting error? It is probable that the word was incorrectly read by the student because he did not know how to spell it. Some authorities in this area have concluded that most typing errors are reading errors and are not due to deficiencies in learning the skill but to deficiencies in related language skills. Thus it may be argued that those who will make the most accurate typists are those who prior to training have the best command of the reading and spelling skills necessary for producing good work on the typewriter. The evidence also suggests that rather than devote time to a search for tests of typewriting aptitude, it might be more profitable to study methods of teaching, particularly with reference to the problem of maintaining the motivation of the pupil. Learning studies of typewriting have done little to develop techniques for maintaining the motivation of the pupil, although it is recognized that at certain times as when the pupil reaches a plateau in his learning curve, further learning may depend upon maintaining the pupil's morale.

Certain tests of so-called general clerical skills have also been developed for the prediction of success in simple clerical jobs. Most of these tests measure the speed with which certain simple perceptual tasks can be undertaken. Number checking and name checking are typical item types and usually involve the comparison of two columns of names of numbers in which opposite entries sometime match and sometimes do not. The examinee must identify those entries which do not match. Most of these tests have been validated against ratings in simple clerical jobs, and the correlations thus produced have been positive and range up to 0.7, which are promising, although they should not be accepted at their face value, since the variables measured by the ratings are usually obscure. One point to be noted is that one would not expect these tests to be of value in predicting achievement in general clerical courses, since these courses do not call for speed in simple tasks but are concerned more with general principles of office operation.

Selection in Liberal Arts Colleges

The reader who wishes a detailed account of the problem of predicting achievement in college should refer to the excellent review by Garrett (14) of 194 studies of this problem. The discussion presented here must be limited to only the more important generalizations which emerge from these studies.

The early studies of the prediction of scholastic success at the college level were mainly concerned with the prediction of over-all success in a liberal arts program. In some cases, the criterion of success was the completion of a four-year program; in others, it was the average grade over a period of one or more semesters. The current trend is to use average first semester or first year grades, since grades in successive years of college tend to be highly intercorrelated.

At the present time, the evidence indicates that the best single measure for the selection of the college student is his average grade in high school. Study after study has indicated that the average high school grade is a better predictor of college grades than either subject-matter tests or psychological tests.

High school and college averages are more closely correlated than is either with test scores. For the prediction of second semester grades, the first semester grades are by far the best criterion. The value of high school grades for predictive purposes is undoubtedly a result of the fact that they represent a combination of ability and motivational factors operating in much the same way as they will operate in college. The advantages of these circumstances seem to outweigh the factors that tend to reduce the validity of high school grades.

Great disparity has been found between the college grades of groups of students who came from different high schools but who had similar high school grades. As a result of this fact, many of the larger colleges and universities have adopted the practice of keeping careful records of their students grouped according to the high school from which they originated. In a single study (18) it was shown that the best method of predicting a student's college grade was to determine the college grades of those former students from the same high school who had the same high school grades as the student in question. It seems probable that the differences in the quality of students coming from different schools do not represent differences in native ability but differences in motivational factors, study habits, and other complex factors which make for academic success.

In general, correlations between high school grades and first year college grades are between 0.5 and 0.6, depending upon such circumstances as the extent to which it is possible for the college concerned to select its students. Where a collegiate group of students has been highly selected the resulting restriction in range of ability reduces the correlation between high school grades and college grades.

Next to high school record, subject-matter tests and particularly the general achievement type of test have been established to be the second-best predictor of college grades. Much to the surprise of many psychologists, subject-matter tests, such as those furnished by the New York Board of Regents, have been shown to be superior to intelligence tests for the prediction of college grades. Other subject-matter tests which have been carefully studied in this connection are the Cooperative English Tests, which have been found to be particularly valuable as a predictor of academic success, possibly because they represent a fortunate combination of items measuring subject-matter knowledge and items measuring various thought processes.

The value of subject-matter tests is only slightly less than high school record for the prediction of college grades, and a series of subject-matter tests having acceptable reliability coefficients may be expected to correlate between 0.45 and 0.60 with average first year grades in college.

Tests of scholastic aptitude rank below high school grades and below achievement tests as predictors of measures of college success. Successful instruments for this purpose include the American Coun·

cil on Educational Psychological Examinations, the Ohio State University Psychological Examinations, and numerous others. Such tests tend to have better predictive value in small institutions than in large private institutions as a result of differences in range of ability.

It has been frequently suggested that the relatively poor prediction of college grades which can be made from scholastic aptitude tests, achievement tests, or high school grades is a result of the unreliability of college grades. There is little evidence, however, to support such a point of view. Later in the chapter evidence will be examined pertaining to the possibility that other factors besides intellectual abilities are important for college success.

Factors other than validity must also be considered in the choice of instruments for the selection of college students. While achievement tests have high validity, the unfortunate effect which they have on the high school curriculum raises serious questions concerning the wisdom of using them in any college selection program. The combination of high school grades and the scores on a scholastic aptitude test will probably provide as satisfactory a selection device as can be obtained at the present time. Unfortunately, it is not known whether measures of the broad outcomes of education such as were developed in the Eight Year Study (33) can be used satisfactorily for predicting college sucess.

Garrett's review of research on the prediction of college success (14) brings out an interesting fact which seems to have remained unnoticed. It is that the tests developed twenty-five years ago are no less efficient than those which have been more recently developed for predicting college success. This seems to indicate that further progress in improving predictions of college success is going to be achieved only with great difficulty. In the meantime, college registrars are likely to continue to use instruments which have demonstrated their worth over the last two decades.

It has become a common practice among colleges and universities to require certain patterns of high school credits for admission. Such a requirement has usually been set up on an armchair basis without any reference to investigation or quantitative data. Study after study has shown, however, that there is practically no relation between pattern of high school credits and success in college. There is some evidence to show that, in distinct contrast to the operation of average high school marks or intelligence test scores, the requirement for entrance of a specific high school credit bars as many superior as inferior individuals, and admits as many inferior as superior ones. After reviewing the available evidence, one might conclude that the present common practice of selecting college entrants on the basis of minimum credits in certain fields of high school work is an inexplicable and useless ceremonial.

Similarly, the advantage of studying certain subjects in high school as background for specific college courses seem to have been greatly overemphasized. While students who have had high school courses in chemistry, physics, zoology, and foreign languages do slightly better in the corresponding first year college courses, there is some evidence that the initial advantage is not maintained.

Consequently, it may be said that the practice of college admissions offices of requiring certain high school courses or certain prescribed sequences lacks support of any kind from careful systematic investigation.

One important study (7) has shown that students who have been subjected to the experimental type of curriculum in high school tend to be slightly more successful in college than students of comparable ability from high schools which offer the traditional type of curriculum. It is not clear whether such slight superiority is a consequence of superior motivation, superior study habits, or superior integration of knowledge. In any case, differences are so small that they do not provide a useful basis for college admission.

The Effect of Guidance on Predictions

Numerous writers have pointed out that the validity of predictions of scholastic success should be materially reduced in those institutions which have sound guidance programs. It is argued that a good guidance service will enable many students to succeed who otherwise would have failed. By guiding a student into those courses for which he is best suited, it should be possible for a student to achieve greater success than he would otherwise have achieved.

Although there have been a number of studies of this problem, the results appear to be in conflict. This conflict is undoubtedly more apparent than real and a consequence of the fact that some studies have been undertaken on general samples of the college population, while other studies have been undertaken with special groups.

Both Darley (9) and Sarbin (34) conducted studies of the validity of predictions of academic success based on counseling and other procedures. In Darley's study an investigation was undertaken of University of Minnesota students transferred out of the general college and admitted to professional schools. Two groups of these transfer students were studied. One group passed through the usual administrative procedure, while the other was passed through a counseling procedure. The predictions made on the basis of the counseling procedure were considerably more accurate than those based on the usual administrative procedure. Insofar as the student follows the counselor's advice, this finding indicates that a guidance program may make substantial changes in a given student's chances of success. The Darley study, however, does not provide evidence that the predictions of academic success made from a counseling procedure are superior to those made from the usual measures of scholastic success. A study of this problem by Sarbin indicated that case studies which took into account numerous variables had approximately the same validity as admission tests which measured only three or four.

Attempts to lower the validity of predictions of failures by proper counseling procedures do not seem to have been too effective. In one study (19), it is reported that in the fall quarters of 1939 and 1940, students entering the Iowa State College directly from high school with low academic averages were grouped together in a pre-admission guidance program. They were subjected to a counseling procedure which included tests and interviews, and were not permitted to register for a full academic load nor for certain subjects which tend to cause difficulty to freshmen. The students also met with a counselor in a combined study methods and remedial reading course. In spite of these aids, the performance of these students was decidely unsatisfactory, and 70 per cent of the group terminated their college work by action of the scholarship committee. In another experiment also conducted at Iowa (21), similar conclusions were drawn.

Consequently, there is as yet little evidence that counseling techniques can either upset predictions of academic achievement or provide predictions which are better than those obtainable from measures which have been validated for predicting academic success.

The Prediction of College Achievement in Individual Subject-Matter Fields

The early studies of the prediction of academic success were concerned mainly with the prediction of over-all scholastic aptitude. More recently, studies have tended to take up the matter of differential predictions of academic success in specific areas by measuring the aptitudes required for those areas. The American Council on Education Psychological Examination permitted some differential prediction insofar as different subject-matter fields require varying amounts of the verbal and quantitative variables. There seems to be some merit for guidance purposes in classifying college students according to whether their main strength is in the verbal or numerical groups. On the American Council Psychological Examination, the L-scores (linguistic) tend to be more highly correlated with English, foreign languages, history, and science, and the Q-scores (quantitative) correlates most highly with mathematics. The Psychological Examination, however, does not provide differential predictions between broad courses such as agriculture or engineering.

It will be recalled that at the high school level, specific tests designed for predicting achievement in specific courses provide more accurate prediction than tests with broader purposes. The same is true at the college level. These tests usually contain materials which resemble those to be learned in the course where predictions are to be made. Where this is not done (15, 39), predictions in specific courses tend to be poor.

The study of differential predictions raises an interesting problem. The evidence indicates that students with high verbal ability but low qualitative or numerical ability have a much better chance of entering colleges than students with low verbal ability but high quantitative or numerical ability. Such a situation, which is not the result of any conscious policy, is likely to discriminate against some of those with high ability for solving quantitative problems.

The Prediction of Scholastic Success in Professional Schools

During the last ten years, professional schools have shown an increasing interest in the use of tests for selection of students. One of the major difficulties in the validation of tests for admitting students to professional schools is the selection of a criterion of success. If selection tests are validated against first year grades, they may not be valid for predicting success in the final years, since the abilities and skills required for success in early phases of professional training are often different from those required for success in the final phases. There is much wisdom in using the criterion of scholastic success which Thurstone has frequently used; namely, graduation, but unfortunately most of the aptitude tests for professional schools have been validated against first semester of first year grades in professional schools.

Engineering. Numerous studies have been made of the measurement of those factors which make for scholastic success in engineering schools. These studies may be summarized by saying the predicted grades in the first two years of engineering school may be expected to correlate between 0.6 and 0.7 with actual grades if predictions are made from tests in mathematical and scientific fields. The Iowa Placement Tests in mathematical and scientific fields have been shown to be about as valid as any of the available tests for predicting success in engineering schools and to be considerably more valid for this purpose than general scholastic aptitude tests. The Pre-Engineering Inventory, a test originally financed by the Carnegie Foundation for the Advancement of Teaching, has been proposed as a device for selecting engineering students. It is probably as valid as any of the better batteries for selecting students of engineering.

Medicine. In 1940, Kandel (20) wrote: "In the selection of candidates for the study of medicine, greater progress has been made than for any other professional field." This was written at a time when the Moss Medical Aptitude Test was being widely used for the selection of medical students and a whole series of studies had demonstrated the validity of such tests of medical aptitude (12). The validity of the combination of the Moss Medical Aptitude Test and premedical grades was established at about 0.7 for many medical schools, which is near the ceiling of validity for scholastic predictions. Here, as in other fields, grades in preprofessional courses and scores on interest inventories have been shown to have substantial validity for the prediction of scholastic success in medical school.

Since Kandel wrote the above statement in 1940, the position has changed. The Association of American Medical Colleges discarded its testing program, and after trials with various sponsors has now assigned responsibility for the program to the Educational Testing Service. Limited information is as yet available concerning the predictive value of the new battery. However, since its primary purpose seems to be more that of selecting "well educated citizens" than that of predicting grades in medical school, its usefulness cannot be evaluated in terms of correlation with grades. A review of early studies of the predictive value of the battery (30) indicates that it has little value for predicting grades in medical school.

Law. Interest has been shown in aptitude tests for law students as well as in aptitude tests for medical and engineering students. Pre-law grades have been shown to be the best available predictors of scholastic success in law school, though law aptitude tests have some validity. The Ferson-Stoddard Law Aptitude Test correlated approximately 0.5 with law school grades in two separate studies. The Iowa Legal Aptitude Test correlated to about the same degree with first year law grades. Combinations of legal aptitude tests with pre-law grades have produced correlations above 0.65, with subsequent grades in legal areas. In the field of law, as in other professional fields, the best predictions of success are obtained by combining previous grades with scores from an aptitude test, and such a multiple correlation accounts for approximately half the variability of the student's law grades. It should be remembered that the other half of the variability is produced by unidentified variables. Since 1948, a new selection test has been developed as a cooperative enterprise of several law schools under the leadership of the Educational Testing Service. This new test seems to have predictive value comparable with that of its predecessors.

Dentistry. Studies of the prediction of success in dentistry have as yet yielded few profitable results. Small positive correlations have been found between various phases of dental training and tests of mechanical aptitude. Tests of general ability have been found to predict, to some degree, grades in dental school. Recently the Association of Dental Schools has instituted a testing program which includes performance tests of motor skill, but the program is still experimental and it is too early yet to expect any report on the validity of the tests. It is encouraging, however, to note that the dental testing program, unlike some of the other programs discussed in this paper, is established on a genuinely experimental basis.

Other Professional Fields. Studies have been carried out to determine factors which can be used in the prediction of success in other professional schools such as nursing, business administration, pharmacy, and social work. The evidence in these fields supports the general contention that the best method of selecting students for professional schools is to combine a measure of previous scholastic success with a measure of special aptitude for the field.

In concluding this section on prediction in professional fields, it may be said that the present tendency to develop different aptitude tests for each professional field is resulting in a series of devices which are very cumbersome in a guidance program. It would be hardly practical for guidance workers to administer to the same individual a premedical aptitude test, a pre-law aptitude test, and a whole series of professional aptitude tests. The multiplicity of these testing devices represents a most unhealthy trend in the guidance movement. On the other hand, a short comprehensive battery built on a rational basis may be expected to provide predictions for each field on the basis of a single series of tests.

The Prediction of Success in Graduate School

Of all the major areas in which work has been done on the prediction of academic success, least work of quality has been undertaken in the area of predicting success in graduate school. One reason for this state of affairs is that during the years preceding the Second World War, most graduate schools had difficulty in maintaining their enrollments and little could be done about selecting graduate students. Two major research projects, however, were initiated during these years. One was by Dr. W. S. Miller of the University of Minnesota; and the other by the deans of the graduate schools of Harvard, Yale, Princeton, and Columbia in cooperation with the Carnegie Foundation for the Advancement of Teaching. This project, largely through the efforts of Mr. Charles Langmuir and Dr.

W. S. Learned, developed a series of examinations designed to measure the student's knowledge in broad areas of study and called the Graduate Record Examination. The nature of these tests was described in Chapter IV. In the early days of the project, a healthy emphasis was placed on the fact that the program was experimental and that research had to be done before the examination should be made available for widespread use.

Studies undertaken indicated that the Graduate Record Examination had limited validity for the selection of graduate students. The verbal factor test was the most valid, though its validity was lower than that which is ordinarily acceptable in the prediction of achievement.

Of course, it must be remembered that these results do not apply to the recent edition of the Graduate Record Examination, which is a product of the Educational Testing Service and which differs from previous editions both in structure and in what it claims to measure. These recent editions *may* have much greater selection value than the first form of the test. The new profile tests are at least patterned after tests which have had value as selection devices in academic situations. It appears that they are designed to measure thinking skill in particular areas rather than information.

The second major research project into the prediction of success in graduate school has been conducted largely by Dr. W. S. Miller at the University of Minnesota. This project consists of the validation of a single analogies test which is both a test of information over wide areas of study and a test of thinking skill. The test, which takes fifty minutes to administer, seems to be at least as valid as the original eight-hour Graduate Record Examination for predicting grades according to data provided in the manual and other studies which have been undertaken (26).

Other investigations have shown that, next to undergraduate grades, high-level verbal-reasoning tests are fairly effective predictors of success in graduate school. Undergraduate average grades may be expected to correlate with graduate grades in similar subjects to the extent of 0.5.

Consequently, in summarizing this section it may be said that the best method available at present for selecting graduate students is to place the main emphasis on the undergraduate scholastic record and a secondary emphasis on a high-level verbal-ability test.

Nonintellectual Factors in Academic Success

The voluminous studies in the area of predicting scholastic success indicate that the best of the currently available aptitude tests may be expected to correlate with high school grades about 0.5, and in certain cases correlations as high as 0.7 have been found. There seems no doubt that it is possible, through unusual diligence, for a student to do acceptable work in a well-known liberal arts college though his intelligence quotient is below 105. High school students with much lower intelligence quotients make satisfactory academic records and may enter smaller colleges from which they eventually graduate.

Even if the factor of unreliability of college grades is taken into account, the data suggest that there may be important factors other than those measured by tests of intellectual aptitude which result in variation in college performance. In the last ten years considerable effort has been devoted to the study of these factors.

At the elementary school level little is known about motivational and other personality factors which affect school achievement, largely because useful measures of these variables are not available. However, clinical psychologists report numerous cases of children who were retarded at school as a result of emotional disturbances or of situations involving tension in the home. The fact that the school does not provide experiences which interest certain pupils may also cause retardation, but evidence for this statement is derived largely from the experiences of those who work closely with pupils. Studies of pupils tested provide little information which the school guidance worker can apply. In an investigation by Lewes (23) of gifted children of superior and inferior educational achievement, the traits found with greater frequency in the low scholastic group were lack of interest in school work, inattention, and an interest in physical and motor activities. However, the reader should be cautious in the interpretation of these results, since the traits characteristic of the low achievement group may be the result rather than the cause of poor achievement.

In a study of the relation of academic success to nonintellectual factors (23), the Rorschach was administered to a group of successful and unsuccessful boys and girls in the eighth and ninth grades.

Unsuccessful students showed a statistically significant greater number of signs of color shock and shading shock; a greater frequency of animal responses, said to indicate the amount of stereotypy in thinking; a lower frequency of Fc responses, which are said to indicate careful awareness of the outer environment, and fewer signs of adjustment. These findings are consistent with independent Rorschach studies of college groups, but the reader should be cautioned that all too often promising studies based on the Rorschach Test have been repeated with contradictory results.

In the absence of personality measuring instruments suitable for the school child, a number of studies have been conducted with instruments built mainly for adults. The Minnesota Multiphasic Personality Inventory has been used widely for this purpose, but Gough (16), who has reviewed such studies, finds that scores derived from this instrument are uniformly valueless for predicting achievement. Many of these studies may be expected to have produced negative results, since they do not seem to have been based on any theory concerning the way in which personality variables are related to achievement.

Garrett (14) has reviewed studies of the relationship of measures of personality characteristics to achievement in college and tabulated the results. The correlations expressing these relationships appear to be mostly close to zero, which probably reflects the inadequacy of measures of personality The data give some support to the belief that the introverted and withdrawn student tends to achieve slightly higher grades than the student of equal ability who is the outgoing type.

It seems that introversion provides a condition which favors academic success, possibly by reducing the tendency for the student to be distracted by outside events. This hypothesis is substantiated by three Rorschach studies (24, 27, 28) which indicate that the successful college student is less responsive to outer stimuli than the poor student. In one study (28) an evaluation of general adjustment made by means of a rating sheet applied to the Rorschach results was found to correlate 0.49 with grades and to a negligible extent with the scores on the American Council on Education Psychological Examination. An examination of the protocols indicated that the most successful students tended to have certain neurotic trends in their personality and were somewhat overambitious intellectually. Similar results have also been found in another study by Thompson (35). These studies suggest that projective techniques may eventually prove to be valuable aids in the counseling of college and precollege students and particularly in helping to solve the problems of those who have high scholastic aptitude but relatively low scholastic achievement. However, one cannot be sure at this time that these results with the Rorschach can be reproduced in other educational situations or even when the test is administered by other personnel.

Attempts to develop tests of persistence have had a long history. However, from the early efforts in this direction in 1934 and 1941 (32, 36) to the more recent ones (13) the results of research do not indicate that measures of persistence are likely to predict achievement.

Studies of the relation between scores on interest tests and academic success have been of limited value because they have been based largely on interest tests which were developed for nonscholastic predictions. The value of interest tests for prediction has already been considered in a general way in the chapter on interest tests. The Kuder Preference Record has been found to provide small but statistically significant correlations with grades in academic fields that correspond with the areas of interest, and other types of interest tests produce similar results. The Strong Interest Inventory has been shown to predict academic success in various professional fields, and as far as prediction within a liberal arts program is concerned, the Strong Inventory seems to have small value for predicting differences in the level of achievement in different subject-matter areas. Other interest blanks have also been shown to have limited use for that purpose. Attempts have been made to produce a scale for the Strong Interest Inventory which might measure studiousness. Correlations of academic success with this scale in early studies varied from 0.11 up to 0.55, depending on the particular group tested, but later studies do not seem to have fulfilled these early promises.

One of the promising approaches to the study of the role of interests at the college level was developed by Detchen (11), who selected from the Kuder Preference Record items which discriminated between the good and poor students on the Comprehensive Social Science Examination given at Chicago University. The resulting interest scale had considerable validity in predicting grades in social sciences and, used in combination with the American Council on Education Psychological Examination and a social science placement test, it produced better predictions than those obtained by either of these instruments alone.

Probably the most notable recent contribution to the measurement of nonintellectual variables related to achievement is the work of McClelland and his associates (25), which has already been discussed. The projective test which this group has developed not only predicts grades, but also provides a measure of motivation which is sensitive to changes in motivational conditions. Under conditions where the student can be presumed to be highly motivated, the test yields higher scores than when the student is working under conditions which result in poor motivation.

This section on factors other than intellectual aptitudes which make for academic success may be concluded by the statement that while it is agreed that factors other than scholastic aptitudes are of great importance, yet most of these factors have not been adequately identified and measured. While it seems fairly clear that the social qualities of an individual have relatively little to do with his academic success, it is also evident that interests and motives play a very important part. The present writer feels that educational counselors have tended to underestimate the importance of these nonintellectual factors and too often have placed excessive reliance on standard measures of scholastic aptitude in counseling the pupil.

Planning to Use Aptitude Test Results

It has already been emphasized that more tests are given in schools than are ever used. It is therefore important that the way in which scores are to be used should be carefully thought through at the time when plans are first made to administer tests.

The varieties of tests which have been considered in this chapter and the last serve three main purposes. These are (1) selection for specific educational programs from which not all pupils can profit, (2) the individual guidance of the pupil designed to assist him in making major decisions, and (3) the provision of information necessary for helping the teacher in curriculum planning. The uses of information derived from tests for each one of these purposes will be given brief consideration.

The application of test results for the selection of pupils for a particular educational program is a relatively simple matter once it has been demonstrated that the instruments to be used are satisfactory for this purpose. Usually, the scores from the various selection instruments are added together in such a way that the combined score produces the most efficient prediction of success in the program for which it is desired to select pupils. It is then common practice to select students from as near to the top of the list as possible. Occasionally it may be possible to set a lower limit on test scores when experience has shown that those who score below a certain lower limit are unable to profit from the program. In any case, since test scores provide only *rough indications* of a pupil's ability to profit from a particular curriculum, the selection procedure involves the acceptance of the best risks and the rejection of the poorest risks. A certain fraction of the best risks will, nevertheless, fail to achieve the goals of the program.

The use of tests in guidance is a much more complex matter than their use for selection, although guidance is the major purpose to which test results are applied in most schools or colleges. The varied backgrounds of school personnel who administer tests and use scores make it difficult to state generalizations concerning how test scores should be used. However, it can be said emphatically that whoever uses and interprets aptitude test scores should be familiar with findings concerning their predictive value and should also know their limitations. He should also have had some training and supervised experience in counseling.

A consideration of the topic of the use of test scores in guidance plunges the reader immediately into one of the most controversial issues in applied psychology, namely, the usefulness of various counseling procedures. It is inevitable that the way in which counseling is undertaken must determine very largely the way which tests and test scores are used.

At the present time, the counseling procedures that are commonly observed in schools and colleges which have an organized counseling program involve a preliminary interview which is used as a basis for determining the general nature of the counselee's problem. Then a battery of tests is administered, and, usually for the sake of administrative convenience, the same tests are administered to all. Finally, the counselee meets again with his counselor to work out some solution to his problem, taking into account test scores and all other relevant data. Much of the counseling which is undertaken in this framework involves the giving of information to the pupil in order to help him solve his problem.

In this type of counseling program, the counselor usually helps the counselee on the basis of test scores and other information to arrive at decisions. This process involves a great deal of judgment on the part of the counselor, and this introduces an element of unreliability, for judgments are subject to error. However, counselors would find support for this procedure in the common observation that a test score can have different meanings according to the other characteristics of the pupil. For example, a score derived from a group intelligence test administered in New York City may differ in significance according to whether the pupil comes from a Spanish-speaking or an English-speaking home. If each measured characteristic must be interpreted in terms of the other characteristics, then the process of interpreting test scores is necessarily complex and requires the counselor to exercise judgment.

There are psychologists who disagree with the systematic use of test scores in the type of guidance program that has been described. These psychologists are those who have been influenced deeply by the observation of clinicians that psychological patients are unwilling to accept information about themselves unless it is consistent with what they already believe. For this reason, these psychologists would reject the use of any uniform battery of tests to be administered to all who seek guidance. Rather would they administer individually selected tests at times in the guidance process when the pupil felt the need for the information which the test can supply. At such times, the pupil is more likely to accept and use the information which the test provides than when it is administered as a part of a uniform routine. There is certainly merit to this point of view, for it is all too easy to present the pupil with facts about himself which he will not accept, but it is also expensive and administratively inconvenient to adopt completely individualized testing schedules.

The central issues concerning how information derived from tests should be used in helping the pupil arrive at wise descisions cannot be discussed adequately at this time, but the student should leave a course in educational measurement with an appreciation of the fact that helping the pupil use the knowledge derived from test scores is no simple matter. Those who wish to pursue the matter further should take further courses in the area of counseling and guidance.

The third use of aptitude test results is for helping the teacher plan a program with objectives which the pupil is capable of achieving. With this end in view, reading readiness tests are administered in the first grade, group aptitude tests are administered at all levels, and sometimes other devices such as interest inventories are administered. The writer feels that each school faculty should plan a program of testing designed to provide the faculty with certain basic information about the pupils. As a part of such a program, group intelligence tests may be administered in certain grades, but not in every grade, as sometimes occurs. Other tests should be included only insofar as there is a real need for the information they supply, and the faculty might well consider participating in such information-gathering programs as the public opinion poll conducted in high schools by Purdue University. At certain times, a school may consider making a study of the extent to which specific objectives are being achieved and to relate actual achievement to that expected on the basis of aptitude tests. All such studies invigorate a school faculty and can provide substantial help in curriculum planning.

Summary

Conclusions from the data discussed in this chapter are summarized in the following paragraphs:

1. Intelligence quotients measured during the grade school period provide rather poor predictions of academic achievement during that period, and for practical purposes are of only small value for predicting academic achievement in college.

2. Measures of various aspects of intelligence, such as verbal reasoning and quantitative reasoning, provide better predictions of academic success in particular fields than are provided by measures of general ability.

3. At the high school level, fairly satisfactory predictions of academic success in particular areas can be made from tests designed to predict success in those areas.

4. The best single predictor of general academic success in college is the student's high school performance. The particular sequences he has had in high school, however, bear no relationship to college success, and little advantage is gained in a specific course in college by taking the corresponding course in high school.

5. Subject-matter tests and tests of scholastic aptitude have some value in predicting success in high school and in college, but they are less valid than measures of previous educational achievement for this purpose. It is probable that the most satisfactory method of predicting general academic success in college is to combine a measure of high school success with a measure of scholastic aptitude.

6. At the college level, prediction of academic success in specific subject-matter fields can be made with greater accuracy than over-all predictions.

7. The development of long aptitude tests for various professional fields represents an unhealthy development in the testing movement since it is resulting in a series of cumbersome instruments which require much time to administer when a single testing program would serve the same purpose. A single comprehensive battery could provide fairly satisfactory predictions of success in most professional fields. The subtests in such a battery would be weighted differently for each professional field. Initial work on such an approach seems particularly promising.

8. The best single predictor of academic success in professional fields is the average grade in preprofessional college work. Average grades are better than test scores for making such predictions.

9. The best predictor of grades in graduate schools is the average undergraduate grade. A verbal reasoning test, such as the Miller Analogies Test or other intelligence tests, may be of some value in the selection of graduate students.

10. Motivational factors probably play a major role in determining academic success both in high school and in college. Measures of interest especially designed for the purpose have been found to correlate with college performance but not as well as measures of aptitude.

11. Accuracy of prediction is also limited considerably by the

fact that the stimulus situation in which the student's response is to be predicted is known only in general terms.

12. The use of aptitude test results should be carefully planned. Aptitude tests should not be administered unless they serve some clearly defined purpose and unless personnel are available who have the knowledge and skill necessary for the proper utilization of scores. For this reason, it is most desirable that teachers and prospective teachers should obtain training in counseling techniques if they are to use aptitude tests for purposes other than selection or curriculum planning.

References

1. Allen, M. M., "The Relationship Between the Kuhlman-Anderson Intelligence Tests and Academic Achievement in Grades 3 and 4," *Educational and Psychological Measurements*, 4, 1944, 161–168.

2. Bennett, George K., *Stenographic Aptitude Tests*, New York, The Psychological Corporation, 1939.

3. Bennett, George K., Seashore, Harold G., and Wesman, Alexander G., *Manual Differential Aptitude Test*, New York, The Psychological Corporation, 1952.

4. Benson, V. E., "The Intelligence and Later Scholastic Success of Sixth-Grade Pupils," *School and Society*, 55, 1942, 163–167.

5. Billhartz, W. H. Jr. and Hutson, P. W., "Determining College Ability During Junior High School Years," *School and Society*, 53, 1941, 547–552.

6. Bond, E. A., *Tenth-Grade Abilities and Achievements*, New York, Bureau of Publications, Teachers College, Columbia University, Teachers College Contributions to Education No. 813, 1940, pp. 67 + VI.

7. Chamberlin, Dean, Chamberlin, Enid, Crought, Neal E., Scott, William E., *Did They Succeed in College?* New York, Harper and Brothers, 1942, pp. 291.

8. Crawford, A. B. and Burnham, P. S., *Forecasting College Achievement*, Part I. General considerations in the measurement of academic promise. Yale University Press, 1946, pp. 291.

9. Darley, J. G., "A Study of Clinical Predictions of Student Success or Failure in Professional Training," *Journal of Educational Psychology*, 29, 1938, 335–354.

10. Deemer, Walter W. and Rulon, Phillip J., *The Stenographic Skills Test*, Cambridge, Massachusetts, The Educational Research Corporation, 1942.

11. Detchen, L., "The Effect of a Measure of Interest Factors on the Prediction of Performance in a College Social Sciences Comprehensive Examination," *Journal of Educational Psychology*, 37, 1946, 45–52.

12. Douglas, H. R., *Prediction of Success in the Medical School*, University of Minnesota Studies in the Prediction of Scholastic Achievement, 2, 1942, 1–16.

13. Edmiston, R. W. and Jackson, Lewis A., "The Relationship of Persistence to Achievement," *Journal of Educational Psychology*, 40, 1949, 47–51.

14. Garrett, Harley F., "A Review and Interpretation of Investigations of Factors Related to Scholastic Success in Colleges of Arts and Sciences and Teachers Colleges," *Journal of Experimental Education*, 18, 1949, 91–138.

15. Goodman, C. H., "Prediction of College Success by Means of Thurstone's Primary Abilities Tests," *Educational and Psychological Measurement*, 4, 1944, 125–140.

16. Gough, Harrison G., "Factors Relating to the Academic Achievement of High School Students," *Journal of Educational Psychology*, 40, 1949, 65–68.

17. Harris, D., "Factors Affecting College Grades: A Review of the Literature 1930–1937," *Psychological Bulletin*, 37, 1940, 126–166.

18. Hoffman, W. S., "Predictive Selective Admissions," *School and Society*, 45, 1937, 829–831.

19. Holmes, J. L., "Scholastic Progress of Students Entering the Iowa State College with Low High-School Averages," *Proceedings of the Iowa Academy of Sciences*, 51, 1944, 383–387.

20. Kandel, I. L., *Professional Aptitude Tests in Medicine, Law, and Engineering*, New York, Teachers College Bureau of Publications, Columbia University, 1940, pp. 78 + X.

21. Kay, G. F. and Stuit, D. B., "The Effect of Special Procedures for Students of Low Scholastic Aptitude," *School and Society*, 55, 1942, 281–284.

22. Keys, N., "The Value of Group Test I.Q's for Prediction of Progress Beyond High School," *Journal of Educational Psychology*, 31, 1940, 81–93.

23. Lewes, W. D., "A Comparative Study of the Personalities, Interests, and Home Background of Gifted Children of Superior and

Inferior Educational Achievement," *Psychological Bulletin,* 37, 1940, 525 (Abstract).

24. Margulies, H., *Rorschach Responses of Successful and Unsuccessful Students,* Archives of Psychology, No. 271, 1942, pp. 61.

25. McClelland, David C., Atkinson, John W., Clark, Russell A., and Lowell, Edgar L., *The Achievement Motive,* New York, Appleton-Century-Crofts, Inc., 1953, pp. 384 + 24.

26. Miller, W. S., *Manual for the Miller Analogies Test,* New York, The Psychological Corporation, 1947, pp. 11.

27. Montalto, F. D., "An Application of the Group Rorschach Technique to the Problem of Achievement in College," *Journal of Clinical Psychology,* 2, 1946, 254–260.

28. Munroe, Ruth, *Prediction of the Adjustment and Academic Performance of College Students by a Modification of the Rorschach Method,* Applied Psychological Monographs, No. 7, 1945, pp. 104.

29. Osborne, Agnes E., *The Relationship Between Certain Psychological Tests and Shorthand Achievement,* Teachers College Contributions to Education No. 873, New York, Teachers College Bureau of Publications, 1943, pp. 58.

30. Ralph, Ray B. and Taylor, Calvin W., "The Role of Tests in the Medical Selection Program," *Journal of Applied Psychology,* 36, 1952, 107–111.

31. Rosenfeld, M. A. and Nemzek, C. L., "Long Range Predictions of College Marks," *School and Society,* 47, 1938, 127–128.

32. Ryans, D. G. "A Study of the Observed Relationship Between Persistence Test Results, Intelligence Indices, and Academic Success," *Journal of Educational Psychology,* 29, 1938, 573–580.

33. Smith, E. R., Tyler, R. W., and the evaluation staff, *Appraising and Recording Student Progress,* New York, Harper and Brothers, 1942, pp. 550 + XXII.

34. Sarbin, T. R., "A Contribution to the Study of Actuarial and Individual Methods for Prediction," *American Journal of Sociology,* 48, 1943, 593–602.

35. Thompson, Grace M., "College Grades and the Group Rorschach," *Journal of Applied Psychology,* 32, 1948, 398–407.

36. Thornton, G. R., "The Use of Tests of Persistence in the Prediction of Scholastic Achievement," *Journal of Educational Psychology,* 32, 1941, 266–273.

37. Travers, Robert M. W., "Significant Research on the Prediction of Academic Success," pp. 147–190 in *The Measurement of Student Adjustment and Achievement,* edited by Donahue, Wilma

T., Coombs, Clyde H., and Travers, Robert M. W. Ann Arbor, University of Michigan Press, 1949, pp. 256.

38. Turse, Paul L., *Turse Shorthand Aptitude Test,* Yonkers, New York, World Book.Company, 1942.

39. Wallace, Wimburn L., "The Prediction of Grades in Specific College Courses," *Journal of Educational Research,* 44, 1951, 587–597.

APPENDIX A

The Computation of the Standard Deviation

The computation of the standard deviation of a distribution is determined by finding the value of the following expression:

$$\sqrt{\frac{\Sigma(X - \overline{X})^2}{n - 1}}$$

In this expression the symbol Σ means to add. That part of the expression which follows the symbol Σ indicates what is to be added. The part in parentheses $(X - \overline{X})^2$ indicates that each score X is to have the mean or average score $\overline{X}$ subtracted from it and each of those differences is then to be squared. Finally the squared differences are to be added together.

Since n indicates the number of cases, it follows that the denominator is one less than the number of cases.

The difficulty with this formula is that it involves a great amount of computation. It is very tedious to subtract each measure from the mean and then to square the difference, so alternative formulae have been developed which eliminate some of this work. These formulas all look more complicated than the one just given, but they do reduce the amount of work involved in making the computations. The following formula is given because of its widespread use in machine computation. Most persons who wish to compute a standard deviation have at least a comptometer available to them.

$$\text{Standard deviation} = \sqrt{\frac{\Sigma X^2 - n\overline{X}^2}{n - 1}}$$

This formula indicates that each one of the scores is to be squared and the squares are to summed (ΣX^2). From this sum is subtracted the product of the square of the mean and the number of the scores. The remaining operations indicated by the formula are self-explanatory.

Table 1 shows the computations of the standard deviation of a distribution of scores on the basis of this formula. The values computed may be entered in the formula as follows:

$$\sqrt{\frac{1850 - 50 \times 5.88^2}{49}} = \sqrt{\frac{1850 - 1728.72}{49}} = \sqrt{\frac{121.28}{49}} = 1.57$$

The resulting value is the standard deviation of the distribution of scores.

TABLE 1

Method of Computing Standard Deviation

Magnitude of Scores	Number of Scores of Each Magnitude	Total Value of All Scores of Each Magnitude	Total Value of the Scores of Each Magnitude Squared
9	3	27	$243 = (9^2 \times 3)$
8	4	32	$256 = (8^2 \times 4)$
7	10	70	$490 = (7^2 \times 10)$
6	14	84	$504 = (6^2 \times 14)$
5	9	45	$225 = (5^2 \times 9)$
4	6	24	$96 = (4^2 \times 6)$
3	4	12	$36 = (3^2 \times 4)$
	$n = 50$	$\Sigma X = 294$ (Total of all scores)	$\Sigma X = 1850$ (Total of each score squared)

Mean of all scores $= \overline{X} = \dfrac{294}{50} = 5.88$

If a calculating machine is not available the arithmetic can be simplified by changing the scale shown in the left column of Table 1 to a new scale of values. It is clear that the amount of scatter of the scores is unchanged if the same constant is added to all scores. For example, the standard deviation of the scores in Table 1 would remain unchanged if 60 were added to each score so that the left column listed values from 63 up to 69. This fact can be used in reducing the amount of arithmetic involved in the calculation of the standard deviation. In Table 2 new values have been assigned to the scores so that now they vary from $+3$ to -3, with 0 approximately at the mean. The remaining computations are then carried out in the same way as before. The values entered in the formula are as follows:

$$\sqrt{\frac{122 - 50 \times 0.12^2}{49}} = \sqrt{\frac{121.28}{49}} = 1.57 \quad.$$

The value of the standard deviation is necessarily identical with the value previously calculated.

TABLE 2

Calculation of Standard Deviation Using a New Scale
of Values for Simplifying the Arithmetic

Original Magnitude of Score	Number of Scores of Each Magnitude	New Assigned Magnitudes	Total Value of All Scores of Each New Magnitude	Total Value of Scores of Magnitude Squared
9	3	+3	9	27
8	4	+2	8	16
7	10	+1	10	10
6	14	0		
5	9	−1	− 9	9
4	6	−2	−12	24
3	4	−3	−12	36
			$\Sigma X = -6$	$\Sigma X^2 = 122$
			$\overline{X} = -\dfrac{6}{50} = -0.12$	

APPENDIX B

The Estimation of Reliability

When two forms of a test have been administered to the same population, or when the same form has been administered on two occasions to the same population, the estimation of the reliability of the test is a relatively simple matter, for it involves only the computation of the correlation between the scores. However, the estimate thus computed must be interpreted with the cautions given in the main body of the text.

The problem of estimating reliability becomes somewhat more complex when it is desired to estimate it from a single form of a test which has been administered only once. Let us assume that the items in the test have been so divided as to produce as nearly as possible two comparable forms which may be referred to as subtest 1 and subtest 2. The reliability of the total test can then be estimated from the formula.

$$\text{Estimated reliability} = 1 - \frac{\sigma^2_{1-2}}{\sigma^2_{1+2}}$$

In this formula σ_{1-2} is the standard deviation of the differences between the pairs of scores, and σ_{1+2} is the standard deviation of the scores produced by summing the two part scores. This method is particularly simple to apply since it does not involve the computations usually involved in the calculation of a correlation coefficient.

If the correlation between the two halves of the test r_{12} has been calculated, it is evident that the coefficient thus produced is an estimate of the reliability of a test half as long as the total test. The total test must have a reliability greater than the reliability of half the test. The reliability for the total test can then be estimated by entering the value found for half the test in the following formula:

$$\text{Estimated total test reliability} = \frac{2r_{12}}{1 + r_{12}}$$

It must be remembered that this formula, like the previous one, cannot be meaningfully applied to speeded tests.

Various formulas developed by G. F. Kuder and M. W. Richardson provide a basis for estimating reliability from a single administration of a single form of a test. These formulas vary in complexity and those that are most complex involve the fewest assumptions. If it is assumed that all items measure the same factors,[*] that all item intercorrelations are equal, and that each item has the same variance, the reliability of the test may be estimated from the following formula:

$$\frac{n}{n-1} \times \frac{\sigma^2 - \Sigma pq}{\sigma^2}$$

In this formula n is the number of items in the test, s is the standard deviation of the scores and, for each item, p is the proportion passing the item and q is the proportion failing (that is, if p were 0.47, it would mean that 47 per cent of those tested passed the item; for this item q would be 0.53 and $pq = 0.47 \times 0.53$). In the use of this formula it is necessary to compute the product pq for each item and then to sum these products.

If the person estimating reliability is willing to make the additional assumption that all items in the test are equal in difficulty, then the following simplified formula may be used:

$$\frac{n}{n-1} \left[1 - \left(\frac{\overline{X} - \dfrac{\overline{X}}{n}}{\sigma^2} \right) \right]$$

In this formula $\overline{X}$ is the average number of items answered correctly, σ is the standard deviation of scores and n is the number of items.

[*] This assumption states that the test must be homogeneous.

Index

Abbott, A., 137, 146
ability to apply scientific principles, 101
ability to interpret data, 97
Abstract Reasoning Test, 364
accounting tests, 154
achievement, definition of, 15
achievement tests, cooperative, 44
Adams, M., 362
age equivalents, 46
age of maximum growth, 378
Allport, G. W., 212, 248, 253, 285, 310
alternatives of test item, 179
American Council on Education Psychological Examination, 348, 354, 373, 380, 382, 387, 388, 391, 397
American Psychological Association, 116
Anderson, G. L., 243, 248
Anderson, H. H., 243, 248
Anderson, R. G., 370
aptitude, definition of, 54
arithmetic, outcomes of teaching, 26
arithmetic achievement, 4
Army Alpha Examination, 345–346
Army Trade Screening Tests, 174
artificiality of test situations, 58
assembly and reproduction of objective tests, 187–188
assessment, definition of, 7
Association of American Colleges of Medicine, 361
Association of Dental Schools, 393
Atkinson, J. W., 249, 406

attitudes, 251–286
changes in school, 265–272
criteria for selecting statements, 261
defining object of reference, 253
disguised methods of measurement, 281–284
effect of movies on, 268–272
genesis of, 251
inconsistency in, 252
Likert method of construction, 263
relation to opinions, 254
Thurstone and Chave technique, 257–262
towards teaching, 256

Barr, A. S., 125
Bateman, R. M., 266, 285
Bennett, G. K., 370, 404
Bennett Test of Mechanical Comprehension, 358–259, 365
Benson, V. E., 404
Berman, I. R., 296, 310
Bernreuter, R. G., 224, 249
Beverly, C., 146
Billhartz, W. H., 377, 404
Binet, A., 307, 332, 333, 334, 335, 336, 337, 344, 345, 369, 375
Binet Test
illustrative items, 337–338
validation in terms of teacher judgments, 334
biographical records, 366–368
Bloom, B. S., 88, 93
Bogardus, E. S., 254, 285
Bond, E. A., 404
Bonney, M. W., 315, 326